AMAZONS IN AMERICA

AMAZONS IN AMERICA

AMERICA

MATRIARCHS, UTOPIANS, and
WONDER WOMEN in U.S. POPULAR CULTURE

KEIRA V. WILLIAMS

Louisiana State University Press

Baton Rouge

Published by Louisiana State University Press
Copyright © 2019 by Louisiana State University Press
All rights reserved
Manufactured in the United States of America
First printing

DESIGNER: Mandy McDonald Scallan
TYPEFACE: Whitman
PRINTER AND BINDER: Sheridan Books. Inc.

Library of Congress Cataloging-in-Publication Data
Names: Williams, Keira V., 1976–
Title: Amazons in America : matriarchs, utopians, and wonder women in U.S.
    popular culture / Keira V. Williams.
Description: Baton Rouge : Louisiana State University Press, 2019. | Includes
    bibliographical references and index.
Identifiers: LCCN 2018035868| ISBN 978-0-8071-7047-2 (cloth : alk. paper) | ISBN
    978-0-8071-7086-1 (pdf) | ISBN 978-0-8071-7085-4 (epub)
Subjects: LCSH: Women—United States—Social conditions. | Matriarchy—United
    States—History. | Popular culture—United States—History. |
    Amazons—History.
Classification: LCC HQ1073.5.U6 W55 2019 | DDC 305.40973—dc23
LC record available at https://lccn.loc.gov/2018035868

Some material from chapters 3 and 5 appeared previously as "From Oz to Amazon
Island," *Journal of Popular Culture* 50, no. 5 (2017). It is used here by permission.

CONTENTS

ACKNOWLEDGMENTS

Thank you to the following for funding assistance and/or for the use of collections: the Dibner Library of the History of Science and Technology at the Smithsonian Institution, the Library of Congress, the Newberry Library, the Popular Culture Association, the Texas Tech University Humanities Center, and the University of Chicago Special Collections.

Thank you for support (feedback, reference letters, snacks, drinks, hugs, and/or vacations): the Twinstitute, the A-Team, the Cougar Rodeo, my writing group at TTU, Bryant Simon, Aliza Wong, and Lisa Yaszek, whose thoughtful comments turned this messy manuscript into something readable. An additional shout-out to Lolly for slogging through that long, terrible first draft that I immediately slashed in two as soon as she read it.

This one's for Juicy, our beloved matriarch who left us too suddenly and too soon. I miss you every minute.

AMAZONS IN AMERICA

INTRODUCTION
THE MULTIPLE MEANINGS OF MATRIARCHIES
IN AMERICAN HISTORY

> A myth no sooner comes into being than it is modified through a
> change in the narrator. Some elements drop out and are replaced by
> others, sequences change places, and the modified structure moves
> through a series of states, the variations of which nevertheless belong
> to the same set.
>
> —CLAUDE LEVI-STRAUSS, *The Naked Man* (1971)

N 2016, the United Nations celebrated the seventy-fifth birthday of Wonder Woman by naming her an Honorary Ambassador to Women and Girls.
That spring, Wonder Woman—"beautiful as Aphrodite, wise as Athena,
swifter than Hermes, and stronger than Hercules"—permeated American popular culture anew after she appeared on the big screen for the first
time in *Batman vs. Superman: Dawn of Justice*. The following year, women protested the inauguration of Donald Trump wearing the superheroine's familiar
star-spangled getup. In the summer of 2017, Wonder Woman sold out theaters
with her very own feature-length film: *Wonder Woman*, directed by Patty Jenkins, garnered critical acclaim and quickly became the "highest-grossing superhero origin film" in Hollywood history. That fall, just after Hillary Clinton
received the "Wonder Woman Award" from the Women's Media Center, American girls followed suit: according to data collected by Google, the Amazing
Amazon was the most sought-after Halloween costume in the United States
that year. The character's enormous popularity earned actress Gal Gadot a
larger role in *Justice League*, DC Comics' ensemble superhero film of November 2017, as well as her own franchise of forthcoming movies, indicating that
the cultural fixation on this character is likely to continue for some time.[1]

The explosion of interest in Wonder Woman in recent years is part
movie-marketing genius and part feminist resurgence during a time in which
the nation's politics have shifted jarringly to the right. But Wonder Woman
is more than just a generic symbol of women's empowerment; rather, the

1

character brings with her an entire body of feminist theory that served as her very reason for being. Creator William Moulton Marston's original *Wonder Woman* and her many incarnations over time are examples of the continual re-creation of matriarchalism, an under-studied branch of American gender theory. Matriarchalism is a constellation of ideas about the history and nature of female power. It is a theory of history that posits that the earliest human societies were women-centered. It is a theory of biology premised upon discernible emotional, behavioral, and interpersonal distinctions between the sexes. It is a theory of social organization that assumes women-centered societies would necessarily be structured differently. It a theory of economics based on the idea that such societies would entail alternative systems of labor and distributions of wealth. It is a theory of politics that argues that female power would remake nations. And, crucially, it is a theory of gender that argues, depending on the creator and the era, that a matriarchal system is either the key to the ultimate achievement of ideals of equality and democracy, or it is the direst threat to the American way of life.

Matriarchalism has a long and varied history in the United States that scholars have yet to fully explore. Historian Cynthia Eller has studied the academic development of and archaeological evidence for what she calls the "matriarchal myth," or the belief in universal, prehistoric matriarchal societies, which is a primary premise of most versions of American matriarchalism. Initially proposed by male anthropologists in the 1860s and 1870s, matriarchalism quickly made the leap to feminist circles; although it was largely discarded as a scholarly theory by early 1900s, it came roaring back three-quarters of a century later via feminist archaeology. Eller found that this myth is "primarily a Western phenomenon," a recurring interest of scholars in Europe and North America in the late nineteenth and late twentieth centuries.[2]

However, despite its erstwhile acceptance in academia, matriarchalism has been a near-constant staple of American popular culture for 125 years; indeed, scholar Sara Jones argues that "Amazons are everywhere, once you know what you're looking for." Matriarchalism has spawned a wide range of texts, indicating that theories about female power have been a frequent, and often even a primary, preoccupation in American popular culture from the late Victorian era to the early twenty-first century. In *Amazons in America*, I chart the multiple manifestations of matriarchalism in the United States, with the goal of understanding the ways in which these texts reflect and refract the gender politics of the long twentieth century.[3]

Several avenues of inquiry led me to these questions. At the time that I read Eller's *The Myth of Matriarchal History,* I was conducting research at the Smithsonian on William Moulton Marston and *Wonder Woman.* I became fascinated by the comic as a matriarchalist text, as the Amazing Amazon hails from an all-female island that is a beacon of love, peace, and democracy. As I sought comparisons to the superheroine's origins, it dawned on me that, rather than being the narrow province of a few feminists with optimistic theories about the distant past, matriarchalism permeates American popular culture, and it has for some time.

In their examination of fictional feminist utopias, Jane L. Donawerth and Carol A. Kolmerten write that the first goal of feminist scholarship is to "recover texts." Once I began to search, I slowly uncovered an unbroken trajectory of American texts—some obscure, some very well known—that were centered on ideas about matriarchal power from the 1890s to the present. In each era, matriarchalism was deployed as a popular means of making sense of contemporary issues, specifically questioning the traditional gendered tenets and biological assumptions of the nature of power and exploring women's potential as social, economic, and political leaders. In keeping with Donawerth and Kolmerten's first task of feminist scholarship, this book charts that trajectory.[4]

The second task, according to Donawerth and Kolmerton, is to go beyond contributionist history and "to reevaluate forgotten, neglected, underrated women writers and their works." This is another broad goal of *Amazons in America,* with a few caveats. First, it has not only been "women writers" who have produced forgotten feminist works. Indeed, while it may have been the key to their financial success (or at least to their publishing contracts), the fact of male authorship may well have kept some of the texts examined herein out of the recognized feminist canon. Second, to fully examine matriarchalism as a feminist theory, we must examine its many negative permutations, or antimatriarchalist texts, as well, not simply the versions celebrated by contemporary feminist proponents of female power. In other words, it is a primary argument of *Amazons in America* that the texts that deride female power are as crucial to understanding the historical import, the theoretical significance, and the real-world consequences—such as imperialism, racism, xenophobia, mother-blaming, and policy making—of matriarchalism as those texts that promote it.[5]

The third task of *Amazons in America* is twofold: to make sense of the multiple meanings of matriarchalism over time, and to situate this theory within the historiographical tradition of US women's history. Matriarchalism is a comprehensive branch of feminist theory that encompasses history, culture, gender, race, socioeconomic organization, familial systems, and labor, among other things. While I do not enter the anthropological and archaeological debate over the existence of prehistoric or ancient matriarchies, *Amazons in America* fits within several other vital scholarly conversations within the fields of feminist theory, women's history, and political history. As numerous historians, feminist theorists, and media studies scholars have shown, a primary feature of the broad history of feminism in the United States is one of progressive gains followed by periods of intense resistance and renewal of patriarchal oppression, or what it known as the "backlash" model. The trajectory of matriarchalism in the United States generally follows this tumultuous time line of organized feminist progress and antifeminist backlash laid out by previous scholars. That is, feminist matriarchalism has flourished in American popular culture during the eras associated with socioeconomic and political progress for women—the early twentieth century, the World War II era, and the late 1960s to the 1970s. Likewise, antimatriarchalism—or theories which posit that innate female characteristics make women ill-suited to power, so much so that female influence over others is conceived as a broad social threat—has reigned in eras in which feminism was at a low point in terms of organization and popularity, particularly during the Cold War and in the last two decades of the twentieth century. A focus on matriarchalism as a branch of feminist thought and theory, then, is also a case-study investigation of the backlash model of feminist history.[6]

Additionally, in the past generation of historiography, the term *maternalism* has come to define a major theoretical approach to understanding women's history, particularly women's political history. In their foundational 1990 study of maternalism and the development of welfare states in Western societies, Seth Koven and Sonya Michel define the term as "ideologies that exalted women's capacity to mother and extended to society as a whole the values of care, nurturance, and morality." With this study, Koven and Michel formally opened the debate on the historical role of maternalism, broadening the definitions of "politics" and "the state" to include women's voluntary organizations and movements and launching inquiry into the question of how "a discourse [that was] grounded in normative gender roles could still be about agency." In short, they examined how gender essentialism—the belief in allegedly natural

4

womanly qualities such as compassion, caretaking, and nurturance—within maternalist rhetoric could paradoxically be used to further the causes of equality and female liberation. More recent analyses of the deployment of maternalist rhetoric have shown how this kind of language could be used contradictorily, to serve both feminist and reactionary ends. Scholars have also found that feminist maternalism, like American feminism itself, has often been exclusive in terms of race and class, and has thus helped to maintain some traditional hierarchies while attempting to tear down others. The trajectory of matriarchalism that I chart herein is also the story of some of the successes and failures of maternalist politics in the modern United States.[7]

Because maternalism—the rhetorical mobilization of women's claims to power based on maternity—and matriarchalism—a set of beliefs about the origins, history, and nature of female power—are both branches of feminist theory that are heavily concerned with contemporary ideas about motherhood, the two concepts have overlapped occasionally in US history, particularly during the Progressive era. But they are not two sides of the same coin; instead, some matriarchalists explicitly rejected motherhood as the primary foundation of claims to female power, while others strategically deployed a maternalist rhetoric of motherhood as the ideal organizing principle of matriarchal societies. This tension within feminist matriarchalism, and between feminist matriarchalism and antimatriarchalism, gets at some of the debates within the study of maternalism and the relationship between sex, gender, motherhood, political rhetoric, and the state. Following matriarchalism as a unifying, evolving set of beliefs about gender and power, with maternalism as an occasional premise of that set of beliefs, *Amazons in America* offers a historical analysis of the precarious theoretical position of gender essentialism and of relying upon the social construction of American motherhood, which has been a major source of historical inequality and oppression, to advocate for female social, economic, and political power.

Since Koven and Michel formally opened the study of maternalism in 1990, the growing body of related scholarship has helped to build a historiographical bridge between studies of feminism as a set of social movements and analyses of representations of motherhood within US history. These are not separate strands of history; rather, the evolution of feminist thought, theory, and action is invariably linked to the history of how American cultural producers have envisioned and promoted ideas of motherhood. Popular culture is an ideal realm through which to analyze both. Scholars like Elaine Tyler

May, in her groundbreaking work on the Cold War, and Ruth Feldstein, in her examination of liberal politics from the New Deal to the Great Society, have linked ideas about motherhood, feminism, popular culture, and the state to produce new interpretations of the role of gender in American politics in the middle decades of the twentieth century. In this vein, *Amazons in America* is a cultural analysis of a lengthier time line, picking up American matriarchalism at its roots in the 1870s and following its various permutations to the present. Because the primary intent of matriarchalism is to describe, defend, and promote specific visions of female power, the matriarchalists that I examine necessarily engage with the feminisms of their time, and they strategically represent motherhood in specific ways.[8]

As the vital scholarship on maternalism seeks to address feminist legal scholar Catherine MacKinnon's famous 1989 challenge that feminism has "no theory of the state," so, too, does this study of matriarchalism. Matriarchalist texts belie MacKinnon's claim, as they add up to over a century of popular theories and publications that envision states built upon the tenets of contemporary feminisms. Women's reproductive status has historically served as both a site of subjugation and of power, and thus this status is not a personal issue, but rather a "central concern of the state," in matriarchalist texts. In her study of feminist utopias, Frances Bartkowski argues that these works must be read as "implicit critiques and remappings of the state," and while not all fictional matriarchies are feminist utopias, they each entail specific visions of what female-powered states might look like, including their development over time, their relationships with other societies, their economic bases, and their day-to-day sociopolitical functions.[9]

As a study of matriarchies in US popular culture, then, *Amazons in America* thus taps into various strands of historiography, including analyses of maternalism, the relationship between feminist movements and popular representations of motherhood, and feminist theories of the state. Because *matriarchy* is a term that has been applied to so many different types of social systems that it can seem almost devoid of inherent meaning, a note on definitions is useful here. The term is derived from the Latin *matri* (mother) and *archon* (ruler); synonyms include "matriarchate," "gyneocracy," "gynecocracy," "gynarchy," and "gynocentric society." "Mother rule" seems a simple enough definition, but the devil is in the details, particularly the details of what is meant by "rule." Scholars have used "matriarchy" to denote allocations of power ranging from the symbolic or cultural (goddess worship), to the social (female-led welfare organizations and service to society), to the economic (control of production and property), to the political (formal governing power). Heide Gottner-Abendroth, a German anthropologist of matriarchal prehistory, defines the term as more than a simplistic "parallel" of patriarchy: "The Greek work 'arche' has a double meaning. It means a 'beginning' as well as 'domination.' Therefore, 'matriarchy' is accurately translated as 'mothers from the beginning.'"[10]

This is not an unproblematic definition, given its reliance upon motherhood. Recent anthropologists and archaeologists thus often prefer to avoid the word *matriarchy* altogether in favor of more precise terms like *matricentric* (societies organized around the mother), *matrifocal* ("women holding a preeminent place in kinship structures"), or *matrilineal* (descent, kinship, and usually property traced through the mother's bloodline). Feminist scholars in particular prefer these more precise terms in order to "speak of the sexes as being on an equal footing, egalitarian, or 'linked' rather than 'ranked,' in a 'partnership' rather than a 'dominator' relationship."[11]

This linguistic sidestep allows scholars to avoid the negative connotations of *matriarchy* as a kind of female tyranny comparable to that of patriarchies in history. Anthropologist Peggy Sanday argues that the traditional "Western definition of matriarchy" as "rule by women," or the "female twin" of patriarchy, is misguided, although she still uses the term in her field research because that is the self-descriptor used by her subjects, the Minangkabau of West Sumatra. She explains that, rather than simply representing a "pre-patriarchal evolutionary stage," matriarchy, among her research subjects, denotes "societies founded on principles of gender balance and a gift-giving economy"; this definition, according to Sanday, "reflects a maternal social philosophy for a global culture that seeks peace and stresses the importance of nurturing the young, the old, the sick, and the poor."[12]

However, not all American matriarchalists in the past century and a half have relied upon maternity as the basis for a claim to formal female power, and some feminist matriarchalists have articulated theories of and calls for sex equity that are not based on essentialist notions of gender. For our purposes here, then, I will use the broadest definition of the term that encompasses each of the theories and texts that I examine. Eller provides this definition in her examination of matriarchal archaeology: "'matriarchal' can be thought of then as a shorthand description for any society in which women's power is equal or superior to men's and in which the culture centers around values and life events described as 'feminine.'" Following this, I use "matriarchalist" to refer broadly to popular sets of beliefs about the origins, history, and nature of female power.[13]

Readers should note that while most of the producers of matriarchalist texts have been preoccupied by patriarchal comparisons—meaning that they use matriarchalist theories comparatively to make arguments about gender and power within contemporary society—many of them make these comparisons through the depiction of single-sex societies. Even when men are absent from matriarchalist texts, patriarchy is the point of comparison for each female-powered system; readers are presumed to live in the contemporary Western world, and each text is premised upon ideas about the differences between the sexes, whether those differences are depicted as biologically determined or socially constructed. In *The Second Sex*, Simone de Beauvoir explained the prevalence of sex dualism: "Being different from man, who sets himself up as the Same, it is naturally to the category of the Other that woman is consigned; the Other includes woman." The literary conceit of many of the matriarchalist texts in US popular culture is that this perspective is flipped: men are often the "other," especially in texts in which men appear only as token interlopers or not at all. Brian Attebury has explored the use of single-sex societies in science fiction as a "fascinating series of thought experiments." Using the all-female society of Whileaway in Joanna Russ's *The Female Man* (examined in Chapter 8 here) as an example, he argues that while "there may be no men" in the fictional utopia, "men are present throughout" the novel for readers, "in the form of the unlamented past, the pressure no longer felt, the horrible example, the stolen prerogative." Likewise, male citizens or patriarchal examples are not textually required for the comparative arguments made in the matriarchalist fiction examined herein, as readers can rely upon their own patriarchal experiences to complete the comparison.[14]

Because matriarchal prehistory is a primary preoccupation of many American matriarchalists, let me be clear that I am not a historian of ancient or prehistory, nor do I seek to enter the debate over the historical existence of matriarchal societies. More to the point, the primary subjects of this book—the scholars and authors who have produced popular versions of female-led societies—have not been interested in adhering to strict definitions, historical narratives, or standards of evidence. Because each author and text offer a diverse set of the characteristics of female-centered societies listed above, I use *matriarchy* as a kind of catchall term. That said, it will not be left to the reader to determine the differences between them; in each chapter, I examine the intricate details of each of these pop cultural matriarchies as a means of understanding the gendered and racial dynamics of that era, and I compare these popular versions of matriarchalism in order to explore the changes in American ideas about female power.[15]

I begin *Amazons in America* with an examination of the academic roots of American matriarchalism. In Chapter 1, "Gynecocracy in the Gilded Age," I explore the development of mid-nineteenth-century anthropological matriarchalism, beginning with Western European influences on American academics. Using a schema laid out by the Swiss scholar Johann Bachofen, anthropologist Lewis Henry Morgan's work with the Iroquois Nations in New York described an indigenous American matriarchy that was more equitable and democratic than Victorian patriarchy, and his publications would have profound resonance in feminist circles.

In Chapter 2, "Mother-Rule in the Modern World," I examine how American suffragists like Elizabeth Cady Stanton and Matilda Joslyn Gage co-opted Morgan's matriarchalism, bridging academic theory and political ideology in their bid for voting rights. Gage, in particular, served as a crucial link between ethnography and popular culture in her writings, especially through her influence on her son-in-law, a popular children's literature author.

In 1893, the same year that Gage published a lengthy work of global women's history, millions of Americans became acquainted with matriarchalism through a thoroughly unrelated venue. In Chapter 3, "White Queens and African Amazons," I examine the darker side of nineteenth-century matriarchalism as an evolutionist discourse of international imperialism. I track this process through the figures of the so-called "African Amazons" of the Dahomey Village at the 1893 World's Columbian Exposition in Chicago. These women represented the negative counterparts to the much-touted role of elite white women in Western civilization on heavy display at the World's Fair.

By the end of the 1890s, however, a new version of matriarchal popular culture emerged that, in the guise of fantastical children's literature, counteracted the racist evolutionism of the World's Fair. In Chapter 4, "Witches, Wizards, and Women of Cast Iron," I examine how feminist ideas about matriarchal precedents and women's rights became very popular through the fictional witches and princesses created by Matilda Joslyn Gage's son-in-law, L. Frank Baum, the author of *The Wonderful Wizard of Oz* series. In this chapter, I trace how matriarchalism transformed from an academic theory, feminist political ideology, and racist discourse into a staple of American popular culture via Baum's publications.

In Chapter 5, "Like Coming Home to Mother," I return to a more unsavory version of American matriarchalism through an analysis of how the feminist and racist matriarchalist ideas examined in the previous chapters coalesced in the utopian writings of sociologist Charlotte Perkins Gilman. A thorough product of her time, Gilman combined contemporary theories of gender equality with a xenophobic discourse of evolutionism in her fictional explorations of matriarchal socialism.

In Chapter 6, "The Amazing Amazon," I return to children's popular culture with an examination of the unique theories of the psychologist William Moulton Marston, the creator of the *Wonder Woman* comic. Wonder Woman was Marston's matriarchalist Trojan horse: when the Amazing Amazon saved the day, she was enacting Marston's gendered prescription for social evolution, explicitly inspired by feminist utopias like those produced by L. Frank Baum and Charlotte Perkins Gilman, but revamped for the World War II–era audience.

Wonder Woman, however, was not without her detractors, particularly in the postwar period that emphasized nuclear, patriarchal family structures. Thus, in Chapter 7, "Vipers, and Momarchies: Mid-Century Antimatriarchalism," I examine the Cold War–era fears of momism, in which middle-class, white American mothers dominated their husbands, emasculated their sons, and ruled the suburbs. Out of these fears, however, came the matriarchalism of the women's liberation movement, the subject of Chapter 8, "Goddesses, Earth Mothers, and Female Men." In this chapter, I chart the rise of a new version of matriarchalism in which anthropologists and novelists posited a revised theory of universally matriarchal prehistory. At the same time, radical feminist matriarchalist utopias began to appear in science fiction, particularly in the works of James Tiptree Jr., Joanna Russ, and Suzy McKee Charnas.

Racist and sexist fears combined again in the second half of the twentieth century, embodied by the specter of the "black matriarchy," the subject of Chapter 9, "Mammies, Matriarchs, and Welfare Queens." The "black matriarch" was famously publicized in the 1960s by Assistant Secretary of Labor Daniel Patrick Moynihan, who, in his research on the roots of African American poverty, cited the "tangle of pathology" in black families, which allegedly took the form of a racialized matriarchy resulting from the rise of single black motherhood. This matriarchal figure became a media staple as part of the broad-based backlash against feminism, the movement for racial civil rights, and the war on poverty in the final decades of the twentieth century.

Finally, in the Epilogue, "Madeas and the Manosphere," I explore how this long and varied American matriarchal tradition has culminated in a bifurcated matriarchal discourse in the early twenty-first century, as evidenced by, on the one hand, the continued production of feminist matriarchalist texts that call upon this genealogy, and on the other, paranoid fears of female power, such as those expressed by the current Men's Rights Movement.

Although the historical time line of American matriarchalism seamlessly spans the 1870s to the 2010s, with distinct versions of the theory manifesting in popular culture in each decade, this trajectory was not easy to reconstruct. While some of the historical figures examined herein are now well known thanks in large part to the volumes of scholarship on Charlotte Perkins Gilman and, more recently, Jill Lepore's masterful biography of William Moulton Marston, their connections to each other are not, and they were largely unaware of their own matriarchalist genealogy; more often than not, they failed to cite each other. Given her interest in Native American social organization, particularly among the Iroquois nations, Matilda Joslyn Gage most likely read Lewis Henry Morgan's publications, but she did not reference his work in *Women, Church and State*. When Gage left the organized suffrage movement, Susan B. Anthony actively helped to erase her legacy, and Gage's matriarchalist influence on future feminists was lost for decades. The burial of the intellectual history of matriarchalism thus began in its first generation.

In the following generation of matriarchalists, Charlotte Perkins Gilman does not appear to have read Gage; she cited sociologist Lester Frank Ward instead. During this same era, Gage only appeared in vague imagery in Baum's *Oz* series, which she inspired. By the 1930s, Gilman was ill, reclusive, and out of print, and William Moulton Marston, the creator of *Wonder Woman* who was known for being cagey about authorship, never cited the fictional feminist matriarchies of the previous generation, although there is clear evidence in the comic that he read these works. Gage and Gilman were both rediscovered by Women's Studies scholars in the 1970s as part of a resurgence of feminist matriarchalism in the United States, but even the producers of the new matriarchalist fiction seemed unaware that they were treading ground that had been thoroughly explored by authors other than Gilman. This continual remaking of matriarchalism thus recalls Claude Levi-Strauss's arguments about how myths change structure over time, while retaining the same basic premises.[16]

On the other hand, antimatriarchalism has long enjoyed a wide currency in the United States. This is partially, but not completely, due to the cyclical nature of organized feminism in American history; opposition to matriarchalism flourished, for example, in the 1950s and the 1980s, when feminist organization was at low points. Bigotry has, of course, always been alive and well in the United States, and thus explicitly sexist—mid-century momism—and racist—the "black matriarch"—versions of matriarchalism garner major media attention, because they uphold patriarchal power dynamics. And with the presidency of Donald Trump, who strategically deployed the rhetoric of misogyny that characterizes the Men's Rights Movement in his campaign and later named Men's Rights sympathizers as his presidential advisors, antimatriarchalism will surely continue to make headlines.

But part of the blame for the lack of knowledge and awareness about matriarchalism as a core feminist theory in American history can be placed on feminists themselves. For instance, the organized suffragist blockade of Gage's work after 1890 meant that matriarchalism was quickly and easily co-opted by racism and imperialism. Then as now, feminist matriarchalism bore the burden of racism, as white proponents espoused the racialized theories of their time, ignoring or explicitly deriding women of color in the process. As with the tension between sex differences and equality that undergirds feminism, there are other enduring internal contradictions within the premises of feminist matriarchalism. Cynthia Eller, the historian of matriarchal mythology, was moved to publish her critique because of what she believed was the concept's fundamental historical inaccuracy, but she was also motivated by the feminist dilemma this mythology embodied:

> There is a theory of sex and gender embedded in the myth of matriarchal prehistory, and it is neither original nor revolutionary. Women are defined quite narrowly as those who give birth and nurture, and who are closely allied with the body, nature, and sex—usually for unavoidable reasons of their biological makeup. This image of women is drastically revalued in feminist matriarchal myth, such that it is not a mark of shame or subordination, but of pride and power. But this image is nevertheless quite conventional and, at least up until now, it has done an excellent job of serving patriarchal interests.[17]

In other words, essentialism—the theory that there are innately female characteristics that inescapably differentiate women from men—is a problematic premise that has bred others. As historians of turn-of-the-century feminism and others have shown, notions of gender essentialism and racism are thoroughly intertwined, and this problem permeates matriarchalism throughout its history.

Antimatriarchalists consistently rely upon "essential" gendered and racialized characteristics to argue against female power. While some feminist matriarchalists openly wrestle with this concept in their writing, others uncritically use "feminine" attributes as the very basis of their arguments, creating what Nancy Cott calls a "paradox" within feminism that shows few signs of resolution in the early twenty-first century. Cott charts the dilemma of advocating for gender essentialism and/or the elimination of gender roles in the Progressive era as a clear parallel to modern feminism. This is a major source of tension between forms of matriarchalism, and this problem of essentialism within matriarchalism is no mere pop cultural plot device. Rather, it is a core conflict that characterizes the way women have historically structured and been structured by the state as inferior objects in need of control or protection, as threats to the prevailing system, or as equal subjects.[18]

In *Amazons in America,* I examine this tension in order to understand the evolution of the gendered premises of female claims to power in the United States. Because we do not yet enjoy the experience of sex equality in this society, much less liberation from patriarchy and the various oppressive structures with which it is entangled, these academic theories and pop cultural imaginings serve as historical traces, or clues to how different groups and individuals have envisioned alternative forms of gendered power over time. The texts of American matriarchalism—both the negative versions that envision female power as a destructive force, and the feminist versions that argue that women are the key to the realization of ideals like freedom, equality, and democracy— offer a new interpretation of the history of gender dynamics in the modern United States. *Amazons in America* explores the popular history of this theory with the goal of understanding not just how we have envisioned female power in the past, but why it is that we cannot seem to progress beyond mere visions into actualizing intersectional female power in the present.[19]

1

GYNECOCRACY IN THE GILDED AGE

The Intellectual and Historical Foundations
of American Matriarchalism

This rediscovery of the primitive matriarch(y) . . . has the same importance for anthropology as Darwin's theory of evolution has for biology
and Marx's theory of surplus value has for political economy.
— FRIEDRICH ENGELS *Origin of the Family,*
Private Property, and the State (1884)

HE latter half of the Victorian era featured many new theories
about human origins that reframed knowledge about the past and
had major implications for prevailing concepts of human identity,
including gender roles. In the United States just before the turn
of the twentieth century, there emerged a full-blown discourse of gendered
power, known as matriarchalism, that was both academic and popular. Matriarchalism, in its original form, was an academic theory that posited one
or more of the following: prehistoric human societies were universally matriarchal; all societies, in their "primitive" forms (to use the terminology of
this theory's nineteenth-century progenitors), underwent a matriarchal stage
before transitioning to patriarchy; and the female rule that characterized matriarchal societies was qualitatively different from the nature of rule within
male-dominated societies. Linked by some to Darwinian evolution, matriarchalism was embraced by scholars ranging from anthropology, to biology, to
history.

Matriarchy was, of course, not a new concept in the nineteenth century.
Discrete matriarchal myths have been identified throughout much of human
history, from ancient Greece to the Americas during the era of European colonization. Yet these myths did not consolidate into a body of academic theory
until the late nineteenth century, and this theory solidified and spread quickly
following the publications of its initial proponents.[1] In this chapter, I examine
the primary ideological roots of matriarchalism, which include mythology,

archaeology, evolutionary theory, early anthropology, North American ethnography, and socialist history.

The burgeoning academic interest in matriarchalism in the second half of the nineteenth century was the product of a confluence of factors that, taken together, thoroughly challenged long-standing truth claims about the human past at their very origins. This matriarchalist moment spawned theories that arose in direct contrast to several standard operating conceptions of the world. In particular, the idea of a universally matriarchal prehistoric past contradicted the belief in the biblical account of human history. Matriarchalism presented a twofold contradiction: it challenged the biblical account by positing that human history was far older than the book of Genesis indicated, and, by definition, matriarchalism argued that male dominance was not a natural or original state of social organization. Although challenges had been posed to the concept of biblical time in previous centuries, the mid-nineteenth-century theory of biological evolution and archaeological evidence for "extreme human antiquity"—the argument that humanity was hundreds of thousands of years old—inaugurated a full-blown intellectual paradigm shift. Matriarchalism became, for a time, a crucial part of this shift, largely due to the combined historical theories of Charles Darwin, Charles Lyell, Karl Marx, Johann Jakob Bachofen, and Friedrich Engels.[2]

In the mid-nineteenth century, the Darwinian concepts of evolution by means of natural selection and the descent of humans from animal species via common ancestors combined with Lyell's theory of a virtually unknown human prehistory of thousands of years to produce widespread scholarly interest in prebiblical societies. The influence of evolutionary theory cannot be overstated; within a generation, its reach went far beyond science. Many thinkers of the era were concerned with the connection between science and society, including Karl Marx, who famously lauded Darwin's work as "a natural-scientific basis for the class struggle in history." One of Marx's goals was to apply Darwin's theories of "historical evolution in Nature" to the sociopolitical history of humans, which he and Friedrich Engels had been investigating since the 1840s.[3]

Taken together, Darwinism and Marxism represented a full-scale assault on Western "truths." Darwin provided a theory of the process of evolution by means of natural selection, while Marx applied his understanding of this Darwinian process to the socioeconomic struggles of human history. Interpre-

tations of their theories would come to represent core components of early anthropology, specifically in the form of evolutionism, or the teleological belief
that all human societies progressed, albeit at different paces, along a clearly
delineated time line of human progress from simple/savage to complex/civi-
lized. According to historians of anthropology, the preoccupation with human
origins according to the Darwinian model, and especially the Western interest
in "primitive" societies, helped to transform the discipline into a science. Historian J. W. Burrow argues that while "Darwin was certainly not the father of
evolutionary anthropology," he was "possibly its wealthy uncle."[4]

In the 1860s, this amalgamation of revisionist history was the primary
theoretical context of a new gendered vision of the development of human
societies. The first scholar to articulate this was Johann Jakob Bachofen of
Switzerland. Bachofen explicitly set out to challenge the Western belief in the
natural, biological imperative of patriarchy. His investigation of the archives,
mythology, and archaeology of Europe in the 1850s led him to a universalizing
theory of "gynecocracy," or female supremacy, based on his findings that the
origins of ancient cultures and societies were woman-centered. He compiled
his research into a series of lectures and eventually a manuscript, which he
marketed to publishers with the argument that "the position of women in
human society is of paramount significance for the insight into the cultural
condition of every age." In 1861, this work was published as *Mother Right: A
Study of the Religious and Juridical Aspects of Gynecocracy in the Ancient World.*[5]

The primary significance of Bachofen's work is his gendering of the time
line of the evolution of human societies. Representing the anthropological
wing of the mid-nineteenth-century challenge to biblical accounts of the human past, Bachofen argued, based on his research on Egyptian, Greek, and
Roman myths, that patriarchy was, historically speaking, quite young. According to Bachofen, "mother right," or the matriarchal organization of the family
and society, was an early stage of sociocultural development that defined all
human societies. In short, he argued that "Amazonism is a universal phenomenon," part of the dynamic and often violent relations between the sexes that
characterized each period of human history. Rather than a hindrance to progress, these relations were, for Bachofen, the catalyst of social evolution.[6]

Within his time line of human history, Bachofen charted five major stages,
three of which were explicitly matriarchal. "Unregulated hetaerism," featuring
widespread concubinage due to the absence of the organizing cultural institution of marriage, was a lowly stage characterized by the brute rule of men.

Male tyrants ran clans, but inheritance of power and rights was, by necessity, matrilineal, because humans had not yet discovered the paternal function in reproduction. Bachofen's low estimation of this stage of "primitive promiscuity" is clear, but there was one positive social good within it: motherhood, "the only light in the moral darkness."[7]

This maternal instinct was the basis for the second stage of history, Demetrian matriarchy or "gynecocracy." In this "first period of Amazonism," which represented a "step forward toward civilization," women chose husbands and ruled over them. During the "Mother-age," the brutes of hetaerism were transformed into boys governed by the guiding hands of mothers. Indeed, maternity became the organizing principle of society: "It is the woman's vocation to tame man's primordial strength, to guide it into benign channels.[8]

According to Bachofen, this first matriarchal stage was followed by the Dionysian age, in which men grew powerful once again. But "one extreme followed the other," and eventually from this came a second Amazon stage, an overcorrection in power relations between the sexes in which women rebelled against male dominance yet again, resulting in the warlike, "unnatural exaggerated matriarchies" found in ancient Greece, Asia Minor, and some European tales of conquest.[9]

Ultimately, the oppression of males that characterized this final Amazonian stage sowed the seeds of the destruction of matriarchy. The "rise of father right," Bachofen explained, began with the men's rebellion against the Amazons. Bachofen seemed, at times, to be of a divided mind on the value of this final transition to patriarchy, yet he ultimately deemed the development of patriarchy "the progress of civilization," a phrase that seemingly indicates that this was, in his estimation, a positive evolution. Bachofen explained this using a cosmic metaphor, arguing that gender relations were like those between the moon and the sun. The development of the "highest stage of the male principle of nature" mirrored that of the natural world: "The earth's development is a striving to copy faithfully the cosmic prototype of the celestial bodies. And this process is completed only with the domination of man over woman, of the sun over the moon."[10]

Thus ascended the Apollonian age, enacted through the patriarchal conquest of the Amazons, spurred on by the discovery of paternity, and represented by classical Greece. The fact of paternity was to be given a primary role in almost all subsequent matriarchalist theories; the discovery of men's role in reproduction, according to most proponents of matriarchalism, had a profound effect on gender relations and thus social organization. The primacy of paternity was, however, a supposition that was not based on archaeological or historical evidence. Bachofen, for one, did not concern himself with any formal standards of proof. As a classicist, he relied upon mythology as sociological evidence, deeming it an "authentic, independent record of the primordial age, a record in which no invention played a part." According to his methodology, myths could be used to shore up spotty archaeological evidence, and vice versa. For Bachofen, reports of encounters with Amazons throughout history were not isolated incidents or representations of male fears and fantasies. Rather, their prevalence, and their common characteristics—the global and timeless "homogeneity of matriarchal ideas"—proved that matriarchy was a universal prehistoric phenomenon.[11]

Bachofen's theory of matriarchal evolutionism must be understood within the context of Victorian gender relations, the stirrings of early Western feminism, and European colonialism. Although he did not present a uniformly positive narrative of the evolution of human societies from matriarchy to patriarchy, Bachofen's work indicated a parallel between the rise of male dominance and the progression of history, and his clear correlation of the "feminine nature principle" with "primordial" and "primitive" life implied that the development of patriarchy was a necessary precondition for "civilization" as he and his Victorian counterparts defined it. His occasional ambivalence about these developments notwithstanding, Bachofen's time line would later be deployed by other scholars as scientific evidence of the value of white, male domestic dominance and global imperialism. As the field of anthropology grew, so too did matriarchalism, but its perceived value and historical meaning varied according to the patriarchal proclivities of its proponents.[12]

Although Bachofen was the originator of the matriarchalist theory of prehistory in the second half of the nineteenth century, *Mother Right* failed to get academic acclaim or reviews in major journals. This dismissal, however, does disservice to Bachofen's innovation. As the first theorist to posit that conflict between the sexes accounted for historical change over time, Bachofen can be seen, in the words of one scholar, as "the Marx of feminism." Despite some dissent from other anthropologists, by the 1880s the matriarchal nature of "primitive" ancient societies was "generally agreed upon" within the field. Although later British anthropologists watered down his narrative of early female power—they argued that he was mistaking matrilineage (descent through the mother's line) for matriarchy—Bachofen's work was to have enormous impact on American anthropology just a decade later, when matriarchalism resurfaced in the United States. Rather than relying upon ancient myths and artifacts, American anthropologists identified the potentially troublesome existence of extant matriarchal "others" in the United States, and they used Bachofen's brand of gendered evolutionism in their analyses.[13]

In the American context, Bachofen's theories presented an interesting dilemma. Of course, as with Darwin and Marx, *Mother Right* was part of the challenge posed by any work about human antiquity to the biblical conception of history. The gendering of the human historical time line, as well, was threatening to notions of power, position, and place in Victorian cultures. In the United States, this threat was not merely academic, as there existed thousands of indigenous women who defied any natural notions of male dominance and feminine weakness. It is within this context of trying to make sense of these coexisting social systems, which contradicted the Victorian conception of proper gender roles, that we must understand the development of American matriarchalism.

American ideas of matriarchy are at least as old as the colonial concept of "America" itself. Beliefs about gender roles and matriarchal power dynamics helped white conquerors, colonists, and citizens to make sense of indigenous peoples, and this was true for many centuries. Early European colonizers fearfully noted the existence of powerful women among tribes throughout the Caribbean and North and South America, from Christopher Columbus in the Caribbean, to Hernan Cortes in Mexico, to Cristobal de Acuña and Gaspar de Carvajal in South America. Christopher Columbus was reputed to be "obsessed" with the myth of the Amazons, twice reporting that he "had encountered, or narrowly missed, such beings" on the Caribbean island Matinino. These "Amazons," he wrote to Queen Isabella, "perform(ed) no work of their sex, for they use(d) bows and darts" to attack his crew. In 1510, across the North American continent, Spanish readers were introduced to an island in the Pacific ruled by an Amazon queen in the romance novel *Las Sergas de Esplandián.* Life soon imitated art: from western New Spain, Hernan Cortes wrote to the king that "an island populated by all women" had been sighted in 1523. Lest this sound attractive to the conquerors, the captain explained that these women practiced regular male infanticide; they sustained their population by allowing men to visit from the mainland, "and if those who became pregnant bear women, they keep them, and if men, they throw them from their company."[14]

Two decades later and much further south, Jesuit missionary Cristobal de Acuña echoed Columbus and Cortes in his 1541 description of a veritable nation of "manlike" Amazonian warriors in the rain forests along the great interior river of South America:

> The Amazons are women of great valour, and they have always preserved themselves without the ordinary intercourse with men; and even when these, by agreement, come every year to their land, they receive them with arms in their hands, such as bows and arrows, which they brandish about for a time, until they are satisfied that the Indians come with peaceful intentions. . . . The daughters who are born from this intercourse are preserved and brought up by the Amazons themselves, as they are destined to inherit their valour and customs of the nation; but it is not so certain what they do with the sons.

In 1542, Dominican friar Gaspar de Carvajal confirmed this account, explaining that resistance to Spanish contact was due to native rule by violent women: "We ourselves saw these women, who were fighting in front of all the Indian men as women captains . . . the Indian men did not dare to turn their backs, and anyone who did turn his back [the women] killed with clubs right before us." The women were so striking that Francisco de Orellana, the leader of the 1542 expedition, named the mightiest river on the continent after these "Amazons." Taken together, the written European observations of powerful indigenous women add up to a consistent record of matriarchal groups throughout the Americas during the era of conquest.[15]

In the land that would become the United States, the existence of powerful women in indigenous societies was similarly well documented, as was the general Spanish fascination with these women, by the time of French and British colonialism. This fascination was part fear—the women they observed were almost always reported to be heavily armed—and part fantasy, as many observers were careful to speculate upon the more prurient details of the purported sex lives of these all-female societies. For conquerors, traders, and settlers, these gendered observations could serve as further justification for territorial takeover.

But this conquest was not just of land. As Europeans built social structures in the Americas, they found that they had to remake and reinforce what they considered to be natural hierarchies on the "gender frontier," and detailed descriptions of matriarchies served as cautionary tales about the importance of securing European-style patriarchy in the North American colonies. Historians have shown that colonial reports often used an explicitly gendered language of conquest that relied upon feminized representations of Native American men. Likewise, reports of Amazons throughout the Americas in the sixteenth century were not idle observations. Rather, they served the clear political purpose of colonial subjugation and/or annihilation: Amazon sightings appeared in official records, letters to European kings, and publications that were meant to explain the savagery, and therefore inhumanity, of the indigenous women, and, by extension, of all of the native inhabitants of the "New World."[16]

Early in the North American colonial endeavor, Europeans understood that, just as male roles determined social and political power in their own societies, so too did dominant female roles influence the power dynamics of indigenous societies. Even to the least observant colonists, this was particularly noticeable amongst the Nations of the Iroquois, for several reasons: geographical location, prolonged and sustained colonial contact, and, most significantly, the obvious matrilineal structure of Iroquois society. As early as the 1630s, European observers noted that, much to their consternation, Iroquois women exercised economic freedom and political power by traveling long distances to trade on their own and being frequently involved in clan and tribal decision making. Other European settlers noted more formal means of female power within Iroquois society. Marie de l'Incarnation, one of the founders of the Ursuline Order in New France, described "captainesses," or deputy chiefs, who made local political decisions and selected diplomats, while the Jesuit priest Pierre de Charlevoix concluded in 1721 that women were the "chief authorities" among the Huron tribes. This leadership was also intertribal: David Cusick, the Tuscarora artist and author, relayed in 1828 the story of an ancient "Fire Queen" who mediated between warring tribes, who respectfully called her "the mother of the Nations." Bemused, and sometimes admiring, European observations of powerful indigenous American women thus abounded throughout the colonial and into the early national period.[17]

The fullest articulation of the colonial fascination with indigenous matriarchies is found in Joseph-Francois Lafitau's *Moeurs des Savages Ameriquains* (1724). Although anthropologists debate the merit of his methods—some call him an original ethnographer, while others counter that he was little more than a travel writer—Lafitau clearly anticipated a primary premise of nineteenth-century anthropology with his teleological narrative of civilization. In his approach to Native Americans, Lafitau reflected the Enlightenment perspective that distant cultures and lands represented "functional equivalents of the European past." He contrasted indigenous American societies with ancient, "primitive" ones, placing social development along a time line that indicated that the "noble savages" of the eighteenth century could, in the future, become "civilized," just as European societies had reportedly evolved over the course of human history. The Kahnawake of Saint-Louis du Sault, the tribe with whom he lived from 1712 to 1717, became for Lafitau "what the Egyptians were for Herodotus: the image of a culture which threw light upon the ancient world and vice versa."[18]

As evidence for his ancient comparisons, Lafitau delineated various contemporary social practices of American Indians, such as polytheism and direct communication with deities, which, he argued, mirrored those of the early inhabitants of Greece and Asia Minor. Principal among these was matrilineal inheritance, which Lafitau suggested reflected the power structure of ancient Lycian society. The original societies of the Aegean featured warrior women who ruled their husbands, a form of social organization that they possibly inherited from an extensive Amazon empire, which, he argued, included a tribe that "corresponded exactly with the Wolf Clan of the Iroquois and Huron." In fact, Lafitau ultimately claimed that the Iroquois, because of their matrilineal social structure, were descendants of the Lycians, whom he believed migrated to the Americas at some point via a land bridge, a hypothesis that explained the origins of the people of the New World without violating biblical tenets.[19]

The Iroquois were matriarchal in several ways, Lafitau explained. There was the matter of their origin story: the major Nations of the Iroquois traced their descent to a common mother. In contrast to those Europeans who believed that any women who worked in agriculture must be slaves, Lafitau explained that indigenous female labor was instead a visible manifestation of their control over the means of production, as fertile fields were passed down through the women of the clans. Political power accompanied these economic roles, as women deliberated in their own separate councils and advised chiefs, whose titles and positions were determined by the matriarchs of their clans. Separation from men, in this case, did not indicate inequality for women. Indeed, Lafitau's description of women's roles encompassed nearly all possible means of power in Iroquois society:

Nothing is more real, however, than the women's superiority. It is they who really maintain the tribe, the nobility of blood, the genealogical tree, the order of generations and conservation of the family. In them resides all the real authority: the lands, fields and all their harvest belong to them; they are the soul of the councils, the arbiters of peace and war; they hold the taxes and the public treasure; it is to them that the slaves are entrusted; they arrange the marriages; the children are under their authority; and the order of succession is founded on their blood. The men, on the contrary, are entirely isolated and limited to themselves. Their children are strangers to them. Everything perishes with them.

Lafitau extrapolated from his personal observations of and interactions with the Mohawks to construct a universalizing theory of the progress of civilizations which posited that human societies each progressed through a series of discrete stages. The West, according to this schema, represented the pinnacle of social, political, and economic development, whereas "savages," like Lafitau's version of the Iroquois, had only a comparative, temporal relevance as a "surpassed" culture, "a superseded moment of an heroic tale of social progress that culminates in the modern commercial self."[20]

Lafitau's study was significant for many reasons, not the least of which that he provided a model of early ethnographic fieldwork in North America. His progressive time line from savagery to civilization offered something of an "evolutionist blueprint" for scholars of the nineteenth century. He also bears the distinction of offering the first published foray into American matriarchalism, although his analysis was hardly read or referenced at all in North America for over a century. Confirmation of his early observations, however, is scattered throughout Euro-American accounts of the Iroquois Nations through the end of the nineteenth century. Mary Jemison, in her famous captivity narrative, described equality within the families, clans, and labor relations of the Seneca in the 1760s. Various colonial records of the mid-eighteenth-century reference Susanna, a frequent trader who served as a savvy negotiator between New York Indian commissioners and her Kanahwake chief. And many documents mention Molly Brant, a Mohawk clan mother and wife of a superintendent of Indian affairs who was famous as an Iroquois diplomat and key British ally during the American Revolutionary era. Federal and state records attest to the continued power of Iroquois women, as do interviews and memoirs. The gendered power dynamics of the Iroquois Nations, originally noted by Dutch colonists in the 1640s, largely survived into the nineteenth century, despite centuries of colonial, and later, US governmental, attempts to transform them. North America thus had a lengthy and well-documented cultural tradition of matriarchy within its borders by mid-century, when Bachofen began writing of human evolution and ancient matriarchalism.[21]

This continued fascination with indigenous gender roles was more than simply an attempt to understand, and thus learn how to control and/or destroy, Native American groups, although it certainly was that. It also indicated explicit American attempts to come to terms with these differences during an era in which white women's roles were very clearly defined. Indigenous women wielding political power gave lie to the Victorian "cult of domesticity" in which female biological destiny was solely to be wives and mothers. By the second half of the nineteenth century, this fascination reflected growing concerns about the nation, particularly in terms of race, class, and gender. Specifically, challenges to the social order came from four major fronts: the so-called "Indian Question," or the perceived problem of Native American habitation of land desired for settlement by the United States; abolition and the securing of rights and opportunities by and for African Americans; the growing labor movement and working-class resistance to the prevailing political and economic systems; and the women's movement for universal suffrage at the state and federal levels.

In the context of these concerns, the survival of "mother right" among the Seneca, the westernmost of the Iroquois Nations, became a renewed subject of academic fascination in the 1870s, well over a century after Lafitau published his study. Rev. Asher Wright, a missionary stationed among the Seneca on the Cattaraugus Reservation in 1874, observed that women's public and private power were intertwined. "No matter how many children, or whatever goods (a husband) might have in the house," Wright explained, "he might at any time be ordered to pick up his blanket and budge; and after such orders it would not be healthful for him to attempt to disobey." This power extended beyond the traditional Iroquois longhouses. Indeed, women had power among the clans to strip chiefs of power and to nominate new ones.[22]

Wright's observations were key to the late nineteenth-century development of an American version of matriarchalism. Although his descriptions were not new "discoveries," his timing was significant. He helped to reinvigorate the image of Iroquois women as enduring "North American Amazons," which countered both prevailing ideas about gender and the declension narrative of postcolonial indigenous cultural decimation or assimilation. This image would influence the work of anthropologist Lewis Henry Morgan, who used it to present an American version of Bachofen's matriarchal prehistory as well as to critique contemporary social relations.[23]

There was, in fact, a specific purpose to Wright's letters about the Seneca: he recorded his descriptions in response to a query from Morgan, who was preparing a book about the evolution of human societies. Morgan sought more detail from Wright about clan characteristics among Native American tribes. Using Wright's responses, his own fieldwork, and contemporary anthropological theories of prehistory, Morgan combined the eighteenth-century ethnographic approach of Lafitau and other missionaries with the nineteenth-century evolutionist historical time line of Bachofen to produce a major work of American matriarchalism.

Morgan was trained as a lawyer, a profession that would lead to his later work as an anthropologist. In the 1840s, Morgan represented the Seneca Nation in a land-grant case regarding a congressional removal treaty that threatened the reservation. After his successful defense of the Nation, the Seneca, in gratitude, adopted Morgan, giving him the name *Tayadaowuhkuh*, or "One Bridging the Gap," presumably in reference to his ability to move between two cultures. Morgan's close ties with the clan transformed him from their attorney to their chief anthropologist.[24]

The following decade, Morgan used his notes from his time working with the Iroquois to write *League of the Haudenosaunee Iroquois* (1851), which would come to be known as "the first scientific account of an Indian tribe." Morgan's painstaking research secured his place as one of the most significant social scientists of the nineteenth century. In this work, we can see the beginnings of his matriarchalist theory, as he stressed the importance of matrilineal descent and inheritance, the keystones that served as "the bond of union between several tribes of the same nation," binding "together the tribes of the same emblem in the different nations."[25]

Morgan then turned to the questions of Iroquois family and clan relations, which inspired his *Systems of Consanguinity and Affinity of the Human Family* (1871). Although his basic premises clearly echo Lafitau's to the modern reader, Lafitau was so rarely read or referenced by nineteenth-century anthropologists—copies of *Moeurs des Sauvages Ameriquains* were difficult to find, and there was no published English translation until 1974—that Morgan had to investigate and rediscover these indigenous characteristics for himself. Like Lafitau, Morgan came to believe that the family systems of the Iroquois were so complex as to indicate migration from an ancient culture, possibly the Tamils of India. Over the course of the 1870s, Morgan developed his own evolutionist theory of kinship systems, arguing that, like cultures and humans themselves, they evolved predictably through specific stages over time.[26]

This historical theory, a combination of the implications of the recent discovery of human antiquity and the application of Darwinian evolution to social systems, culminated in the publication of Morgan's *Ancient Society, or Researches in the Lines of Human Progress From Savagery through Barbarism to Civilization* (1877). As the subtitle indicates, social evolutionism was his primary premise. According to Morgan's version, Native Americans could serve as valuable educational tools on the ways of the ancients. Previous theorists like Lafitau had much to say about "primitives" and "others" as ancient throwbacks and negative comparisons to contemporaries, and similarly, Victorian anthropologists like Morgan were concerned with the evolutionary order of societies, depicting nonwhite, non-Western "others" as "calibrated stepping stones on a path illustrating evolutionary progress from 'savagery' through 'barbarism' to the apotheosis of white, male Western 'civilization.'"[27]

Scholars have long analyzed the racism inherent in this kind of historical thinking, a problem I will tackle more specifically in ensuing chapters. Just as significantly for Morgan, this linear evolution was fundamentally gendered. Through his fieldwork among the Iroquois, Morgan came to understand that the matrilineal clan was not just a cultural "domestic unit." Rather, it was the entire principle upon which the tribes' political and economic structures were built. Moreover, this was not true of just the Iroquois. The archaeological and ethnographic "richness" of North America, Morgan explained, justified his use of fieldwork among Native American tribes as evidence for all of human experience. He concluded "that the history and experience of American Indian tribes represented, or less nearly, the history and experience of our own remote ancestors when in corresponding conditions."[28]

Using Native Americans as his primary sources, Morgan compared his observations to other scholars' analyses of both ancient and far-flung "savages." These comparisons served as the foundation of his model of "ethnical periods," or the seven stages of social evolution from savagery to civilization that all human societies, regardless of their historical era or geographical location, purportedly underwent. He argued that there were two basic forms of government: one based on kinship and personal relationships, and another based on property rights and ownership. Morgan concluded in *Ancient Society* that most American tribes, according to his model of stages, exist in the "Upper Status of Savagery," with power structures based on kinship. Within this "status," Morgan argued that the "gens," or what we might now call a "clan," was the basic unit of social organization, followed by "the successive stages of integration" of "the phratry, the tribe, and the confederacy of tribes, which constituted a people or nation."[29]

Within the "savage gens," according to Morgan, women held a unique position. The communal nature of ancient society provided for a particular kind of gendered power, "the phenomena of mother right and gynecocracy." Because maternity could easily be established in tribes in which paternity was still misunderstood, mothers held ultimate power in these clan-based societies. This reproductive rationale for a mother-based power structure was not an original supposition on Morgan's part, based as it was on Bachofen's speculation. The specific stages of this evolutionist model, however, are all his own: according to Morgan, the matrilineal clan stage was followed by the "phratry," or the "brotherhood" stage, which was characterized by several gendered developments: the establishment of paternity; "segmentation" of the matrilineal gens; and, eventually, monogamy, oppression of women, and the prevalence of private property ownership.[30]

Morgan's major contribution to matriarchalism was not his gendered time line, which will by now be familiar to readers. Rather, it was his estimation of the evolution that he described; in short, it was the value judgment that he placed upon the transition from matriarchy to patriarchy, and his firm insistence on the positive socioeconomic attributes of the matriarchate. The oppression of women and children within family units represented, for Morgan, the deterioration of societies rather than civilized progress. Although, like Bachofen, Morgan avoided the wholesale denigration of patriarchy or the romantic idealization of matriarchy, he cited this patriarchal transition as the catalyst for social and even imperial destruction: Greece and Rome had, among other things, the "failure to develop and utilize the mental, moral and conservative forces of the female intellect" to blame for their decline. In the "status of barbarism," patriarchal power and private property ownership spawned the separation of societies into economic classes, which "antagonized the democratic principles created and fostered" by the gens organization of societies. Morgan targeted "aristocracy," whose "burdensome character upon society has been demonstrated" for "several thousand years," as an unwanted result of the advance of societies from "savagery to civilization" and from matriarchy to patriarchy. Combining class and sex relations, he argued that inequality led to social decline.[31]

Morgan's historical narrative was a kind of warning to contemporary societies, a cautionary tale, ignored by most of his readers, that the tyranny of a patriarchal, property-based system of power would inevitably cause societal downfall as it had so often in the past. Morgan concluded with a suggestion that his contemporaries learn from this past, and in fact use it to correct the present. Morgan refrained from an analysis of contemporary patriarchy, yet there is in his work a discernible nostalgia for the "ancient gentes," which were, according to his findings, matriarchies.[32]

Morgan's critique of contemporary society was timely. The year that *Ancient Society* was published was a tumultuous one for American hierarchies of class, race, and ethnicity, featuring as it did the Great Railroad Strike, a corrupt political compromise that returned the South to "home rule" and ushered in Jim Crow, and the 1,700-mile pursuit of the Nez Percé Indians across the Far West by the US Army in an attempt to enforce a federal order removing them from their Oregon land. Hierarchies based on gender and sex were under fire, as well, as we shall see shortly.[33]

The academic context of Morgan's work was no less contentious. Although the concept of universal prehistoric matriarchy would enjoy the status of "orthodoxy" until it fell out of favor two decades later, Morgan was frequently attacked by other anthropologists, particularly those who supported theories of prehistoric "father right" over "mother right." Indeed, this criticism of his magnum opus fostered American ethnography, as other budding anthropologists flocked to the field in search of evidence for or against Morgan's matriarchal theories. Those matriarchalists who saw patriarchal society as a triumph of civilization dismissed him, but some like-minded academics lauded his work; in 1880, Bachofen himself dedicated a book of essays to "Herr Lewis H. Morgan in Rochester (New York) . . . out of gratitude for the manifold instructions which I received."[34]

Morgan's most lasting impact as a matriarchalist was not discipline-specific, nor was it merely academic. Rather, it was sociopolitical. Friedrich Engels, in *Origin of the Family, Private Property, and the State* (1884), cited Morgan frequently and devoted an entire chapter to his analysis of the "Iroquois Gens."

In the 1880s, Engels was heavily influenced by the intertwined concepts of evolution, human antiquity, and the matriarchalist emphasis on sex relations as the key to economic developments, especially the ownership and inheritance of property. Engels's text was fairly unoriginal in that his major contribution was to combine three major discourses of the era: he and Marx's materialist-economic model of history, Darwin's evolution, and Morgan's matriarchalism.[35]

More so than any of his predecessors, Engels transformed the dim matriarchal past into an ideal. For Engels, the early stages of human history were characterized by both communism and gender equality:

> Communistic housekeeping . . . means the supremacy of women in the house; just as the exclusive recognition of the female parent, owing to the impossibility of recognizing the male parent with certainty, means that the women—the mothers—are held in high respect. One of the most absurd notions taken over from eighteenth-century enlightenment is that in the beginning of society woman was the slave of the man. Among all savages and all barbarians of the lower and middle stages, and to a certain extent of the upper stage also, the position of women is not only free, but honorable.

Most contemporary scholars, Engels argued, projected their own gender biases onto the past to justify the inequalities of the present.[36]

Engels relied upon Morgan's ethnographic evidence to present an indigenous American solution to contemporary capitalism. Using Wright's analysis of gender relations among the Seneca, which he got from Morgan's publication of Wright's letters in *Ancient Society*, Engels connected gender, power, and economics, arguing that the communal household served as the foundation of female power. And this power was, in his estimation, truly feminist, based as it was on notions of sex equality. Engels cautioned that the "savage" position of women contradicted the evolutionist narrative of sex relations in "civilized" societies: "The lady of civilization, surrounded by false homage and estranged from all real work, has an infinitely lower social position than the hard-working woman of barbarism." The transition from communistic households had dire consequences for women; it constituted nothing less than the "world historical defeat of the female sex."[37]

Engels presented the matriarchal past as a distant ideal that threw into high relief the problems of patriarchal capitalism. Engels's contribution to American matriarchalism was based on his audience: through *Origin*, this discourse reached socialist readers, thereafter wedding the concept of a matriarchal, communistic past to political visions of a Marxist future. His influence in the United States, however, was not limited to the socialist or communist faithful. At the time that Morgan and Engels were deploying matriarchalism as a means of exposing the dark devolution of Victorian society, American feminism was solidifying as a movement.[38]

Organized feminism existed in the United States from at least the 1840s, when activists attended the first women's rights conference at Seneca Falls, New York, a town named after the matriarchal nation that so intrigued Lewis Henry Morgan. It is likely not an accident of history that, like Morgan, some of the major feminists of the second half of the nineteenth century—Susan B. Anthony, Matilda Joslyn Gage, Elizabeth Cady Stanton, Sojourner Truth— were raised in Iroquois territory. While Morgan was developing his theory of gynecocracy, American feminists, still burning from the exclusionary gendered language of the Fourteenth Amendment, were beginning to agitate for suffrage through organized channels.[39]

In 1869, as Morgan was finishing his first major work on the Iroquois, Wyoming became the first US territory to grant the vote to women via legislation. Utah Territory quickly followed Wyoming's lead the following year. By the 1870s, two women's suffrage organizations had formed: the American Equal Rights Association, which advocated for universal suffrage via federal amendment, and the National Woman Suffrage Association, which advocated for state-by-state suffrage, either by legislation or by amendments to state constitutions. In 1872, activist Susan B. Anthony was arrested for illegal voting in New York. In 1876, she and Matilda Joslyn Gage disrupted the United States Centennial celebration at Independence Hall in Philadelphia when they approached the stage unannounced to present Acting Vice President Thomas W. Ferry with the "Declaration of Rights of the Women of the United States." Two years later, the Senate Committee on Privileges and Elections held hearings on a proposed constitutional amendment that extended suffrage to women. Although the proposal was dismissed by legislators, many of whom pointedly read the newspaper during the hearings to indicate their lack of interest in universal suffrage, feminist activism reached a broader audience through federal actions like this.[40]

The timing of Morgan's matriarchal theory was, for these activists, auspicious. It is not at all surprising that those feminists who read Morgan wholly embraced his theory of matriarchal prehistory as a justification for their own political activism and goals—widely accepted female power in the past legitimated its usefulness in the present. Thus, Morgan's Seneca name, "One Bridging the Gap," had many contexts: his legal work for the Native American land rights, his academic publications on indigenous societies, and his enormous popularity with American feminists.

After the publication of Morgan's *Ancient Society*, matriarchalism became popular in the United States. Not surprisingly, it first took root among a handful of leaders of the suffrage movement, who read Morgan's ethnography with much interest. In particular, Matilda Joslyn Gage, who, along with Susan B. Anthony and Elizabeth Cady Stanton, was a major leader within this movement, relied upon Morgan's matriarchalist arguments. At the time that *Ancient Society* was published, Gage was already beginning to develop the corresponding theories that would make up her own magnum opus. Morgan's explication of gynecocracy provided the final piece of an emerging theory of American feminist matriarchalism that would come to resonate in US popular culture for the next century.

2

MOTHER-RULE IN THE MODERN WORLD
Victorian Feminist Matriarchalism

> A strange identity of thought pervades all parts of the world . . . all
> evince proof of the wide psychic undercurrent which seething through
> women's souls is overthrowing the civilizations built upon the force
> principles of the patriarchate, and will soon reinstate the reign of
> truth and justice.
>
> —MATILDA JOSLYN GAGE, *Women, Church and State,* 1893

THE first American feminist credited with taking up the theory of matriarchalism is Elizabeth Cady Stanton in her speech "The Matriarchate, or Mother-Age" (1891). Stanton's starting point was Morgan's theory of ancient matriarchy, particularly his claim that women's status was a key indicator of a society's health and progress. The trajectory of Morgan's theories from the academic realm of early anthropology to the sociopolitical realm of the suffrage movement and feminism, which was a crucial transition in the development of the American matriarchalist tradition in popular culture, is the subject of this chapter.

By the end of the nineteenth century, according to Stanton, academic questions about human antiquity and the evolution of social systems were no longer up for debate. She began her speech by generalizing the "fine calculations of historians as to the centuries of human growth," assigning sixty thousand years to the state of savagery, twenty thousand to barbarism, and five thousand to civilization. Stanton deplored the blind acceptance of patriarchy as a universal, historical condition; citing Bachofen and Morgan, she challenged this widely believed "fallacy," arguing that the "facts" of human social evolution were only significant insofar as they indicated "how long a period, in proportion, women reigned supreme, the arbiters of their own destiny, the protectors of their children, the acknowledged builders of all there was of home life, religion, and later, from time to time, of government."[1]

Stanton's time line of history was explicitly based on Morgan's schema of social organization. She traced how women rose to power via reproduction, controlling property and family lineage, and participating in tribal governments in which "their opinions had equal weight on all questions." Like Morgan, she cited examples from "American aborigines," including the Zuni and the Iroquois, as well as from ancient Greece, and she extrapolated to all of world history: "As far back into the shadowy past as human thought penetrated . . . we behold woman in all her native dignity, self-poised and self-supporting, her own head and hands her guidance and protection."[2]

Maternity, for Stanton, was the key to the original organization of human societies. Rather than just one factor in the historical processes that led to "civilization" as her contemporaries defined it, Stanton argued that "the necessities of motherhood were the real source of all the earliest attempts at civilization . . . maternity has been the all-inspiring motive or force that impelled the first steps toward a stable home and family life." Man in primitive societies "simply invented and improved weapons of warfare" in his quest for food, "but the woman, handicapped as she appeared to be by child-bearing, became on this very account the main factor in human progress." In short, "the man's contributions at this early period are nothing as compared to woman's," as her many duties "as mother, bread-winner, protector, defender of a group of helpless children" elevated all of early womankind to "intellectual and inventive supremacy, and made her the teacher and ruler of man."[3]

While prehistoric men occupied their time with weapons, hunting, and warfare, women, Stanton claimed, were responsible for most of the early milestones in human history, including the development of agriculture, the growth of the healing arts and medicine, the domestication of animals, and the cultivation of "the sentiments of kinship and all home life." Although she mentioned the supposed link between the establishment of paternity and the simultaneous rise of monogamy and private property ownership, this, for Stanton, was not a sufficient explanation for the transition in gendered power. "Woman's supremacy" was "undisputed, accepted as natural and proper wherever it existed," and so challenges took time to succeed. Rather than a violent rupture in power dynamics, "this invasion of the mother's rights was a slow process," Stanton argued, that was "for long periods resisted." Specifically, she claimed that one could trace the defeat of matriarchal systems to Christianity.[4]

Stanton's targeting of organized religion was her primary contribution to the developing feminist discourse of matriarchalism. She did not, however, arrive at this conclusion on her own. In fact, although her speech is often cited and included in anthologies of feminist documents, Stanton did not formulate her brand of revisionist history under the sole intellectual influence of well-known academic matriarchalists like Morgan. Although she has been largely lost to history, Stanton's friend and fellow activist Matilda Joslyn Gage first advanced the idea of the ancient "matriarchate" ten years earlier, in an 1881 article. While Stanton's speech is more likely to appear in modern collections, Gage's feminist matriarchalism is the version that would leave an indelible impression upon American popular culture.[5]

Matilda Joslyn Gage's brand of matriarchalism was a product of her lifelong beliefs in equality, feminism, and anticlericalism. Born in 1826 into an activist family, Matilda Joslyn was exposed to radical ideas when her family would host reformers on the lecture circuit in upstate New York. Parlor discussions centered on the evils of slavery, as the Joslyn home was a safe house for the Underground Railroad and a frequent respite for traveling abolitionists. Other family conversations to which young Matilda Joslyn was privy were about women's rights, as female participation in the abolitionist movement became a "burning issue" by 1850. These experiences were so ingrained that Gage later stated that she thought she "was born with a hatred of oppression."[6]

In 1845, Matilda Joslyn married Henry Gage, and the couple settled in Fayetteville, New York. Henry ran a dry goods store, and his wife soon became pregnant. Even as she had five children in quick succession, Gage maintained an interest in contemporary social problems. In 1845, she was inspired by *Narrative of the Life of Frederick Douglass* (1845), the memoir of the fiery, ex-slave orator whom she had seen speak in Syracuse two years earlier. Gage also read Margaret Fuller's women's rights treatise *Woman in the Nineteenth Century* (1843). According to her biographer, reading these two revolutionary works in tandem solidified Gage's belief in the intertwined roots of racial and gendered oppression, and she concluded that contemporary Christianity was "the bulwark of the slave's oppression, and perhaps of woman's as well." Throughout her domestic duties, Gage maintained the radical politics of her childhood; her home, like that of her parents, became a station on the Underground Railroad.[7]

Gage found her calling when she attended and spoke at the 1852 National Woman's Rights Convention in Syracuse, New York. At this convention, she met Susan B. Anthony, who became her close collaborator for the next three and a half decades. At twenty-six, Gage was the youngest woman to speak at the convention. In her first public address, she listed examples of historical figures who demonstrated women's "peculiar fitness for governing," an interesting choice of opener that anticipated her later position as a women's historian. Gage's expansive historical knowledge impressed the more established feminists, and a new spokesperson was born.[8]

Emboldened by the audience's response to her lecture and angered by the frequent antifeminist vitriol in the press, Gage turned to writing, then to lecturing on the women's rights circuit, and finally to organizing abolitionist and women's petitions, campaigns, and events in the 1850s. True to her abolitionist roots, Gage concentrated wholeheartedly on the issue of slavery during the Civil War. As a young feminist, she consistently championed unpopular causes, including the rights of immigrants, free love, and the rights of Native Americans. This broad conception of rights was the crux of Gage's sociopolitical philosophy, and one that later distinguished her from many of her more singular-minded, suffragist colleagues in women's rights circles.[9]

After the Civil War, Gage threw herself into the suffrage movement, as securing the vote became the primary focus of the broader women's movement. In order to document women's contributions as part of a justification for voting rights, Gage wrote the three-volume, one-thousand-page *History of Woman Suffrage* (1876–1885) with her sisters-in-arms Elizabeth Cady Stanton and Susan B. Anthony. With a small group of other leaders, she helped to form the National Woman Suffrage Association, and she became a full-time activist, participating in many campaigns, including the very public disruption of the 1876 Centennial Celebration of the Declaration of Independence. Denied participation in the opening ceremony, Gage and Anthony stormed the stage in front of a crowd of 150,000. As they fled the security guards, the women threw copies of their own "Declaration" to the crowd. A decade later, Gage made headlines again as part of a group of women from the New York State Women's Suffragette Association who hired a boat to crash the unveiling of the Statue of Liberty, a ceremony to which only two women were invited; the activists protested the hypocrisy of a feminine symbol of freedom in a nation in which women could not vote.[10]

After these stunts, Gage became one of the suffrage movement's official historians. As she conducted research, Gage began to uncover the untold details of women's history, and she became a matriarchalist as she discovered buried contributions and overt oppression of powerful women in almost every society that she studied. During this same time, as part of her intellectual quest, Gage became very interested in Theosophy, a New Age–type spiritualism that combined Western science and Eastern philosophy, centered on the charismatic figure of Madame Helena Petrovna Blavatsky. Like matriarchalism, Theosophy is best understood within the context of the many theories that sparked a crisis in religious belief in the late Victorian era. Blavatsky promoted the idea that all world religions stemmed from a single source—the "secret doctrine" or "ancient wisdom"—and these belief systems were corrupted over time. The goal of the Theosophical Society was to recover and reclaim this foundational knowledge.[11]

Although Theosophy had some strange features, the initial appeal for Gage seems to have been its primary stated objective, which was to "form a 'Brotherhood of man,' without distinction of race, creed, sex, caste, or color." Theosophists argued that there was partial truth in every world religion; in their comparative studies of belief systems and science, they tended to focus on Eastern religions and ancient civilizations, particularly those of Egypt and India, and this emphasis influenced Gage's investigation into world history. Blavatsky's promotion of the goddess worship of ancient cultures offered to followers like Gage an alternative to the patriarchy of Victorian Christianity, which called for circumscribed gender roles, and theosophical elements began to crop up in Gage's public lectures, including one on ancient Egypt in 1880. By 1885, Gage had become a member of the Theosophical Society of Rochester, New York, and her newfound spiritualism infused her broadly conceived feminism in her speeches and writings.[12]

But Gage's anticlerical vision of a "radical, far ranging woman's movement" was destroyed in 1890 when the National Woman Suffrage Association merged with the more conservative American Woman Suffrage Association, which was supported by the Women's Christian Temperance Union (WCTU). Incensed by this alliance with a Christian organization, which she saw as the primary progenitor of patriarchy in Western societies, Gage abandoned most of her fellow activists, as Anthony and her many followers pursued the vote through what they saw as the most expedient means possible. For Gage, this merger was ill-conceived, immoral, and self-defeating for women. She argued that it was a capitulation to the sources of the "fourfold bondage" of women: "State, Church, Capitalist, Home."[13]

As Gage sought different activist avenues for her broad conception of rights, she grew more radical, while the suffrage movement grew more conservative and narrowly focused. Gage was adamant about "the absolute necessity of religious freedom as a prerequisite for authentic women's liberation," and she threw herself into an investigation of "intellectually and morally repulsive" religious conservatism, that primary "danger of the hour" that plagued American society and jurisprudence and had invaded the suffrage movement via the WCTU. Disillusioned yet emboldened by the contentious split with the NWSA, Gage went on to form the little-known Woman's National Liberal Union, a "Free Thinker-Anarchist-Feminist organization" based on the premise: "That the church is the enemy of liberty and progress and the chief means of enslaving woman's conscience and reason, and therefore as the first and most necessary step toward her emancipation we should free her from the bondage of the Church." Three years later, this principle became the basis of Gage's major work of women's history.[14]

As Gage grew ever more anticlerical, she read widely in works on human antiquity, mythology, and matriarchalism. In an article published in 1881, Gage provided the outlines of the first explicitly feminist version of American matriarchalism, and after over a decade of research, she expanded upon her claims in a lengthy treatise, *Women, Church and State* (1893). Gage dedicated the book first to her deceased mother, and then to "all Christian women and men, of whatever creed or name who, bound by Church or State, have not dared to Think for Themselves." This dedication was double-edged, serving also as an insult to those former feminist sisters who had betrayed Gage by capitulating to the influence of the church in their single-minded quest for suffrage.[15]

In the first chapter, entitled "The Matriarchate," Gage stated unequivocally that the doctrine of female inferiority contradicted historical evidence: "Such assertions are due to non-acquaintance with the existing phase of historical knowledge, whose records the majority of mankind have neither time nor opportunity of investigating." Clerical ignorance was no longer excusable, Gage argued, because in the second half of the nineteenth century, "the spirit of investigation has made known many secrets of the past, brought many hidden things to light." Gage cited newly discovered records from societies as diverse as "Babylonia and Chaldea," to the Zunis and the "Astecs," to "Darkest Africa," that suggested the existence of ancient, universal, matriarchal social systems. Gage deemed this social form the "Matriarchate or Mother-rule," in which, "except as son and inferior, man was not recognized in either of these great institutions, family, state or church." True to her academic matriarchalist predecessors, Gage used everything from the "Hindoo" Vedas to the archaeological artifacts left by the Mississippian Mound Builders to make a firm argument for the universality of this sociopolitical form across time and space.[16]

Everywhere she looked, Gage found traces of the matriarchal past, which she painstakingly described like an art historian uncovering pentimenti on a painting. In Catholic worship of the Virgin Mary, for example, she saw echoes of prehistoric worship of the "eternal feminine," which most ancients, she argued, "recognized as the creative power." In Egyptian worship of Isis, Gage found "the earliest law-maker, through whose teachings the people had risen from barbarism to civilization," and who demonstrated how to grow and harvest grains, thus "rendering the long stability of the Roman Empire possible." The persuasive property-owning wives of "old Aryan Scriptures," the Vestal Virgins in Rome, the reverence of the "old Berserkers" in ancient Scandinavia for their earthly and heavenly "Holy Women"—each was evidence of universal matriarchal history.[17]

Following the lead of academic matriarchalism, Gage argued that this original womanpower stemmed from the basic facts of reproduction, and she viewed motherhood as an obvious source of power. In matriarchal societies, she argued, "the right of the mother was therefore most natural," and the relationship between mothers and children was the organization of family and society. This natural right, however, did not translate into singularly domestic power, as the "cult of true womanhood" in Victorian America would have it. Gage was a devoted mother herself, but she had a higher goal: "There is a word sweeter than mother, home or heaven: that word is liberty."[18]

Here, Gage's deployment of maternity as an organizing principle of society contrasted with the maternalism of her time. In the late Victorian era, women's organizations often framed their political positions within the language of "true womanhood" by emphasizing the social usefulness of women's allegedly biological imperatives to caretaking and self-sacrifice. Using maternal rhetoric as a springboard to public activism proved to be enormously effective among white, middle-class women; by the end of the nineteenth century, "tens of thousands of urban middle-class women" had joined various women's clubs, and by 1910, the General Federation of Women's Clubs (GFWC), the clearinghouse of these organizations, boasted 800,000 members. These female reformers relied heavily upon "moral suasion" and maternalist rhetoric to seek state funds and even intervention.[19]

In the United States, maternalism manifested itself via a broad coalition of women's charitable organizations that relied upon claims to motherhood and maternal characteristics as a means of promoting social services via the private sector, influencing public policy, and, in the cases of those functions of women's organizations that were later co-opted by the government, participating in state formation. As "municipal housekeepers," or women who argued that their inherent responsibilities of childcare and housekeeping encompassed not just their homes, but also their neighborhoods and cities, they located their power within the rhetoric of the "cult of domesticity" that had been used in the past to deny women political rights and responsibilities, and in doing so, they left an "unmistakable stamp" on the welfare state that emerged by the New Deal era. In particular, Gage's nemesis, Frances Willard of the Women's Christian Temperance Union, was a master of maternalist rhetoric in the late nineteenth century, and the organization she headed became increasingly influential after its founding in 1874. The WCTU's tagline was "Home Protection," which the organization used to lobby for change within the public sphere.[20]

This essentialist use of motherhood contrasted with the general rhetoric of late Victorian suffragists, who relied upon the language of equal rights in their demand for the vote. These two positions became increasingly intertwined after the 1890 merger between the suffrage organizations and the WCTU. Although many suffragists continued to claim political rights as natural rights, maternalism became a vital part of suffragist popular culture, and maternal rhetoric offered a "unifying theme" for various women's organizations after 1890, so that by 1920, "motherhood was a central organizing principle of Progressive-Era politics." Maternalism, rooted in essentialist ideas about femininity in Victorian culture, and feminism, premised upon the basic argument of sex equality, thus uneasily coexisted within the suffrage and women's movements at the turn of the twentieth century. As part of her ongoing effort to combat gender essentialism, Gage did not idealize mothers as "angels in the house" who could then apply their otherworldly qualities to cleaning up society. Rather, she believed that maternity had its practical uses as an organizing principle for families and societies.[21]

And, Gage argued, one need not look far afield for such societies. Like Lewis Henry Morgan, Gage found democratic matriarchal systems in her own backyard in upstate New York, in the numerous "reminiscences of the Matriarchate" among the Iroquois Nations. Echoing Morgan, Gage explained that Six Nation women had "superiority in power," controlling property and offspring. This domestic power further translated into public authority, as women served as "final adjudicat[ors]" regarding elections of chiefs, sales of land, treaties, and "questions of war."[22]

Although *Women, Church and State* is a major work of women's scholarship, Gage was not simply entering an academic debate; she was making a political argument. The matriarchal tendencies among the Iroquois were, for Gage, the key to American principles. Citing the esteemed nineteenth-century writer, historian, and statesman George Bancroft, Gage argued that "the form of government of the United States was borrowed from that of the Six Nations." She explained that the Iroquois originated the first conceptions of inherent rights, natural equality of condition, and the establishment of a civilized government upon these bases.[23]

Morgan had come to these same conclusions through his ethnographic work with the Haudenosaunee, but Gage's experience was notably different. She visited tribes not as an academic, but as a woman seeking answers to her own oppression. There were clear connections, not just comparisons, between the treatment of Native Americans and the oppression of women. Specifically, Gage exposed the link between American ideas of citizenship and white masculinity in her study of land policy. As early as 1869, she wrote that the Iroquois council's denouncing the recent Indian Act in New York and the simultaneous women's rights convention in Washington were "two forcible commentaries upon our so-called republican form of government." She continued to explore connections between oppressions throughout her career as an activist and writer.[24]

Gage spent time with Iroquois women, who taught her their maternal creation myth and explained their many rights and responsibilities. The local matriarchs were sufficiently impressed by Gage's understanding of their culture that, after several visits to the reservation near Syracuse, Gage was adopted into the Mohawk clan in 1893. She later explained: "I received the name of Ka-ron-ien-ha-wi, or 'Sky Carrier,' or as . . . the Seneca would express it, 'She who holds the sky.'" Gage claimed that the adoption and her new name would allow her admission into "the Council of Matrons," where, after a vote, she would be allowed "a voice in the Chieftainship,'" although she does not seem to have exercised this right. From the Mohawk women, Gage learned natural medicine, which she began to use in her counsel to her children and grandchildren, cautioning them against the Western, male medical establishment. These experiences heavily influenced her analysis of world history; as cultural, social, and political models, Gage wrote, "the world is indebted to the Iroquois."[25]

Gage's time amongst the Haudenosaunee further inspired her condemnation of gendered inequality in contemporary America, and she presented a clear culprit for historical regression. The "barbarism" of Christianity, she argued, had dragged with it "myriad institutions" of oppression, and this was particularly true from a gendered perspective. Gage did not equivocate when it came to the question of the fate of the matriarchate. The Christian Church, and its close corollary the Western state, were to blame. The ascendance of Christianity ushered in the "Patriarchate," which was characterized by various negative historical factors, including polygamy, an emphasis on multiple births per woman, regarding wives as property, "the sale of daughters as a legitimate means of family income" through marriage, "the theory of a male supreme God in the interests of force and authority, wars, family discord, the sacrifice of children to appease the wrath of an offended (male) deity," the "destruction of girl children," and prostitution. Gage led her readers slowly through history, detailing the suppression and destruction of female power and the development of a false doctrine of natural patriarchy.[26]

Of particular interest to Gage was the treatment of witchcraft, which encapsulated her gendered argument about the church's role in world history: "When for 'witches' we read 'women,' we gain fuller comprehension of the cruelties inflicted by the church upon this portion of humanity." The label of "witch" was indisputably gendered: "What was termed magic, among men, was called witchcraft in woman. The one was rarely, the other invariably, punished." She explained: "The witch was in reality the profoundest thinker, the most advanced scientists of those ages. The persecution which for ages waged against witches was in reality an attack upon science at the hands of the church. As knowledge has ever been power, the church feared its use in woman's hands, and leveled its deadliest blows at her." In Gage's examples, accusations of "witchcraft" denoted medicinal and scientific advances by women throughout history, redefined by the church, like all instances of female intellect, as heretical evil.[27]

Torture and execution were the tools of enforcement of this new system. Gage estimated from historical records that "nine millions of persons" were executed for witchcraft between the late fifteenth and the late eighteenth centuries, the majority of whom were women. The social paranoia over witchcraft was not some ancient relic; indeed, Gage argued, citing Luther's statement that he would "burn all" witches, that it increased over time into the modern period. Over time, women complied for fear of torture, which included methods such as boiling in oil and iron-collared "Witches' Bridles." Eventually, women submitted to the new norm of female passivity: "Ignorance was regarded as an especial virtue in woman, and fear held her in this condition. Few women dared to be wise, after thousands of their sex had gone to death by drowning or burning because of their knowledge."[28]

Oppression was accompanied by the rewriting of history to erase women, and this erasure concerned Gage most of all. The destruction of female power in history was a devastating historical process, but Gage concluded on a hopeful note, citing contemporary developments in scientific thought and human inquiry. Gage saw great potential in her contemporaries: "Woman is showing her innate wisdom in daring to question the infallibility of man. . . . She is not obeying 'too well.'" Opportunities in education and social activism had emboldened women of the late nineteenth century, as they learned "that not self-sacrifice, but self-development, is [their] first duty in life." And despite the recent tumult in her relationships with feminist colleagues, Gage still cited the potential of women's suffrage to defeat the final retrograde hold of the church over the state.[29]

Whereas Morgan ended his matriarchal history with a warning, Gage ended with a prediction. Indeed, reading the conclusions of *Women, Church and State*, one gets the feeling that Gage—despite her abandonment by her fellow activists, her advanced age, and her increasingly poor health in the 1890s—believed that nothing less than a revolution was at hand. The changes she predicted were not simply the product of so-called Western advancement or feminism. Gage believed a global change, such as the ones she charted in history, was coming to the Victorian world. In this movement, the United States, with its traditions of rights stemming from the Nations of the Iroquois, would lead the way: "In no other country had the conflict between natural and revealed rights been as pronounced as in the United States. . . . We note its beginning; its progress will overthrow every existing form of these institutions; its end will be a regenerated world.[30] In short, Gage offered this impressive investigation of world history as support for her prediction of a coming American matriarchy.

Women, Church and State was well reviewed, but not widely read, due to its academic nature, length, and controversial subject matter. As a lifelong activist who was accustomed to intermittent poverty, Gage did not expect to profit from the sales of her book, and she anticipated antagonistic reactions from those opposed to women's rights. It was a theme she addressed frequently, including in her first public address in 1852: "We need not expect the concessions demanded by women will be peaceably granted; there will be a long moral warfare before the citadel yields." And no one was more interested in this kind of ideological warfare than Anthony Comstock, the famous moral crusader of the late Victorian era, who deemed *Women, Church and State* "salacious" and threatened to arrest the members of Gage's hometown school board if the book was allowed in the school library. He argued, "The incidents of victims of lust told in this book are such that if I found a person putting that book indiscriminately before the children I would institute a criminal proceeding against them for doing it."[31]

Gage was delighted by this, as Comstock's reaction mirrored those of the patriarchs examined in her book. With her characteristic tartness, she responded that Comstock was a "mentally and morally unbalanced" man who did not know "right from wrong or the facts of history from the 'tales of lust.'" If ignorance was a sin, she told the local newspaper, then "Anthony Comstock (was) a great sinner." She later described the invigorating effects of the controversy: "You wish to know the effect of this Comstock-Catholic attack upon me? It has acted like a tonic. I have not been well through the summer, not having recovered from over-work on *Women, Church and State,* but the moment I learned of Comstock's letter and read the falsities so freely printed in regard to my book, I grew better and feel myself able to meet all enemies of whatever name or nature."[32]

In addition to Comstock's strict (and sexist) moral code, another objection to Gage's version of matriarchalism mirrored the popular late Victorian accusation that women who sought power and/or equality were, in effect, trying to become men. The obscure Ohio teacher and matriarchalist author Mary E. Bradley Lane challenged this claim by offering fictional characters whose power was rooted in female biology; rather than becoming men, these powerful women simply replaced them. Lane's *Mizora: A Prophecy* was serialized in the *Cincinnati Commercial* in 1880–1881 and published as a novel in 1889. In Lane's novel, the men of the distant land of Mizora, located at the temperate center of the Earth and reached via a mysterious whirlpool in an "unknown sea," destroyed themselves through warfare, leading to a Bachofen-esque female revolution that established a matriarchy. The Mizoran women found that they were better rulers than the men as they eliminated disease, crime, war, and poverty; the government became the "beneficent mother who furnished everything" to such an efficient degree that all were educated and well-fed, and "life was so harmonious and perfect that it was a pleasure to contemplate."

The visitor/narrator of the novel, Vera, learns that the Mizoran women, in their mastery of the biological sciences, discovered how to reproduce on their own, whereupon they took the advice of a "prominent scientist" to "let the [male] race die out" in order to avoid the reinstallment of patriarchy and to embark upon their successful experiment in matriarchy. One character "solemnly" explains, "Know that the MOTHER is the only important part of all life." Lane thus offers an all-encompassing form of maternalism that posited the power of women to not only rule men, but to replace them altogether. Although the novel was not well known or widely read, Lane hit upon a common charge that female rule necessarily entailed the subjugation, or even the eradication, of men.[33]

A related cultural response to matriarchalism with which Gage was familiar was the idea that, rather than women trying to become or replace men, they were instead trying to make men become women. In 1893, the same year that Gage published *Women, Church and State,* Julian Robinson published the pornographic novel *Gynecocracy: A Narrative of the Adventures and Psychological Experiences of Julian Robinson Under Petti-Coat Rule.* Upon meeting his governess and her female charges, the narrator, Julian, expects to "be shorn of my manhood and made effeminate and good-for-nothing." In a series of female-driven sex scenes involving dominance and submission, most of Julian's fears do come true. But this novel went beyond mere titillation; the most brutal and frequent "punishment" endured by the narrator under the gynocratic hand of his governess is enforced transvestism, including the wearing of "a chemise, long stockings, drawers, petticoats, a corset which did not fit," and "a pair of Mademoiselle's own laced drawers" around his neck. This cross-dressing was accompanied by physical violence and sexual humiliation. Julian quickly becomes Mademoiselle's "wretched petticoat-slave"; "completely emasculated," he feels his "virility ebbing away," but, to his own surprise and to the horror of many male readers, he loves it. Sex, he claims, gives women "such power over men," so much so that he argues that "this world is woman's earth, and it is petticoated all over." Julian concludes: "Theirs is the dominion, turn and twist the matter as you will." "I love my bondage and I love my tyrant," he says of his cruel mistress, who ends the novel by yelling at him to stop writing and "go to [her] bedroom at once, Sir!" Julian, clad in his "lady's stocking and drawers," follows her orders dutifully. This, then, was the popular stuff of matriarchy when Gage published her lengthy history: a sadistic woman and a "trembl[ing]" man.[34]

While *Gynecocracy*, as pornography, and *Women, Church and* State, as scholarship, were not for general audiences, the fear of matriarchy was widespread at the turn of the twentieth century, and capitalizing on this fear was an explicit strategy of antisuffragism. Some of the most widely circulated images of suffragettes in the United States were produced by antagonistic groups, and a common theme was "sexual inversion," or the alleged masculinization of women and the feminization of men that would result from women flocking to the polls. One oft-used image featured a man caring for three small children; the postcard had one of two captions that read either "Don't worry—The Worst is yet to come" or "Holding His Own—Ma's at the Movies." The specter of men doing housework and childcare—one memorable postcard featured a man with a halo feeding a bottle to a baby, with the caption "Suffragette Madonna"—was a primary representation of the suffrage movement, as was the image of large, masculine women browbeating men, often brandishing gender-specific weapons such as a rolling pin or a broom at their husbands. "What is a suffragette without a suffering household?" asked one image of a haughty woman clutching a ballot while her husband cared for a crying baby and a little girl, who glared accusingly at her mother. Others depicted women in men's clothing, such as the "Pantalette Suffragette" and the "Suffragette Coppette." If admitted to the masculine sphere of political participation, then, women would usurp all of men's roles, become domineering matriarchs, and imprison their husbands within the household.[35]

As in much of the academic matriarchalism of the late nineteenth century, this popular fear of female political power was clearly tied up with social evolutionism. Horace Bushnell, in his published opposition to suffrage, wrote that, if given the vote, women would become "large-handed, big-footed, flat-chested, and thin-lipped," and that would be "the end of our newborn, more beneficent civilization." The belief in universal prehistoric matriarchies was frequently used as evidence that female political power was dangerous, even savage. In an 1894 article, physician James B. Weir explained that "matriarchy" was not an "advanced thought," but rather it was "as old as the human race," and "a return to it at the present time" would be "distinctly and emphatically and essentially retrograde in every particular." Like communism, the "doctrines of the matriarchate" were "degenerate beliefs" representing a "reversion back to the mental habitudes of our savage ancestors." Espousal of these doctrines indicated viraginity, the contemporary diagnosis applied to women who displayed "masculine" traits. Its "mild form" was the tomboy, although the perceived ailment could progress to female tranvestism, homosexuality, and, "unquestionably," suffragism. The extension of the vote to women would cause a rapid decline of civilization, Weir warned: "I see, in the establishment of female suffrage, the first step toward that abyss of immoral horrors so repugnant to our cultivated ethical tastes—the matriarchate, with all of its accompanying licentiousness and gross sexual indulgence." He implored women to abandon the quest for rights and embrace essentialism: "In my opinion woman, as long as she remains *sana mens in sana corpere,* will never give up the brightest jewel in her crown, domesticity, for a wornout, obsolete, savage bauble like matriarchy."[36]

In a second installment in the *American Naturalist* in 1895, Weir used the latest anthropological theories of prehistory, evolutionary science, and psychology to offer a cautionary tale about gender and civilization. Early societies, he argued in "The Effect of Female Suffrage on Posterity," featured such "primitive" things as widespread nudity, "laxity in sexual relations," general promiscuity, and father-daughter incest, all ruled over and approved of by a "matriarchate" of female governmental power. Weir's true concern in this essay was not gendered power in prehistory, but rather its nightmarish mirror image in the present. These early "savage" societies, Weir argued, featured "female suffrage in its primitive form, brought about, it is true, by environment, and not by elective franchise."[37]

Weir's brief history lesson was meant to show his readers that "the 'New Woman' was born many thousands of years ago," for the ancient matriarchs and the suffragists shared many characteristics. Victorian women were succumbing to this "atavistic desire (matriarchy)" because "atavism invariably attacks the weak" and "individuals of a neurasthenic type." Various powerful women throughout history—Joan of Arc, Catharine the Great, Elizabeth I— were, in Weir's expert opinion, "masculo-feminine" aberrants, "pronounced viragint(s), with a slight tendency toward megalomania." Rule by these malignant matriarchs invariably featured "political corruption, cruelty of government, sexual immorality—nay, downright, impudent, open, boastful indecency," in addition to general decadence and degeneracy.[38]

This was no idle fear on Weir's part, he repeatedly assured his readers. Rather, it was a horror of history repeating itself before his expert eyes. Weir believed that feminists of the time—he mentioned Susan B. Anthony by name—had the goal of "a social revolution, in which the present form of government will be overthrown and matriarchy established in its stead." His primary concern was for those future generations who would invariably suffer under the savage tyranny of the matriarchate wrought by female suffrage: "The simple right to vote carries with it no immediate danger," he explained. "The danger comes afterward; probably many years after the establishment of female suffrage, when woman, owing to her increased degeneration, gives free rein to her atavistic tendencies, and hurries ever backward toward the savage state of her barbarian ancestors." He concluded: "I see, in the establishment of equal rights, the first step toward that abyss of immoral horrors so repugnant to our cultivated ethical tastes—the matriarchate."[39]

As a suffragist, Gage was a part of the movement that gave rise to this first reactionary version of American antimatriarchalism, and because she offered historical precedent for women's contemporary claims to political equality, her research was a direct challenge to antisuffragists like Weir. Her arguments were also a departure from the reigning maternalism of the era, as Gage did not couch her claims to female power in paeans to women's allegedly innate attributes that would make them ideal social housekeepers. It was not necessary, however, for the mainstream women's movement to formulate a response to Gage's challenge. By the early 1890s, Gage had severed her ties to the women's suffrage organizations, and Susan B. Anthony was in the process of muting Gage's past contributions to the movement altogether.

At the time of publication, *Women, Church and State* was the lengthiest published work of American matriarchalism, and it was the first feminist work of its kind. Although its publication in 1893 caused some controversy, Gage's "secession" from the suffrage movement resulted in her being written out of the pages of history—literally, in the case of *The History of Woman Suffrage,* when Anthony, who outlived both Gage and Stanton, erased Gage as coauthor of the volumes and reduced her former ally to a footnote. Gage, then, was excluded from history like so many of the historical women about whom she wrote, and to add insult to injury, this exclusion was initiated by a feminist colleague. For her part, Gage refused thereafter to be connected in any way with Anthony and Stanton, writing in 1893 that the two women were "traitors" like "Benedict Arnold."[40]

Although she was subsequently lost to history until the new wave of Women's Studies scholars, particularly when her biographer, Sally Roesch Wagner, unearthed her work in the 1970s, Gage's revolutionary ideas lived on through an unexpected source: *The Wizard of Oz* series of children's books, authored by her son-in-law, L. Frank Baum. Seven years after the publication of *Women,*

Church and State, Baum would use his mother-in-law's ideas to create a fantastical fictional matriarchy. Feminist matriarchalism would also be co-opted by some American socialists in the two decades following Gage's work, although Gage was rarely cited as a source. The theory proved amiable to multiple interpretations; in 1893, the very year that *Women, Church and State* was published, long before Baum could put pencil to paper, matriarchalism in the United States took a decidedly distasteful turn. Co-opted by the prevailing discourse of social evolutionism, matriarchalism became a part of the racist project of international imperialism.

Between the 1860s and the 1880s, then, various academic strands combined to produce a new and potentially revolutionary gendered conception of human history, social organization, and political power, and Gage was a key figure in the development of this discourse. The "rediscovery" of matriarchal prehistory, proclaimed Engels, "has the same importance for anthropology as Darwin's theory of evolution has for biology and Marx's theory of surplus value has for political economy." The various intellectual sources—the secular concept of human antiquity, Darwinian evolution, Bachofen's analyses of ancient myths, Engels's application of each of these to socioeconomic history— combined with Morgan's ethnography of the Iroquois Nations and the emerging context of American feminism to produce a comprehensive discourse of matriarchalism that was the unique product of its time and place. Engels argued that "the matriarchal gens has become the pivot on which the whole science turns," and he was correct: although it has largely been forgotten now that once it burst upon the American scene in the 1870s, matriarchalism became a major component of the social sciences of the late nineteenth century, and from there it spread to feminism and popular culture via Gage.[41]

Yet the final product was more than the sum of its parts; matriarchalism could be mobilized in the United States in the service of various ideologies. Bachofen himself recognized this potential problem. An understanding of matriarchal history "can be achieved only on one condition," he explained in the "Introduction" to *Mother Right:* "The scholar must be able to renounce entirely the ideas of his own time, the beliefs with which these have filled his spirit, and transfer himself to the midpoint of a completely different world of thought." He cautioned: "The scholar who takes the attitudes of later generations as his starting point will inevitably be turned away from an understanding of the earliest time." This is, of course, what Bachofen did in *Mother Right* (although he was not especially self-aware in his warning), and it is also what happened as matriarchalism went mainstream in the 1890s.[42]

Judith Walkowitz argues that many Victorian academics relied upon historical and anthropological theories of ancient and indigenous societies to define and justify contemporary sexual tensions and gendered hierarchies. Anthropologist Adam Kuper agrees, arguing that theories about primitive society are "illusions," but they are also useful myths that serve "political functions" and "feed a variety of ideological positions." The psychosocial endeavor of imagining and defining "savages" extended beyond academia; matriarchalism inspired many reactions connected to different "social interests," and these connections generated multiple pop cultural manifestations in the fin de siècle United States. The academic interest in matriarchalism in the second half of the nineteenth century, and its general popularity at the turn of the twentieth century, can be explained by the fact that this theory could be deployed in the service of all manner of contradictory ideologies. In direct opposition to Gage's goal of tolerance, equality, and a theosophical sisterhood of humanity, American matriarchalism made its first major headlines as a vital part of the racist, imperialist project represented by the International Columbian Exposition in Chicago in 1893.[43]

3

WHITE QUEENS AND AFRICAN AMAZONS
Imperial Matriarchalism at the Chicago World's Fair

> The fact of the natives' simplicity, despite their detractors, fills me
> with an abiding hope that if at the outset these particular, amiable
> and amenable tribes of East Africa have sagacious, peaceful, fair treat-
> ment, and their natures are enlarged and they are led at a gradual pace
> to accept the ways of civilization, there is much to hope for in their
> intellectual unfoldment.
>
> —MAY FRENCH SHELDON, *Sultan to Sultan* (1892)

FIFTEEN years after Morgan's publication stirred the debate on matriarchalism within American anthropology, and just one year before
Gage published *Women, Church and State,* Americans clamored to
read *Sultan to Sultan* (1892) by the "famous female globetrotter" May
French Sheldon. As an unexpected bridge between anthropological techniques
and budding imperial ambitions, French Sheldon offered an "innovative ethnology" of her expedition to East Africa. No mere explorer, French Sheldon
explained that she was instead a kind of feminine conquistador. Her goal, she
wrote, was to better acquaint her readers "with the possibilities of the natural
primitives whom I am proud to call my friends and be called friend by, and
to demonstrate that if a woman could journey a thousand and more miles
in East Africa, among some hostile tribes, unattended by other than Zanzi-
baris [sic] mercenaries, without bloodshed, the extreme measures employed
by some would-be colonizers is unnecessary, atrocious, and without the pale
of humanity." In short, French Sheldon argued that white women could play a
matriarchal role in Western colonialism, providing a guiding, feminine hand
that would result in a better kind of imperialism. In this role, she called herself
the "White Queen."[1]

According to this new version of matriarchalism represented by women
like French Sheldon, when matriarchy characterized a society of people of
color, particularly those very people who had been recently and/or were soon
to be colonized by the West, it was evidence of savagery. In the hands of

elite white women, however, matriarchal power could, some argued, be a key strategy within the new era of colonialism at the turn of the twentieth century. In other words, successful subjugation hinged on the feminine touch, with white women as the power brokers between Western societies and colonial subjects. This racist brand of imperial matriarchalism was widely disseminated through the strange mix of academic theories and popular culture represented by the 1893 Chicago World's Fair, where French Sheldon was widely celebrated.

Historian T. J. Boisseau uses French Sheldon's self-descriptor "White Queen" to denote the "imperial feminist figure" of the early twentieth-century women's movement who "was capable of representing her race, class, and nation on a global stage in a way that connoted sovereignty, authoritarian power, and racial prestige." In a broader study of the racialized discourses underpinning the development of feminism during this time, Louise Newman agrees, arguing that French Sheldon was just one of many white women of the late Victorian and Progressive eras that "offer[ed] themselves as the epitome of social evolutionary development." But the rhetoric used by French Sheldon and others was not simply imperialist. French Sheldon made a specific appeal to power that places her firmly within an ideological time line with the likes of Bachofen and Morgan as, in her publications and public lectures, she mobilized a new form of matriarchalism. French Sheldon, "the elegantly arrayed lady . . . fresh from the wilds of Africa," was the white face of imperial matriarchalism, a discourse that depended upon intertwined arguments about gender, race, and power. It also hinged upon the imagined presence of dangerous, dark-skinned matriarchs, represented by the so-called "African Amazons" of the Dahomey Village exhibit at the World's Fair. In this chapter, I juxtapose the "White Queens" and the "African Amazons" at the 1893 World's Columbian Exposition in Chicago as a means of understanding the role of matriarchalism within American ideas about imperialism at the turn of the twentieth century.[2]

Inspired by the success of the Paris exposition of 1889, the World's Fair in Chicago that coincided more or less with the four-hundredth anniversary of Columbus's expedition to the Americas was a significant breakthrough in the dissemination of national ideals and international ambitions. The Fair was meant as both a celebration of the triumph of Western civilization and an example of innovation itself, featuring scientific advancement, technological achievements, and colonial conquests. Representatives, artifacts, technology, and artwork came from thirty-six countries and forty-six American states and territories, totaling over five thousand exhibits that were viewed by some 27 million visitors over the course of the Fair's six-month run.[3]

In a first draft of the system of classification, G. Brown Goode of the Smithsonian Institution laid out the evolutionist mission of the Fair: "to expound, as far as may be, the steps of the progress of civilization and its arts in successive condition; to be, in fact, an illustrated encyclopedia of civilization." Thomas Palmer, President of the World's Columbian Exposition, echoed this mission when he called the Fair "the clearing-house of civilization." To this end, anthropological experts were carefully chosen to manage this presentation. Frederick Putnam, the esteemed Harvard anthropologist, was deemed the most "competent" man to head up Department M: Ethnology. Putnam's exhibits were, according to one journalist, "in one sense the basis of all of the rest of the fair exhibits." The "white man's burden" of imperialism, with its dual goals of education and uplift, therefore became a major theme of the Fair as Putnam, his assistants, and the rival anthropologists of the Smithsonian exhibits worked hard to present "realistic" scenes depicting the experiences of subjugated peoples. This was no mere display; the "burden" lived and breathed at the Fair in the exhibits of live groups from around the world. With a young Franz Boas as his primary assistant, Putnam argued that the living exhibits were meant to be mutually beneficial: fairgoers viewing the various ethnic villages participated in the "scientific study of the first historic people," while the "natives" themselves were "allowed every opportunity for improvement by observation of the benefits of civilization and education."[4]

Deemed the "Educator of the People" by the *Chicago Tribune,* the World's Fair thus instructed both the attendees and the people on display about the benefits and responsibilities of Western civilization. Although some scholars argue that there was no clear organizing logic of these exhibits beyond a vaguely geographical arrangement, the "origins and progress of civilizations" had been the primary theme of international expositions since the celebration of the Industrial Revolution at the Great Exhibition in London in 1851. Moreover, many fairgoers in Chicago thought they discerned a pattern. Marian Shaw, special World's Fair correspondent for *The Argus* of Fargo, North Dakota, described the displays of the Anthropological Building: "Beginning with the cliff dwellers and other primitive races, one can trace the progress of mankind in all stages of civilization and barbarism through the ages until he reaches the wonderful works of the nineteenth century." In short, evolutionism, regardless of the intention of the organizers, provided an ideological perspective through which to make sense of the many wonders of the Fair.[5]

While most of the official exhibits of the Exposition were "of a serious nature," "designed to educate, uplift, provide enjoyment, and stimulate commerce," the Midway Plaisance—the mile-long stretch connecting Jackson Park, the primary Exposition site on the shore of Lake Michigan, to Washington Park to the west—was a different sort of adventure altogether. The Midway trafficked in sensationalism, from the lions on horseback and the chariot drawn by tigers courtesy of Hagenbeck's Zoological Arena Company, to the jewel of the Midway invented for this occasion, the Ferris Wheel. "Upon the whole," concluded journalist Julian Hawthorne, "it is the most magnificent and satisfactory plaything ever yet devised for the delectation of mortal woman or man."[6]

Unlike the more formal exhibits in the "overcivilized" White City, which focused heavily on artifacts from various countries and states, the displays of the Midway, the "Bohemian wing of the Fair," were heavily populated. Chicago Fair organizers combined "commercial pressure" with "anthropological interest" in "colonial exhibits" that lined the Midway Plaisance, the first exhibits of living people at a US fair. Although these kinds of living displays had been featured at previous expositions, most recently in Paris in 1889, an American, the famous circus showman P. T. Barnum, claims to have come up with the idea of displaying "every accessible people . . . on the face of the globe" in 1849. On Chicago's Midway in 1893, attendees viewed the "definitive form" of living ethnological and colonial displays. Wide-eyed fairgoers came upon various human displays of conquered or soon-to-be-conquered peoples from around the globe, often called "types" to denote their status as objects of scientific and anthropological inquiry. A stroll down the Midway could include the "Wild East show" at the Bedouin Sheikh's camp, a "paradise of ethnology" which "showed all the features of home life in the desert" in the Turkish Village; the scantily clad "girls" doing the *danse du ventre* on the "Street in Cairo"; and the spectacle of the Algerian "torture dance," which involved iron skewers. "There is," warned journalist Amy Leslie, "a spice of adventure, something rakish and modestly questionable about this legalized harlequinade of other people's habits."[7]

The contrast between the Midway Plaisance and the White City was stark. In her 1894 novel *Sweet Clover*, Claire Louise Burnham described passing from the "mile-long babel" of the Midway to the "great, beautiful silence" of the

White City as passing "out o' darkness into light." This juxtaposition of "dark" and "light" combined with the arrangement of this "highway of surprise" to enhance the evolutionist effect. Fair attendees easily picked up on the teleology, following the exhibits as if reading a historical narrative. Julian Hawthorne, son of novelist Nathaniel Hawthorne, explained to would-be fairgoers that "you have before you the civilized, the half-civilized, and the savage worlds to choose from—or rather, to take one after the other." Marian Shaw saw the inhabitants of the Midway as a kind of living history:

> Although the nations of the earth are not seen here in their highest degree of culture, one meets with a civilization so strange and bizarre that he seems as if transported, now to medieval times, now to a period still more remote. These people are they, who, in the mad race of nations for power and pelf, seem to have been left far behind, and, compared with the nations of today, are like untutored children.

A walk along the Midway at night, opined the *Chicago Record*, was an exercise in "survival of the fittest." The comparative cultures of this "mad race of nations" from the "ends of the earth" were noted by many visitors to the Exposition who felt they had viewed "the very origin of civilization."[8]

The colonial exhibits served a didactic, almost missionary purpose: the perceived lack of civilization in these societies—which happened to be located in European colonial regions and in areas upon which the United States turned its newly imperial eye in the 1890s—revealed the depth of the moral duty of Western societies to aid their reputedly backward neighbors. Although poet Rudyard Kipling would not coin the phrase "the white man's burden" until the end of the decade, the racial "burden" of territorial control and expansionism was a familiar concept to white America, given the context of the return to "home rule" in the South post-Reconstruction that bred the rise of Jim Crow and the recent, final push into western lands controlled by Native Americans. The Fair itself was conceived in commemoration of Columbus's "discovery" of the "New World," the cataclysmic event that precipitated the decimation of the indigenous American population. White colonization, removal, and destruction of American Indian tribes continued unabated throughout the nineteenth century as the citizens of the new nation pursued the expansionist mission of "manifest destiny." Just two months before the congressional vote that gave Chicago the hosting rights to the Fair, the assassination of Chief Sitting Bull and the subsequent massacre of almost three hundred Lakota Sioux at Wounded Knee marked a major, violent showdown between the US Army and Native Americans. Following this final territorial triumph of continental expansion, the United States census declared the frontier officially closed.[9]

At the 1893 annual meeting of the American Historical Association, held in Chicago in tandem with the Fair, historian Frederick Jackson Turner famously lectured on what would come to be known as his "frontier thesis." Turner explained that the Census Bureau's recent declaration had significant implications for the nation's future. American society and politics, he memorably argued, were born of the processes of "crossing a continent, in winning a wilderness, and in developing at each area of this progress out of the primitive economic and political condition of the frontier into the complexity of city life." If, as he claimed, the American spirit was determined by the "perennial rebirth" of westward expansion and conquest, Turner assured his listeners that it would not die out with the closing of the North American frontier. Rather, he proclaimed, "American energy will continually demand a wider field for its exercise."[10]

Turner's paeans to the nation's indomitable, imperialist psyche had both racial and gendered implications. One of the most popular features of the Fair's six-month run, Buffalo Bill's Wild West Show, was a colonial exhibit on a grander, and more action-packed, scale, as well as a testament to Turner's white, masculine, "pioneer force in American culture," available for fifty cents just a few steps beyond the fairgrounds. Advertised as "The Affair" beside the Fair, Cody's extravagant troupe performed twice daily, rain or shine, to a crowd of 18,000, showcasing the "Primitive Horsemen of All Races" and the Great Sioux Wars of the 1870s. Deemed by one boy in attendance "a great show for a paleface," the Wild West show was a wild success, and many visitors to the Fair, such as the young reporter Theodore Dreiser and the renowned anthropologist Franklin Hamilton Cushing, enthusiastically paid separate admission to watch the frontier conquest enacted before their very eyes.[11]

Cody's gendered frontier trafficked heavily in stereotypical ideas of white masculinity—the official program for his show in Chicago deemed him a "genuine specimen of Western manhood" and "one of the finest types of manhood this continent has ever produced"—and indigenous hostility and brutality. Yet even in Cody's hypermasculine show, the role of gender in American expansionism was changing, and not just due to the presence of the eagle-eyed Annie Oakley. In one particularly poignant performance, Cody removed his hat and bowed low before Susan B. Anthony, who was in attendance by special invitation. The famous feminist stood, bowed, and waved her handkerchief "enthusiastically" in response, bringing "the audience to its feet in a thunder of applause and cheers." This moment, juxtaposing as it did the violence of Indian suppression and a romantic exchange between a cowboy icon of the American frontier and the white female face of American feminism, can be seen as a metaphor for the transition in matriarchalism in the early 1890s.[12]

Although she was denied a position on the Board of Lady Managers, Anthony's speeches at the Fair also indicated this transition. Deeming herself "an object lesson of the survival of the fittest" for surviving decades of "ridicule and contempt" aimed at the women's movement, Anthony reported that the Fair's suffrage "exhibit has done more in six months to help the cause than anything else could have done in twenty-five years." She lectured about women's unique powers, and she tapped into the Progressive, maternalist discourse of women as domestic "social housekeepers" and international "mothers of civilization" in her bid for suffrage, a message that resonated with those concerned about Turner's "wider field" for the "exercise" of the American impulse for expansion. Underscoring her role as a "white queen" in the evolutionist order, Anthony observed of the African warrior women on the Midway: "I wonder if humanity sprang from such as this? It seems pretty low-down, doesn't it?" The headline regarding this exchange proclaimed: "EQUAL RIGHTS HERE: Susan B. Anthony Finds the Long Sought Purpose at Last—DOWN IN DAHOMEY VILLAGE, The Dear Old Lady Sees the Girls that Bear Arms and Says Our Girls Could Fight Too."[13]

Despite the antimatriarchalist fears that characterized this kind of media coverage, Anthony had many admirers at the Fair, including May French Sheldon. Unlike Anthony, French Sheldon was explicit in her endorsement of the matriarchalist discourse of American imperialism at the Fair; it was, in fact, her primary claim to fame. Fresh off the lecture circuit following her three-month expedition in East Africa from the coast to Mount Kilimanjaro in 1891, French Sheldon contended that the innate strengths of Victorian true womanhood—piety, purity, domesticity, morality—plus women's reputed skills of patience and nurturance, could serve as the key forces behind, and were in fact ideally suited to, the civilizing mission of Western colonialism. As an antidote to the vulgarities of male colonialism, women could accomplish the task sans forceful subjugation or bloodshed. In this way, white women could serve as the front-line matriarchs of Western imperialism.[14]

According to her account, French Sheldon proved her own argument time and again in eastern Africa. When she met local chieftains and leaders, wearing "an elaborate court dress made of bright white silk and satin," "a waist-length platinum blonde wig," and "hip pistols, a ceremonial sword, and a leather whip," by her own reports (and, it is worth noting, no one else's), they greeted her as a "White Queen" and dubbed her "Bebe Bwana," which she translated from Swahili to "Woman Man," "Woman Master," or "Lady Boss." One historian deems this get-up "the literal embodiment of Britannia," but her US citizenship was not lost on contemporary observers. "Who," asked the *New York Times*, "but an American woman would have conceived the idea of making a Worth gown help her win her way into the interior of Africa?"[15]

As her biographer has shown, French Sheldon skillfully combined the attributes of "true womanhood" with the purportedly masculine traits of thirst for exploration, fearlessness, and authority over dark-skinned male "savages." This latter characteristic was illustrated in the most oft-quoted section of *Sultan to Sultan*, in which French Sheldon moved through the "rebellious throng" of her African porters, both pistols cocked and pointed at any man who dared to dissent. But despite the moniker "Woman-Man" and her porters' persistence in calling her "sir," French Sheldon was no conquistador in drag; her femininity mattered very much to her cause. "My method of procedure," she stated, "was to harmonize and attract towards me rather than to bully and subdue them by any rough methods." French Sheldon argued that men had doomed colonialism through macho behavior and violent masculinity, and she therefore refused the requests of all "professional and scientific men" who wished to tag along on her journey, arguing that she would "show how easy it was for a woman to travel about on friendly terms with the natives where a man would probably have to make his way by force."[16]

White men would thus hurt her cause, while black men had, according to French Sheldon, a different sort of masculinity altogether. French Sheldon found African men to be essentially impotent, "prone to indulge in personal bedeckment," and happy to "do all the strutting about and fancy work" while the women performed the labor. She claimed that she subdued the African men in her caravan, as well as others she encountered, fairly easily. Fannie Williams later explained in *The Chautauquan*:

In speaking to her followers, or in giving her orders, she was always careful to stand above them, and look down upon them; and discovered that she had much more command over them when taking this position. They finally came to accept this as her invariable custom, and always brought her a box to stand upon; or if on the march, would escort her to a boulder or a high rock, when she wished to proclaim her directions. Once when marching through an African desert where there were no boulders, they formed a phalanx of kneeling slaves, and she stood upon their backs.

French Sheldon mobilized racist stereotypes to her own ends, as part of her imperial matriarchalist bid for female power that could help to resolve American anxiety about its role in colonialism. Brutal takeover of foreign lands violated basic American principles of sovereignty and democracy, but the softer civilizing mission that French Sheldon embodied provided a way out of this conundrum: when white women shouldered the "burden" of global racial uplift, they would nurture and teach the savages, leading them "at a gradual pace to accept the ways of civilization." In short, her 1891 adventure was not, French Sheldon reiterated, a mere exploratory mission; beneath the US flag flying above her tent, she wrote of the ways in which she would improve colonialism through the development of infrastructure and industrial training so that Africans could then practice the "self-help" that was so germane to American capitalist identity.[17]

French Sheldon's writings were immensely popular, as were her subsequent appearances on the lecture circuit in Europe and the United States. Pundits of the time named her "Lady Stanley" after Henry Morton Stanley, the famous Western explorer who coined the phrase "Darkest Africa." One year after the publication of *Sultan to Sultan*, French Sheldon was invited to the World's Columbian Exposition in Chicago, where her occupation was listed in the registry of members of the International Congress of Anthropology as "African explorer." French Sheldon was widely celebrated in the Windy City, winning two awards, giving several lectures, and enjoying a reception in her honor, to which she wore her famous Bebe Bwana costume, sans the waist-length wig. Visitors to the White City could hardly miss French Sheldon, as her adventures were highlighted in three separate buildings.[18]

In a well-attended lecture in the Woman's Building, French Sheldon told the crowd that her aim in Africa "was ever to protect the natives, to meet the men of tribal importance in their own sultanates, as a woman of breeding should meet the highest officials in any land." The solution to the "African problem," she argued bluntly, was for women to teach civilization through "the establishment of industrial manual training stations," medical clinics, and the mere "presence of practical, honest, sober, decent, industrious white men and women, whose daily life will carry the highest precepts of enlightenment." She concluded with her intention to return to "lend [her] efforts to a 'common-sense' method of colonization, and substantiate the principles many explorers look askance at, and criticise as too Utopian for Africa."[19]

The reception of French Sheldon as the spokesperson of imperial matriarchalism at the Fair was glowing. She was not merely brave, although, according to Fannie Williams of the *Chautauquan*, she certainly was that: "The prestige of a white woman, the first who had ever passed that way, and who seemed like a supernatural being sent from the heavens; the unconscious influence over these rude savages of the refinement of her deportment and manners; and above all, a certain commanding dignity, saved her from danger." The broader significance of French Sheldon's journey was as a new kind of colonizer; her feminine influence was, it seemed, infectious, as "her example" was "worshiped in every possible way by these poor ignorant savages." Williams concluded, "They had learned to fear the white man, and to expect nothing from him save oppression and cruelty, but with a woman it was different."[20]

In French Sheldon's brand of matriarchalism, appeals to woman's "essential" nature were key; although she did not deploy motherhood specifically as a rhetorical tool, her language echoed maternalist rhetoric, relying as she did upon allegedly innate, maternal attributes such as patience, persuasion, and nurturance. Yet her travel tales also contain incidents of stereotypically masculine forms of control and violence. Her paeans to women's gentle hand in the civilizing mission notwithstanding, French Sheldon, by her own admission, had to discard her attempts to control her porters through "kindness or moral suasion," instead finding that "discipline could only be maintained by chastising serious offenders in the accepted way," by which she meant whipping. Moreover, French Sheldon "worshiped" Stanley, whose violent exploits during his explorations were well documented, even celebrated, in the American press, and she apparently later served as both an alleged double agent and an explicit endorser of King Leopold II's brutal administration of the Congo Free State. The gendered and racial essentialist premises of French Sheldon's imperial matriarchalism, therefore, did not seem to have basis in her own experience, as she frequently approached her African interests in the masculine manner on which she built a career deriding. Despite these contradictions, French Sheldon was treated as an ethnological expert and an imperial mouthpiece, and in *Sultan to Sultan* she duly included measurements, such as precise longitude and latitude for locations and chemical analyses of stones she collected, to lend an academic air to what was otherwise an elite woman's travelogue.[21]

French Sheldon's matriarchalism was echoed by other white women at the Fair. Bertha Palmer, the president of the Board of Lady Managers of the Fair, lamented the "oppressive bonds" placed upon women of other cultures" that perhaps the "movement for the advancement of women, inaugurated in connection with the World's Columbian Exposition," could help to remedy. The international nature of the Fair provided an opportunity for the real-time enactment of imperial matriarchalism, Palmer acknowledged when she wrote of the "foreign sisters of the Midway Plaisance": "In some ways they are ignorant and I think we owe it to our cause that we visit these women and invite them to our buildings and spend time and money on teaching them our ways and manners." To this end, the Board of Lady Managers commissioned two murals, "Primitive Woman" and "Modern Woman," to contrast the hard labor and darker skins of the former with the white robes and gentility of the latter.[22]

Thus, while one oft-photographed statue in the White City, in age-old gendered imagery of territorial conquest, represented "The Virgin West" as a white woman, the Fair also broadcast the message that the status of some women was changing, such that elite, white women could play a key role in the racialized power structure of the new colonial world. *World's Fair Puck*, which was specially printed and sold on the grounds in Jackson Park during the Exposition, offered this image several times: first in "On With the Dance! The American Woman Leads the World," in which a pale woman in a gleaming white ball gown functioned as a maypole, directing the movements of people of various ethnicities who were tethered to her by ribbons, and again in an image of the Fair as a Victorian lady brandishing a flag over rows and rows of men in the military uniforms of different nations.[23]

When women like May French Sheldon claimed international power via their allegedly civilized whiteness, they also located the root of the problems of "savage," darker-skinned peoples within the matriarchal tendencies of overbearing women. One cover of the *World's Fair Puck* depicted a pair of white women in full Victorian dress, watching a group of retreating African women from a safe distance beneath parasols. Under the heading "A Privileged Race," the two commented upon the group's near-nudity with knowing pity. Said Anabel, "Just look at those African women! I should think they'd hate to go out with such scanty clothing." Replied Madge, "Well, you know, people with their complexions don't tan easily." The white female gaze of the "mothers of civilization" was thus complemented by the troubling presence of African women, and this juxtaposition was a key component of imperial matriarchalism at the Fair.[24]

On the Midway Plaisance, matriarchalism was a subtle part of the broader discourse of social evolutionism, or the teleological narrative of human evolution from "savage" to "civilized." Near the western entrance to the Midway, almost at the end of the mile-long stretch, lay the Dahomey Village, the largest exhibit from West Africa at the Fair. Citing the "enthusiastic" support of the French government, Xavier Pené, the French manager of the Dahomey Village, explained that, beyond mere profit, he had "a more elevated goal: *l'intérêt Colonial*, and also the interest of the indigenous people who had been able to judge, for themselves, the grandeur of France, and the progress of civilization in the United States, Portugal, Spain, etc." To this end, Pené recruited over sixty people representing a "diverse mixture of tribal and regional groups" from French Congo, French Guinea, and Benin. The sign over the village, just beneath the flag, read "Benin-French-Colony-West-Africa-Coast," and the French flag flew over the village. As the Fair's "only major black exhibit," the village inhabitants' origins were erased, and they summarily became "'savage Dahomeyans." Moreover, the women were advertised as "Amazons," people who occupied one of the lowest rungs of social evolution. The village would prove to be one of the most profitable exhibits on the Midway.[25]

The Dahomey Village became, according to one historian, the "standard" of colonial displays at international expositions. As such, it represented the "pornography of power" that "was so vital to the efforts of imperialists trying to build public support for their expansionist schemes." Visitors to Chicago in 1893 could walk the evolutionist time line from savage matriarchy to civilized patriarchy, beginning with the thatched huts of the Dahomey Village and walking eastward along the Midway Plaisance to the White City. This was commodified racism for mass consumption, but it was also the first form of commodified matriarchalism in American popular culture. Commodification in Chicago occurred in tandem with colonialism, as the violent takeover by French forces in Dahomey provided a broader context in which fairgoers could feel that their voyeurism was, in fact, part of the civilizing experience.[26]

Newspaper-reading Americans were likely familiar with the Dahomey region of West Africa, made famous by reports of the French wars of conquest in the early 1890s. The exotic descriptions in the papers were meant to titillate, horrify, and inspire American support for the French colonial endeavor. In the months leading up to the Fair, the *Chicago Tribune* argued that while the "Savage African Tribe" may be of "profound interest to the anthropologist" because of their peculiar customs, American readers of the "civilized world" should take interest in them "in the hope that they will not be allowed much longer to practice the awful enormities for which they have become famous." These "enormities" included wanton torture and execution, as well as a penchant for fighting to the death in warfare. Even more shocking to readers was the fact that both sexes participated in this violence: "the amazons or women warriors of Dahomey are world-famed."[27]

The combination of racism and ethnocentrism as justification for colonialism is obvious in these accounts, but ideas about gender played a role, as well. In Dahomey, the sex of the region's warriors caused prurient interest among European, and later American, audiences; indeed, the curious gender roles were a major component of representations of Dahomey as dangerous. Various visitors described the "Amazons" in the late eighteenth and early nineteenth centuries, but they achieved their most lasting fame among Western audiences by way of Sir Richard F. Burton. In his widely read *A Mission to Gelele, King of Dahome* (1864), Burton described the women of the court of King Gelele:

> The four soldieresses were armed with muskets, and habited in tunics and white calottes, with two blue patches, meant for crocodiles. They were commanded by an old woman in a man's straw hat, a green waistcoat, a white shirt . . . and a sash of white calico. The virago directed the dance and song with an iron ferrule, and her head was shaded by way of umbrella, with a peculiar shrub. . . . Two of the women dancers were of abnormal size, nearly six feet tall, and of proportional breadth, whilst generally the men were smooth, full-breasted, round-limbed, and effeminate-looking. Such, on the other hand, was the size of the female skeleton, and the muscular development of the frame, that in many cases femineity could be detected only by the bosom. I have no doubt that this physical superiority of the 'working sex,' led in the Popo and Dahoman race to the employment of women as fighters. They are

the domestic servants, the ploughboys, and the porters . . . the field hands, and market cattle of the nation, why should they not also be soldiers?

Burton was not alone in his fascination; the "Amazons" were noteworthy to almost all European men who published accounts of their time in Dahomey. Burton explained that "Mother" was their "official title," and with maternity came a measure of political power: "For each monarch, in the dynasty there is an old woman mother," and the mothers of "high officials" held sway, as well. These were not ornamental women in the king's court; according to colonial accounts, the Amazons served as powerful matriarchs within the monarchical system of Dahomey.[28]

By the end of the First Franco-Dahomeyan War in 1890, the French public was well acquainted with these fearsome women. In early 1891, one entrepreneurial Brit capitalized on this fame with an exhibition at the Jardin d'Acclamatation in Paris featuring twenty-four "amazons." The women performed military-inspired dances and combat simulation to a drumbeat provided by two Dahomeyan men. According to one reporter, the women's faces were "at first calm and almost smiling," but by the end, they showed "a sort of martial ecstasy resembling delirium." The show toured Europe for two years, up to the eve of the World's Columbian Exposition in Chicago. By this time, the French were fighting in Dahomey again, and the reports coming out of these battles detailed rampant brutality. The opportunistic reprinting of Burton's memoir in the early 1890s and the newspaper reports of the ongoing Dahomey resistance proved to be riveting reads. As the Dahomeyans fought back against French conquest, they were depicted as untamable Amazons, a narrative that tapped into the matriarchalist evolutionist time line, positioning Dahomey as a barbaric society in need of civilizing rather than a sovereign kingdom challenging Western invasion.[29]

As this war raged on and Chicago prepped for the upcoming World's Fair, the *Tribune* covered the "famous Amazons" at length: "This guard of the King is distinct from the harem, and those composing it have made a vow of celibacy. The Amazons are recruited from the children of the chiefs, or the captured girls. . . . Numbering about 1500, made up of two battalions, the Amazons "accompany the King in war, but never engage in battle except on his special order. They are courageous and even ferocious." Like "wild beasts," the "Amazons" reportedly tore animals apart to "devour [their] meat warm and palpitating," and according to some reports, they even occasionally dabbled in human sacrifice. By 1893, wrote one observer, "for twenty years the Amazons and sacrifices of Dahomey ha[d] caught the Caucasian fancy." By the time the Village was erected in Chicago, these "cruel" and "cunning" women had transformed in the popular imagination from an auxiliary fighting force to living evidence of the barbarism of female dominance.[30]

As proof of the "contrast in the extremes of humanity," the Dahomey Village was meant to be "expressive of the lowest savagery about whom we could readily believe all the stories of the Amazon army and of cannibalism," according to Professor Putnam himself. For an admission fee of twenty-five cents, paying customers entered the Dahomey Village, which "teem[ed] with savage awfulness quite too utterly shocking," where they could listen to "native music" and view a "Fetish Amazon war dance" performed by the topless women. Visitors reported strong reactions to the "half-naked blacks" and fiercely dancing warriors. Marian Shaw and her companion tried to avoid the more "vulgar" exhibits, and thus she stayed only briefly in the Dahomey Village, where the music of the "twenty-one Amazonian warriors" was to them "as nerve-torturing as any [they] have heard." Shaw's disgust notwithstanding, this combination of sex and violence was, of course, the selling point, and sell it did; the *Chicago Standard* recommended that, if an attendee had only two days to visit the Fair, the Dahomey Village should be scheduled on the first day, so as not to miss it.[31]

The combination of bare-breasted women armed with weapons and allegations of cannibalism were enough to draw a large crowd to the Village on most days. Lest fairgoers misunderstand the evolutionist message on display, one guidebook explained: "The habits of these people are repulsive; they eat like animals and have all the characteristics of the lowest order of the human family." Another reporter mused: "Wonderful study in civilization this—the forty or fifty savages in the pavilion, and the surrounding fringe of whites, representing half a dozen nationalities, but all belonging to another order of existence: Man the savage and man the thinker—here he comes face to face, in striking contrast." And for the many children who visited the Fair, an "off-hand sketch" in Jenks's *Century World's Fair Book for Boys and Girls* showed a "Little Dahomey Boy and His Playthings," which included a saber and what appears to be a wooly mammoth, indicating the boy's reputed place in the historical time line of evolutionism.[32]

As in the European colonial accounts, much that was written about the

Dahomeyans of the Exposition explained their savagery in gendered terms. One "official guide" delineated the "marked contrast between the men and women, the latter being much larger, fiercer looking and altogether more savage in their appearance than the former, who are rather inclined to be effeminate." Observers frequently remarked upon the women's "battle scars"; historian H. D. Northrop described their heads as being "seamed by a large knife as a sort of badge of humiliation and subjection," and Hubert Howe Bancroft claimed that the presence of the "supremely hideous" women increased the "barbarity" of the Dahomey "spectacle." They were "just the sort of the people" that the Fair organizers and managers refused to "banquet or surfeit with receptions," such was their dangerous potential.[33]

Of the group, the women were always described as the most terrifying. The "Amazons" were "feather decked and sword girded, bearing the scars of hasty carvings, and savage as tigresses," and "none of them seemed to know the meaning of fear." Even their basic customs, according to the *Chicago Record*, were violent—simple greetings between the women allegedly involved facial slaps. The *Chicago Tribune* reported that "Akile and other amazons" put out a fire in the village by pulling the burning reeds and shingles off with their teeth, explaining: "That's the way they fight fire in Africa. They tear burning structures to pieces with their hands and teeth as readily as a Chicago hook and ladder company." In a caption underneath a photographic image of "Four Amazons," one guidebook explained:

> Hideous looking as they were, the Dahomeyan Amazons became objects of attraction and even admiration. This feeling could not have been caused by their beauty, but may have arisen from their fighting qualities and points in physique which every patron of the ring and turf is quick to discover and appreciate. The reputation of these black women is of the most sanguinary character. . . . It is said that they are absolutely ignorant of fear; and they are credited with being educated to the use of war-like weapons and schooled in the tactics of their savage battles from childhood, so that when they fight it is to kill or be killed. The bodies of several of the women in the Dahomeyan Village were frightfully scarred, the results of contests in which they had become enraged. In several of the gala day processions through the Exposition grounds these people approached the frenzy that borders on blood-shedding, but were restrained from actual violence.

This observer concluded hopefully: "Under the protectorate of the French over their territory it is believed a little of the mildness and virtues of civilization may be introduced."[34]

Claims to authentic "savagery" aside, the villagers were, in fact, skilled and seasoned performers; some of the Dahomeyans had learned how to enact "wildness" via stage managing and "careful fashioning" for Western audiences at previous international expositions. In his history of the Fair, Reed notes that among the many inaccuracies and misrepresentations inherent in the Dahomey Village, the most popular was the martial nature of its female inhabitants, as "the famed female warriors of Dahomey were considered the king's wives, and would not have left Dahomey to journey to the United States under any circumstances."[35]

Displays of ancient "savagery," then, were performances crafted for a specific audience. As other historians have pointed out, the exhibition of Africans had a long history in Europe, and much of this popular fascination had to do with gender and, more specifically, sex. Victorian scientific racism revealed a fascination with women's anatomy, "repeatedly locat[ing] racial difference through the sexual characteristics of the female body." The most infamous example of this was the display of Saartjie Baartman, the so-called "Hottentot Venus" from South Africa whose diminutive height, near-nudity, reputedly large labia, and prodigious rear end made her, for a short time in the early nineteenth century, "the greatest phenomenon ever exhibited" in Great Britain. As part of the burgeoning trade in imperial artifacts, including "human curiosities," Baartman's perceived threat as a "dangerous savage" from South Africa was defused; as an indentured servant presented for consumption by entertainment-seeking Londoners, she was transformed into a "Hottentot," a subhuman sexual object, rather than a Khoisan subject of colonialism. She was one of the "most talked-about women" in London and Paris, and she became one of the primary gendered symbols of nineteenth-century European colonialism in Africa.[36]

Despite some reports to the contrary, no "Hottentots" were displayed in Chicago, but many of the female colonized subjects of the World's Fair endured a similar tension between being depicted as barbaric beasts and as objects for the sexual consumption of spectators. Fairgoers' graphic reports of disgust along the Midway notwithstanding, whiteness was not a prerequisite for assessments of beauty at the Fair. While observers reserved their most derisive description for these "African Amazons," this disdain was not replicated in accounts of the other "exotic" and foreign women along the Midway.[37]

Indeed, the first act along the Midway just beyond the White City was the "World's Congress of Beauty" featuring "40 Ladies from 40 Nations" representing all "types of loveliness" recruited by a reporter turned "Chicago beauty collector." This popular sideshow showcased "every quality of beauty," with the notable exception of Dahomeyan women. "Fettome, A Bedouin Woman," and her cohort were, according to one description, "as intelligent as their lords" and "by no means bad-looking," while "Miriamna, a Woman from Ceylon" was a "wee bit of a woman" who "had a dignity of her own which she maintained under all circumstances" as she served tea in the Ceylon Tea Room of the Woman's Building. The "Boushareens" of Soudan were described as "stalwart and fine-looking"; explained the observer: "Once in a while a type of the African is presented to the white race and is counted as handsome." These women were, according to the author of *The Photographic World's Fair and Midway Plaisance*, "a great deal happier at the Fair than they were in their own often-raided part of Africa."[38]

Above all the people of the Midway, the women of Samoa, where the United States had a naval station and would, just a few years later, have an official territory, were the most revered. "Allalauia, the Samoan girl," was the belle of the Midway Ball, "molded in such statuesque perfection as never a corseted, French-heeled belle of civilization could hope to cultivate." She and the other "Samoan Girls" were admired as some of the "finest specimens of physical development"; indeed, before they left Chicago, one of the women, "pronounced by the authorities on art as possessing very nearly the recognized ideal of womanly proportions," was used as a model for the Art Institute of Chicago. The reverence reserved for these "dusky sirens" was one aspect of the gendered dimension of the "noble versus nasty savage" approach to Western imperialism.[39]

Because of the key function of sex in both scientific racism and imperial matriarchalism, the Dahomeyan women, by comparison, represented to white fairgoers the utmost in savagery. Explained one observer, the Dahomeyan women's "demeanor rather conveyed the impression that they were bad and glad of it," with looks to match: "Of the sexes, the women, battle-scarred Amazons from the King's army, were the larger and fiercer looking. Anything but attractive were these she-warriors, and about as devoid of all femininity, even of the uncivilized type, as could be well imagined." Journalist Julian Hawthorne concluded bluntly, "There are no beauties among the Dahomeyans." Others explained that the "Dahomean mother is, in feature and figure, the incomparable nightmare of the human race"; it was therefore "impossible to conceive of a notch lower in the human scale than the Amazon, or female warrior, represents." To underscore their subhuman unattractiveness, one guidebook included the Dahomeyan "warlike 'ladies'" with the Hagenbeck Animal Show under the heading, "Glimpses of Foreign Life"; another reporter likewise deemed the women "as degraded as the animals which prowl the jungles of their dark land." While other dancers along the Midway were served up as Orientalist pornography for white consumption, the armed African Amazons were treated as frightening throwbacks on the evolutionist time line, dangerous women who threatened the expansion of Western "civilization."[40]

Accordingly, there were palpable fears of miscegenation at the fair, reflecting the broader "sexual dangers of U.S. colonialism." Although a *World's Fair Puck* cartoon represented this fear as a white woman in danger, recoiling in fear from the nearly naked "savage" in front of the "Cannibal Exhibit," much of the concern over "race-mixing" centered on the unsettling presence of the Dahomeyan women. The problematic potential of miscegenation was nowhere more evident than in the reports of the Midway Ball, or, as some called it apprehensively, the "Ball of the Midway Freaks." Critic Amy Leslie expressed concerns for the safety of the white people who planned to attend the Ball, as the "intimate collision of nations" might well result in violence. She warned: "Have the ball, by all means, but prepare for sanguinary chromatics in the picture." Others were more overt in their sexual critiques of the Ball, where "the belly dancers and every other depraved jiggling half-dressed woman of the Midway" would "dance with the senior officers of the fair." This "situation," lamented a *Chicago Tribune* reporter, was thus "full of horrifying possibilities":

It should cause a shiver in the composite breast of the Board of Lady Managers when they consider what may happen if Director-General Davis should lead out some fascinating Fatima at the head of the grand procession . . . or if Mayor Harrison, who belongs to all nations, should dance with the whole lot. Will they suppress their partners' contortions by protest or by force, or, following the fashion of the country, will they, too, attempt Oriental contortions? Suppose that President Higginbotham finds as his vis-à-vis an anointed, bare-backed Fiji beauty of a Dahomeyite amazon bent upon the extraordinary antics of the can-

nibal dance, is he to join in and imitate her or risk his head in an effort
to restrain her?

These warnings served to keep "hundreds of amusement-seekers, particularly
ladies," away from the Ball, a "gathering of as motly [sic] and crude a host of
citizens as cosmos could choose to breathe upon."[41]

The Ball proceeded as planned, and it was, according to Leslie, "a nightmare of discomforts, hilarity and barbaric splendor." In a setting featuring elaborate rugs, tapestries, silk bunting, flags, and greenery representing
the global reach of the Midway, the tuxedoed men of Chicago danced until
nearly dawn with "black Amazons with bushy hair and teeth necklaces" in the
"strangest gathering since the destruction of the Tower of Babel." Although
Leslie described the Dahomeyans at the Ball as "of course" representing "everything savage . . . with a vehemence of physical exertion and spiritual ecstasy
overwhelming in diabolism," and flirtations and alcohol both flowed freely, the
Tribune's worst fears of violence or miscegenation were not realized.[42]

The organizers took care to prevent sexual attraction across the color line.
The problem of nudity was resolved in a particularly colonial manner: women
from the Midway, like the "Amazon" Aheze, were given special coverings. In
a lengthy front-page article the day after the Ball, the Chicago Tribune detailed
their attire: "Short skirt and low bodice made of small American flags; sea-
weed necklace and snakeskin amulets, twine string headdress, and bare feet."
This was apparently a tried and true method for covering the bodies of the
African women, and one that was used multiple times during the Fair. A reporter for the Chicago Record mused on the Fourth of July: "John Hancock little thought that some day the wild people from Dahomey would celebrate the
anniversary of American independence by wearing red, white and blue flags
around their dusky thighs." The flag, the ultimate national symbol and talis-
man of territorial expansion, thus defused the perceived threat in the bodies
of these women by desexing the "savages," disempowering the Amazons, and
rendering them decent for "civilized" company in an obvious metaphor for
imperialism.[43]

Reactions to the Dahomey Amazons thus encapsulated the gendered logic
of the Fair. These women represented the lowest scale of the evolutionist time
line, as evidenced by their matriarchal savagery, which contrasted starkly with
the "mothers of civilization" in the White City such as May French Sheldon,
the White Queen. Other human exhibits, while not occupying the same place

on the evolutionist time line as Western societies, indicated the benefits of colonialism, exemplified by, for example, the reputed gentleness of the Javanese and the beauty of the Egyptian dancers. "The Exposition speaks of the advancement of civilization," wrote one correspondent for the *Chicago Standard*. "It is time," he argued, "to bring civilization to the savage people on display." The African Amazons were a kind of ultimate test of civilization. According to another reporter, "There is an educational aspect," a "living object lesson," to the exhibit. He concluded: "If you want to realize as never before how much you have to be thankful for in being born in a civilized land and a member of a Christian family and people, go to Dahomey encampment. . . . If Christianity can educate and elevate and civilize these people, it can work a miracle indeed."[44]

One way to work this "miracle" was to tame the savage matriarchy, a task accomplished not just through actual conquest of Dahomey by the French, but also by shipping the "Amazons" to Chicago, housing them in a human zoo, making them perform for white audiences, and clothing them in the flag of the United States. Although many of the other inhabitants of colonial exhibits went home or traveled on to tour Europe after the Fair, this American taming of the Dahomey matriarchy would continue beyond the World's Columbian Exposition.

As in representations of colonized women at the Fair, a key tactic in controlling a subjugated group was the sexualization of its women. In Chicago, despite the much-remarked-upon exposure of their bodies—unlike any other group of women at the Fair, the "Amazons" were generally bare-breasted— the Dahomeyan women were never depicted or described as desirable sexual objects. Rather, they were violent, dangerous matriarchs to be viewed with great caution from a safe distance. But this representation changed after the Fair, a shift that reflects the immediate colonial context. The country of Dahomey itself was viewed as more dangerous to Westerners in 1893, as it was an African power that seemed to be at least partially successful in resisting the French. By 1894, however, France controlled the region after heavy losses. As the inhabitants of the Dahomey Village decamped from Chicago in the winter of 1893–1894, and as the French made a final successful push into the region, the "Amazons" transformed into sexual objects.[45]

This representational transformation was complete by the opening of the California Midwinter International Exposition in San Francisco in January 1894, just two months after the closing of the World's Columbian Exposition. The Midwinter Fair, as it came to be known, was the brainchild of M. H. de Young, the editor of the *San Francisco Chronicle*, who had the idea after attending the Chicago Fair. The California Fair would feature selected exhibits from Chicago, such as the Dahomey Village, the Street in Cairo, and the "Esquimaux," in addition to some new displays, such as a herd of buffaloes and a Forty-Niners Camp. Evolutionism was again the organizing logic of the exhibits, as the Dahomey Village was "situated at the extreme western end of the north drive" of the Midway, an international promenade which was, as in Chicago, "crowded with representatives of all nations in their national costumes, jostling one another as they move along with the throng or attempt to stem the human tide."[46]

According to the *Official History* of the Midwinter Fair, the "cynosure of all eyes" was the Dahomey Village. As they prepared for opening, the officials argued that a realistic replication of the village was crucial to their endeavor, as "there has been nothing at Chicago in the line of people from a foreign land who have been so much talked about." Admission to the Village was twenty-five cents, and the "great attraction" was, of course, its women, whom one reporter compared to a famous American heavyweight bare-knuckle boxing champion: "The people from Dahomey were led by an Amazon of some 50 years' standing, with a Sullivan jaw and a cannel-coal complexion. Her costume included nothing but a calico skirt and a little brief authority."[47]

Although eventually the Dahomey Village in San Francisco featured the same inhabitants as the one in Chicago (their ship was delayed, and they did not arrive until May of 1894), the presentation on the West Coast was different in tone. The Sullivan-esque Amazon described above notwithstanding, the Dahomeyan women were almost exclusively represented as more sexual and less violent in San Francisco; they were disarmed, as it were. No longer threatening to the Western imperial enterprise, this colonial containment was represented in gendered terms. As objects for sexual consumption, in contrast to the Chicago Fair, the Dahomeyan Amazons were frequently photographed in San Francisco. Eschewing the charge of pornography that plagued topless photographs, the *Official History of the California Midwinter International Exposition* opened its chapter on "The Concessions," San Francisco's version of the Midway, with a widely reprinted photo of the bare-breasted women. In "Pyramid of Dahomey Women," one woman stands in profile, looking down at three others. All are bare-breasted, and three of the four are resting their heads in their hands wearily, as if they are bored. Although weapons are visible, they are loosely grasped as props rather than brandished as threats against Western civilization. Robert Rydell, a historian of world's fairs, deems the image simply "a pyramid of bosoms," as the women's breasts are the focal point of the photo. Images such as this and "Dahomey Girls in Picturesque Poses" visually contained the "Amazons"; castrating cannibals no more, they were passive sexualized objects, "sit[ting] calmly before the camera with their breasts bare," while other photographs from the exhibition showed the Dahomey men "waving their weapons."[48]

Situating the Dahomeyans within familiar stereotypes of femininity and masculinity apparently made them more palatable; although most guidebooks and official histories of the World's Columbian Exposition failed to include a single photograph of the "Amazons," the Dahomeyan women appeared in six photographs in the *Official History of the Midwinter Fair* alone, more than any of the other inhabitants of the ethnic exhibits. The Village was immensely profitable in San Francisco, enough so that after the California Midwinter Fair, the Dahomeyans were sent on to perform in various other venues, even splitting so that there were two groups "leasing out their services to exhibitions and holiday resorts" as well at major national and international expositions, where they "still appeared in a more official role as part of French imperial exhibitions."[49]

Beyond these "colonial exhibits," the Dahomey Amazons would live on in American popular culture through another medium. An accident of timing—the African inhabitants of the Dahomey Village in Chicago were late in arriving—gave birth to another American representation of the Dahomeyan women. The ship carrying the villagers arrived in May, but because the Midwinter Fair opened in late January, Fair organizers hired local African Americans as stand-ins. The ruse worked, as a reporter for *The Examiner* took these "false Dahomeans" for the real thing, observing that their performatively poor English, dancing, and degree of undress marked them as African. One of these "sham" Dahomeyans was Caribbean-American comedian Bert Williams, who would become a major vaudeville star, the first African American with a lead role on Broadway, and the best-selling black recording artist before 1920. Williams got his start in various West Coast minstrel shows, one of which he performed in an "absolute dive" called, ironically enough, the Midway Plaisance. There Williams met George Walker, who was to become his comedic partner in a series of shows based on the "coon" formula, which played on racist stereotypes. Both men were hired to play Dahomeyan villagers at the Midwinter

Fair when the Africans were delayed.[50]

Once the "villagers" arrived in May, Williams and Walker were let go, but they took advantage of their free access to the Fair to interact as much as possible with the Dahomeyans, eventually writing a show inspired by the experience. In 1903, Williams and Walker took their musical *In Dahomey* to Broadway—one of the first black musicals to open on the Great White Way—with music by Will Marion Cook and lyrics by famed poet Paul Lawrence Dunbar, who, like Walker, had attended the World's Columbian Exposition in Chicago and seen the original Dahomey Village firsthand. The musical, originally titled *The Cannibal King*, tells the story of a group of African Americans affiliated with the Dahomey Colonization Society who travel to West Africa in search of a missing heirloom. There, the first people they encounter are the "Amazons." The women are mute but fierce as they execute a military drill, and then they are shoved offstage in what is primarily a drama about men and their missing property. The musical was a modest hit in the United States, and after fifty-three performances in New York, *In Dahomey* went to London, where its popularity increased after the all-black cast was invited to perform at the birthday celebration for the Prince of Wales. *In Dahomey* was initially met with some confusion by British audiences, but Williams and Walker saved the production when they changed the finale to a rousing rendition of "God Save the Queen." With this revision, the African Amazons were fully tamed, and the rightful matriarch of the play became the titular white queen of the incongruously added national anthem of Great Britain.[51]

Through these juxtapositions between the "White Queens" and the "African Amazons," imperial matriarchalism went mainstream as an endorsement of Western colonialism. White, evolutionist, and racist, imperial matriarchalism represented a departure from the feminist matriarchalism of Matilda Joslyn Gage. But even as imperial matriarchalism permeated American popular culture as a justification for expansionist ambitions, Gage's theories would spawn a different kind of matriarchalism that would become enormously popular for well over a century, as we shall see in the following chapter.

4

WITCHES, WIZARDS, AND WOMEN OF CAST IRON

American Matriarchalism Goes Mainstream

> "What has happened?" the Scarecrow asked a sad-looking man with
> a bushy beard, who wore an apron and was wheeling a baby-carriage
> along the sidewalk.
>
> "Why, we've had a revolution, your Majesty—as you ought to know
> very well," replied the man; "and since you went away the women have
> been running things to suit themselves. I'm glad you have decided to
> come back and restore order, for doing housework and minding the
> children is wearing out the strength of every man in the Emerald City."
>
> —L. FRANK BAUM, *The Marvelous Land of Oz* (1904)

ONE of the many reporters covering the spectacle of the World's
Columbian Exposition was a recent Chicago transplant named
Lyman Frank Baum. As a correspondent for the *Chicago Evening
Post* and a new citizen of the Second City, Baum was enthralled
with the Fair. He visited it many times, and its lasting impression is evident
in his later fiction. But unlike many of the millions of spectators who flocked
to Chicago in 1893, Baum did not wholly internalize the imperialist and racist
messages that characterized the Exposition.

Although the Fair was a major catalyst to his ever-active imagination,
Baum's other primary influence during the early 1890s was much more personal. Baum was the son-in-law of Matilda Joslyn Gage, who published her
matriarchalist text, *Women, Church and State,* in 1893, the year of the Exposition. In fact, Gage lived with her daughter, Maud, and Maud's husband, Frank
Baum, off and on throughout the research and writing phases of the book, and
Gage paid her daughter's family a lengthy visit in Chicago to attend the World's
Congress of Religions at the Fair. Gage's tome was well reviewed, but it was
academic, controversial, and not widely read. Her son-in-law, however, would,
in just a few years, achieve notoriety as a best-selling author of children's literature, and his most well-known fiction, *The Wonderful Wizard of Oz* series,
would be rife with the various theories—Theosophy, antiracism, feminism,

and matriarchalism—espoused by his mother-in-law. Gage was written out of contemporary history, but her legacy lived on in Oz.

Like Gage and Morgan, Baum was born in the Mohawk Valley in New York in 1856, just as Morgan was developing his theories about matriarchal history and Gage was hitting her stride in the suffrage and abolitionist movements. Unlike his future wife, Baum grew up privileged, especially after speculation in the Pennsylvania oil industry made his father a rich man. In his late teens, Baum began what would become decades of bouncing between jobs, working in family retail, chicken-breeding, playwriting, and acting. In the early 1880s, while Baum was sampling careers, young Maud Gage, the beloved daughter of Matilda Joslyn Gage, was preparing to enter Sage College, the women's college at Cornell, to fulfill her mother's dream that she become a doctor. At school, Maud had many friends, including her roommate, Josie Baum, who set Maud up on a date with her cousin. Matilda Gage intimidated her daughter's suitors, and Baum's cousin Frank, the young chicken breeder turned actor with a life-long interest in writing, was no exception. Maud proved to be as strong-willed as her mother, however, and her relationship with Baum grew serious.[1]

In 1882, when Maud decided to drop out of college to marry her boyfriend, Gage was initially livid, concerned as she was about the uncertain future of the would-be actor. Gage warmed to Baum, however, as it became clear that he was devoted to her daughter. After the wedding, Maud left Sage College to travel with her husband's current play, but the tour turned sour as the troupe headed west and paychecks dwindled. Following this acting failure, Frank, in an attempt to support his young bride and, eventually, their four sons, went to work with his father and his brother in the family petroleum products business. The company was, for a while, very successful, but it lost a major battle with the oil cartel controlled by John D. Rockefeller, and Frank was an irresponsible spender and poor planner. This financial downfall prompted Maud Baum to take on the role of money manager in the family in a move that, according to one of Baum's biographers, "mirrored" Maud's parents' relationship.[2]

The young Baums struggled financially, as Gage had predicted they would, and Frank tried various means of supporting his family. After the decline of the family oil interests and the death of his father in 1887, he grew disenchanted, and, reportedly on the advice of the legendary newspaper editor Horace Greeley, he looked westward. Baum wrote to his brother-in-law in South Dakota of his "western fever," complaining that the East was too "crowded" and its "competition ke[pt] a man down." "In this struggling mass of humanity," he complained, "a man like myself is lost." Soon thereafter, Baum and the family moved to Aberdeen in the Dakota Territory, where he opened a variety store, Baum's Bazaar, dedicated to selling nonnecessities. Matilda Gage, who spent the winters with her daughter's family, ventured to South Dakota to visit her children and to stock the store with books on feminism and Theosophy.[3]

Although it did well at first, Baum's Bazaar was forced to close on New Year's Day, 1890. Baum, displaying his characteristic optimism, took the opportunity to fulfill a lifelong dream and became the editor of a local paper. One month after his store went under, Baum debuted the first issue of the *Aberdeen Saturday Pioneer,* in which he set himself apart from other local media with his explicit Republican politics and outrageous satire. His three primary themes reveal the direct influence of Gage: of his twelve editorials, eight address Theosophy and the occult, two address suffrage and gender issues, and two criticize contemporary capitalism.[4]

Baum's voice in the paper is most evident in these editorials and in his satirical column entitled, "Our Landlady," featuring the fictitious Sairy Ann Bilkins, through whom he lampooned all manner of political issues. A prominent point of discussion in the forty-eight "Our Landlady" columns was the women's suffrage referendum in South Dakota, which had been admitted as a state in November 1889. Baum became secretary of the local suffrage organization in May of 1890, just as his mother-in-law split with the National Woman Suffrage Association and the national organization identified South Dakota as a state in which a suffrage amendment had a good chance of passing. In the paper, Baum used his fictional creation Sairy Ann Bilkins to show his support for women's rights. She attended a suffrage convention in 1890, and she even ran for mayor as an opposing candidate to local bigwigs, warning that she had secured the women's bloc. Through Bilkins, Baum argued: "It's the conceit o' men as is the biggest stumblin block tar universal sufferin o' women."[5]

In his own editorials, as well, Baum used the paper as a suffrage platform, covering Susan B. Anthony's state-by-state campaign in the West. "If our politics are to be masculine forever," he wrote in 1890, "I despair of the republic." In an editorial about American diversity and tolerance, he continued his plea: "We must do away with sex prejudice and render equal distinction and reward to brains and ability, no matter whether found in man or woman." Western women, in particular, deserved the vote, according to Baum. The archetype of the strong, pioneer woman is one he described at length in an editorial advocating for suffrage in South Dakota, arguing that "a young lady's highest ambition is to become a breadwinner" and a "bright example" of "independence."[6]

Gage's influence on Baum is also evident in his writings dealing with Native Americans, although his stance in this case does not lend itself to an easy analysis. In *Women, Church and State,* Gage argued that the indigenous matriarchy of the Iroquois represented the pinnacle of American ideals of democracy and equality. As any student of US history knows, this was, to put it mildly, a minority opinion among white Americans in the late nineteenth century, an era that featured virulent racism, forced relocation, and outright violence against Native Americans. The year during which Baum ran the *Aberdeen Saturday Pioneer* was an especially violent one for US-Indian relations in the region. Racist panic about Indian attacks reached a high point in the Dakotas in the fall of 1890, as Lakota rumors about the arrival of a Messiah sparked a religious ritual known as the Ghost Dance. The Ghost Dance spread through the region, and various camps of Sioux were reported to be dancing wildly and experiencing visions. These activities, par for the course for Christian religious revivals, were nevertheless interpreted by local whites as war dances in preparation for an attack. By November of 1890, area newspapers were running headlines like "Indians Nearly Crazy" and "War Is Certain."[7]

In the *Aberdeen Saturday Pioneer,* Baum was more tempered. Although he ran "boilerplate reports" of the Ghost Dance, he warned readers that accounts were exaggerated. Indeed, he explained, the "Indian scare" was "false and senseless," and media reports of it were profit-making ventures, rather than accurate, real-time reporting: "Probably papers who have so injured the state by their flashy headlines of Indian uprisings did not think of the results of such actions beyond the extra sale of a few copies of their sheets."[8]

Baum's calmer approach was not popularly adopted, and panic reached a high point in late November, when the governor of South Dakota put the local company of the National Guard on high alert in response to rumors of "roving bands of Lakotas moving off the reservations." Buffalo Bill Cody himself was dispatched to "secure the person" of Sitting Bull; the Hunkpapa Lakota Sioux chief and medicine man had famously participated in the defeat of General Custer at Little Big Horn in 1876, surrendered to the US government in 1881, toured for a while with Buffalo Bill's Wild West Show, and then, in November of 1890, joined the Ghost Dance. Cody was supposed to retrieve Sitting Bull from the dance at the Standing Rock reservation in late November, although this plan was overridden at the last minute. The panic subsided long enough for Baum to warn his readers again: "The Indian scare was a great injustice, and when we realize that it was the work of sensational newspaper articles, we are tempted to wish that the press was not so free, and could have some wholesome strictures laid upon it."[9]

Bands of Lakota began to move through the southern and central parts of the state, and South Dakota began to arm itself in early December. The ensuing violence resulted in the death of Sitting Bull, who was killed in his camp during a raid by the US Cavalry. Along with the massacre of the Lakota Sioux at Wounded Knee two weeks later, Sitting Bull's death was national news, and while many white American rejoiced at the death of the "savage," others were dismayed by the outright assassination of a chief who had not posed a threat to white civilization for many years. Baum's editorial eulogy on December 20 enumerated the various injustices to Sitting Bull and his tribe, including theft, treachery, deception, and murder. Baum wrote of the Great Chief's final stand: "The proud spirit of the original owners of these vast prairies, inherited through centuries of fierce and bloody wars for their possession, lingered last in the bosom of Sitting Bull. With his fall the nobility of the Redskin is extinguished, and what few are left are a pack of whining curs who lick the hand that smites them." Baum scholars, however, have focused on the next, troubling part of this editorial. Following the evolutionist, "survival of the fittest" logic of Western civilization to its (il)logical conclusion, Baum offered a shocking call for extermination: "The Whites, by law of conquest, by justice of civilization, are masters of the American continent, and the best safety of the frontier settlers will be secured by the total annihilation of the few remaining Indians." Baum concluded, "Their glory has fled, their spirit broken, their manhood effaced; better that they should die than live the miserable wretches that they are."[10]

This editorial has quite understandably been read by scholars as evidence of Baum's racism and his belief in manifest destiny and the inexorable advance of American civilization a la Frederick Jackson Turner. Yet another interpretation is possible here, if readers take Baum's eulogy within the context of his other editorial writings, which were often satirical and explicitly critical of American injustices and hypocritical professions of equality. At the very least, if the editorial did represent the editor's true feelings about race, he was certainly critical of the American, evolutionist notion of progress; "civilization," in this editorial, is vengeful and violent.[11]

Given the level of influence that Gage, an adoptee into the Mohawk Nation and outspoken admirer of Native American social systems, had on the Baum household, it is surprising, perhaps even improbable, that Baum would spout such open racism in his newspaper. When placed within the context of his other columns that month, Baum's Indian editorials look more like misunderstood satire rather than a cheer for "civilized" progress. In "Our Landlady," for instance, the fictional Mrs. Bilkins discusses the Ghost Dance with an Indian chief, who pleads fearfully, "Don't hurt us, Miss Bilkins." He explains that his people had heard rumors of an imminent attack—a reversal of the white panic permeating Aberdeen: "Candidate-afraid-of-his-Pocketbook was in the camp this mornin' an' said the rumors o' the whites risin' that we'd heard was all true. He said that the whites was all starvin' in Dakota, an' the government wouldn't give 'em any rations, an' so they was comin' to rob us Injuns of what we had. I tell you the Injuns is pretty badly skeert an they're leavin' their homes an' bandin' together for mutual pertection." Of the Ghost Dance, he says: "We live in a free country. We Injins can vote an' you wimmin can't, and don't you fergit that. Religion is as free as water an' much more plenty. If there's any fault found with our runnin' our religion to suit ourselves we'll jest join the independents." This advocacy for religious tolerance and the threat of using the crucial right of voting to combat racism, veiled as it was in familiar satire, offers a different context for interpretation, making Baum's Sitting Bull eulogy look less like a racist, genocidal screed and more like a scathing, if misfired, critique of federal policy and actions.[12]

Gage's spiritualist influence on Baum also comes through in his newspaper. In an 1887 letter, Gage wrote that Maud and Frank were reading various texts by the founder of Theosophy, Madame Blavatsky. Although he did not formally join the Theosophical Society until 1892, in the late 1880s, under Gage's tutelage, Baum's interest in the philosophy grew steadily. Through his editorials, Baum attempted to educate his readers on the benefits of this new spiritual movement. He explained that Theosophists were "searchers after truth," and were therefore not a "menace" to Christianity, but over time, his anticlericalism became more pronounced. In October of 1890, he argued:

The people are beginning to think. While everything else has progressed, the Church alone has been trying to stand still, and hang with a death-grip to medieval or ancient legends. It teaches the same old superstitions, the same blind faith in the traditional bible, the same precepts of salvation and damnation. And all this while the people have been growing more liberal in thought, more perfect in comprehension.

Baum's spiritualism was not limited to Theosophy; in his editorials, he endorsed various aspects of the occult, including clairvoyance.[13]

In this same vein, the *Aberdeen Saturday Pioneer* also serialized fiction by the popular English author Edward Bulwer-Lytton. Bulwer-Lytton was significant to Baum, for his fiction had, for almost fifty years, served as a kind of thematic guide to the occult. Another author in whom Baum was interested was H. Rider Haggard, the author of the controversial *She: A History of Adventure* (1887), which was partially inspired by a Bulwer-Lytton novel from the 1860s. Perhaps most significant for our purposes is the fact that Haggard's *She* was an internationally popular matriarchalist novel. Various European novelists responded to the matriarchalism of Bachofen and British anthropologists in the 1870s and 1880s by envisioning fictional female societies; of these, H. Rider Haggard's *She* was by far the most widely read. In *She*, Haggard combined various Theosophical elements, including the wisdom of ancient civilizations, immortality, and self-reliant journeys through unfamiliar lands—all themes that would later surface in Baum's children's literature, as well. In an unwitting nod to Bachofen, who cited matriarchal mythology as "hints from the ancients," Baum quoted a "friend" who "declared" that Haggard "was undoubtedly a reincarnation of some ancient mystic, and therefore throughout his brain lingered some latent and inexplicable knowledge which prompted the ideas from which 'She' emanated."[14]

Baum's unorthodox feminist, racial, and spiritual views notwithstanding, the *Aberdeen Saturday Pioneer* was an initial success, but a major wheat crop failure, a harsh winter, prairie fires, and a drought hit South Dakota that year. As "hard times" became a common phrase in Aberdeen, Baum's general optimism and occasionally controversial columns proved to be less popular. He suspended his editorials for five months, and when he returned in mid-October of 1890, Baum again addressed provocative topics, including direct attacks on the church and local ministers. His criticism of the Aberdeen school system, in which he argued that salaries were unjustifiably high as the region and the nation slid into a depression, proved to be his undoing, and he left the paper the following month.[15]

In the winter of 1891, mirroring the problems with the local economy, Baum's health was poor and his career was failing. Matilda Gage, in fact, had to step in to care for both, putting Baum to bed with chest pains and publishing the final issues of the newspaper while Maud prepared to give birth to their fourth son. After the baby's arrival and Baum's recovery, the family needed a change. At the time, Chicago was deep in preparations for the upcoming World's Columbian Exposition, set to open in May of 1893. Baum, on a post-recovery exploratory mission to examine potential opportunities accompanying the Fair, was hired by the *Chicago Evening Post*.[16]

The entire family packed up and moved to the city. Gage's influence on Baum continued during the Chicago years, as he and Maud studied, passed the requisite tests, and were admitted into the Theosophical Society in the late summer of 1892. In the fall of 1893, Gage joined her family in Chicago to attend the Fair's Parliament of the Religions of the World, in which Theosophy had controversially been included along with the major world religions. There Gage and Baum heard Hindu leader Swami Vivekananda's impassioned plea for tolerance in his welcoming speech. This was, of course, a challenging message at a major Exposition that featured open racism and promoted international imperialism.[17]

The mystical beliefs of Theosophy would later find voice in the fantastical world of Oz, and one can find many other allusions to the Fair in Baum's later fiction, as he visited many times during its six-month run. Baum later wrote, "Who can forget Chicago in 1893 and the people of all nations?" He was fascinated by the White City, the inspiration for the Emerald City of Oz (both were illusions, as the White City was not, as it appeared, made of marble, while the emerald effect in Oz is achieved through colored glasses), as well as its "alter-ego," the Midway, peopled by exotic cultures like the land of Oz itself. Baum made the front page with his piece on Thomas Edison, the "wizard of Menlo Park," who debuted his motion picture device, the Kinetoscope, at the Fair—a scene that Baum re-created seven years later when the Wizard of Oz projects various images in his throne room to disguise the fact that he is a mere man. Likewise, Hagenbeck's Animal Show, featuring lions, tigers, and bears, among other beasts, was inspiration for the many talking animals of Oz.[18]

Baum's stint as a newspaperman in Chicago was financially unsuccessful, as Maud, the family accountant, soon determined that his salary did not cover their expenses. Chicago's brief economic boom ended with the Fair, and the depression gripping the nation descended upon the Second City. Baum returned to retail, this time as a traveling china salesman, and although the

family struggled, his time in Chicago was an important one for his development as a writer. In 1895, Matilda Gage came across a contest for the writing
of a children's book; the prize was $500, and she urged her family members
to join the competition. She instructed Baum via letter: "Now you are a good
writer and I advise you to try. . . . If you could get up a series of adventures or
a Dakota blizzard adventure where a heroic teacher saves children's lives . . .
bring in a cyclone from North Dakota." She urged him to concoct "a fiction
which comes with a moral, without however any attempt to sermonize."[19]

Predictably, Frank missed the deadline, but he did start writing. As Gage
grew weak and eventually ill enough that she had to move in with the family
in Chicago full-time, Baum kept writing. He had some successes, and over the
next five years, he honed his ideas and themes. During the next few years, a
handful of Baum's stories were published, and that was enough to encourage
him to keep writing.[20]

Although Baum's *Mother Goose in Prose* (1897) and *Father Goose: His Book*
(1899), his original takes on the famous children's rhymes, did fairly well, in
1898, family tragedies abounded: Maud's older brother had a baby, Dorothy
Gage, who died at the age of five months old, and Matilda Gage's health began to decline. In March of 1898, Gage suffered a devastating stroke, and she
passed away soon thereafter. "Your mother," Frank wrote to his brother-in-law
in a grief-stricken anticipation of the famous refrain from *The Wizard of Oz*,
"will never be able to go home."[21]

In her will, Gage made Baum her literary executor and divided her property equally among her four children, but to Maud alone she left all of her
"woman suffrage papers, books and documents." She requested cremation,
and Maud Baum traveled to Gage's childhood home in Fayetteville, New York,
to scatter the ashes. During this difficult time, alone in Chicago with the boys
as their mother traveled east, Frank unexpectedly had his "big idea." "Suddenly," he wrote his publisher, "the one [story] moved right in and took possession" of his creative mind. He continued: "I grabbed a piece of paper that was
lying there and I began to write. The story really seemed to write itself. Then,
I couldn't find any regular paper, so I took anything at all, including a bunch
of old envelopes." He wrote an entire book with one pencil, the stub of which
he later framed.[22]

The passing of the influential family matriarch and the mother of American feminist matriarchalism thus resulted in a children's fantasy that was
to become "America's first native fairy tale." Baum's fantastical books—

eventually, there would be fourteen of them—depict a matriarchal utopia the likes of which American audiences had never seen. Both Gage and Baum had tried various media through which to disseminate their ideas: speeches, essays, historical tomes, editorials, and satire. In 1898, following Gage's advice to avoid overt "love or religion . . . or political" stories, Baum hit upon the medium through which their shared vision could be spread. In Gage's version of world history, societies evolved from matriarchal utopias into patriarchal dystopias; in Baum's fantastical creation, Oz underwent the opposite transformation, from a patriarchal dystopia riven with conflict and slavery, to a matriarchal utopia featuring diversity and equality. In homage to his mother-in-law, Baum used the platform of children's literature to represent the perversions of patriarchy, the natural power of women, and the equality that he and Gage believed resulted from matriarchal rule.[23]

The tale of Oz begins in a desolate place: the isolated landscape of tornado-prone Kansas, a nod to Frank and Maud's brief, unhappy time there when he was a traveling actor at the beginning of their marriage. It seems that the only thing Kansas and Oz have in common at the outset of the series is that they are both patriarchies; but for this, the comparison between the two lands is stark. While Oz is populated with fantastical characters, Americans, with the exception of young Dorothy, appear to be a pretty sad lot. Aunt Em, once a "young, pretty wife" with sparkly eyes and rosy cheeks, had turned gray, and the same is true of Uncle Henry, who is "weak and nervous" to boot. Henry's neurasthenia is characteristic of the male characters of Baum's series; under the sham rule of the so-called Wonderful Wizard, Oz is peopled with inept men.[24]

In fact, many of the male characters in the series deal with classic symptoms of fin de siècle masculine crisis. Dorothy's companions were all males— the Scarecrow, the Lion, and the Tin Man—experiencing peculiarly gendered emotional problems. The Scarecrow's lack of brains is not just problematic; it is also apparently emasculating. A crow explains to him, "If you only had brains in your head you would be as good a man as any of them, and a better man than some of them." The Scarecrow's other marked characteristic has gendered implications, as well: being made of straw, he is unable to feel anything, and he cannot be hurt.[25]

Dorothy's other traveling companions are similarly afflicted. The Tin Man was so made because the Wicked Witch had each of his appendages, and eventually his torso and his head, cut off one by one with an enchanted ax. Without a heart, he is unable to love, and he weeps frequently over this affliction. The Cowardly Lion is a fearful, sniveling mess, and it is this character that perhaps most illustrates Baum's satire of contemporary masculinity. Despite his enormous size, he is unintimidating enough that Dorothy's first interaction with him is to slap him, yelling, "You ought to be ashamed of yourself!" The Lion lacks courage, and he makes up for this shortcoming with stereotypical masculine bluster: "I learned that if I roared very loudly every living thing was frightened and got out of my way."[26]

Baum's most obvious representation of patriarchy is the Wizard himself, a "Great and Terrible" leader who "does not like to see anyone, and usually gets his own way." Various characters along the Yellow Brick Road attempt to describe him to Dorothy, and he is universally seen as omniscient and terrifying. The Wizard introduces himself as "Oz, the Great and Terrible," to which the girl replies that she is "Dorothy, the Small and Meek." Despite this description, however, Dorothy—a girl of no more than twelve in the novel—has more power than this much-feared ruler.[27]

To get back to Kansas, the Wizard commands Dorothy to take down the formidable Wicked Witch of the West. For this adventure, Dorothy dons a "pure white" dress, the mark of her increasing power—in the color palette of Oz, sorceresses wear white—and, after facing a pack of wolves, a flock of crows, a swarm of bees, a band of flying monkeys, and enslavement, she defeats the Wicked Witch with a mere bucket of water, which "melt[s] her away like brown sugar." Dorothy becomes both liberator, as she frees the Wicked Witch's slaves, and ruler, as she commands the King of the Winged Monkeys to take her back to the Emerald City to face the Wizard.[28]

Like the Cowardly Lion, the Great and Powerful Oz turns out to be all bluster, reduced to simply "The Great Humbug" in the final chapters. The Wizard explains "meekly" that he has "been making believe" all along. His power, he tells the travelers, comes from a mix of ventriloquism, the fear he carefully instilled in the people, and alteration of perception by having the citizens of and visitors to the Emerald City wear green glasses so that they would not see that it was really just a boring white—Baum's clearest allusion to the White City of the World's Columbian Exposition, where the buildings gleamed so brightly on sunny days that vendors did a booming business in "colored eyeshades." The unmasked Wizard soon flees for Omaha, and the Scarecrow temporarily becomes the king, although he is ineffectual and, in subsequent stories, easily overthrown. And, of course, Dorothy held the power to accomplish her utmost desire all along: to get home to Kansas, all she has to do is clap the heels of her silver shoes together and say her wish out loud.[29]

Dorothy is not the only powerful girl in this series—she is not even the *most* powerful girl. The rightful ruler of all of Oz is, in fact, a princess named Ozma. When the Wizard usurped the throne, he hid Ozma "by means of a magical trick" which "managed to prevent her being discovered." This trick was to have the magical "old hag" Mombi turn Ozma into a boy named Tip. Tip, upon learning this history, experiences his own crisis of masculinity. Glinda the Good Witch explains: "You are not a girl just now, because Mombi transformed you into a boy. But you were born a girl, and also a Princess." Tip's first reaction is to yell, "I want to stay a boy," and he struggles not to burst into tears.[30]

The boy Tip, "small and rather delicate in appearance," is "parent" and "dear father" to various characters, particularly Jack Pumpkinhead, whom he created. When Glinda reveals the truth about Tip's sex and royal birthright, Tip's best friend Jack gasps, "If you become a girl, you can't be my dear father anymore!" But this sex transformation is, in the end, accomplished with little masculine anxiety, and with this emasculation comes great power: birthright restored, Ozma (the mother) is far more authoritative than Tip (the father) could have ever been. Ozma's "magical sex change" receives little commentary in the fantasy tale; what matters to the characters is that "she's a girl now, and the sweetest, loveliest girl in the world."[31]

In Ozma, Baum presents the rightful matriarch of Oz. Ozma is a benign ruler commanding the heads of each of the countries of Oz, as "the little rulers are all captains, and Ozma's the general." Baum explained that she was a "beloved" leader: "She is said to be the most beautiful girl the world has ever known, and her heart and mind are as lovely as her person." The transition from male to female rule in Oz is thus met with resounding applause.[32]

In Oz, good women and girls support each other in their leadership. Ozma and Dorothy become fast and close friends when Ozma liberates Dorothy from imprisonment by an evil ruler, and Ozma makes appearances in many books in the series as Dorothy's protector. In *Dorothy and the Wizard in Oz* (1908), Ozma checks on Dorothy in her "enchanted picture" each afternoon, and if the young girl is in danger, Ozma can save her by wishing her back to Oz via the Magic Belt, perhaps an allusion to the famed belt of Hippolyta, the Amazonian queen of Greek mythology. The two budding matriarchs occasionally travel together in full royal splendor in a gem-encrusted chariot drawn by the bow-bedecked Cowardly Lion and the Hungry Tiger—a direct reference to one of the acts in Hagenbeck's Animal Show at the Chicago World's Fair, which featured "ermine mantled and crowned lions driving triumphal chariots around the arena, drawn by royal tigers."[33]

The *Oz* series is also populated with minor female rulers, but Baum did not present all women as natural leaders, a point he made very clear when an army of female revolutionaries plots to take over Oz in *The Marvelous Land of Oz* (1904). The Army of Revolt is led by General Jinjur, who explains to Tip/Ozma that her army, "composed entirely of girls," has planned a coup for one primary reason: "Because the Emerald City has been ruled by men for long enough." Baum may well have been baiting the ghost of his mother-in-law with this impending feminist revolution, as Jinjur's second reason hinges upon female stereotypes: "The City glitters with beautiful gems, which might far better be used for rings, bracelets and necklaces; and there is enough money in the King's treasury to buy every girl in our Army a dozen new gowns. So we intend to conquer the City and run the government to suit ourselves."[34]

Armed only with "long, glittering knitting-needles" stuck in their hair, the girls' entire military strategy relies upon perceptions of feminine weakness and beauty. "What man would oppose a girl, or dare to harm her?" Jinjur asks. And she was right: "no man could face the terrible weapons of the invaders," for "the Royal Army of Oz was too much afraid of women to meet the onslaught." The Guardian of the Gate "simply turned about and ran with all his might through the gate and toward the royal palace, while General Jinjur and her mob flocked into the unprotected City." Jinjur "gaily" taunts the Scarecrow and his friends, "You see how foolish it is to oppose a woman's wit."[35]

Jinjur's rule ushered in a domestic revolution in which "men were sweeping and dusting and washing dishes, while the women sat around in groups, gossiping and laughing." One man explained that since the "revolution," Jinjur and her girls "have been running things to suit themselves," and "doing housework and minding the children is wearing out the strength of every man in the Emerald City." Despite Jinjur's attraction to the many gems of the Emerald City, her real fear, it seems, is of being forced back into the private sphere. When she learns of Ozma's return, she moans, "after having ruled as Queen, and lived in a palace, I must go back to scrubbing floors and churning butter again! It is too horrible to think of! I will never consent!" Defeated by Glinda's army, however, Jinjur and her rebels return to domesticity, "rushing one and all to the kitchens of their houses" as "the men of the Emerald City cast off their aprons."[36]

Although some scholars have read Jinjur's failed revolution as a jab at the contemporary suffrage movement, others are more measured in their estimation of these scenes. According to Baum scholar Nancy Koupal, "Baum's awareness of the differing philosophies within the suffrage camp made him a sophisticated commentator on the movement itself, as well as a critic of its opposition, which helps to explain why Baum scholars often find his treatment of women perplexing and seemingly inconsistent." Jinjur, in fact, does not retreat meekly back to the domestic sphere. In *Ozma of Oz* (1907), readers learn of her fate. She marries a man who owns nine cows, and becomes "happy and contented and willing to lead a quiet life and mind [her] own business." But when Ozma asks about Jinjur's husband, she replies that he is at home, "nursing a black eye" that she gave him when he milked the wrong cow.[37]

Low-grade violence, vanity, and snobbery are thus common traits of the minor queens of Oz, but other female characters in the series represent even more drastic threats to equality. These various wicked women, besides being generally nasty, are liars, bigots, and slaveowners. The Wicked Witch of the East, killed by Dorothy's house at the beginning of *The Wonderful Wizard of Oz*, is particularly memorable (or at least her shriveling feet are), but because she dies at the outset of the series, not much is known about her. Her sister, the Wicked Witch of the West, is the most famous of the witches, although she also dies in the first book. She is a power-hungry, notorious slaveholder with one eye, "as powerful as a telescope," that can see all of Oz. Tellingly, as she contemplates how to deal with Dorothy and her companions, the Wicked Witch of the West thinks like a patriarch, according to Matilda Joslyn Gage's view of the development of dystopic, gendered power. "I can still make her my slave," the Witch muses, "for she does not know how to use her power." She revisits this idea again during her death scene; as she melts into a "brown, melted, shapeless mass" on the floor, she cries, "I have been wicked in my day, but I never thought a little girl like you would ever be able to melt me and end my wicked deeds."[38]

While the Wicked Witch of the West is singularly powerful in her resistance to the patriarchal forces of the Wizard, other evil female characters gain power through what gender studies scholars have deemed the "patriarchal bargain," or the sociocultural constraints that "exert a powerful influence on the shaping of women's gendered subjectivity and determine the nature of gender ideology in different contexts." In Baum's contemporary late Victorian society, the patriarchal bargain generally consisted of women's capitulation to the "angel of the house" role in exchange for economic support, protection, and power within the domestic sphere. This kind of "female conservatism," in which women embrace and even enforce oppressive roles, is an ironic one in which "women, through their actions to resist passivity and total male control, became participants with vested interests in the system that oppressed them." During eras in which ideas about gender are in flux, as at the turn of the twentieth century with the increasing power of the suffrage movement in the United States, these bargaining women may resist change for fear of seeing "the old normative order slipping away from them without any empowering alternatives." Thus, in Baum's fictional world, many of the evil, powerful women support sexist, misogynistic gender norms of vanity, snobbery, and jealousy of other women as a trade-off for a measure of power of their own.[39]

On the other hand, echoing both Gage's reconceptualization of the role of presumed witches in world history and Theosophy's emphasis on the divine feminine, Baum's good witches are nurturing mother figures who consistently work to advance the feminist utopian vision of Oz. Baum contrasts civilization, in which there are no witches, to the barbarism of Oz, in which witches are the most powerful beings. Dorothy, in her attempt to understand the role of witches in Oz, protests that Aunt Em told her "that the witches were all dead—years and years ago." The Good Witch of the North replies that witches are a matter of geography, as they no longer exist in "civilized countries."[40]

However, Baum, as usual, was toying with the contemporary notion of civilization. In *The Road to Oz*, he explained what he meant by this: "to become civilized means to dress as elaborately and prettily as possible, and to make a show of your clothes so your neighbors will envy you, and for that reason both civilized foxes and civilized humans spend most of their time dressing themselves." Indeed, Dunkiton, a ridiculous land even by Ozian standards, is populated by "clever donkeys" who are the "center of the world's highest civilization." Baum thus satirized popular Western notions of civilization and evolutionism, and in doing so, he elevated the female rule associated with barbarism in accordance with the theory of matriarchalism.[41]

Good witches such as the famous Glinda, the Witch of the South, help Dorothy and the supporting cast of characters throughout their journeys, providing insight, protection, and love. Glinda is the most powerful of the witches; the Scarecrow explains that "nothing that goes on in the Land of Oz escapes her notice." Glinda busies herself by studying sorcery, striving "to find a remedy for every evil and to perfect her skill in magic." She is able to control the behaviors of animals and objects, and in her palace she keeps the Great Record Book, "on the pages of which are constantly being printed a record of every event that happens in any part of the world, at exactly the moment it happens." The Book gives her the omniscience that the Wizard could only pretend to have, as well as elevates her to the primary record-keeper of Oz—a position usually held by men, as Gage pointed out time and again in *Women, Church and State*, a book which was her own valiant attempt at remediating the patriarchal control of the telling of history. In fact, Baum's biographer speculates that Glinda is a stand-in for Gage: "Glinda," he suggests, is short for the honorific "Good Witch Matilda."[42]

In later books, Glinda proves to be a most impressive sorceress and military strategist, but she prefers diplomacy to warfare, as readers discover in Baum's final Oz book, when Glinda takes a pacifist position in the face of a violent coup. Glinda is a safe and authoritative mother figure throughout the series, rescuing beloved characters from various dangers and whisking them to her palace, where they are often bathed, clothed, fed, and put to bed, like small children. Tellingly, there is no corresponding father figure in Oz.[43]

As this matriarchy matures over the course of Baum's fourteen books, Oz transitions from a conflicted, patriarchal land to an equal, matriarchal society. This trajectory from dystopia to utopia is the reverse of the evolution of world history traced by Gage in 1893, although the equations of patriarchy/dystopia and matriarchy/utopia are the same. The evolution of Oz from a patriarchal dystopia to a matriarchal utopia tracks with the increasing public presence of the suffrage movement in the first two decades of the twentieth century. Baum's authorship of these books spanned from 1898, when Gage died in his home while working on another book about patriarchal religion, to the passing of the Nineteenth Amendment by Congress in 1919. In conjunction with the slow gains of the suffrage movement, Oz increasingly grew into a land of gender equity.

By establishing a matriarchy, ruled over by the ethical Princess Ozma, with crucial help from her mortal companion Dorothy and Glinda, Baum's fairyland did more than give women power that they did not have in turn-of-the-century America. Female rule in Oz has far-reaching effects; in fact, it eradicates all possible social problems. Slavery is outlawed, and all of the beings of Oz—humans, witches, animals, robots, animated objects like sawhorses and china—have equal rights. This political equality notwithstanding, it should be noted that the good matriarchs of Oz are always depicted as white-skinned.

Indeed, the most popular of these characters—Glinda, Ozma, and Dorothy—are conventionally beautiful according to Victorian standards, an interesting creative choice for an author who quickly became known for the many fantastical characters he created. In utopian literature, authors often use narrators to establish a conventional point of view against which to contrast the imagined society. Dorothy serves this purpose in *The Wonderful Wizard of Oz* as an emissary from the United States. Her whiteness thus functions conventionally and invisibly, and conforms to her basic role as a narrator in utopian fiction, although Baum flips the script by making her female, like Lewis Carroll's Alice. While he obviously had a financial reason to make Dorothy white—white readers were more likely to identify with her—Baum was thus also following genre conventions. It is worth mentioning here that this same reason does not apply to the other matriarchs in the novels, and so their whiteness is, at best, a blind spot and at worst, a reflection of contemporary racist matriarchalism, in which white femininity imbued a special form of power. Given the context of his personal life and politics, the whiteness of his fictional matriarchs is more likely a reflection of his own racial privilege and that of the suffrage movement with which he was associated than it is an intentional narrative argument for white supremacy.[44]

Baum's fiction otherwise thoroughly promotes ethnic and racial diversity. In the series, whiteness does not confer privilege, nor do other characters automatically occupy lower rungs on the social ladder because of color (or species, for that matter). Diversity is explicitly celebrated in each book. As the Scarecrow says to Jack Pumpkinhead, "I am convinced that the only people worthy of consideration in this world are the unusual ones." The Cowardly Lion echoes this sentiment: "Let us be glad . . . that we differ from one another in form and disposition." This represented a challenging message during a historical era that featured the violent end of the "Indian Problem" (witnessed by Baum in lurid detail in South Dakota), the development of Jim Crow, and rampant nativism. In *The Magic of Oz* (1919), two characters debate creating a hybrid animal by combining several creatures; "the queerer, the better," they say of their potential creation. Even Uncle Henry, the ineffectual patriarch from Kansas, realizes that Oz "is a queer country, and we may as well take people as we find them."[45]

Baum's Oz books, according to one scholar, represent a "queer utopia"—"queer" meaning, in the context of children's literature, "odd," although the term is not devoid of its sexual connotations—which "display[s] an antinormative sensitivity in their celebration of the unique, the eccentric, and the downright peculiar." In Oz, rights accompany diversity; all inhabitants of Oz have a political voice via equal access to Ozma, who listens patiently to her subjects and always responds in a fair manner. Individualism and self-reliance, as many scholars have argued, are integral to Oz, but solidarity and collective activism are just as salient to the plot of each book in the series. Baum intended to offer his readers, in veiled fictional form, a quintessential Theosophical "Universal Brotherhood of Humanity, without distinction of race, creed, sex, caste, or color."[46]

As it developed over two decades, Oz became Baum's statement against the "four-fold oppression" described by Gage: "the church, the state, the capitalist, and the home." Organized religion is completely absent, the state is a benign monarchy that exists to protect and promote individual freedom, and the economic system is a prosperous form of agrarian socialism. This economic organization mirrored the growth of socialism as a formal political philosophy in the early 1900s. Membership in the Socialist Party grew consistently between its formation in 1901 and the election of 1912, in which Socialist candidate Eugene Debs won 6 percent of the national electorate. That year represented an all-time high in Socialist Party membership, and the numbers remained steady for the next several years. The Socialist Party received another boost in membership, and votes, because of its pacifist stance during World War I. However, when Baum was working on *Glinda of Oz* (1919), his final book in the Oz series, the postwar Red Scare was thoroughly, deliberately crushing American socialism; this backlash made Baum's works all the more radical for his time.[47]

In some ways, Baum's Oz echoed the fictional socialist utopias of the era, the most famous of which was Bellamy's best-selling *Looking Backward*. Baum was no stranger to reversals of fortune, and he was known to critique contemporary capitalism. "Mammon rules the world and not morality," he editorialized in 1891, "and again we say, look at the condition of modern society, and in fear and trembling ask yourself—Where will the end be?" Although industrial capitalism's production of a middle class in the nineteenth century impressed him, he warned in 1899, one year before the publication of *The Wonderful Wizard of Oz*, that he lived in a "civilization as full of terrors as it is of surprises—and no man can guess where it will finally lead us." One biographer argues that his experiences unequivocally showed Baum "the futility of the American dream."[48]

To be clear, however, Baum did not identify as a socialist. Rather, his critique of the capitalist class system, poverty, and scarcity fit into the basic Theosophical tenet of promoting equality and tolerance as a means to "embracing endless supply and prosperity." Regardless of Baum's own political behavior, this Theosophical goal is achieved in Oz through monarchical socialism. Ozma is, for all intents and purposes, an "absolute monarch with unlimited power," yet she "seems almost deliberately to have refrained from exercising her vast powers." The economic system of Oz relies upon the equal distribution of goods and resources, and the organizing principle, or the "First Law of Baum's Utopia of Oz," is love. The Tin Woodman explains that money, and by extension capitalism, are considered "vulgar" in Oz, as "no one in all Oz cares to have more than he can use." Labor, he continues, is also divided equitably: "But no one works more than half his time, and the people of Oz enjoy their labors as much as they do their play." Moreover, "there were no cruel overseers set to watch them, and no one to rebuke them or to find fault with them. So each one was proud to do all he could for his friends and neighbors, and was glad when they would accept the things he produced."[49]

Oz is a classless society, save the royal family and court, and this economic system results in a very happy and healthy population. This is due to the benevolent rule of women, and the comparison to the contemporary capitalist United States was explicit. At the beginning of the series, Baum indicated that the sad land of Kansas, and by extension, the United States, was capable of reform, when Dorothy explains to her friend the Scarecrow, "No matter how dreary and gray our homes are, we people of flesh and blood would rather live there than in any other country, be it ever so beautiful." And then she states her famous mantra for the first time: "There is no place like home." But later in the series, Dorothy, and in fact her entire family, choose the utopia of Oz over home. Dorothy's Aunt Em, a former farmwife in Kansas turned royal guest in Oz, explains: "I've been a slave all my life. I guess we won't go back to Kansas, anyway. I'd rather take my chances with the rest of you."[50]

This moment of choice is significant, as it disrupts the usual narrative arc of the genre. Scholars of children's literature use fantastical elements to toy with readers' expectations, but a key narrative component of those expectations in this genre is a "return to ideological and cultural normativity," as when Alice wakes up from her dream of Wonderland. But when Dorothy and her family choose to remain in Oz, the utopia is made to seem real, because it is no mere fantasy for the characters. In Baum's series, there is no conclusive return to the contemporary United States. Rather, Oz—diverse, socialist, matriarchal Oz—becomes the new norm.[51]

Baum reportedly did not see anything extraordinary about Oz when he finished the first book, yet *The Wonderful Wizard of Oz* was an "instant success" that became the best-selling children's book of the Christmas season upon its publication in 1900. The first book in the series would remain a best seller throughout the following century. A *New York Times* reviewer noted its "stray bits of philosophy that will be a moving power on a child's mind," and presciently predicted that it would become a major subject of study. While none of the other books sold quite like the first, many were popular, and they provided a more stable income than the family had ever experienced. Making Oz into a series was not, Baum claimed, his idea at all. In his "Author's Notes" at the beginning of each book, he mentions that readers fairly badgered him into writing more. Baum repeatedly tried to end the series, especially during a long hiatus between 1910 and 1913 in which he pretended to readers that communications with Oz had been permanently disabled and he, as the "Royal Historian of Oz," could no longer report on the now-invisible land. Yet he continued to produce new books, and to promote Oz's unique version of matriarchalism, throughout the 1910s.[52]

For most of that decade, Baum produced an average of one new book every year, and he constantly returned to Oz, in live theater, on the radio, and briefly and unsuccessfully in film versions. In 1919, when he succumbed to a lifelong heart condition, Congress was just a few weeks shy of approving the amendment, named after Gage's old friend-turned-enemy Susan B. Anthony, granting women the right to vote. His final two books in the series were published posthumously.[53]

Through the failed patriarchs and powerful women of *The Wizard of Oz*, American matriarchalism, once an esoteric academic theory, went mainstream. Baum's Oz is a socialist, matriarchal monarchy based on the fundamental ideal of equality—an ideal that Gage said was inherent in the rule of women, but was nowhere to be found in the late Victorian United States, in which sexism, racism, and xenophobia reigned. Oz is set apart from other matriarchies not because of its fantastic nature—as we shall see, the Amazonian world of *Wonder Woman* similarly featured magical powers and many imaginative beasts. Rather, its singularity stems from Baum's unique combination of various ideologies that advocated for universal equality, including Gage's matriarchalism, Republican suffragism, Theosophy's promotion of tolerance and diversity, and socialism's elimination of class exploitation and conflict. Children's literature proved to be the ideal medium for Baum's gender and racial politics. Without the disguise of fantasy, this would have been a controversial message during an era in which Jim Crow permeated the South, immigrants were assigned ethnic quotas, popular opposition to suffrage grew in tandem with its acceptance in various states, and, by the end of Baum's life, the postwar Red Scare assaulted American socialism.

Baum, according to Edward Wagenknecht in *Utopia Americana*, constructed the first fairyland "out of American materials." The core "materials" that Baum used were, in fact, originally created indirectly first by Morgan and, more directly, by Gage. But few of them were to become lasting components of American matriarchalism. Gender equality would, of course, play a major part in future fictional feminist matriarchies, but racial and class equality would fall out of the equation fairly quickly. Through Morgan, to Gage, to the World's Fair, to the "Royal Historian of Oz," we can track the circuitous route of the fledgling American matriarchalist tradition. After Baum, this route— much like Dorothy's journey through Oz—takes some unpleasant turns, as the racist evolutionism of the World's Fair and the feminist matriarchalism of Gage combined to produce what is perhaps the most famous fictional matriarchy of the Progressive era, Charlotte Perkins Gilman's *Herland* (1915).[54]

5

LIKE COMING HOME TO MOTHER

Progressive Era Matriarchalism

When we say MEN, MAN, MANLY, MANHOOD, and all the other
masculine derivatives, we have in the background of our minds a huge
vague crowded picture of the world and its activities . . . of men everywhere, doing everything—"the world."

. . . But to these women, in the unbroken sweep of this
two-thousand-year-old feminine civilization, the word WOMAN
called up all that big background, so far as they had gone in social development; and the word MAN meant to them only MALE—the sex.

—CHARLOTTE PERKINS GILMAN, *Herland* (1915)

B
Y the early twentieth century, American matriarchalism had several
branches: the anthropological approach to "primitive" and prehistoric cultures via gendered evolutionism; the feminist revision of
world history that argued for contemporary gender equality; the
imperial matriarchalism represented by the white "mothers of civilization"
and the "savage Amazons" at the 1893 Chicago World's Fair; and fictional matriarchy as the model for equality, diversity, and peace in the works of L. Frank
Baum. In the 1910s, as Baum continued to churn out his matriarchalist fiction
for children, another branch of the theory developed, and it was one that exhibited elements of each of its progenitors.

Although she is primarily known now as a writer, Charlotte Perkins Gilman was known in the early 1900s as one of the foremost theorists of the
"first wave" of feminism. Gilman was also possibly the most famous producer
of explicitly matriarchalist popular culture in the United States in the early
twentieth century, although by the 1920s, her work fell into obscurity which
would last several decades. In the 1970s, Gilman posthumously achieved newfound fame, riding the crest of "second-wave" feminism and the new brand of
matriarchalism that accompanied it, which I examine in Chapter 8.

Since then, scholars from various disciplines have produced many volumes devoted primarily to Gilman's fictional output, most of which are about

her harrowing short story "The Yellow Wallpaper" (1892). Yet the bulk of her writing—seventeen books, the entire contents of the monthly journal *The Forerunner* from 1909 to 1916, and over one thousand essays—was nonfiction. Gilman is, in fact, better characterized as a sociologist who wrote some fiction. And the contemporary academic theories that informed her sociological approach were evolutionism, socialism, and matriarchalism.[1]

Matriarchalism thus expanded into several theoretical branches during the early twentieth century as both Baum and Gilman were writing their very different matriarchalist texts. Through Gage and Baum, matriarchalism showed potential as a nonracist brand of feminist theory during a time when mainstream, white feminism relied upon evolutionism and social Darwinism to publicly extend the feminine sphere of influence while maintaining racial hierarchies. In the 1910s, even as Baum envisioned a matriarchal fantasy land featuring gender and racial equality, Gilman offered a fictional feminist utopia that both incorporated and went beyond the racism of imperial matriarchalism by eliminating people of color altogether.

Although they were feminist contemporaries in the 1890s, Gilman was a generation younger than Gage, and there is no evidence that the two met or even read each other's work. While Gage was working on *Women, Church and State*, Gilman was chafing against the gendered social system in her own writing. In many of her published works, Gilman combined, wittingly or not, the many versions of matriarchalism that we have examined herein. Like Bachofen, she firmly believed in the universality of matriarchal social systems in prehistory. Like Morgan, she espoused the evolutionist theory of "primitive," extant matriarchies among Native American groups. Like Gage, Gilman argued that matriarchy entailed equality and democracy in any given society. Like French Sheldon, Gilman relied upon both gender essentialism, or the belief in women's supposedly innate tendency to serve society, and racism, particularly the evolutionist belief in a hierarchy of cultures and races. Finally, like Engels and Baum, she theorized that matriarchal socialism was the key to eliminating class conflict and related social problems.

As with previous pop cultural matriarchalists, Gilman's personal experiences informed her work. She had a troubled childhood, especially after her father abandoned the family. According to one biographer, Gilman learned that the way to maintain contact with her father was to write him for lists of books, and "he responded as if he were supervising a student's research project," suggesting works on ancient empires, histories of the United States, and, "prominently," works of matriarchalism. Her "heroic mother," who remained "loyal as a spaniel" to her estranged husband, was distant and withholding, further exacerbating Gilman's sense of abandonment. From her childhood, one of Gilman's many biographers argues that she learned a lesson that would later influence her sociological theories of gender: motherhood was a burden.[2]

In her autobiography, Gilman makes it clear that these parental dynamics forced her to grow up quickly, and as a result, she developed a strenuous literary work ethic. Although her primary interest was in writing, in 1884, she wed Charles Walter Stetson, and she also became involved in the suffragist movement, even writing a suffrage column for Alice Stone Blackwell, the famous feminist and socialist. Over time, however, the more Gilman settled into her domestic duties, the more depressed she became, a condition that grew more pronounced once she became pregnant with their daughter Katherine. Gilman later wrote that Walter tried to help: "A lover more tender, a husband more devoted, woman could not ask." Gilman's own defense of her husband notwithstanding, Judith Allen writes that Stetson was a "committed 'masculist,'" referring to Gilman's term for men who opposed women's rights; he reportedly found suffragists "tiresome." In this interpersonal context, as she neared the end of her pregnancy, Gilman's condition worsened. A typical diary entry recorded a "well-nigh sleepless night," during which she was "cold, hot, restless, nervous, hysterical."[3]

Domesticity appears to have been the precipitating context, and motherhood the exacerbating factor, that led Gilman to a full breakdown. The first month postpartum went well, due to the live-in presence of a baby nurse. But, wrote Gilman, "after her month was up and I was left alone with the child I broke up so fast that we sent for my mother." Charlotte became a "mental wreck": "Here was a charming home; a loving and devoted husband; an exquisite baby, healthy, intelligent, and good . . . and I lay all day on the lounge and cried." In an attempt to break the saga of sleepless, weeping nights, Charlotte traveled alone to San Francisco, which she described as "heaven" and "paradise," only to return back home to recurring "miserable weakness" on the East Coast.[4]

After this trip, it dawned on her that her depression was context-specific: "This was a worse horror than before, for now I saw the stark fact—that I was well while away and sick while at home." Gilman then sought the "rest cure" for "nervous prostration" from Dr. S. Weir Mitchell. His prescription was, in Gilman's words: "'Live as domestic a life as possible. Have your child with you all the time.' (Be it remarked that if I did but dress the baby it left me shaking and crying—certainly far from a healthy companionship for her, to say nothing of the effect on me.) 'Lie down an hour after each meal. Have but two hours' intellectual life a day. And never touch pen, brush or pencil as long as you live.'"[5] The cure for Gilman's disorder, according to the popular "nerve specialist," was thus suspiciously like its cause.

Suffice it to say that this domestic treatment did not work for Gilman, and she and Walter separated after four years of marriage. This was the "cure" Gilman needed; she was "finally free," and their separation resulted in a "surprising output of work." Four years later, after trying to make ends meet as a single mother, she made the decision to relinquish custody of her nine-year-old daughter Katherine to Walter, who had remarried to one of Gilman's former friends. Gilman later explained that this was an attempt to avoid the mistakes made by her own parents: "Since [Katherine's] second mother was fully as good as the first, better in some ways perhaps; since the father longed for his child and had a right to some of her society; and since the child had a right to know and love her father—I did not mean her to suffer the losses of my youth—this seemed the right thing to do." Regardless of her selfless motivation, she was "furiously condemned": "To hear what was said and read what was printed one would think I had handed over a baby in a basket." Although it afforded her the freedom to write and to join public life as an activist and sociologist— her biographer argues that Stetson's second wife's "care of daughter Kate permitted Gilman's career as a public intellectual"—this rejection of motherhood was both physically liberating and psychologically devastating for Gilman.[6]

Gilman turned thirty and left her husband in the same year, and her liberation from domesticity catalyzed what would become a prolific writing career. Specifically, during that year, Gilman wrote two texts, a short story and a poem, that contained the seeds of her developing matriarchalism. Almost as soon as she separated from Walter, Gilman began the work of fiction for which she is most famous today, "The Yellow Wallpaper," an autobiographical short story about a woman taking the rest cure and enduring what she deemed the "inevitable result" of enforced domesticity: "progressive insanity." *New England Magazine* published "The Yellow Wallpaper" in early 1892, and it made "a tremendous impression." Various doctors wrote in to respond; one argued that "such a story ought not to be written" because it might drive readers "mad," while another "wrote to say that it was the best description of incipient insanity he had ever seen." Charlotte was pleased that her story had reached doctors' desks, for her "real purpose" in publishing it was "to reach Dr. S. Weir Mitchell, and convince him of the error of his ways."[7]

"The Yellow Wallpaper" was a graphic critique of the psychological dangers of domestic oppression, which would become a primary component of Gilman's brand of matriarchalism over the course of her writing career. While she was working on her more famous short story, she also published her first poem, "Similar Cases" (1890), which represented the other major component of her developing matriarchal theory: gendered evolutionism. "Similar Cases" represents the influence of several theories that Gilman had discovered in California, and the poem is widely recognized as a satirical critique of resistance to social change, but it also contains a subtle gendered argument about the evolution of human civilization. Neolithic Man's "civilization" in the poem is an ugly adventure of warfare, land grabs, and disease, a depiction which echoes the gendered critique of colonialism espoused by contemporary imperial matriarchalists; indeed, shortly after the publication of "Similar Cases," May French Sheldon left London to traipse around Africa in her ballgown and blonde wig. Over time, the "mothers of civilization" ethos of imperial matriarchalism would come to have a profound effect on Gilman's thinking.[8]

Gilman's developing matriarchalism was not influenced by the colonial arguments of White Queen-style feminism alone. Her critique of modern "civilization" also represented the influence in Gilman's post-divorce life of the Nationalist movement, with which she became heavily involved after 1890. Nationalism was a form of gradual socialism made famous by Edward Bellamy in his utopian novel, *Looking Backward: 2000–1887* (1888). This movement appealed to late nineteenth-century reformers for its emphasis on cooperation over competition and especially its advocacy of a "peaceful, gradual, evolutionary change" to socialism rather than the violent, revolutionary class conflict of Marxism.[9]

Matriarchalism within socialism predated Edward Bellamy via the 1884 publication of Friedrich Engels's *Origin of the Family, Private Property, and the State*. While Engels was critical of utopian socialism, he recognized the potential of Nationalism to "articulate and spread a global socialist alternative." Although later critics derided the "untouched" Victorian gender roles and the bourgeois urban fantasy of *Looking Backward*, Bellamy's advocacy of female economic independence brought many women to his movement. When she became involved with Nationalism in California in 1890, Charlotte Perkins Gilman believed that the movement was "true Americanism," a vital source of democracy in an unequal society. Gilman's "Similar Cases" first appeared in the official journal of the Bellamy movement, and Nationalism proved to be an able springboard to public recognition for Gilman, as she became a frequent fixture on the lecture circuit. However, Gilman's concern about the place of gender roles within socialist systems eventually turned her off of Nationalism. The apparent "backwardness" of the contemporary socialist movement on the "Woman Question" led Gilman to combine feminism, socialism, and evolutionism to create her own brand of matriarchalism.[10]

Gilman's early matriarchalism was the natural product of her self-described "failure" as a proper Victorian wife and her disappointment in the gender politics of socialism, but she also had a major academic influence. At a suffrage convention in 1896, she met Lester Frank Ward, the "father of American sociology." Gilman was familiar with Ward's early work, and he with hers, as he had written her a supportive response after reading "Similar Cases" in the *Nationalist*. Likewise, Gilman had been struck by a short article of Ward's called "Our Better Halves," published in *Forum* in 1888, in which he laid out what he would later call his "gynaecocentric theory." This theory, lauded by Gilman as "the greatest single contribution to the world's thought since Evolution," rested upon the premise of universal matriarchy in prehistoric societies.[11]

First in an 1888 lecture at which Gage's former friend Elizabeth Cady Stanton and other suffragists were present, and shortly thereafter in the *Forum* article, Ward argued on behalf of female superiority across species, using the examples of hawks, reptiles, fish, and insects. He claimed that heredity and the transmission of acquired characteristics were primarily female genetic endeavors, while men were only secondary evolutionary conduits. Over the course of evolution, humans had, in effect, reversed this power dynamic to their own detriment: "Woman is the unchanging trunk of the great genealogic tree; while man, with all his vaunted superiority, is but a branch, a grafted scion, as it were, whose acquired qualities die with the individual while those of woman are handed on to futurity. There is no fixed rule by which Nature has intended that one sex should excel the other, any more than there is any fixed point beyond which either cannot further develop." According to Ward, the primacy of females in the hereditary passage of traits meant that, despite the prevalence of patriarchy, the progress of civilization was due to women. As a reform Darwinist who believed in the genetic transmission of acquired characteristics, Ward argued that the natural superiority of females in other species had interesting implications for human gender relations and evolution.[12]

Ward later expanded upon this "gynaecocentric theory" in *Pure Sociology* (1903). In this work, he again challenged the presumed naturalness of patriarchy, arguing that "androcentric" (male-centered) theory was hegemonic, a "world view" that had been so "deeply stamped upon the popular mind" that it amounted to a stable "social structure." He went on to cite some of the major matriarchalists, including Bachofen and Morgan, but his ignorance of Gage's *Women, Church and State* allowed him to erroneously claim the originality of his premise that "the facts of amazonism that are so often referred to as so many singular anomalies and reversals of the natural order of things, are never looked at philosophically as residual facts that must be explained even if they overthrow many current beliefs." Ward would be the first to derail the genealogy of American matriarchalism by not acknowledging Gage; his omission of preexisting feminist matriarchalism enabled him to position himself as its progenitor.[13]

According to Ward, scientists ignored the overwhelming evidence for "the matriarchate" in the natural world because, as Bachofen had warned a half-century before, they presumed late Victorian patriarchy to be the baseline measurement of gender relations. Instead of natural selection as the driver of evolution, Ward offered instead sexual selection, or the females' power to select male mates, as the core of his gynaecocentric theory. Ward's theory combined gendered evolutionism with reform Darwinism, which posited that human behavior could affect the course of natural selection and direct evolution, to produce a form of matriarchalism that Gilman would seize upon with gusto.[14]

The primary contribution of Ward's gynaecocentric theory was his firm rejection of the evolutionary justification of female oppression based on the alleged sex traits of physical weakness and diminished intellect, and his essay sparked some angry responses from contemporary biologists. On the other hand, suffragists and feminists, not surprisingly, responded favorably. Ward's work provided for Gilman the primary bridge between the three major ideologies to which she subscribed: feminism, socialism, and evolutionism. As she developed her own ideas on the Nationalist lecture circuit in the1890s, Gilman appropriated two of Ward's primary terms—"gynaecocentric" (woman-centered) and "androcentric" (male-centered)—and fully incorporated them into her own sociological theory. Gilman first articulated her theory in *Women and Economics* (1898), which she wrote in just six weeks, at the same time that she was falling in love with her cousin, Houghton Gilman, and considering a second marriage.[15]

In this work, Gilman combined various theoretical forces of the era—feminism, evolutionism, socialism, and matriarchalism—to develop her own explanations for the causes of and solutions to women's oppression. Combining Ward's terms *gynaecocentric* and *androcentric,* and his theory of sexual selection, Gilman offered a "biological basis for feminism in reform Darwinist terms." Relying upon Morgan and Ward, Gilman took the theory of universal matriarchal prehistory as fact, explaining that prehistoric men co-opted women's roles as agriculturalists and manufacturers in order to control the food supply, the economy, and, eventually, women themselves. The goal was the control of resources, but it led to a system of male sexual selection, with the result of female oppression.[16]

Gilman stressed that patriarchy was not a deliberate goal in this social evolution. To Ward, she wrote, "As to the Overthrow: Not telic. Not sudden. Not a conquest by man." Gilman believed that the development of male social supremacy occurred "not by any act of cruelty on the part of man but [because of] the increasing desirability of woman's services." In other words, women's essential capacity for service to the community—providing food beyond individual needs and subsistence—was "at the root of our great race tragedy, the subjugation of the female." For Gilman, female power was the key to the development of human societies; she accepted matriarchal prehistory as a given in her later works, arguing that the earliest iteration of law and government was "maternal," based on "lines of common love and service." Upon the transition to patriarchy, based on male seizure of control of the food supply at some unnamed prehistorical moment, men also took control of women and "instituted the custom of enslaving the female."[17]

Gilman coined the phrase "sexuo-economic relations" to describe the resulting perversion of power dynamics in modern human societies. Men controlled resources and women's labor, which was unpaid, and therefore rendered women captive: "The female of the genus homo is economically dependent on the male. He is her food supply." This inequality was unnatural, according to Gilman, who, like Ward, used examples from various species to prove her case. "In no other animal species is the female economically dependent on the male," she wrote. "In no other animal species is the sex relation for sale," as exemplified by the "evil" marriage market in which woman is "the supply" and man "the demand."[18]

Although Gilman did not cite Gage, or give any other indication that she had read her work, she argued that the economic oppression of women was mirrored by the suppression of their public power, using the primary example of the development of Christianity. "In dim early times," Gilman wrote, "she was sharer in the mysteries and rites; but, as religion developed, her place receded, until Paul commanded her to be silent in the churches." Unlike Gage, however, Gilman saw this perversion of natural sex equality as a prerequisite to the attainment of civilization. But she then diverged from many of the anthropological matriarchalists, as civilized patriarchy was but a stage on Gilman's proposed social evolutionary scale; the development of male dominance was necessary to achieve civilized status, but, she argued, its time was over. As Western societies had reached a sufficient level of civilization, the consequences of continuing this socioeconomic and political oppression of women would be dire: "The inevitable trend of human life is toward higher civilization; but, while that civilization is confined to one sex, it inevitably exaggerates sex distinction, until the increasing evil of this condition is stronger than all the good of the civilization attained, and the nation fails." Gilman argued that in order for the human race to continue evolving—indeed, for it to survive—the balance between male and female power must be righted.[19]

Gilman used the women's and socialist movements to elaborate upon practical solutions, including state organization of household industries, which would free up half of the population to devote time to public works: "The economically independent mother, widened and freed, strengthened and developed, by her social service, will do better service as mother than it has been possible to her before." This, then, was the solution: collectivize housework and childcare, so that women could put their maternal instincts to use in society. Based on the examples of ancient social organization and contemporary movements for equality, Gilman concluded: "When the mother of the race is free, we shall have a better world, by the easy right of birth and by the calm, slow, friendly forces of social evolution." In her early sociological publications, Gilman used prehistoric matriarchalism and gender essentialism to advocate for sex equality.[20]

Gilman scholar Ann Lane explains that over time, Gilman "went beyond Ward's theories to envision a fully structured, cooperative, socialized world." In various subsequent publications, such as *The Home: Its Work and Influence* (1903) and *The Man Made World, or Our Androcentric Culture* (1911), which she dedicated to Lester Ward, Gilman honed her matriarchalism. She wrote to Ward in 1908 as she tried to work out the transition from universal matriarchy in prehistory to modern patriarchy:

Assume a matriarchal settlement under exceptionally good conditions. . . . Assume an excess of females. . . . Having now good conditions and surplus females, the male becomes increasingly valuable. The
dominant females, already the industrial power and used to tribal communism, now establish a voluntary polygyny agreeing to maintain one
male to each small group of females. If this were done, the male being
now supported by the group of females and held in high esteem, is in a
position to develop naturally, the excessive indulgence, cruelty, pride,
etc. which would so lead to the more injurious effects of unchecked
masculine rule.

She concluded her "simple and genetic" hypothesis cheerily with a shorthand
version: 'Good conditions—excess females; excess females—male at premium.
Male at premium—females establish polygyny. Polygyny—overdevelopment of
maleness. Predominant maleness—androcracy. Androcracy—the world as we
have it. . . . How's that?'"[21]

Gilman tested her matriarchalism on the lecture circuit and in meetings
with the members of Heterodoxy, a radical women's group that she frequented
for many years. Heterodoxy's multigenerational members had diverse political views, but they were united in their commitment to feminist issues, and
the group provided a space of female community in Greenwich Village for
several decades. Gilman dropped out for a time in the 1910s in protest of the
group's support for World War I, but Heterodoxy continued to serve as a key
social context in which she encountered like-minded women. Although the
two never considered themselves to be friends, it was through Heterodoxy
that Gilman met Margaret Sanger, the famed birth control crusader. Sanger's
arguments about the control of reproduction would have a major influence
on American matriarchalism, as is evident in Gilman's own ideas about motherhood in her later matriarchalist fiction and in the psychological theories of
William Moulton Marston, the creator of the matriarchalist comic *Wonder
Woman*.[22]

All the while, as Gilman lunched with the ladies of Heterodoxy and deliv-
ered public lectures on her sociological theories, she maintained an interest
in writing poetry and fiction. Between 1909 and 1916, Gilman put her work
in *The Forerunner*, the journal that she wrote, edited, and published herself.
Although her explicit intent in this journal was didactic, not literary—she
explained that the "subject matter, for the most part, is not to be regarded as

'literature,' but as an attempt to set forth certain views of life which seemed to the author of real importance to human welfare"—Gilman frequently published her own fiction in *The Forerunner*. As it was the primary mouthpiece over which she had complete creative control, in 1911, Gilman used her journal to offer her initial fictional foray into matriarchalism.[23]

In the novella *Moving the Mountain*, Gilman presented her version of what she called a "baby Utopia, a little one that can grow," which was achievable through "no other change than a change of mind, the mere awakening of people, especially the women, to existing possibilities." She promoted the novella as follows: "Those who believe this world is a good place, easily made better, and who wish to know how to help it, will enjoy reading this book. Those who do not so believe and wish may not enjoy it so much, but it will do them good."[24]

Moving the Mountain opens on "a gray, cold, soggy Tibetan plateau," where Nellie Robertson discovers her long-lost brother John after thirty years. Before his journey, John was a young patriarch who supported his father's prohibition against educating his sister. After finding John, Nellie's task is to teach him the ways of the new world, including the many sociopolitical implications of the revolution in gender roles. The rapid changes of the past thirty years—"more changes than an ordinary century or two"—make John, who is 55 when he is discovered in Tibet, "feel like a child." John is astonished by the accomplishments of women, so much that, on the return journey from Tibet, he asks Nellie what has happened to the men; he is worried that they were all gone, or that they were "all doing the housework." Nellie explains that men and women do the work that they prefer. He groans, contemplating "this awful place I was coming to, with strange, masculine women and subdued men."[25]

To John's surprise, the world is transformed into something like a "great clean beautiful house—richly furnished." Nellie's husband explains that Ward's theory of sexual selection—"the female is the race type; the male is her assistant"—gained enough traction that it caused a gender revolution. The precipitating event, according to Nellie, was that "the women woke up," got organized, and changed things quickly: "They saw their duty and they did it." In a line reminiscent of French Sheldon's imperial strategy, Nellie argues that American women decided that the way to deal with social problems was to "substitute improvements" rather than "restrain and prevent and punish." In this method, they were ideally suited: "As women had learned this in handling children, they began to apply it to grown people—the same children, only a little older." They professionalized the duties formerly relegated to women—

housework, childcare, food preparation—to address the economic problems of poverty and labor conflict.[26]

The results were rapid and encompassing. Within ten years of John's disappearance, the United States became socialist. The "New Religion" of social service thoroughly replaced the repressive Christianity of Progressive America; according to Nellie, in this new world, there is no longer a concept of sin, nor are there prisons, poverty, racism, sexism, disease, accidents, deforestation, or crime. Life expectancy is one hundred years of age, and all humans are "more agreeable" because they are better fed through a system of clean food production managed by experts rather than by individual "ignorant housewives." People live cooperatively in clans of family, friends, and acquaintances in apartment buildings with ample gardens, "nurseries and child gardens," and meeting and entertainment spaces, cared for by professional food and housekeeping services. Just as other industries became "specialized," the "New Women" also "specialized the baby business": "All women who wish to, have babies; but if they wish to take care of them they must show a diploma" that certified capability as a "child-culturist." Motherhood is considered a professional industry; those women who are "good with children" work for the governmental "Department of Child Culture" to care for the nation's young while their parents work.[27]

Women brought about this "new grip on Life," and they rose to the top through their natural tendency toward social work. Although women were natural leaders, the new system featured gender equality; as Nellie's husband explains to John, "Nothing has interfered with our position as human beings; it is only our sex supremacy that we have lost." This utopia is not for all, however; Gilman's argument for female fitness to remake civilization rested heavily upon xenophobia and racism. In concordance with the tenets of evolutionism and reform Darwinism, Gilman advocated for eugenics. In *Moving the Mountain*, selective breeding ensures a uniform population, so that "certain classes of criminals and perverts were rendered incapable of reproducing their own kind." *Moving the Mountain* thus rested upon two of the primary tenets of imperial matriarchalism: gender essentialism, in which women's allegedly unique capacity for nurturing and service could uplift society, and racism, in which this responsibility rested solely with white women as the pinnacle of human civilization. Unlike the imperial matriarchalists, however, Gilman believed that socialism was the key to human advancement, and she continued to plot out this trajectory in a series of fictional works in the mid-1910s.[28]

Four years later, Gilman made the full transition to explicit matriarchal-ism with what later scholars called the "mother-text" of early feminist utopias when she serialized her novel *Herland* in *The Forerunner*. As in *Moving the Mountain*, she uses a male narrator as her foil, but this time, the three male characters are clear archetypes, not "in the least 'advanced' on the woman question": Van, the narrator, is a sociologist with a scientific perspective on human life; Terry is a wealthy, aggressive explorer; and Jeff is a chivalrous doctor. Gilman juxtaposes these men against an all-female utopia, which they stumble upon during an "expedition" into what Gilman possibly meant to be the Amazon region. From their "savage" guides, the men hear tales of a "strange and terrible Woman Land in the high distance." Joking about this mysterious land, which they initially call "Feminisia" before they settle upon "Herland," the three men set off in Terry's steam yacht to locate the "undiscov-ered country of a strictly Amazonian nature." They expect to find an "awfully primitive" society with the women kept as "sort of a national harem." To their shock, they find a "CIVILIZED country" where they assume "there must be men."[29]

The women's lack of fear of the masculine intruders makes their subse-quent seizure of the men surprising; it is, as one scholar argues, a complete inversion of "those characteristics of 'masculine' and 'feminine' which have be-come embedded in a destructive pattern of dominance and submission." The Herlanders carry the men "like children" into a main building, where they are anesthetized and imprisoned. Despite a bath, a restful sleep, and clean clothes, the captive men feel "like a lot of neuters." Also inverting the usual script of white men observing dark-skinned natives, the women go to work immedi-ately to civilize the men, all the while taking notes—"miles of them!"—like good ethnographers.[30]

The Herlanders explain to the unwelcome visitors that there had not been a man in their civilization for two thousand years. Van narrates: "What hap-pened to them first was merely a succession of historic misfortunes such as have befallen other nations often enough"—such as wars, depopulation, slav-ery, and natural disasters, particularly a volcanic eruption that filled the pas-sage from Herland to the sea. The slaves revolted, turning on their masters, but they succeeded only in replicating the inequality against which they had rebelled. Eventually, "this succession of misfortunes was too much for these infuriated virgins," and "so the young women, instead of submitting, rose in sheer desperation and slew their brutal conquerors," so that "there was lit-

erally no one left on this beautiful high garden land but a bunch of hysterical girls and some older slave women." The genocidal violence of this female
revolution belies Gilman's reliance upon gender essentialism, a problem that
she did not address in the text. At some point in the early postrevolutionary
history, one of the women had a child, and the virgin births continued among
the population.[31]

Without men, the rebellious women had not expected to survive beyond
the existing generation, so "to them the longed-for motherhood was not only
a personal joy, but a nation's hope." Daughters, who "grew up as a holy sisterhood," took motherhood seriously, spending "their whole ardent youth looking forward to their great office." Motherhood became the "Crowning Office,"
and children the "RAISON D'ETRE" of Herland. To advance their civilization, the women professionalized childcare. They co-mother, and after a year
of breastfeeding each child, the mother usually returns to work, leaving her
daughters in the expert hands of the co-mothers, "whose proud child-service
was direct and continuous, was lovely to see." Children are educated in this
setting, which is the beginning of the "lifelong learning" practiced by all members of society to avoid "atrophy in the disused portions of the brain." Mothers
are never far from their children, but neither are they burdened with being
their sole caretakers, educators, and role models. As one scholar explains, this
fictional model was "an idealized validation of the socially acceptable motherhood Gilman both missed as a child and escaped as an adult, as well as an
ideological program."[32]

The primacy of motherhood spawned a new religion, a "sort of Maternal
Pantheism," as the women "lost all interest in deities of war and plunder" and
focused on their "Mother Goddess," who represented maternity "magnified
beyond human limits." Out of the essential traits of motherhood developed
the "central theory of a Loving Power," which became their organizing principle (and which would also inspire the world of Wonder Woman two decades
later). Here, Gilman calls upon the matriarchalism of Victorian anthropology,
positing an ancient, universal, woman-centered society that had been reborn
in Herland. As Van begins to understand the primal role of maternity in Herland society, he has a "queer feeling, way down deep," a "stirring of some ancient dim prehistoric consciousness":

> It was like—coming home to mother. I don't mean the underflannels-
> and-doughnuts mother, the fussy person that waits on you and spoils

you and doesn't really know you. I mean the feeling that a very little child would have, who had been lost—for ever so long. It was a sense of getting home; of being clean and rested, of safety and yet freedom; of love that was always there, warm like sunshine in May, not hot like a stove or a featherbed—a love that didn't irritate and didn't smother.

Van's assessment notwithstanding, Gilman's use of motherhood as the crux of the political, social, and economic systems in Herland ultimately replicates the "ideological structures of patriarchy" which place female value in the womb.[33]

In this way, Gilman thoroughly echoes the gendered premises of Progressive women's activism. Although she rejected motherhood in her personal life—and indeed, this rejection helped to spark her career as a lecturer and writer—and she thoroughly condemned "matriolatry," or the idealization of Victorian maternal domesticity, in her 1903 book *The Home*, Gilman's theories increasingly came to rely upon maternalism. Gilman eschewed the Victorian construction of womanhood that relegated mothers to the domestic sphere, but she endorsed the attendant sex characteristics of this construction— nurturance, empathy, morality, cooperation, orderliness, cleanliness—as both the key to female power and as the organizing principle of society. In this, she echoed other female activists and reformers of the era. While women's organizations like Gage's old foe, the Women's Christian Temperance Union, had traditionally used maternalist rhetoric in their political lobbying efforts, maternalism reached its height as a primary premise of female Progressive politics in the 1910s. Jane Addams of Hull House argued that the necessities of keeping their homes, neighborhoods, schools, and cities clean, safe, and free of disease spurred women to the broad application of their capabilities: "Women are pushed outside of the home in order that they may preserve the home." Addams argued for female suffrage on the premise that the private and public spheres had merged, famously concluding, "Politics is housekeeping on a grand scale."[34]

Because of her personal experiences—a cold relationship with her mother, postpartum depression, and her decision to give her first husband full guardianship of her young daughter—motherhood was a tricky subject for Gilman, and she took her time developing her own form of maternalist rhetoric. In a 1913 essay published in *The Forerunner*, Gilman explained how the "New Mothers of a New World" would remake the nation:

A new standard is rising—the woman's standard. It is based not on a personal selfishness but on the high claims of motherhood, motherhood as a social service instead of man-service. This new motherhood shines before us like a sunrise. Women as world builders, women recognizing the need of stronger, nobler people and producing them, women saying to men—"You have had your day—you have worked your will—you have filled the world with warfare, with drunkenness, with vice and disease. You have wasted women's lives like water, and the children of the world have been sacrificed to your sins. Now we will have a new world, new-born, new-built, a mother-world as well as a father-world, a world in which we shall not be ashamed or afraid to plant our children.

Gilman thus posited that American women were poised to remake the world because of their status as mothers. In the official program of the Woman Suffrage Procession, a parade of with over 5,000 participants who marched down Pennsylvania Avenue in March of that same year, Gilman explained, in a quote that was widely distributed as a postcard featuring a healthy baby under the slogan "Votes for Mothers," that the divide between women's private maternal concerns and the public sphere of politics was an illusion: "Politics governs even the purity of the milk supply. It is not 'outside the home,' but inside the baby." Finally, in *Herland*, published in 1915, Gilman envisioned an entire world based around the female principles that she, like other maternalists of her era, believed would remedy the ills of the Progressive era.[35]

Accordingly, in *Herland*, motherhood is the keystone around which society is organized, and the women professionalize all domestic duties, enacting a "conscious effort to make it better" in all aspects. The confused men agree that this maternal set-up ushered in a utopia, featuring a "country as neat as a Dutch kitchen" and a perfected environment that is an "enormous garden" in which every tree bears fruit and all regions look like parks. This idyllic landscape produces a "perfect" food supply for the three million Herlanders through careful cultivation and composting. There is no smoke, dirt, or noise in Herland; Van explains, "Everything was beauty, order, perfect cleanness, and the pleasantest sense of home over it all."[36]

This "pleasant sense" applies equally to the population. There is no class system in Herland; all women are sisters, and they are horrified when the men explain about poverty. Decisions affecting the country are made cooperatively or by council, although Herland also has a "Land Mother" who serves as something of a mediator in public discussions. Because Herlanders are taught "Peace, Beauty, Order, Safety, Love, Wisdom, Justice, Patience, and Plenty" from birth, concern for community and a socialist economy developed; private property and "home" are foreign concepts, as the women perform all major life tasks cooperatively. Van concludes that they simply "had no horrible ideas."[37]

Most modern scholars beg to differ with Van's assessment, pointing out Gilman's explicit racism in *Herland* as part of the debate over Gilman's use of the word *race*. Judith Allen argues that by this term, Gilman meant the human race, and Allen criticizes historian Gail Bederman for her "overliteral" argument that the "race work" that Gilman espoused was white supremacy, making Gilman part and parcel of the racist white feminism of the early twenty-first century. My reading of Gilman's use of "race" indicates slippage between the two meanings, and whatever she meant by the term itself, it is clear that she heartily endorsed some of the tenets of the racism and xenophobia of her era. In her utopian fiction, Gilman unquestionably relied upon the racist assumptions of evolutionism to explain the differences between nations and cultural groups.[38]

In *Moving the Mountain*, Gilman resolved the "race problem" through selective breeding, assimilation, and training camps for immigrants. In *Herland*, her solution is even more chilling, based solely on eugenics, resulting in a wholly white population of women. Here, Gilman is not especially original in her replication of the racist feminism of her era; in fact, Mary E. Bradley Lane anticipated Gilman's claims by some twenty-five years in her serialized novel *Mizora*. The "lovely blonde" matriarchs of Mizora believed "that the highest excellence of moral and mental character is alone attainable by a fair race," and so, in addition to letting men "die out," Mizoran women "eliminated" those with "dark complexions." Upon her return, the narrator concludes sadly, "The world to which I have returned is many ages behind the civilization of Mizora."[39]

Gilman's Herlanders are likewise deliberate eugenicists, although the failure to reproduce men is not so much deliberate as a happy historical accident for these matriarchs. Race, however, is a different story. Their whiteness, like that of the Mizorans, is presented as evidence of their advanced evolutionary status. The women were, Van explains, originally of superior racial origins. Before the ancient volcanic eruption, the "best civilization of the old world" reached the land through the passage to the sea, making the women of "Aryan stock." To maintain their race, in both senses of the word, as a human and as a white race, the women purposefully avoided contact with other groups in the Amazon Basin, and they became "Conscious Makers of People" through "negative eugenics," or the forgoing of motherhood among those women deemed unfit to breed. Gilman went beyond the parental education paradigm of eugenics to the "negative" eugenics via selective breeding. This protocol enabled Herlanders to represent what Gilman called "race purity," with the additional eugenic result of no disabilities, no errant behavior, and no criminals. Thus, Gilman's matriarchalism, like French Sheldon's, is not simply or coincidentally white; rather, whiteness is a precondition for this utopia, as the success of this society depends upon selective breeding and elimination, offering an "evolutionary discourse about white civilized womanhood."[40]

Notions of race and gender are thoroughly intertwined in Gilman's fiction. In her matriarchal utopia, rather than positing a feminist awakening as the impetus to social change, Gilman relied upon the racist tenets of white gender essentialism that positioned women as natural, refined, and nurturing, and men as devolved, often dumb, and potentially violent. According to Van, when Terry, frustrated by being "neutered" in sexless Herland, attempts to rape Alima, the object of his affection, he simply "put in practice his pet conviction that a woman loves to be mastered, and by sheer brute force." In this obvious showdown between Victorian gender roles and Herland's matriarchal norms, Terry is easily subdued, bound, and anesthetized in short order by the women who burst in at Alima's cries for help. With these characterizations, Gilman was not simply playing to gender stereotypes for dramatic effect; rather, these characters were the embodiment of the gender essentialism and evolutionism that undergirded her brand of matriarchalism. As a caricature of a patriarchal social Darwinist, Terry is the only source of violence in Herland. In fact, he is the only sexual being there. Pfaelzer notes the "utopian chastity" of the Herlanders as Gilman linked sexual desire with other forms of male dominance in society.[41]

Through these characterizations and the violent climax, Gilman rewrote the race and gender of the usual evolutionist time line. The original matriarchal societies that Herland called back to, reinvigorated, and improved upon were more civilized by measures of human health, happiness, peace, and equality than the Western patriarchal societies that were, at the time of Gilman's writing, engaged in global warfare. These pinnacles of democracy were female-centered, but, according to Gilman's fiction, they were also white, a theory that reflected the racial tenets of Victorian evolutionism as seen in the depiction of the Dahomeyan Amazons at the 1893 World's Fair. Like French Sheldon, Gilman positioned white womanhood as key to a successful society.

Accordingly, when Terry brings violence to Herland, despite the racial superiority allegedly represented by his white skin, it is clear that he is a patriarchal throwback who cannot survive in a peaceful matriarchy. At Terry's subsequent trial, the "stern grave mothers" decide his fate: "You must go home!" Jeff, who had become "thoroughly Herlandized" by his relationship with one of the women, elects to stay, reasoning, "Why should I want to go back to all our noise and dirt, our vice and crime, our disease and degeneracy?" Van decides to return home to "Ourland" with his love Ellador, who insists upon accompanying him after he promises not to reveal the location of Herland.[42]

Gilman thus set up a direct comparison between Progressive society and Herland. She clearly relied on the racism and xenophobia of the Progressive era, but we should not dismiss her ideas about race as merely reflective of context. As the direct heir of imperial matriarchalism, race is not incidental to her theories; it is the crux upon which her feminist matriarchalism was based. Lanser contends that "For Gilman, patriarchy is a racial phenomenon" in which it is "primarily non-Aryan 'yellow' peoples whom Gilman holds responsible for originating and perpetuating patriarchal practices, and it is primarily Nordic Protestants whom she considers capable of change." In her writing, Gilman often used racial speculation to explain the endurance of patriarchy, blaming the oppression of women in feudal Europe on the "'ancestor-worshipping' cultures of the 'old patriarchal races.'" White women were civilizers, while all men and people of color were savages requiring patience and careful training, a point Gilman drove home in her next fictional work, serialized in *The Forerunner* in 1916.[43]

Gilman's sequel, *With Her in Ourland*, opens immediately where *Herland* left off. Terry is banished, accompanied by Van and Ellador, the "Wife from Wonderland." The world to which they return is a fraught one; World War I, a potent symbol of the by-products of "patriarchal primacy," rages in Europe. Terry, ever the patriarch, dismisses the horrors of global warfare as "human nature," and he even briefly mentions the "abnormal" female soldiers of Dahomey. Shortly after the arrival of their steamer in Europe, Terry joins the Allies, but the sight of war—"ruins, ruins everywhere"—renders Ellador "like a woman of marble, cold, dumb, sitting still by the window where she could rest her eyes on the far stars." Reflecting Gilman's own pacifism, Elllador makes careful note of the ravages of masculine society, dismayed until she learns of ancient Egypt, where she "found much that pleased her in the power and place of historic womanhood." She also finds comfort in "Burmah," due to "that surviving matriarchate in the island hills," a reference to fin de siècle British colonial accounts of matriarchal societies in India. But as they travel the globe, she becomes increasingly depressed by the patriarchal horrors.[44]

Her outlook does not improve upon arrival in the United States, when she is struck by the "unmotherliness" of the "great rich lovely land." Van hopes that Elllador's "vast storehouse of mother-love can help to set us straight at last," but she struggles to find reason for optimism about the fate of the Western world. Elllador searches widely for positive comparisons to Herland, and she has trouble communicating even with women, finding them so trapped within their circumscribed role as to be inscrutable, with the exception of some accomplished professionals, like a doctor, a missionary, and a biological researcher. She sees hope only in the women's and labor movements, and especially within the Socialist Party: "What a splendid vision of immediate possibilities that is."[45]

Elllador takes meticulous notes on each of the social problems she encounters, and she pinpoints the "root error" of the patriarchal family: "It does seem clear that much mischief has followed from too much father." Proprietary patriarchy led to capitalism, and American paranoia of socialism had caused the nation to err in the opposite direction, so that the mass of citizens toiled in poverty. Elllador corrects Van and his contemporaries on their perverted definition of socialism, explaining that in Herland, all women share the land— "We never divided it up into little bits as you people have"—with the end result of a "balanced plenty" in which "every one has enough." Her solution to the world's ills is as gendered as her diagnosis. She complains that modern nations are like "poor, little, underbred children": "Quarrelsome, selfish, each bragging that he can 'lick' the others—oh, you poor dears! How you do need your mother!" Here, Gilman's Herland makes the transition from fantastical utopia to what Riane Eisler calls a "pragmatopia," or a "realizable scenario for a partnership future." Gilman's prescription, laid out by Elllador, mirrors the imaginary United States of *Moving the Mountain,* in which lifelong training in "democratic thought," the nationalization of resources, and the professionalization of "home industry" would result in a socialist utopia in the near future.[46]

As in Herland, this utopia would be achieved through the dystopian method of eugenics. In a discussion comparing international populations, Van calls the "white races civilized—and lump the others," and this becomes the prevailing organization of peoples in the main characters' discussions of immigration. "You have stuffed yourself with the most ill-assorted and unassimilable mass of human material that ever was held together by artificial means," muses Ellador. The "melting pot" Van describes is, according to Ellador, the scourge of the United States: "It never occurred to you that the poor and oppressed were not necessarily good stuff for a democracy," that they "make monarchy and despotism—don't you see that?" As in *Herland,* the stuff of true democracy, equality, and peace in *Ourland* was white.[47]

Ellador is a firm evolutionist when it comes to immigration. People of color from the allegedly less evolved cultures, according to the evolutionist rendering of reform Darwinism, were redeemable, but this was not a task that could be accomplished overnight. Exhibiting her classic slippage between the definitions of "race," Gilman argued in the novel that "the human race is in different stages of development, and only some of the races—or some individuals in a given race—have reached the democratic stage." Ellador echoes imperial matriarchalism, explaining that others must be uplifted and carefully taught the ways of civilization as Herlanders defined it. Thus, the solution to the "race problem" in Ourland is to separate races according to their relative stages in evolutionary, historical development until selective breeding and democratic training yield a socialist utopia.[48]

Gilman pushed reform Darwinism to its most racist and classist conclusion, the proposition that society could be "remade" in, as Ellador outlined it, just three generations. As readers of *Herland* know, the "perfectly cultivated, richly developed roses" of Herland seemed natural, but they were, in fact, carefully, selectively bred to produce uniform, white purity. This task could also be achieved in the United States, as Ellador, ever the efficient eugenicist, lays out in a detailed trajectory: "It is the people who take three generations to remake. You could improve this stock, say, 5 per cent in one, 15 in two and 80 per cent in three."[49]

As in Herland, women would lead the way: "Anything that brings women out into social relation, into a sense of social responsibility, is good. . . . It does not seem to me possible for women to mishandle food as men do, or build such houses." Gilman thus replicates the gender essentialism of imperial matriarchalism, arguing that the mothers of civilization—the white women of

the United States—will have to remake the "Real World," while Van and Ellador return to Herland, have a son, and "begin a new kind of men." Ellador
concludes, "What a glorious time they will have—cleaning up the world!"[50]

Unlike some of her more famous works of nonfiction, Gilman's matriarchal
trilogy did not reach a wide audience; although *Herland* was her most widely
read fictional work, serializing it in *The Forerunner* meant that it only reached
subscribers. The novella was not reviewed professionally, but it did, like many
of her works in *The Forerunner*, spark some criticism. In the end, *Herland*, like
Gilman's other major publications, generally failed to satisfy her critics or,
for that matter, many of her colleagues; to feminists, she was not committed
enough to suffrage, and to socialists, she was not committed enough to the
revolutionary cause.[51]

One historian estimates that Gilman was at the height of her popularity
between 1912 and 1914, although she was also widely celebrated just after the
publication of *Women and Economics* in 1898. But in the mid-1910s, opponents
of feminism, such as the antisuffragist *New York Times*, roundly condemned
Gilman. Economist Correa Moylan Walsh attacked both feminism and academic matriarchalism, arguing:

> The civilized world is a 'man-made' world: for this statement we have
> the authority of the foremost American feminist, who ought to be on
> her guard lest women do not unmake it. . . . The idea suggested es-
> pecially by the term 'matriarchate' or 'matriarchy,' of mother rule, is
> unobjectionable if confined strictly to the rule of mothers over their
> children; but extended as it generally is, in parallelism with 'patriarchy'
> to mean the rule of women over men (more definitely expressed by 'gy-
> naecocracy'), the implication is false; for there is no evidence, not even
> in Egypt, that women ever ruled over anything but children.

Walsh concedes that "there are some legends of Amazons" who "controlled
their own affairs, got themselves fecundated by their male neighbours, reared
only their female children, and waged war with men," but he reminds readers
that "the one thing uniform about all such legends is that the women were
beaten and their congregations destroyed." Examples among the ancient Lycians, Greeks, or Iroquois, he argued, simply "could not last," as they represented "a state of unequal equilibrium" that opposed the "true nature of
things." According to Walsh, who ignored Gage's major work of women's his-

tory, Gilman offered "perhaps the first" version of a "woman-made philoso-phy of history," which he dismissed as "mainly inductive, going from the past trend of alleged events to the future." Moreover, Walsh contended in his attack on feminism, Gilman's proposed social solutions would result in the "mascu-linization of women and the feminization of men"; that his characterization was a paraphrase of Baum's fictional "women of castiron" and house-minding men was likely unintentional. Walsh was not alone in his criticism. Author Avrom Barnett named Gilman among others who, "in attempting to give their movement a 'scientific' basis, have committed all the atrocities of which the dilettante in science is capable," the primary example of which was "the older feminists' use of the unsound gynaecocentric theory of Ward."[52]

Thus, when Gilman was attacked, it was more specific than the widespread attacks on other feminist theorists of the 1910s; the target was often her ma-triarchalism. In her autobiography, Gilman reasoned that her "little journal" was too controversial for most American readers: "There were some who were with me on one point and some on two, but when it came to five or more dis-tinct heresies, to a magazine which ridiculed even Fashion, and held blazing before its readers a heaven on earth which they did not in the least want—it narrowed the subscription list."[53]

Readership of *The Forerunner* decreased substantially enough by 1916 that Gilman suspended publication. One of her biographers writes that she "did not age quietly," although her fame waned after World War I. Gilman's decline into reclusion and obscurity reflected the conservative backlash against the suf-frage and socialist movements and the antiradical campaigns of the 1920s. In particular, the coordinated red-baiting sponsored by the US War Department targeted feminists like Gilman and Jane Addams, who was deemed a "serious threat" to the nation. Despite *The Woman Patriot's* warning that men should "make way for the matriarchy" after the ratification of the Nineteenth Amend-ment, the primary feminist organizations of the 1910s, particularly NAWSA, with its single-issue focus on the federal amendment, were suffering from "burnout" and in disarray by the 1920s. Membership in these organizations dropped, the Equal Rights Amendment stalled in Congress, and writers like Gilman could not get published. In the late 1920s, Gilman was impoverished, reclusive, suffering from poor health, and writing her autobiography. She wrote most of it in 1926, but an agent was unable to find a publisher for it.[54]

By the 1930s, former suffragist Doris Stevens wrote, "All about us, we see attempts being made, buttressed by governmental authority, to throw women back into the morass of unlovely dependence from which they were just beginning to emerge." Despite this inhospitable environment, Gilman continued to write, and her reactionary belief in racial evolutionism and eugenics grew; convinced of "fundamental ethnic differences" between groups, she argued for aggressive education in national training schools to ensure assimilation and later advocated for birth control as a means of controlling reproduction along eugenicist lines. Citing the melting pot metaphor, she argued that if, through indiscriminate immigration, one put "into a melting pot promiscuous shovelfuls of anything that comes in handy, you do not get out of it anything of value, and you may break the pot."[55]

Gilman also continued to produce fiction, publishing her last novel, *Unpunished* (1929), which was ahead of its time in its depiction of intimate partner violence, but unfortunately very much of its time in its racist depictions of African Americans and Italians. By 1930, Gilman's writing was out of print. She died of suicide five years later upon discovering that she had inoperable breast cancer—euthanasia was her last radical act, and she wrote about her preparations for it at length in her autobiography.[56]

During her lifetime, Gilman was renowned as a sociologist who "produced some fiction on the side," but she later became better known for her fiction, particularly "The Yellow Wallpaper" and *Herland*. She has since inspired an enormous scholarly corpus that now recognizes her "mixed legacy." By this, scholars generally mean her simultaneous significance to American feminism as well as her role in promoting eugenics, xenophobia, and racism. Scholars of race relations often focus on Gilman's nonfiction, while feminist theorists generally focus on her fiction, but reading the two together provides a broader picture of her position in the racial theorizing of her time as well as her central role in the matriarchalism of the Progressive era. Gilman was rediscovered during the revival of feminist matriarchalism in the 1970s, when novelists carried some of Gilman's ideas to "even more radical conclusions."[57]

Importantly, like her feminist legacy, her matriarchalist legacy is mixed. Gilman was a conduit of some of the tenets of previous matriarchalists, especially the feminist belief in matriarchal democracy of Gage and the racist belief in white female superiority of French Sheldon, but she also anticipated future iterations of matriarchalism as it developed in the 1940s and again in the 1970s. The Herlanders worshipped a central goddess and based their society on the rule of maternal love, achieved only through the total elimination of men. Gilman's matriarchs are strong, capable, and intelligent; Van alternately calls the utopian Amazons "wonder-wom[e]n," "ultra-women," and "superwomen." As these familiar-sounding monikers indicate, the matriarchalist ideas of Gilman's fiction would be famously reinvigorated just a few short years after Gilman's death in 1935 in the guise of William Moulton Marston's immensely popular superheroine, Wonder Woman.[58]

6

THE AMAZING AMAZON

Wonder Woman's Matriarchalist Superheroics

> Like the crash of thunder from the sky comes the WONDER WOMAN
> to save the world from the hatreds and wars of men in a man-made
> world! And what a Woman! A woman with the eternal beauty of Aph-
> rodite and the wisdom of Athena—yet whose lovely form hides the
> agility of Mercury and the steel sinews of a Hercules! Who is WON-
> DER WOMAN? Why does she fight for America?
>
> —CHARLES MOULTON, "Wonder Woman Arrives
> in Man's World," 1942

As the major voice of feminist matriarchalism in the first two decades of the twentieth century, Gilman's views were both reflective of and controversial for her time. Marie Howe, the founder
of Heterodoxy, the radical women's group, praised Gilman's "life
of inherited rebelliousness," and one of her smaller rebellions was, in fact,
breaking with Heterodoxy over the issue of World War I. Gilman returned to
the fold postwar, and through these meetings, she maintained connections
with various activists who had ties to the suffrage and feminist movements.
Although there is no evidence of actual collaboration, nor are there extant
sources that confirm discussions of matriarchies in Heterodoxy meetings, Gilman was one of two Heterodites who wrote matriarchal fiction. The other,
Inez Haynes Gillmore, published her novel *Angel Island* shortly before Gilman
serialized *Herland* in her journal, *The Forerunner*.[1]

Angel Island uses the familiar utopian plot device of a shipwreck on a seemingly deserted island to place five men within an all-female society. As the sole
survivors of the wreck, the men worry about becoming "savages" without the
soft touch of women, who "keep up the standards of life." On the island, when
the men encounter and become enraptured by a band of large, winged, beautiful women, they obsess over what to do with them. They resolve to seduce
them, and when that does not work, they decide to capture the "Valkyries."
They succeed, and, when the women fight like "leopardess[es]," the men cut

their wings for good measure, so that they cannot escape. Over time, the wing-less women learn to love the men, but unused to walking in favor of flight, they hobble and stumble in a clear metaphor for women's roles in patriarchal society. The couples pair off, and their offspring are born without wings, save one, a girl named Angela. The women lie around with their useless legs, resignedly discussing their previous lives of flight and exploration while they watch their children run around on healthy, land-loving limbs.[2]

The men grow bored with them, and the "five tottering females" internalize their own apparent weakness, as if their status were natural and not violently enforced, while harboring secret "contempt for the thing that walks." When the men decide that it is time to cut young Angela's wings as a rite of passage—her father decrees that "he could not possibly let her fly when she became a woman, that then it would be 'unwomanly' and 'unlovely' and 'uncharming' and 'unfascinating'"—the women decide to rebel. Because they have so thoroughly conformed to the patriarchal society enforced by the men, rebellion requires a new adaptation. One woman explains: "We must stop wanting to fly, we women. We must stop wasting our energy brooding over what's past. We must stop it at once. Not only that but—for Angela's sake and for the sake of all girl-children who will be born on this island—we must learn to walk." The women teach themselves to walk "with the frank, free, swinging gait of an Amazon," while their children run around them, and Angela flies above. Their wings grow back, not to their former glory, but enough so that the women can escape and force the men to meet their demands. Gillmore ends the novel much as Gilman ends *Herland,* with the hopeful birth of a son in this new equal society—a boy with wings.[3]

Although Gilman's matriarchal fiction is more well-known to twenty-first century audiences because of the rediscovery of her work by scholars in the 1970s, Gillmore's *Angel Island* also had a clear cultural impact. In her tale of patriarchs who indoctrinate formerly powerful women with lies about their own weakness, discover to their dismay that matriarchal power is not something that can be destroyed through physical violence or social norms, and learn to submit to female power in order to achieve gender equality, Gillmore unwittingly scripted much of the mythology of US pop culture's next major matriarchalist text. America's first comic superheroine did not have wings, but she could fly, and her creator, William Moulton Marston, believed firmly in teaching women to exercise their innate power. In his matriarchalist creation of the 1940s, Marston added a hefty dose of unique psychological theory to the elements of existing fictional societies like Oz, *Herland,* and *Angel Island* to create what would become America's most famous pop cultural matriarch: Wonder Woman.

William Moulton Marston was born into a Massachusetts family of means in the spring of 1894. An indifferent student in high school, Marston blossomed at Harvard. Although he claimed to detest history, he displayed an early interest in Greek mythology, which became a full-blown passion in college. His favorite course was Ancient Philosophy, taught by George Herbert Palmer, an avowed suffragist. Marston was particularly receptive to Palmer's mentorship, perhaps because he was in love with a childhood friend and Mount Holyoke undergraduate, Sadie Elizabeth Holloway, a tomboy whose favorite subject was Greek mythology.[4]

Just as Marston discovered his academic passion, psychology was coming into its own as a legitimate branch of philosophy, and he soon fell under its sway, as well. While maintaining a heavy philosophy course load, Marston began to study with Hugo Munsterberg in his famed "emotions lab" in 1912. Their research dealt with physiological measures of deception, and in his junior year, Marston helped to develop a test of deception using systolic blood pressure measurements. The tools he used became, essentially, what we now know as the lie detector test.[5]

Just after graduation in 1915, Marston and Holloway married, and over the next few years, Marston entered Harvard Law School, taught military psychology at Camp Greenleaf in Georgia, and then entered the Philosophy PhD program at Harvard to continue his psychological research. Holloway went to law school at Boston University, and then began working on her MA in Psychology at Radcliffe. Once she graduated, Holloway took a job in sales, embarking on what would be a recurring role as breadwinner in their family. Upon receiving his PhD, Marston went to Washington, DC, to join the Psychology Department at American University, where he continued to advocate for the wide applicability of his lie detector test, but use of his method in a famous murder trial established an unfavorable precedent when his evidence was reversed on appeal. This blow, combined with an unrelated arrest for fraud, cost Marston his professorship at American University.[6]

Some time after he returned to Boston, Marston landed a teaching job at Tufts, where he grew close to an undergraduate named Olive Byrne. Byrne was the child of an absent father and an indifferent mother, Ethel, whose sister, Margaret Sanger, was the famous birth control activist. At Tufts, Olive took a psychology class with Marston. Holloway was not living with him at the time; she was in New York, working as the managing editor of *Child Study*, a psychology journal devoted to parenting. Olive Byrne and Professor Marston clicked immediately, her grades improved immensely under his mentorship, and she became his research assistant in short order.[7]

Marston and Byrne left Tufts at the same time; in 1926, she left for graduate school in Psychology at Columbia, while he was likely fired. Byrne went on to complete her PhD coursework within two years, but she never wrote a dissertation, as personal circumstances intervened. Marston and Byrne's careers had become intertwined, and his mentorship had grown into something else altogether. Not long after Byrne graduated from Tufts and he was (probably) fired, Marston gave his wife an ultimatum: "Either Olive Byrne could live with them or he would leave her." The Marstons had lived apart off and on throughout their marriage, and they had even included a third party, Marjorie Wilkes Huntley, at times in their relationship. This ultimatum, however, caught Holloway off guard, and she "walked out the door and walked, without stopping, for six hours, thinking."[8]

What she was thinking about on this walk, it turns out, was not just her own emotional connection to her cheating husband. Holloway very much enjoyed working outside the home. She had always intended to do so, and she had gotten quite a bit of education in order to achieve that goal. She later explained, "I do feel strongly that every woman should have the experience of earning money and have the knowledge that she can support herself if she wants to." Moreover, at thirty-four years old, Holloway wanted to have children, but she was keenly aware of the "dilemma" of the working mother; it was a problem she was well aware of as editor of *Child Study*. After Marston's ultimatum, she found herself considering potential solutions. Having Byrne move in as their future children's nanny solved the work-life balance problem for Holloway. She made her decision, and soon thereafter, Byrne dropped out of Columbia and Holloway gave birth to her first child, a son they called Pete. Holloway worked up until the eve of the birth, and she returned to work in New York City as soon as possible, leaving her husband and graduate student-cum-mistress-cum-nanny at home with the newborn.[9]

Marston's biographer argues that despite appearances, the family did not function as a matriarchy, and according to his children's reports of him as an often-difficult, heavily drinking man, it is likely that Marston ruled the home as a patriarch. His son Byrne said that Marston was home all the time, smoking, sleeping "half the day," and drinking in the evenings. Sheldon Mayer, Marston's later editor at DC Comics, argued that although Marston "had a family relationship with a lot of women," the dynamic was "male-dominated" rather than matriarchal.[10]

However, matriarchy was the apparent intention, if not the lived reality, of this familial arrangement. Holloway's desire to work dovetailed with Marston's developing psychological theories about human relationships, specifically regarding conflict between the sexes. As he, Holloway, and Byrne worked together on a book on his theories, they were also cultivating a community of like-minded thinkers interested in alternatives to the patriarchal models of sex, marriage, and parenthood. According to Holloway, "all the basic principles" of the life she shared with Marston and Byrne were formed "in the years 1925, '26, and '27 when a group of about ten people used to meet in Boston at Aunt Carolyn's apartment once a week." The "remarkably kinky New Age" group met to discuss many things, including Marston's developing ideas about gendered dominance and submission. Marston's biographer called these meetings something of a "sexual training camp," with distinct theoretical underpinnings.[11]

But it wasn't all about sex; an explicit goal in these discussions of gender roles was female emancipation. The entire group read Margaret Sanger's *Woman and the New Race* (1920). Sanger was affiliated with Heterodoxy in the 1910s and thus serves as a primary link between the matriarchalists Gilman, who was generally reclusive by the late 1920s, and Marston, who was just beginning to develop his theories at that time. Gilman and Sanger moved in the same socialist circles in the early 1910s, although the lack of focus on feminist issues within American socialism led both of them to focus their activism elsewhere. Sanger published *Woman and the New Race* just after the ratification of the Nineteenth Amendment, and her writing was to have a profound effect on Marston's thinking in the 1920s, the age of the "New Woman."[12]

In *Woman and the New Race*, Sanger advocated, as always, for birth control. She did not base this claim on the simple right to personal choices, as modern-day reproductive justice activists would; rather, she argued that the prohibition against birth control was related to larger socioeconomic trends. The most oppressive force in the world was involuntary motherhood, which, according to Sanger, was closely associated with broad social problems such as contemporary inequities of labor and the violence of war. In a brief overview of world history, she argued that "behind all war has been the pressure of pop-

ulation"; she explained that territorial disputes, expansionism, and imperialism often stemmed from overpopulation and consumption. Attendant social
and political institutions thus developed to protect and promote involuntary
motherhood; echoing Matilda Joslyn Gage, Sanger argued that the church
and the state were intertwined forces of gendered oppression. Sanger also espoused academic matriarchalism, arguing that Christianity "turned back the
clock two thousand years for women," destroying the "great freedom, power,
and influence" that they had achieved in prehistoric societies and early empires in Egypt, Greece, and Rome.[13]

Like Gilman, Sanger believed that change was in the hands of the very
women who had settled into the powerless position of "breeding machine and
a drudge." She advised: "The brutal, unavoidable fact is that she will never
receive her freedom until she takes it for herself." The path to revolution, in
fact, was simple: birth control would liberate women, and "then, through the
understanding of the intuitive forward urging within her, she will not stop at
patching up the world; she will remake it." And in a section that heavily influenced Marston, Sanger summed up her argument: "What effect will the practice of birth control have upon woman's moral development? . . . it will break
her bonds. It will free her to understand the cravings and soul needs of herself
and other women. It will enable her to develop her love nature separate from
and independent of her moral nature." She continued: "Love is the greatest
force of the universe; freed of its bonds of submission and unwanted progeny,
it will formulate and compel of its own nature observance to standards of purity far beyond the highest conception of the average moralist."[14]

This emphasis on love as the life force of individuals and societies appealed
to Marston's group of friends, as did Sanger's evaluation of the various changes
of the 1910s and 1920s, particularly the piecemeal repeals of the "semi-official
witch hunting" represented by the Comstock laws, which had served to censor
Gage's book three decades before. According to Sanger, suffrage, women's new
roles in the workforce, and the "arousing of public conscience" as represented
by the early feminist movement "have all operated to give force and volume
to the demand for woman's right to control her own body that she may work
out her own salvation." Chains of bondage, the self-emancipation of women,
the belief in women's unique strength and goodness, and women as leaders in
a new sociopolitical ethic of love: these ideas would turn out to be so foundational for Marston that he would later furnish new employees with copies
of *Woman and the New Race*, explaining that by reading it, they would know

everything necessary about Wonder Woman, the character he would create some fifteen years after reading Sanger.[15]

So while the Marston family may not have functioned consistently as a matriarchy, with the women in obvious positions of power, the threesome of Byrne, Holloway, and Marston had a fairly clear structure, if not a hierarchy, throughout the 1930s. Byrne's presence in the household was key to Holloway's emancipation; Byrne raised the children and occasionally wrote free-lance for women's magazines like *Family Circle,* while Holloway worked full-time earning most, and sometimes all, of the family money. The women controlled the finances, while Marston, not unlike L. Frank Baum, dabbled in various, largely unsuccessful business ventures. "Many classmates can testify with me that it is very hard to earn a living," Marston wrote in a Harvard Class Report in 1930. "The only thing to do is to have a wife, like mine, who will go to work and support you." And all the while, Marston honed his psychological theories exploring the question of women's liberation from bondage so that they could lead the world.[16]

While the Holloway-Byrne-Marston threesome worked out their new arrangement, they were also writing Marston's first major work of psychological theory. Marston dedicated *Emotions of Normal People* (1928) to five women: his mother, his aunt Claribel in Chicago, Marjorie Wilkes Huntley, Holloway, and Byrne. In this book, Marston argued that the emotions that were socially defined as "abnormal"—particularly "the love parts," including homosexuality, fetishism, dominance/submissive practices, and various other "appetitive compulsions"—were, in fact, "completely normal," because they are impulses within the central nervous system that are naturally generated in response to appropriate stimuli. Citing his many years of blood pressure–based deception analysis, mental health studies of New York schoolchildren and Texas prisoners, and various tests performed in his student clinic at Tufts, Marston set out to scientifically describe and quantify the basic "nodal points of primary emotion" in humans, of which there were four: dominance, submission, compliance, and inducement (which would come to be known as DISC theory). He argued that "sex differences in adult dominance" were balanced, such that women's dominance was "nearly on a par with that of men." This balance was, in his estimation, a relatively recent development supported by anecdotal evidence such as the increased participation of women in sports.[17]

After a lengthy explanation of his experimental evidence and theoretical conclusions, *Emotions of Normal People* shifts from a pseudoscientific textbook to a political manifesto advocating nothing less than a gendered revolution. Using his theory of basic human emotions, Marston concluded that "there seems little reason to doubt that women, as a sex, are many times better equipped to assume emotional leadership than are males." Women's status of "dominantly enforced weakness" in a "predominantly male civilization" had arrested their development, keeping them dependent and reinforcing weakness as an adaptive sex behavior, an argument similar to the one made three decades prior by Gilman. But, Marston argued in the 1920s, women were "nearing the point where they will be able to provide for themselves quite as well as men can provide for them," and they were "beginning to develop both power and willingness to help themselves."[18]

Thus, he claimed, women would soon be able to dominate men and teach them that, rather than the masculine mode of aggression and force, "love (real love, not 'sex appetite') constitutes, in the human organism, the ultimate end of all activity." Women would lovingly dominate, he predicted, and men would happily submit. This "emotional re-education" would be taught by "Love Leaders" who would be, according to Marston, necessarily female: "We have already seen that males cannot be counted on, unless the male organism changes radically. The only possible candidates for love leader training, therefore, are women." Marston was not suggesting, however, that women were innately more compassionate than men; even the highly developed "Love Leader" would need to be "taught to use her love power exclusively for the benefit of humanity and not for her own destructive, appetitive gratifications." This teaching of "love mechanisms" should occur on all fronts, including in the workforce, in domestic labor like housecleaning and childcare, and even in the bedroom.[19]

Despite, or perhaps because of, its radical conclusions, Marston's treatise did not find a wide academic audience, and those who did read it found Marston's experimental evidence to be thorough but strange. F. Aveling, writing for the *Journal of Philosophical Studies*, avoided reviewing the more controversial aspects of the text, saying simply that there were "additional chapters" at the end. Those reviewers who did address these chapters had mixed reactions. Describing Marston as "an American psychologist and neurologist whose work is quite unknown," the *Saturday Review* called *Emotions of Normal People* an "important," "daring," and "very stimulating" work, but the reviewer cautioned that Marston "has thrown down challenges which many may consider outrageous." The lengthiest and most enthusiastic review appeared in the *Journal of*

Abnormal and Social Psychology, written by none other than Olive Byrne, who deemed *Emotions of Normal People* "the first logical and sensible treatise on human emotions that psychology has ever offered." She did not, of course, reveal their relationship, and hers was the only glowing review of the book. Much to his chagrin, *Emotions of Normal People* did not revive Marston's academic career.[20]

Throughout the 1930s, with a family supported primarily by his wife's salary, Marston attempted to popularize his unorthodox theories through various venues. He "patched together odd jobs," including adjuncting at universities, touting himself as the "world's first consulting psychologist," and writing. In 1931, with Holloway as coauthor, he published *Integrative Psychology: A Study of Unit Response,* a serious tome of over five hundred pages that was likely a last-ditch attempt to reinvigorate his career. Like *Emotions of Normal People,* it was largely ignored.[21]

Disenchanted with academia after the tepid reception of his psychological texts and his inability to keep a teaching position, Marston next attempted a more creative dissemination of his theories via his erotic historical novel *Venus With Us* (1932). Through the tale of Florentia, a teenaged vestal virgin and the true love of Julius Caesar in ancient Rome, Marston illustrated how dominance and submission—in such forms as sexual withholding, voluntary enslavement, bondage via chains or ropes, polyamory, and parent-child interactions—were the true stuff of loving relationships. Caesar, an androgynous beauty with many lovers and a vicious temper, goes by the titular motto, "Venus with us!," and he is heavily influenced by powerful women, of which there are many in the novel. Marston's psychological theories are neatly contained within *Venus With Us,* particularly in the roles of women as Love Leaders directing the actions of men.[22]

Marston continued to try all possible avenues of publicizing his theories. In 1935, after Olive Byrne, under the name Olive Richard, joined *Family Circle* as a staff writer, Marston became known through her gushing columns as the magazine's official psychologist. By the mid-1930s, however, the country was in a major economic depression, and the Marston household, headed by "both Mommies and poor old Dad," was struggling. The growing number of children—Holloway's son Pete and daughter Olive Ann, and Byrne's sons Byrne and Donn, all the "biological children of Bill Marston"—was more than Holloway could support alone. According to their son Byrne, "I don't know what happened about the various teaching positions, but I do remember when

I was really small we were living up in Massachusetts with my grandmother because there just wasn't any money." Despite Marston's many attempts to promote it, this interpersonal matriarchal setup, it seemed, wasn't all it was cracked up to be.[23]

In the late 1930s, Marston tried his hand at self-help literature, using the upbeat discourse of self-improvement to promote his own psychological theories. In *You Can Be Popular!* (1936), he explained that the "definite psychological differences between the sexes," particularly the "certain love emotions" experienced by "normal women" every day, dictated gender-based approaches to social relationships. The following year, Marston published *Try Living* (1937), in which he advised his readers to "live, love, and laugh." In a veiled reference to the sexual subculture of which he was a part, Marston explained that he used to meet with a group of friends, "men and women of diverse races and creeds," in Boston each Sunday night to "discuss human problems," and "they all agreed, despite their divergent backgrounds, that a great share of this world's unhappiness is caused by unfulfilled desires." "LOVE IS THE MOST PRACTICAL THING IN THE WORLD," he fairly shouted at his readers. Two years later, he continued this theme in *March On!* (1939), in which he concluded: "Someday, I sincerely hope, women will demand and create love schools and universities."[24]

Marston's self-help books sold poorly, and in general, despite his predictions, the 1930s were a low point in the popularity of matriarchalism in the United States. In 1939, the most famous fictional matriarchy in American pop culture at the time, Baum's *Wizard of Oz* series, received a makeover in its translation to the big screen. Despite Dorothy's famous mantra, "There's no place like home," Dorothy, and in fact her entire family, choose to live in the utopia of Oz in Baum's stories. This is a telling choice that contradicts the traditional narrative of the genre in which the narrator is discovered to be dreaming. But in the 1939 film, Oz is a "bad dream," according to Auntie Em. Although the Munchkins sing to Dorothy that she will be "history" in the "hall of fame" for her heroic deeds in Oz, they are a figment of her imagination, and one to which she will not return; she exclaims upon awakening in her bed in Kansas: "I'm not going to leave here ever, ever again." Lest the point be missed, Dorothy spells it out to Glinda: "If I ever go looking for my heart's desire again, I won't go any further than my own backyard." This is a heartwarming message about the value of home, to be sure, but it is also a gendered lesson about where young women belong. By the late 1930s, then, the matriarchy of Oz had been fully tamed into a mere dream, and feminist matriarchalism itself seemed to be on the decline.[25]

True to his own positive self-help message, however, Marston did not give up. His loose involvement with the advertising and entertainment industries only increased his belief in the potential of mass media as a platform for his psychological theories. By the late 1930s, a new medium, comic books, had become popular with both adult and child readers. *Detective Comics* hit the stands in 1937, followed by the nation's first comic superhero, Superman, in 1938. Batman debuted the following year. By then, millions of American children were reading comic books.[26]

Marston identified the comics as his ideal medium, and the cultural context, as well, seemed ripe for his theories. The climate of the 1930s does not, at first glance, appear hospitable to feminism; the disarray of feminist organizations, the waning support for married women's labor participation during the Great Depression, and the growth of right-wing organizations all point to a discernible antifeminist backlash. Yet, although they are often overshadowed by their suffragist sisters of the previous generation and the wartime women workers of the following decade, the feminists of the 1930s were active as promoters of social welfare through voluntary organizations and as contributors to the New Deal government. In 1933, Inez Haynes Irwin (nee Gillmore), author of the matriarchal novel *Angel Island*, published a lengthy review of the previous century of women's activism entitled *Angels and Amazons*. She argued that in the arenas of education, industry, social and political organizations, and formal political participation, women had made such strides that equality was almost nigh. She concluded: "The girl of today can do almost everything boys do—and usually does. She works at everything. She plays at everything. She is on the mountain, in the sea, and above the clouds."[27] Irwin was not alone in this sentiment. Despite the lukewarm reception of his theories, Marston, too, believed that American women were poised for major change.

After a decision by the Supreme Court in a case featuring Margaret Sanger, who had replaced Charlotte Perkins Gilman as "the best-known feminist in the world" by the 1930s, the Comstock laws against contraception relaxed, and the economic emergency of the Great Depression, among other things, prompted the American Medical Association to endorse birth control. In *Woman and the New Race*, Sanger argued that birth control was the key to unlocking women's liberation, and Marston heartily agreed with her prognosis for women's empowerment. A few months after the court's decision in 1937, he held a press conference in which he predicted imminent female global supremacy.[28]

On November 10, 1937, Marston held forth for two hours at the Harvard Club of New York. The ostensible reason for the press conference was the recent launch of *Try Living!*, but Marston used this platform to make a bold prediction: within a century, the United States would undergo a transformation into a "sort of Amazonian matriarchy." The *New York Times* detailed how this evolution might occur:

> As to the prediction, Dr. Marston said that within 100 years there would be a beginning toward a matriarchy; within 500 years a definite sex battle for supremacy; and within 1,000 years the matriarchy would begin to emerge and women would take over the rule of the country, politically and economically. His theory is that women, frustrated in love—the one thing in which they have specialized—by husbands who have specialized in success and have come home tired at night, will go out in the future and seek their own success.

The *Washington Post* explained further, quoting Marston: "Women have twice the emotional development, the ability for love, than man has. And as they develop as much ability for worldly success as they already have ability for love, they will clearly come to rule business and the Nation and the world." The result would be "an American matriarchy—a nation of amazons in the psychological rather than the physical sense." Bombastic rhetoric and shameless self-promotion aside, Marston did seem to be on to something; in just a few years, as the United States entered World War II and industries underwent conversion to produce war materials, the labor that would fuel the war, pull the American economy out of the Great Depression, and launch the longest sustained period of economic growth in US history was noticeably female, as millions of women abandoned the domestic sphere to work during the wartime emergency.[29]

By this time, as well, all of Europe was at war, a situation that Margaret Sanger famously explained as the fallout of overpopulation due to oppression of women's basic bodily rights. Marston was, of course, heavily influenced by Sanger's arguments (not to mention her niece, Olive Byrne), and he added to Sanger's formulation his own psychological theories. To Marston, world war represented the illogical conclusion of the perverted masculine impulse to aggressive dominance. This broad context—the development of the comic book industry, contemporary feminism and the promotion of female labor, concern over the growth of global conflict, and, of course, Marston's decade-long search for the proper medium for his theories—gave birth to the world's first comic superheroine.[30]

Critics of the new medium were worried about violence in the comics, and the coverage of this concern provided an outlet for Marston, the erstwhile psychological consultant. In *Family Circle,* Olive Byrne offered Marston a venue in which to promote his theories as a justification for the popularity—indeed, the educational usefulness—of comic books. Comics, Marston argued, singling out *Superman* in particular, represented wish fulfillment, and as such, they could not be "wrong or harmful for children," because the violence therein was always resolved through the patriotic vanquishing of evil. After years of Byrne touting Marston's psychological prowess via her magazine columns, this one hit pay dirt: on the strength of his defense of *Superman,* Marston was hired as a consulting psychologist by Max Charles Gaines, the creator of the comic book, who had assembled an advisory board of academics and child experts to defend his brand against charges of "unwholesomeness."[31]

Marston used his new consulting gig to advocate for a gendered correction to the perceived offenses of the comic book industry. Comics were a unique medium, he argued, whose power was "not a matter of modern theory but of anciently established truth." And the truth that Marston most wanted established, he later explained, was one of gender and sex. When he became a consulting psychologist to DC Comics, in a reversal of his previous endorsement, he immediately identified their "blood-curdling masculinity" as the comics' "worst offense." This was no mere entertainment; rather, the violent masculinity of the comics could have negative psychological effects:

A male hero, at best, lacks the qualities of maternal love and tenderness which are as essential to a normal child as the breath of life. Suppose your child's ideal became a super*man* who uses his extraordinary power to help the weak. The most important ingredient in the human happiness recipe still is missing—*love.* It's smart to be strong. It's big to be generous. But it's sissified, according to exclusively masculine rules, to be tender, lover, affectionate, and alluring. "Aw, that's girl's stuff!" snorts our young comics reader. "Who wants to be a *girl?*" And that's the point; not even girls want to be girls so long as our feminine archetype lacks force, strength, power. Not wanting to be girls they don't want to be tender, submissive, peaceloving as good women are. Women's strong qualities have become despised because of their weak ones. The obvious remedy is to create a feminine character with all the strength of a Superman plus all the allure of a good and beautiful woman. This is what I recommended to the comics publishers.

In 1940, he pitched his solution—a female superhero—to Gaines at DC Comics. Gaines agreed that Marston could have a six-month trial run in an existing comic, and Wonder Woman was born. That is, "Suprema, the Wonder Woman," was born, but her name was quickly shortened.[32]

By early 1941, then, Marston was hard at work translating his theories to the comic superhero format. In a letter to DC editor Sheldon Mayer that accompanied his first script, Marston emphasized that they must stay true to his "universal theme," the "great movement now under way," which he defined as "the growth in the power of women." He demanded bluntly: "I want you to let that theme alone—or drop the project." In this letter, Marston was long-winded about the connection between the back-story for his new character and the contemporary gendered context:

> Bear with me while I mention the under-meaning here. Men (Greeks) were captured by predatory love-seeking females until they got sick of it and made the women captive by force. But they were afraid of them (masculine inferiority complex) and kept them heavily chained lest the women put one over as they always had before. The Goddess of Love comes along and helps women break their chains by giving them the greater force of real altruism. Whereupon men turned about face and actually helped the women get away from domestic slavery—as men are doing now. The NEW WOMEN, thus freed and strengthened by supporting themselves (on Paradise Island) developed enormous physical and mental power. But they have to use it for other people's benefit or they go back to chains, and weakness.

Wonder Woman, then, was to be Marston's matriarchalist Trojan Horse, his means of introducing his psychological theories and gendered predictions for the future of the United States to a new generation via the medium, comic books, that children were consuming at an unprecedented rate.[33]

And so, in *All-Star Comics* in the December 1941–January 1942 issue, readers discovered an extra feature called "Introducing Wonder Woman." Beside an illustration of Wonder Woman in mid-sprint, the legend read:

> At last, in a world torn by the hatreds and wars of men, appears a *woman* to whom the problems and feats of men are mere child's play—a woman whose identity is known to *none*, but whose sensational feats are outstanding in a fast-moving world! With a hundred times the agility and strength of our best male athletes and strongest wrestlers, she appears as though from nowhere to avenge an injustice or right a wrong! As lovely as Aphrodite—as wise as Athena—with the speed of Mercury and the strength of Hercules—she is known only as *Wonder Woman*, but who she is, or whence she came, nobody knows!

The series begins on Paradise Island, the matriarchal land founded by the Amazons, where Wonder Woman carries a wounded American soldier, Steve Trevor, around the all-female society "as if he were a child." Unlike Baum, Marston did not slowly introduce readers to the utopian nature of his fantastical matriarchal society over time. Rather, the benefits of female power were evident in this first story. Paradise Island had "fertile soil," "marvelous vegetation," and "varied natural resources," combined with "no want, no illness, no hatreds, no wars." This idyllic state is inescapably gendered; as long as the Amazons "do not permit [them]selves to be again beguiled by men," they will remain advanced beyond "so-called man-made civilization."[34]

Marston wantonly mixes various ancient mythologies within his stories. Ares, the Greek god of war, and Aphrodite, the Greek goddess of love and beauty, divide up the world in Wonder Woman's origin story. Ares wants his men to "rule with the sword," while Aphrodite declares that her "women shall conquer men with love." Thereafter, Ares becomes known as Mars, the Roman god of war, and he slays weak men and enslaves women, who "were cheaper than cattle" at slave markets. Aphrodite, in response, "shaped with her own hands a race of superwomen," bestowing upon their leader, Hippolyte, her Magic Girdle, which allows her to conquer the men. The Amazons build Amazonia, a "magnificent city," and they are shown "tossing men about" as they repel attackers. Mars sends Hercules to defeat them, but he is no match for the Amazons as long as Hippolyte wears the magic belt. So he plans a "treachery," to "use woman's own weapon against Queen Hippolyte." He seduces her, takes the Magic Girdle, makes war on the Amazons, enslaves them, and loots the beautiful city of Amazonia. In "despair," Hippolyte prays to Aphrodite, who promises to break their chains, so long as the Amazons forever wear "wrist bands" to remember the "folly of submitting to men." After they successfully battle Hercules's men again, the Amazons sail far away and found their new civilization, "A Paradise for Women Only!"[35]

Marston constantly contrasts Paradise Island, the "enlightened land of women," with the "upset world of men" during World War II. On Paradise Island, the Amazons build a utopia, and they sustain their population with the help of Aphrodite, who bestows upon them eternal youth and the Divine Gift when she breathes life into a tiny clay statue that becomes the Princess Diana. Steve Trevor's accidental intrusion spawns a love story, but Wonder Woman does not forsake the island just for romance; in accordance with the orders of Queen Hippolyte, Athena, and Aphrodite, young Diana is sent to preserve "liberty and freedom" in "America, the last citadel of democracy, and of equal rights for women." Marston thus packed into these few introductory pages a hefty dose of his psychological theories, his loose interpretation of the truths inherent in Greek mythology, and his bold predictions for the future.[36]

In February 1942, just after Wonder Woman's debut in *All-Star Comics*, Marston published "Women: Servants for Civilization" in *Tomorrow* magazine. In this article, he provided a defense of the theoretical basis for his new superheroine. Citing his proclamation from 1937 that women would one day rule the world, Marston argued that since the first world war, times had changed, and American women had, "to their own surprise," realized "that they were potentially as strong as men—in some ways stronger." As evidence, Marston cited women's increasing control of wealth and income, the rates of women in the workforce, and the numbers of women who support "wholly, or in part, their husbands and families" (according to his uncited numbers, "two million six hundred thousand of them"). Women's honesty in business, low crime rate, and intelligence—"women can do more work in a given time, and can do it more accurately, than men"—made them ideal "servants for civilization," to replace the current "predatory masters." Sounding much like Margaret Sanger, Marston wrote that, given "the only hope of permanent peace and happiness for humanity on this planet is an increased expression of love, and that women are the primary carriers of this great force, one of the problems we face is to provide women with more opportunity for using their love powers." He argued that the move toward female power was already under way as women learned to emancipate themselves, and then, he predicted, "there will dawn a new era of living, warmed (as it should be naturally and must have been intended) by the love nature and capacity of women, balancing and counteracting that male selfishness which has thrown off-balance the love potentialities of mankind, and brought us to a sorry state."[37]

With these theories as its basis, *Wonder Woman* became Marston's means of teaching readers of the comics how to prepare for the coming matriarchy. In a press release in which he was revealed as the author of *Wonder Woman*, Marston publicized his claims that the fate of civilization rested upon this gender revolution. He declared: "The only hope for civilization is the greater freedom, development and equality of women in all fields of human activity." As in his other writings, Marston envisioned *Wonder Woman* as a teaching tool through which the theories he had first developed in the 1920s could reach a broader audience, only this time, he targeted a new demographic. Comic books, he argued, were America's "most popular mental vitamin," representing an innovative means of educating youth with his "psychological propaganda for the new type of woman who should . . . rule the world." In his careful representations of "the ideal of glorious modern womanhood," Marston was, as Sheldon Mayer put it, "writing a feminist book but not for women."[38]

The most obviously didactic aspect of *Wonder Woman* was the running feature "Wonder Women of History," written by Alice Marble, the women's tennis champion, who reportedly wrote to the publishers to express her approval of Wonder Woman in the spring of 1942 and was promptly hired. The first installment was a four-page feature on Florence Nightingale, who was, according to Marble, inspired "by an ancient statue of an Amazon maiden which she saw in Rome." Other Wonder Women of History included Susan B. Anthony, Matilda Joslyn Gage's former best friend; Annie Oakley, the female star of Buffalo Bill's sideshow at the World's Columbian Exposition; and many others.[39]

Marston's matriarchal fantasy of *Wonder Woman* is rife with the themes that populate previous matriarchies, including *Women, Church and State*, *The Wizard of Oz*, and Gilman's fictional trilogy. Each issue, as in each Oz book, features inept, if generally well-meaning, men who are in need of rescue by women, usually, but not always, the Amazing Amazon herself. In nearly every story, Wonder Woman saves Steve Trevor, and she carries him like a child in each of her first three stories. Wonder Woman's mission is to fight for America, but this battle often takes the form of protecting Trevor, who represents benevolent patriarchy. Trevor himself comments upon this occasionally, protesting that Wonder Woman deserves the credit that is heaped upon him by his superiors. As in Oz, generally harmless men like Steve Trevor are contrasted with their darker male counterparts, the corrupt patriarchs and supervillains. The most brutal male character in *Wonder Woman* is Mars, the god of war. Mars, his minions, and various other villains work for the twin evils of the Axis powers and patriarchal oppression.[40]

Marston wrote at the end of Wonder Woman's first *Sensation Comics* issue in January 1942 that Wonder Woman's "exciting adventures" each month would consist of "best[ing] the world's most villainous men," but many of the threats to "freedom, democracy, and womankind" were women. In one of her first appearances, Diana Prince knocks out Lila, a Nazi spy working undercover within the US Army. Baroness Paula von Gunther, "former head of the Gestapo," is a frequent villain who smokes, wears leopard print, and enslaves young American women before Wonder Woman sends her to prison for rehabilitation and transforms her into an Amazon ally. There are many female characters that represent Marston's argument that women can be just as corrupted by power as men; as in Oz, these vain, evil creatures represent the "women of the patriarchal bargain," who have bought into prevailing sexism as a means of attaining a measure of power over others.[41]

Counterbalancing these wicked men and women are strong women, often of the Amazon variety. On Paradise Island, Marston explains, "love and justice make women strong beyond the dreams of men." Wonder Woman has the "invincible power of perfect womanhood" that she applies to the "supreme tasks of defending democracy and transforming evil to justice and happiness." And Diana is not alone in many of her abilities; Marston emphasizes that Paradise Island houses a race of wonderful women. The Amazons, in their endeavors to become "Aphrodite's Warrior Girls," practice impressive, superhuman athletic training throughout the series. Although Paradise Island is inhabited by a "virile race of wise and beauteous Amazons," Diana is the most wondrous of all. In her first appearance in *Sensation Comics,* she undergoes a "grueling" tournament from "sunrise to sunset" as she outraces a trained deer, bests her sisters at "tests of strength and agility," and finally wins the competition by deflecting dozens of bullets with her bracelets. Wonder Woman is frequently compared to strong men; in one issue alone, male characters compare her to Jack Dempsey, Houdini, and Joe Louis. Her athleticism delighted young readers: she could outrun wild animals, trains, and automobiles; repel bullets—and at least once, flaming arrows –with her bracelets; wrestle lions; walk through fire; lasso an exploding bomb mid-air; singlehandedly force a herd of wild cattle to retreat; go free-diving for days with no helmet; catch crashing planes and steam shovels with her bare hands; and even use her toes as fingers to snatch things from the air.[42]

Wonder Woman excels at more than just physical feats. Marston explains that a key part of Amazon education involves training the two brain hemispheres to "perform two different acts at the same time," so that "Amazon girls are taught to solve difficult mathematical problems with one half of the brain while with the other they conduct a strenuous wrestling match with some sister student." Thus, Wonder Woman is able to physically subdue enemies while directing her speeding, invisible plane in the sky overhead. Multifaceted Amazon training, Marston implies, would result in a matriarchy of women working together to perform unprecedented physical and mental feats.[43]

Strong sisterhood is not isolated to Paradise Island. Although in the first issue, Wonder Woman competes with, bests, and leaves the Amazons to travel to the United States with Steve Trevor, she quickly finds some earthly sisters. In *Sensation Comics,* Marston introduces an entire college sorority to help Wonder Woman, the "powerful being of light and happiness." The Beeta Lambda Sorority of Holliday College is headed by Etta Candy, a short, rotund redhead with an avowed love of sweets, a penchant for humorous exclamations, and a fierce loyalty to Wonder Woman. The Holliday Girls ably assist Wonder Woman throughout the 1940s. They are athletic, as well, representing a more attainable ideal for women's physical strength than the superhuman Amazons; they row, play tennis and basketball, and swim with Wonder Woman on a synchronized team.[44]

And yet, despite her constant rescue of inept men like Steve Trevor, defeat of brutal patriarchs, and assistance from an able army of strong women, the most powerful female figure in the comic is not Wonder Woman. True to Sanger's and Marston's belief in the power of freed motherhood, Hippolyte, Diana's mother and Queen of the Amazons, is by far Marston's supreme Love Leader. Hippolyte is something of a combination of Princess Ozma and Glinda the Good Witch in Baum's series. Like Ozma, Hippolyte is a fair-minded monarch in a peaceful land of plenty, and like Glinda, she has special powers that she employs only in emergency situations. Similar to Glinda's Great Record Book, Hippolyte has the magic sphere, a gift from Athena that "when tuned to any time or place in the world's history its viewplate shows everything that has happened there." The magic sphere also helps Hippolyte to locate anyone at any time in the past, present, or future. She has access to "the secret library of Aphrodite," which contains confidential information like the location of Valhalla, the "Hall of the Slain" of Norse mythology. Thus, like Gage and the suppressed but wise women that populated her *Women, Church and State*, Hippolyte alone has access to the true, full history of civilizations. And physically, although she rarely exercises this power, Hippolyte is stronger even than Wonder Woman, as readers discover in "The Masquerader," in which Hippolyte disguises herself as Wonder Woman to save her daughter from danger. This issue ends with Hippolyte chastising Diana: "Daughter, rouse yourself! Burst your bonds of mind and body!"—the message that Marston hoped to send to the American children whom he believed he was preparing for the matriarchal revolution.[45]

Although Marston was no history buff—he cautioned his readers on the "vagaries of past-dwellers" and "ancestor worship"—like Gage, he had a keen interest in unearthing the historically suppressed power of women. The goddesses in *Wonder Woman* represented his belief that ancient mythology revealed universal truths. In *Try Living*, he connected the worship of male gods to historical problems of gender. Echoing Gage, Gilman, and Sanger, Marston believed that many social and religious practices presumed to have a basis in theology were more accurately aimed at controlling the power of women. This plays out in a few issues of *Wonder Woman*, such as the episode in which Wonder Woman and friends are transported back in time to Salem in 1692, where a Puritan boy falsely accuses a girl of witchcraft. Harrumphs Etta Candy, "If I remember my history, the Salem Puritans hanged people as witches on the complaints of boys like this twerp!" The visitors from the 1940s are put in stocks to be hanged as witches as Wonder Woman explains, "Your superstitious beliefs which cause you to kill innocent victims in cold blood are very evil! There is no such thing as a witch or a sorcerer. Some day you will bitterly regret the grave injustices you have committed!"[46]

For Marston, history itself was uninteresting, even misleading. On the other hand, philosophy and mythology "made Greek hedonism a vital, living thing," and contained truths that one could not access through dry, historical facts. As Bachofen had argued eight decades before, mythology revealed hidden truths about gender and power that had contemporary relevance. Marston believed that if male domination had not resulted in the suppression of women, then perhaps the global conflict that served as the backdrop for *Wonder Woman* could have been avoided. Indeed, one motivation of Marston's comic, true to his belief that his gendered psychological theories applied to all conflict, was to end warfare.[47]

As Marston developed his superheroic plots, he linked love and war in ways he had been unable to in previous works. He wrote to Sheldon Mayer: "You may remember, at the very first, I pointed out that when you touch certain universal truths you create in my script re war and women taming men so they like peace and love better than fighting. This is the entire aim and purpose of Wonder Woman." In his first script, Mars, the Roman god of war, taunts Aphrodite, the Greek goddess of love and beauty, crowing that he has won their eternal battle, because "the whole world's at war," prompting her to send her "strongest Amazon maiden" to "help America." The second installment opens with a lengthy explanation of how "the Spirit of War rules supreme over the entire earth," introducing Mars and his "aide-de-camp, General Destruction." When Wonder Woman defeats Mars after a prolonged battle, she addresses readers directly: "Thus I broke Mars's chains! So must the whole earth break the shackles of its vicious war lords! Do your part—buy war bonds and stamps and help America lead the world to freedom!" For Marston, as for Gilman, the impulse to war was thoroughly gendered, representing masculine aggression. Those who fight with Wonder Woman fight against "women's bondage—that Hitler principle that women must remain slaves!" Wonder Woman's twofold mission is to defend "America from the enemies of democracy and fight fearlessly for down-trodden women and children in a man-made world."[48]

As in Oz, Marston's matriarchy on Paradise Island is a utopia because of the rule of women; according to the tenets of DISC theory, social, economic, and political conflict were by-products of the rule of men. Oz develops into a socialist utopia over the course of fourteen books, but the development of Marston's far less radical matriarchal economics and politics took fewer pages, as Paradise Island serves from the outset as an antidote to the patriarchal excesses of capitalism. In one issue, Marston perhaps unwittingly called back to Gilman's suffragist politicization of milk; six months into her existence as a comic book star, Diana Prince comes across a desperate woman who lost her son to malnutrition and weeps because she cannot afford milk for her daughter. Diana buys the child milk, and in her subsequent investigation of the International Milk Company, she discovers that the Nazis are behind the plot to starve and weaken American children. Wonder Woman leads a "gigantic demonstration against the milk racket," and "the streets are packed for miles with poor mothers and children who follow Wonder Woman while cameras click and newsreels grind." The protest mimics the labor activism of the 1930s as well as the women's movement of the 1910s, and, as Marston's biographer points out, the accompanying illustration recalls the famous suffrage parade of 1913, in which Inez Milholland led women through the streets of Washington, DC, riding a white horse.[49]

The following month, Wonder Woman engages in class warfare again when she discovers that the female clerks at Bullfinch's Department Store were "run down from overwork and insufficient food" due to low wages. The picketing clerks carry signs that read "Our Toil Makes Gloria [Bullfinch] Glamorous" and "Bullfinch Stores Unfair to Girls," as Diana Prince confronts the manager about paying a living wage. Wonder Woman captures Bullfinch, hypnotizes her, and makes her work like one of her own employees. Shortly thereafter, Bullfinch announces that salaries will be doubled and working conditions improved. Marston was no socialist, representing a break with the socialist matriarchalism of Baum and Gilman. Rather, as part of her wartime patriotism, Wonder Woman consistently argues that American capitalism could work better, if only the proper women were in charge.[50]

The problem with capitalism in *Wonder Woman*, like all problems in the comic, is one of gender. The corruptive nature of patriarchal capitalism is a major theme of each issue in which an inhabitant of Paradise Island other than Diana ventures to the United States. In the fall of 1945, "the malice and selfishness of the man-ruled world invade Paradise Island" in "Rebellion on Paradise Island." Several Amazons grow envious of Wonder Woman's American life as she shows them movies of "man's world" in "Sappho Hall" on one of her visits to her home island. The jealous sisters flee for the United States, and, after they've removed their bracelets, they almost defeat Wonder Woman in their quest to join the crooked consumer market. The bracelets, or "Aphrodite's bands," come to symbolize not just former enslavement by men under Hercules, but also a key barrier to the corrupt, capitalist seduction of man's world. Wanta Lynn, a Holliday College student trained on Reform Island, is similarly controlled by "terrible desires" when she removes her bands. She becomes "obsessed by jealous, greedy longing for money," thinking: "I'm strong but other girls are richer, socially prominent. I must have wealth—position— oh! These terrible desires control me whenever I take off Aphrodite's bands!" After saving the day, Wonder Woman concludes: "Strong humans become ruthless self-seekers unless they're bound by love!"[51]

Thus, Marston's utopia is in some ways unlike the others examined in previous chapters. Although Paradise Island itself is depicted as a land of plenty, in which all needs and wants are apparently met by the monarch or the goddesses, Marston was not anticapitalist, and there is nothing to indicate that the Amazons lived in a socialist system. Rather, Marston targeted *patriarchal* capitalism. The characteristic that sets Wonder Woman apart from her various pop cultural contexts—other superhero comics as well as previous fictional matriarchies—is the fact that Marston deployed the superhero formula with a very specific psychological agenda in mind. Marston's self-described "psychological propaganda" is evident in almost every installment of *Wonder Woman*, usually in the form of bondage and messages about love conquering violence. In the comics, Marston had free reign to disseminate his visions of a world of strong women inducing men to submission.[52]

Although he certainly intended the sexual overtones in the many scenes of women and men binding each other in ropes and chains, Marston's version of female dominance differed in substance from "sexual inversion" or the intimidation and humiliation of men by women in antimatriarchalist texts like Robinson's *Gynecocracy*. Robinson's fiction presents women's sole power as sexual, rooted in pleasure. "I do not believe that equality of the sexes will ever be established until the seat of a woman's womanhood is transferred from between her legs to her head," his narrator explains. While "a man exists for something else than for procreation," this was "the beginning and the end of a woman." For Marston, however, dominance and submission were not simply for the purposes of sexual pleasure and power. Rather, he had grander theories regarding gendered liberation and world peace.[53]

Marston's psychological theories permeate the series, sometimes in not-so-subtle forms. In "Battle of Desires," dominance and love take the form of a giant caveman and a winged woman who act out DISC theory. Dominance tries to club the woman, but "love has wings," and she escapes. Other "desires"—"Fear, Friendship, Selfish, Creative"—appear, only to be captured by Dominance. In a scene straight out of the matriarchalist novel *Angel Island*, Dominance attempts to cut their wings, only to have his huge scissors blocked by Wonder Woman's bracelets. A year later, based on the training principle that "if he's bound and controlled he'll be happy and useful," Dominance thanks Wonder Woman for teaching him to do "good work, instead of blowing up things."[54]

In each installment, women—usually Wonder Woman, although her female allies play key roles here, too—serve as Love Leaders. In her first encounter with Baroness Paula, Wonder Woman defeats her by being a "kinder mistress," breaking the chains of her enslaved girls and restoring them to normal. As in this instance, bondage is key to Marston's depiction of submission in *Wonder Woman*. Wonder Woman's magic lasso can "make bad men good, and weak women strong." Over time, Marston began to develop more formal means of taming his corrupt characters. For those who needed intensive training, Marston created Reform Island, also known as Transformation Island, where prisoners are educated in the ways of the Amazons. Reform Island cures various villains, turning the formidable Baroness Paula into Wonder Woman's "best friend and faithful lieutenant." The binding chains that prisoners on Reform Island wear represent Aphrodite's law of love. The inmates at the prison wear "girdles" that teach "loving submission" until they are fully trained in Amazon ways, or in rare cases, when they relapse. Compliance and submission thus trump dominance and inducement; as Wonder Woman explains to Steve, the "only way " to "rule anybody . . . is to do it the way women do it—by inspiring affection!"[55]

As the Amazon training in self-reliance indicates, Marston believed, as did Gage and Gilman, that women's complicity in their own oppression was as damaging to civilization as outright sexism from men. And like both Gilman and Sanger, Marston's entire matriarchal vision rested upon the concept of women's innate capacity for love, a fundamental sex difference that had, of course, served as the basis for stereotypes of feminine weakness, the prohibition on the performance of certain types of labor and the exercise of power, and the enforcement of the maternal primary caretaker and domestic labor status. Thus, Marston's was a specific brand of feminism based on gender essentialism, and evidence of his support for certain sexist stereotypes—such as the feminine quest for beauty, the pleasure of being dominated by men, and the female penchant for consumption—abounds. Despite her enormous power, for instance, Wonder Woman nearly swoons when Steve Trevor calls her beautiful, and she is often jealous of other women around him. For the most part, however, she is her own rival, as clueless Trevor expresses love for Wonder Woman and ignores her alter-ego, the "be-spectacled" and "demure little Army nurse Diana Prince." Trevor occasionally defies their interpersonal power dynamic and attempts to enact the "blood-curdling masculinity" that Marston identified in the male superhero comics. Uncharacteristically, Wonder Woman finds Steve's newfound power attractive, exclaiming: "No—Aphrodite forbids us Amazons to let any man dominate us. We are our own masters—but I confess—I love to have you boss me!" Although she reclaims her Amazonian strength, Wonder Woman surmises that "man's world marriage" must be "thrilling."[56]

Marston's own ideas about natural feminine traits often come through in the comics. On her first trip to the United States, after she dumps Trevor at the hospital, Wonder Woman is "dying" to go shopping, and just over a year later, she muses, "Isn't it silly how we girls love to dress up?" Wonder Woman also can't be trusted in her choice of romantic partners; in "The Crime of Boss Brekel," she falls for a crime boss. Falling into Trevor's arms at the end, she tells him, "When he grabbed me I found his arms weren't as strong as yours. . . . Oh! You're stronger than I remembered!" Yet she always recovers from her momentary lapses into stereotypical feminine weakness; as she reminds herself, episodes like these "just make a girl realize how she has to watch herself in this man's world!"[57]

The racism of the time also permeated the pages of *Wonder Woman*. During the Marston years, *Wonder Woman* was almost exclusively a white world, with the exception of racist images of agents of the Axis. Later in the series, readers encounter racist illustrations of the "natives" of Zani Island. The "deep hostility" toward the Japanese felt by many Americans found its way into *Wonder Woman;* in one issue, a female Chinese character refers to the Japanese as "monkey men" and "dwarves." Moreover, Marston in his scripts, and Harry G. Peter in his illustrations, fluctuated between denigrating and exoticizing women of color. These offensive characterizations of "others" and the overwhelming whiteness of Paradise Island indicate that white supremacy was an unacknowledged component of Marston's matriarchalism. At the same time, the racism in the pages of the comics was not limited to the pervasive prejudices of the time. Rather, when Wonder Woman visits other cultures and rescues them, she often enacts French Sheldon's imperial matriarchalism. The "Redskins" of one issue speak in dialect, perpetrate violence, and bow down to Wonder Woman as a "white goddess of men and beasts," while the Africans of "The Witchdoctor's Cauldron" are depicted as savage caricatures. Although they are dangerous, and some of the "wicked natives" wear swastika loincloths, Wonder Woman, ever the adept White Queen, is able to teach them the error of their ways. The comic thus combined elements of every previous version of pop cultural matriarchalism examined herein.[58]

Wonder Woman, in her various forms—*Sensation Comics, All-Star Comics, Comic Cavalcade,* and her own comic books and newspaper strips—was a runaway success, and she became the unexpected height of Marston's eclectic career. She immediately "sold like crazy," so that by 1944, *Wonder Woman* had over 10 million readers, more than any superhero save Superman and Batman. Despite her enormous popularity, however, the Amazing Amazon also generated controversy from the start. There was, of course, the matter of visual representation; superheroes might fight other men in tights without comment, but a female figure in a revealing outfit lassoing and binding others was another matter altogether. Wonder Woman's outfit is the subject of much comment in the stories themselves, as when one of the Holliday Girls compliments her "ducky costume," but says if Wonder Woman wants to join the band, she'll have to change, because "the dean insists on more above the waist." Wonder Woman, however, argues that she "can do better with fewer clothes."[59]

For those familiar with Marston's life's work, it will not be surprising that the most controversial aspect of *Wonder Woman* centered on issues of bondage and discipline. Marston, of course, mandated that bondage should be a big part of Wonder Woman, and others involved in her creation—illustrators, producers, editors—were well aware of his intention and its undergirding theories. According to editor Sheldon Mayer, "There was a certain symbolism that Marston engaged in, which was very simple and broad; I suspect it probably sold more comic books than I realized, but every time I came across one of those tricks, I would try to clean it up." To Marston, bondage was a crucial symbol of his psychological theory of emotions and of the promotion of matriarchy.[60]

Not all readers bought this rationale. Josette Frank of the Child Study Association of America expressed repeated dismay at *Wonder Woman*. Although the circulation numbers proved the comic's worth, she argued to Gaines, "this feature does lay you open to considerable criticism from any such group as ours, partly on the basis of the woman's costume (or lack of it), and partly on the basis of sadistic bits showing women chained, tortured, etc." In response, Dorothy Roubicek, a DC Comics editor, advised Marston to "veer away from Paradise Island for a while and place Wonder Woman into conventional life. . . . By taking her off Paradise Island, except in rare cases, the chained woman angle is removed." In other words, to remove the offending bondage, Marston needed to retreat from the matriarchy. Roubicek also "hastily dashed off" a letter to Gaines listing various ways to "keep women confined or enclosed without the use of chains" in the pages of the comic, with the agreed-upon goal of reducing the use of chains in the stories "by at least 50 to 75%." In a clearly frustrated letter to Gaines, Marston protested:

> Women are exciting for this one reason—it is the secret of woman's allure—women *enjoy* submission, being bound. This I bring out in Paradise Island sequences where the girls beg for chains and enjoy wearing them; their chains also increasing the girl's strength because her muscles carry that much extra weight continually. This teaches the *power* of submission. And because all this is a universal truth, a fundamental, subconscious *feeling* of normal humans, the children love it. That is why they like Wonder Woman on Paradise Island better than Wonder Woman anywhere else—and I have kept careful tabs, believe me! Children *feel* this as truth and it gives them inner pleasure and relieves their perpetual conflict between the urge for power and the restraint of same by outside authority. For Heaven's sake, whatever else we do, don't let's spoil this one BIG appeal of Wonder Woman!

He dismissed Frank by citing the "danger in letting ignorant people monkey with delicate machinery."[61]

Gaines sent Roubicek to see Lauretta Bender, a psychiatrist at Bellevue Hospital, for an expert perspective. In her report to Gaines, Roubicek stated that Bender sided firmly with Marston, wholeheartedly endorsing his theories and his "clever" handling of this "experiment" in exposing the public to the "real issue at stake in the world (and one she feels may possibly be a direct cause of the present conflict)." Roubicek concluded: "She thinks it is a worthwhile experiment, and believes it would be unwise to interfere with Dr. Marston."[62]

Despite this endorsement, objections continued to roll in, although at least one reader wrote that the "sadistic bits" about which Frank complained were, in fact, his favorite part of the comic. Frank continued to express concern about the "sex antagonisms" in *Wonder Woman*. Exasperated, Marston responded by calling Frank an "avowed enemy of the Wonder Woman strip," and after a few more letters back and forth, "Frank resigned from the advisory board for *Wonder Woman* and *Sensation Comics*, stating to Gaines that although she could tell that he had made an effort to omit "whippings, tortured women in chains, and other objectionable features," she still found "the strip hard to take," featuring as it did "significant sex antagonisms and perversions." In fact, she argued, she would "consider an out-and-out strip tease less unwholesome than this kind of symbolism." Lauretta Bender replaced Frank on the board.[63]

By the time that Frank resigned, Marston faced even more damning criticism of Wonder Woman that attacked her at the very heart of his theories about interpersonal psychology, Americanism, and feminism. In a letter to Gaines in the spring of 1943, advisory board member Professor W. W. D. Sones expressed concern that, instead of being an icon of American democracy, Wonder Woman implicitly endorsed all that the United States was fighting against in World War II. The "submission" that Marston emphasized as a goal, in fact, could make "dictator dominance possible." Sones explained: "From the standpoint of social ideals, what we want in America and in the world is cooperation and not submission." A few days later, Marston responded directly to Sones that the "self-seeking and attendant emotions" that characterized "Hitler, Mussolini, Napoleon, business tyrants, and criminals," which resulted "in war, conflict, etc.," were exactly what Wonder Woman, and Marston himself, were fighting against. War, Marston explained, was simply the "sadistic perversion of erotic feeling"—"LOVE CONTROLLED BY DOMINANCE"— which Wonder Woman consistently opposed. Wonder Woman, then, was the "beneficent mistress" who bound her victims in "love chains" to educate them in the ways of freedom, equality, and democracy.[64]

The charge of anti-Americanism rose its ugly head again in 1945 after Walter J. Ong, a newly minted literary theorist under the graduate tutelage of Marshall McLuhan, published "Comics and the Super State," in which he claimed that superheroes represented totalitarianism. *Time* covered the controversy, citing Ong at length on the "herdist phenomenon" that characterized superhero comics: "Everything is centered on one man—the leader, the hero, the *duce*, the *Fuhrer*. . . . The Superman of the cartoons is true to his sources. He is not another Horatio Alger hero or a Nick Carter; he is a super state type of hero, with definite interests in the ideologies of herdist politics." Under the subheading "Bull-Necked Males," Ong singled out Wonder Woman for the "Hitlerite paganism" represented by the Amazons' Aphrodite worship. Princess Diana was no model for democratic matriarchy. Rather, she was "only a female Superman, preaching 'the cult of force, spiked, by means of her pretentiously scanty 'working' attire, with a little commercial sex." Ong dismissed Marston's matriarchal theory as "nonsense," arguing that she was "incapable of sustaining womanly standards." He concluded, "this is not a healthy sex directed toward marriage and family life, but an antisocial sex, made as alluring as possible while its normal term in marriage is barred by the ground rules."[65]

Marston maintained that Ong was misinterpreting his stories. "My whole strip," he repeatedly explained, "is aimed at drawing the distinction in the minds of children and adults between love bonds and male bonds of cruelty and destruction; between submitting to a loving superior or deity and submitting to people like the Nazis, Japanese, etc." Ong's sexual critique was particularly telling for Marston, who lumped Ong into the same category of critics as people like Josette Frank who just didn't get it: "New slants on life, new enlightenment in the field of morality always meet bitter opposition—usually from persons who read into them their own evil thoughts and intentions." "Evil thoughts and intentions" aside, readers still loved Wonder Woman, although over the following year, sales began to drop, and the Amazing Amazon herself changed substantially. This was not likely due to Ong's critique; rather, the end of the war and personal circumstances surrounding the production of Wonder Woman changed her irrevocably.[66]

For one thing, Marston was no longer the primary writer, and his control over the comic was waning. Although the byline was always "Charles Moulton," Marston consistently sought outside help with his creation, including from his family, Marjorie Wilkes Huntley, and others. In 1944, Marston discovered a talented 19-year-old student, Joye Hummel, while teaching in New York. On the basis of her performance in his course, he hired her to write *Wonder Woman*. Hummel explained: "He believed that I would understand how he wished his heroine, Wonder Woman, portrayed and would be able to incorporate his theories into the stories." Olive Byrne furnished Hummel with her homework, Sanger's *Woman and the New Race*, explaining that "it was all she'd need" to understand Wonder Woman, and Hummel became a frequent collaborator.[67]

It was Hummel who was with Marston on the train from Rye to New York in August of 1944 when he collapsed from polio, the illness that would confine him to a bed for the final years of his life. His doctors were shocked at the late onset of the disease (Marston was in his fifties), and Marston did not take well to his new position as an invalid. Although she had been working for Marston for just a few months at that point, Hummel became a full-time surrogate for him at the office, working in New York with Harry G. Peter during the week and traveling to Rye on the weekends. Hummel's account books, in which she meticulously recorded her payments and visits to Rye, reveal that she wrote more and more of the stories by the mid-1940s.[68]

In 1946, when a biopsied mass revealed that Marston had incurable lung cancer, his family, at Holloway's insistence, never told him of the diagnosis, for fear that "he would fall into a deep depression." Marston lived for nine more months, six of which were productive, as he worked with Hummel from his home to produce *Wonder Woman* scripts. He wrote until the week he died, and his last *Wonder Woman* script featured as many of his favorite characters as he could pack into one story. In it, Wonder Woman captures a team of villains, and in Marston's final panel, Hippolyte proclaims: "The only real happiness for anybody is to be found in obedience to loving authority."[69]

Marston did not live to see this story in print; he died in early May of 1947 surrounded by his family and friends. His obituary in the *New York Times* reviewed his life's work, focusing heavily on lie detection. Although *Wonder Woman* received just a brief mention, the underlying matriarchalist motivation of the comic was explained: "A strong believer in the psychological doctrine of 'live, love and laugh,' he had predicted that the time would come when women would run this country in political and business affairs." Holloway and his four children were listed among the grieving family. Olive Byrne was not.[70]

After Marston's death, *Wonder Woman* suffered a series of devastating blows. Max Charles Gaines had resigned from the company in 1944, and just a few months after Marston succumbed to cancer, Gaines died in a boating accident. Joye Hummel married—Marston's daughter Olive Ann was her flower girl—and resigned shortly thereafter. Various writers filled in to keep Wonder Woman going, including Robert Kanigher, and Holloway, for one, did not approve; she lobbied for the job herself, but she was ignored. DC Comics hired Kanigher, whose assistant later called him a "very wild chauvinist." Holloway returned to her job, Olive Byrne went to work for a while in Margaret Sanger's old clinic, and Wonder Woman evolved with the times.[71]

The postwar period was a rough time for superhero comics in general. Battles with supervillain agents of the Axis no longer sold as they had in wartime, and the adult market of soldiers who received comic books in monthly care packages overseas had shrunk. By 1950, some popular wartime superheroes, including Captain America, the Green Lantern, and the Flash, had been canceled, and only Wonder Woman, Superman, and Batman remained. In a devastating blow to feminist matriarchalism as a staple of popular culture, Robert Kanigher, who wrote Wonder Woman for the two decades after Marston's death, thoroughly revised and then discarded the comic's matriarchal theme. In the new "secret origin of Wonder Woman," the Amazons founded their society not because they were escaping brutal patriarchy, but because they were wracked with grief over the defeat of their men—fathers, brothers, husbands, and sons—in warfare. The men thus did the important work of fighting wars, while the women cried at home. Moreover, the divine inspiration for the Amazing Amazon was no longer a gift of the goddesses. Rather, in Kanigher's version, the Princess Diana received her superpowers from both female and male deities, including Hercules, the Amazons' archenemy in the Marston mythology. The new Wonder Woman alone had powers; there was no sisterhood of Amazons, and Wonder Woman lost her earthly sisters, too, as Kanigher did away with Etta Candy and the Holliday Girls. In a final death knell, Kanigher replaced "Wonder Women of History" with "Marriage a la Mode," a feature on marriage customs ranging from bridal eyebrow-shaving in ancient Japan as a symbol of a woman's "subservience to her husband" to potential grooms wrestling over a bride on "Mombasa Island, Somaliland."[72]

Wonder Woman herself changed, as well. Imbued with new powers, she could fly. But her newfound flight did not help the Amazing Amazon escape the marriage plot. A running theme of the Kanigher era was her internal feminine struggle between career—fighting evil—and marriage—generally to Steve Trevor, although in the 1950s, she had several love interests, including Birdman and Mer-Man. For two decades, Kanigher had Wonder Woman enjoying all sorts of stereotypical feminine situations, from multiple marriage proposals, to babysitting, to being carried across a stream by Trevor in "S.O.S. Wonder Woman."[73]

This drastic character change represented the domestic retrenchment of the postwar period, in which the women who had flocked to the workforce during wartime now retreated, sometimes forcibly, back to the home. The gender roles that Marston had devoted his career to redefining—dominant, masculine breadwinning and submissive, feminine domesticity—reasserted themselves as the nuclear age of "affluence and anxiety" dawned. Times had changed and, to the vocal consternation of Marston's family, Wonder Woman changed with them. In Cold War America, the comics were under attack as a source of psychosocial problems, and in popular culture, fears of female power combined with mother-blaming to produce a new, dual-sided, decidedly sinister form of antimatriarchalism, as we shall see in the following chapter.

7

VIPERS AND MOMARCHIES
Mid-Century Antimatriarchalism

I give you mom. I give you the destroying mother. I give you her justice—from which we have never removed the eye bandage. I give you the angel—and point to the sword in her hand. I give you death –the hundred million deaths that are muttered under Yggdrasill's ash. I give you Medusa and Stheno and Euryale. I give you the harpies and the witches, and the Fates. I give you Pandora. I give you Proserpine, the Queen of Hell. The five-and-ten-cent-store Lilith, the mother of Cain, the black widow who is poisonous and eats her mate . . .

—PHILIP WYLIE, *Generation of Vipers*, 1942

N 1948, almost exactly one year after Marston's death, Frederic Wertham, a renowned forensic psychiatrist and professional rival of Lauretta Bender, Wonder Woman's primary psychiatric defender, launched a sustained attack on what he deemed the "psychopathology" of comic books. In *Collier's*, he cautioned readers about the "Horror in the Nursery," or the dysfunctional behavior that resulted from early exposure to comics. In *The Saturday Review of Literature*, Wertham offered a list of disturbing, violent behaviors committed by children, including using each other for target practice with bows and arrows, threatening to throw each other off of fire escapes, and even murdering other children and adults. The "common denominator," he wrote, was comic books, citing a clear connection between the violence in the comics and juvenile delinquency. At the time, Wertham was just beginning his research on this link, which he would publish as *The Seduction of the Innocent* (1954).[1]

Although his primary target was "crime comics," which became popular after World War II, superhero comics did not escape his condemnation. Wertham agreed with those scholars who charged that superhero comics were antidemocratic, asserting that the stories taught "prejudice" and, depending on the reader, dominance to the point of an endorsement of fascism, or submissiveness to the "blandishments of strong men who will solve all their social problems for them—by force." Wonder Woman, he believed, was a unique kind of "horror type": "She is physically very powerful, tortures men, has her own female following, is the cruel, 'phallic' woman. While she is a frightening figure for boys, she is an undesirable ideal for girls, being the exact opposite of what girls are supposed to want to be." *Wonder Woman* taught children to resolve interpersonal issues through violence, a pattern which manifested as juvenile delinquency in their teens, and she was therefore included as one of the most dangerous comics in Wertham's study.[2]

Wertham's proclamations caused much hysteria, including public bonfires of comic books. The publication of *Seduction of the Innocent* prompted the formation of a Senate Subcommittee on Juvenile Delinquency, which resulted in a national Comics Code Authority to regulate depictions of violence and sex in the comics. Comic characters were reined in, and Wonder Woman came to resemble the lovestruck teens of the flourishing genre of romance comics. But even as her power waned in the early 1950s, popular culture had begun to feature many other dangerous matriarchs to complement the superheroine's corrupt hold on American children.[3]

Of course, comics were not the sole cause of juvenile delinquency, Wertham's crusade notwithstanding. By the mid-1940s, journalists and experts had found another culprit, one located in the very heart of the American home: mothers—or rather "moms," as they would come to be known. News articles began to delineate the link between female-headed households and the rise in teen delinquency. Although motherhood was not a major theme in *Wonder Woman*, during the Amazing Amazon's heyday in the early 1940s, a transition occurred in American views of motherhood that would heavily influence pop cultural matriarchalism. Readers will remember that maternal concerns about the comics as sources of youthful corruption provided for Marston an entry point into the industry, allowing him to position himself as a psychological expert in defense of the medium. His job, via Olive Byrne's column in *Family Circle* and soon thereafter as the consulting psychologist for DC Comics, was to reassure American parents that the comics did not cause juvenile delinquency. After Marston parlayed this role into a new career as the creator of *Wonder Woman*, and as women flooded the labor force in support of the war effort, the perceived threat posed to children shifted away from the comics and increasingly toward mothers themselves. According to mid-century popular culture, maternal overinvolvement and juvenile delinquency came to constitute two of the primary psychological problems in American society.[4]

The emerging doctrine of "momism," or the belief that mothers were developing unhealthy attachments to and domination over their children, particularly their sons, tied cultural fears of matriarchy to motherhood in new ways in the 1940s and 1950s. In previous pop cultural manifestations, motherhood may have provided an original justification for matriarchal power, but maternity as an institution was either ignored, as in Oz and Wonder Woman, or seen as a reformable, positive prerequisite to female equality and advancement, as in Gilman's socialist formulations. In the middle decades of the twentieth century, however, motherhood held a central position in antimatriarchalism via momism, the theory that posited that women could abuse their power as mothers and supplant the authority of fathers to create a kind of perverted matriarchy. In the mid-century United States, paranoia about this perversion manifested as a broad fear of white, middle-class women who overmothered and weakened their sons.

Before *Wonder Woman* was born, even as Marston peddled his matriarchalist theories via academic publications and self-help books, this new branch of maternal antimatriarchalism was developing. Although it would not solidify as a theory until the early 1940s, traces of it can be found in the popular culture of the 1930s. In *The Silver Cord* (1933), Laura Hope Crews played Mrs. Phelps, a heavy-handed matriarch who forces her two sons to choose between their mother and their wives. Although she often claims that she does not have a "selfish hair on her head," Mrs. Phelps is a skilled psychological warrior, pretending to be ill, insulting her daughters-in-law, and guilt-tripping her sons in every scene. Citing the "old saying" that a "boy's best friend is his mother" (a line that would be repeated in a more famous momism horror film a few decades later), Mrs. Phelps skillfully ruins one son's engagement and nearly ends the other's marriage, all in the course of one night. The older son is barely able to flee this smother mother, while the younger is last seen dejectedly laying his head on her breast. Disgusted, his rejected fiancé decides her next move will be to "marry an orphan." The message is clear: selfish, overweening mothers like Mrs. Phelps have the power to wreck lives. This advent of the Bad Mother on screen indicated that the new opposition to matriarchalism was percolating as early as the mid-1930s.[5]

Just a few years later, this new theory would have a name. A self-described "motherless" college dropout turned successful commercial writer, Philip Wylie became frustrated by wartime propaganda after a short time working in the Office of Facts and Figures. Over the course of seven weeks in 1942, Wylie furiously "composed a book of [his] thoughts." Although he took on many institutions in *Generation of Vipers*—religion, consumerism, warfare, government, the military—the most oft-quoted section is Chapter 11, "Common Women." In this chapter, Wylie's "treatise on the matriarchy," he coined the term, *momism*, that would become the shorthand description of the perceived problem of overmothering. Much has been written about Wylie's *Generation of Vipers* as an early manifestation of Cold War–era opposition to feminism, but, as Rebecca Jo Plant points out, the book can also be seen as part of the repudiation of long-standing ideals of "moral motherhood" and "the culmination of an interwar assault on sentimental feminism." It is thus both in keeping with the conflicting ideas about the institution of motherhood found in previous matriarchalist popular culture examined herein, and a rabid departure from these works, as the matriarchy Wylie identified in 1940s America was a singularly destructive force.[6]

Wylie's innovation was not his identification of the perceived problem; he was not alone in suggesting that overmothering weakened sons and led to a host of psychological and behavioral issues. Psychiatrist David M. Levy, for instance, argued in 1943 that "maternal overprotection" yielded a range of "maladjustments" in boys, including violence against family members, misbehavior in school, difficulty forming healthy social relationships, and homosexuality. Rather, Wylie's original contribution to the developing literature was his extension of the problem—in other words, it was his argument about the broad social consequences of maternal behavior.[7]

Wylie opens *Generation of Vipers* by lamenting the "infantile" state of man in a time of global war. Like so many evolutionists, Wylie fears for the stability of contemporary civilization. He ends the opening chapter by calling "civilized men" first "medieval," and then he goes even further back along the alleged time line of human societies, deeming modern humans "cruel bumpkins and dancing savages." The "cancer of the soul" that he identifies in his peers was caused by many things, but in "Common Women," Wylie gets to the heart of the matter: "Momism," or the smothering of sons by their mothers, had produced a nation of dangerously effeminate and weak men. Wylie argues that, although the tendency toward destructive maternity might, in fact, be timeless—"The spectacle of a female devouring her young in the firm belief that it is for their own good is too old in man's legends to be overlooked by any but the most flimsily constructed society"—during World War II, Mom's devious power reached record proportions.[8]

According to Wylie, Mom is the result of American cultural forces that weakened men and empowered women. The modern "American myths and archetypes," according to Wylie, center around the wealthy Prince and his Cinderella. The latter, a slave no more, is, in Wylie's modern American version, a gold digger, social climber, and, eventually, a castrating mother. Wylie makes a historical argument about women's role in American society, explaining that by the 1940s, they were "conditioned to get the hell out of those chores" for which poor Cinderella was so pitied, and after "tens of thousands of years" of "tending babies, feeding fires, twirling flax, and pushing broom-handles," modern American women had become "idle." In this critique, Wylie dimly echoes Gilman's argument that enforced idleness kept women in a state of permanent dependency. But Wylie extends the argument further, blaming women themselves. Just as idle hands are the devil's plaything, so this new "candy-craving class" of women turned to broader pursuits: "Some women in the category instantly set out to compete with men in their own activities. . . . After the original Cinderella was enthroned in the palace, it is doubtful if she set out to instruct the national courts, train the guard, select the priests, and reorganize the peasants. American women think they can do that." In other words, according to Wylie, American women were creating a matriarchy, "in fact if not in declaration." Matriarchs, or "moms," in Wylie's sneering parlance, are the "end product" of Cinderella.[9]

Having "served and observed the matriarchy," Wylie positions himself as something of an anthropologist. Referring back to his historical argument, Wylie explains that "until very recently" in human history, women "died of hard work," but because of their longer lifespans in the 1940s, "megaloid momworship" is evident everywhere. The specter of military men spelling out "mom" on a drill field is but one indication of her elevated status:

> Disguised as good old mom, dear old mom, sweet old mom, your loving mom, and so on, she is the bride at every funeral and the corpse at every wedding. Men live for her and die for her, dote upon her and whisper her name as they pass away, and I believe she has now achieved, in the hierarchy of miscellaneous articles, a spot next to the Bible and the Flag, being reckoned part of both in a way."

Women, Wylie explains, control the majority of wealth in the United States, having achieved this status by convincing men to support them. The "grip of the matriarchy" was first felt with the success of women's suffrage, which, Wylie maintains, caused rapid social decline in the form of "political scurviness, hoodlumism, gangsterism, labor strife, monopolistic thuggery, moral degeneration, civic corruption, smuggling, bribery, theft, murder, homosexuality, drunkenness, financial depression, chaos, and war."[10]

Wylie's antimatriarchalism thoroughly places female power within the "savage" stage of evolutionism. The "common" Mom is a drag on American civilization: "Rather than take up her democratic responsibility in this mighty and tottering republic, she will bring it crashing down." As antisuffragists had warned decades before, her tool of imperial destruction is gender inversion. "Mom" and her "co-cannibals" do not just intimidate men; Wylie intimates that these women are, in fact, reversing the gender order so that they functioned *as* men. "Mom," he explains, had "donned the breeches of Uncle Sam." She is "a great little guy" who had taken "over the male functions," an "American pope" with "captive sons" who dare not threaten her power. Only middle-aged men like Wylie descry "the "gynecocracy" that had produced this "generation of vipers." The mass of men are "feminine tools" of this "dynasty of the dames," duped and subdued into submission by propagandistic paeans to American motherhood that rivaled the work of Goebbels. No mere subtype of American woman, Wylie depicts "mom" as rapacious, emasculating, and nothing less than the cause of World War II. She is a constant and continuous danger, as she reproduced her own kind rapidly:

> I give you mom. I give you the destroying mother. I give you her justice—from which we have never removed the eye bandage. I give you the angel—and point to the sword in her hand. I give you death –the hundred million deaths that are muttered under Yggdrasill's ash. I give you Medusa and Stheno and Euryale. I give you the harpies and the witches, and the Fates. I give you Pandora. I give you Proserpine, the Queen of Hell. The five-and-ten-cent-store Lilith, the mother of Cain, the black widow who is poisonous and eats her mate, and I designate at the bottom of your program the grand finale of all the soap operas: the mother of America's Cinderella.

In other words, as Mom virtually castrates her sons, she empowers her daughters to do the same, ensuring the continuation and consolidation of the American matriarchy that so troubled Wylie.[11]

This argument, it turns out, sold very well. Wylie's scathing takedown of America's "sacred cows" sold almost two hundred thousand copies and went through twenty printings as a hardback. In the mid-1950s, Wylie claimed that he had received between 50,000 and 60,000 letters from readers of *Generation of Vipers*. Although readers responded to the various topics that Wylie excoriated, by far the most famous section was his chapter on momism.[12]

Wylie did not predict that his mother-blaming screed would be the source of his lasting fame; in fact, in his 1945 postscript about the audience response to *Generation of Vipers*, he did not mention momism at all. Yet that was the year that momism came into its own, as the term began to appear in both the media and in academic texts, both of which treated overmothering as a dire social problem and momism specifically as "an essentially accurate, if spiteful, analysis of the middle-class American family." Carl Jung read *Generation of Vipers* "from cover to cover with the most intense interest," and he promised Wylie in 1947 that he was "spreading its fame" in Europe. Although Wylie was flattered by Jung's stamp of approval, even asking him at one point for authentication of "the fact that I do comprehend [Jung's] basic theory," he was very surprised by how firmly the culture latched on to his chapter on women. He explained in 1954 that "the whole thing was a gag" that he found "hilariously funny." He continued: "I didn't expect to become known for the rest of my life as a woman hater. That's the first thing they'll put in my obituary—a woman hater." His satirical intent notwithstanding, Wylie's attack would be the most memorable of the many cultural critiques of matriarchy in the 1940s.[13]

Wylie's diagnosis of momism spread quickly to popular media, as women's magazines like the *Ladies' Home Journal* questioned: "Are American Moms a Menace?" The answer was resoundingly affirmative; weakened paternal influence exacerbated Mom's power such that she transformed her sons into "helpless ninnies" who were "hypersensitive, worrisome, fussy, vain." No longer "sweet, doting and self-sacrificing," the American Mom was "stern, capable and domineering," a clearly "dangerous influence on her sons and a threat to our national security." The magazine included a Freudian list of "don'ts" so as to avoid momism, which included instructions not to rear sons "in an excessively female atmosphere" and the administration of "masculine vitamins" to combat Mom's more pernicious effects.[14]

Within a few years, weak men and world war were not the only things blamed on Mom; she was held responsible for the spread of communism, as well. The *Washington Post* quoted Mrs. William C. Reed, the national president of the American Legion Auxiliary, who claimed that the clamor of Moms for their boys to come home postwar was selfish and misguided. She explained: "This resulted in demobilization at a time when American might in Europe would have held the Iron Curtain back."[15]

Mom's power was linked to masculine fragility in Cold War politics, which featured polar images positing that anything "soft" or "feminine" was a national threat. Edward Strecker, professor of psychiatry at the University of Pennsylvania, former president of the American Psychiatric Association, and special consultant to the secretary of war and surgeons general of the army and navy, was one of the first experts to offer evidence for the link between overmothering and unfitness for military service, and he used Wylie's terminology of momism, which would thereafter permeate academic literature, to do so. In 1945, Strecker gave a lecture entitled "Psychiatry Speaks to Democracy," which would become known as "the Mom lecture" due to his targeting of American mothers. The lecture was popular enough that Strecker published articles and a book based on his premise, an indictment of "the doting 'mom' for her sins against her children and the nation."[16]

Specifically, Strecker was moved to go public with his concern about the amount of psychological neuroses he found in potential army recruits during World War II—over 1,800,000 men were rejected, while another half a million were discharged due to mental illness. In a 1946 article, Strecker argued that it was not "difficult" to determine the source of these psychological problems: "Given the opportunity of having known these young men of 18 to 22 when they were 8 to 12 years old and particularly *having known their mothers*, a competent psychiatrist could have forecast with reasonable accuracy their future military ineffectiveness." He went on to "indict a considerable number of mothers," or the "MOM," as he put it, "who refuses to emancipate the child," binding her offspring to her via metaphorical "silver cords" of varying lengths.[17]

The response to his articles and the success of his lectures prompted Strecker to compile his observations in a book. *Their Mothers' Sons: The Psychiatrist Examines an American Problem* was a "timely warning concerning a system which condemns enormous numbers of men to a miserable, maladjusted life because 'Mom' has never weaned her son emotionally." Strecker opened by defining his terms: "'Mom' as I have used it, and will use it throughout this book, is merely a convenient verbal hook upon which to hang an indictment of the woman who has failed in the elementary function of weaning her offspring emotionally as well as physically." Describing what will sound to twenty-first century readers like posttraumatic stress disorder, Strecker argued that the persistent psychiatric problems he found among veterans were not, as in the case of PTSD, common responses to the experience of warfare, but rather symptoms of "immaturity" based on a failure to cut the "emotional apron strings," or the "Silver Cord" between mother and son.[18]

Momism flourished in what Strecker deemed "our matriarchy," and the consequences were dangerous. The "immature" American men who were unfit to defend the nation were "enwombed psychologically" and therefore the "gravest menace" facing the United States. Moreover, momism, according to Strecker, was Nazism within the home. The Third Reich and the Japanese Empire, he argued, were both "momarchies" that abused and emasculated their citizens to the point of fomenting globally destructive world conflict; "Hitler, Mussolini, and Stalin," he speculated, "probably became too deeply attached to their mothers." And so he addressed American moms directly in the press release for the book: "What is happening to that son of yours? Are you training him to think and act for himself, or are you smothering him with your ideas and your authority? Are you starting him along the road to happiness, or the road to a neurosis? Are you really his friend or his well-meaning enemy?" The potential danger was not simply the psychiatric well-being of America's sons. Rather, the safety of the nation was at stake.[19]

The popularity of Strecker's expert diagnosis of the national disorder of momism led other academics, including sociologists and psychoanalysts, to follow suit. Like Wylie's "treatise on the matriarchy," Strecker's academic work was an "instant bestseller" that generated even more media coverage condemning Mom. "Doting mothers are the ruination of their children and collectively, on that account, a deadly menace to society," began the *New York Times* review of *Their Mothers' Sons*. The "parasitic activity" of "maternal scheming" resulted in neuroses, psychoses, and general insanity, including schizophrenia, "the supreme product of motherhood run wild." The *Times* reviewer took exception with Strecker's tone—"at times the reader gets the impression that Dr. Strecker would improve a revolting situation by the procedure of beating people's brains out"—but not with his conclusions: "There is no doubt that he has performed a genuine service by striking with all his authority at the root of a social ill."[20]

Momism, invented as a joke by Wylie and legitimized as a psychological diagnosis by Strecker, proved to be so popular that by the late 1940s, *Esquire* and *Reader's Digest* openly lamented the development of a "near-matriarchy." In 1947, in *Modern Woman: The Lost Sex,* psychiatrist Marynia F. Farnham and journalist Ferdinand Lundberg warned of the "masculinization" of women as they developed "aggression, dominance, independence and power." That same year, the *Washington Post* reported that "everyone is taking a whack at 'Mom' these days," blaming her for "the Nation's alarming mental illness and juvenile delinquency, for the boyishness of American men, for virtually all adults who are soft, weak, selfish, maladjusted, and incompetent."[21]

Given this media coverage, it did not take long for Mom to make her way into popular culture, and an array of films offered cautionary tales about the devastating effects of maternal power. As one historian of the 1950s has noted, "rarely has family life looked so repulsive in the movies of a decade that also tried to uphold the family as an institution," and the source of repulsion in these films was often the mother. Although the evil stepmothers and queens of the golden era of Disney—hell-bent on domestic slavery (*Cinderella* (1950) or murder (*Snow White* (1937) and *Sleeping Beauty* (1959))—offered some of the most fearsome matriarchs of mid-century cinema, the real danger posed by Mom, according to popular dramas of the era, was to sons.[22]

Alfred Hitchcock provided American audiences with the smothering mother taken to the most extreme conclusion in *Psycho* (1960). Bates's violent disorder is completely homegrown, wrought by his dear old Mom. Alternately calling him "boy," "half a man," and "Mamma's Boy," Mrs. Bates thoroughly controls Norman, who fantasizes in the novel on which the film is based about strangling his mother "with her own Silver Cord," a reference to what Strecker called a continued "umbilical dependence" that kept sons "paddling about in a kind of psychological amniotic fluid rather than letting them swim away with the bold and decisive strokes of maturity from the emotional womb." Just as Mom symbolically castrated Norman, so, too, would he render his female victims ineffectual through murder, committed in Mrs. Bates's clothing, no less. Viewers hear Norman and his mother fight about the female guest at their motel; echoing Dr. Strecker's "cruelest" type of Mom—she "who closes the door of her children's lives against the vista of normal and unwholesome sex and fastens it securely with her silver cord"—Mrs. Bates is distraught at the idea that Norman might have another woman, "a strange young girl" who might be a potential sexual partner, in his life. Despite the vicious fights that viewers hear between Norman and his mother, he quotes the original momism film, *The Silver Cord,* explaining that "a boy's best friend is his mother," and claiming that it is his duty to care for her. Adult Norman duly remains a child, with a bedroom full of tiny furniture and toys, even after her death.[23]

In fact, the momism is so complete in this film that Norman, viewers learn at the end of the film, is Mother—she has, in essence, devoured her young. A decade earlier, he murdered his mother, and via Norman's intense psychological personality disorder, Mrs. Bates repeatedly replicates his crime, inhabiting his body in order to eliminate threats to her influence. The implication here is that she did not simply smother him emotionally as a child, but that even ten years after her death, she controls both his bodily existence and his deranged mind. This diagnosis is scripted directly from the literature on momism. Strecker argued in 1946 that schizophrenia was a "surrogate" for Mom, as "in many schizophrenia patients a true bill of indictment can be drawn against mom—indictment for failure to prepare the child to meet even the minimal demands of adult life." This explanation is echoed by the psychiatrist in *Psycho* who describes Norman's split personality: "He was never all Norman, but he was often only Mother." He concludes: "Like a dutiful son, he cleaned up all traces of the crimes he was convinced his mother had committed. . . . He tried to *be* his mother. And now he is." Thus, although Mother Bates's murdered corpse decays in the cellar, it is really she who has destroyed her son. One of the final shots of the film is of Norman's face merging with his dead mother's skull, the extreme result of momism in which Mom enacts her need to "live through the child."[24]

And Norman Bates, violent creep though he was, was not even the worst outcome of momism. Mom could, as Wylie and Strecker had warned, be a threat to national security. Years before *Psycho,* Alfred Hitchcock ventured into matriarchalism with one of the first big-screen examples of momism as a national danger in *Notorious* (1946), starring Ingrid Bergman and Cary Grant. To make up for her father's treasonous espionage, protagonist Alicia Huberman agrees to "work for Uncle Sam" by meeting, wooing, and eventually marrying a Nazi working in Rio. The Nazi operative, Alex Sebastian, has a strange personal life; his household features his domineering mother and a German scientist who is experimenting with uranium. Of these two, Mrs. Sebastian is the bigger threat. When she discovers Alicia's true identity as an American spy, she sets about slowly poisoning Alicia, sewing calmly as Alicia writhes in pain. At the moment of truth, when Alicia is rescued, it is Mrs. Sebastian who speaks for her impotent son. Momism in this film is a clear and present danger more powerful than, and even perhaps the cause of, Nazism.[25]

As Hollywood's enemy switched from the Third Reich to the Red Army after an alliance with the House Unamerican Activities Committee, films began to detail the links between momism and communism. The opening dialogue in *My Son John* (1952)—"Mother! We're waiting!"—indicates that Lucille Jefferson, the family matriarch, is the center of this narrative. Although she has to be pulled from the window of the car that was taking her two youngest sons off to enlist in the Navy during World War II, it is her titular oldest son John that commands her attention. One film historian describes Lucille as a character from "a moldy textbook on male homosexuality," as she plays the overweening Mom to her "sly, furtive" son. John openly mocks his father's patriotism as well as his mother's love when she nostalgically, if manically, sings him a nursery rhyme that used to be his favorite. His drunken and goofy father questions if John has become "one of those guys we should be alert about," while his mother is slow to suspect her beloved son's new communist persuasion.[26]

It becomes clear why when John and Lucille discuss their values; when John says he loves "humanity" and "the downtrodden," Lucille understands this to be her doing, as part of his good, Christian upbringing. She cries, "You're a part of me, and it's always been my prayer that whatever's good in me would be a part of you." He is her "tomorrow," or so she thinks until the FBI shows up to investigate John for communist activities. She deploys all of the momism tactics, alternately accusing him, guilt-tripping him, and cheering for the good son he used to be. John escapes the FBI as Lucille breaks down and takes to the bed, but John's escape is fruitless—he is haunted by his mother's voice and the sound of college graduates singing "Hail to Mother." In the end, it is Lucille—the matriarch, the only one with any power over the national security threat posed by her son—not the feckless FBI or John's drunken father, who convinces him to confess. Here, then, momism was the source of communist infiltration, but it also, paradoxically, served as its remedy, as only Mom could convince the spy to change his dangerous ways (albeit too late, as he is killed by his former communist comrades on the way to confess to the authorities).[27]

A decade later, Mom was not just the dysfunctional reason behind her son's communism; she was also, according to *The Manchurian Candidate* (1962), the mastermind of Soviet strategy. The first scenes establish the dark tone of this heavy-handed drama featuring Raymond Shaw, the decorated soldier who "despises" his mother, her "disgusting" ambition, and her marriage to a red-baiting senator. In a complicated plot involving recurring nightmares, brainwashing, and dysfunctional family dynamics, Shaw's mother oversees the preparations for global domination: the development of her son into an assassinating automaton, murder in Manchuria, Russian cover-up, recurring psychological fallout for all of the soldiers present, and—until she is stopped at the very end—her own takeover of the US government through her emasculated politician husband. Shaw laments, "It is a terrible thing to hate your mother," but she is so broad a threat that he must defeat her to save himself and the nation. She is destructive domestically—she destroys her son's love life long before she has him brainwashed into becoming an assassin, whereupon she has him murder both his lover and her father—and internationally, as the Russians, the Chinese, and the unwitting Americans all do the bidding of this "red queen." This seemingly proper political wife and doting mother, then, could be more dangerous than the threat of Russian nuclear weapons, the communist takeover of Korea, or the paranoid McCarthyites at home. She was the singular architect of "unspeakable acts" that represented the extent of the damage wrought by an unrestrained mother.[28]

Women thus played a role in the on-screen drama of the Cold War as that most acute potential threat, Moms who colluded with the enemy. In the daily news, however, matriarchal fears became more narrowly geographically focused by mid-century, as "suburban suffering" became a frequent pop cultural concern. The decline in housing construction during the Depression and the war coupled with the rising birthrate and postwar prosperity to create a suburban development boom. By 1960, as many Americans lived in the suburbs as in urban areas, and this new culture was reportedly "a female world, especially during the day." Postwar suburbanization, according to one sociologist, entailed both "a real and symbolic removal of women from the city and the public" to uniform neighborhoods in which housewives had little to no interaction with employed adults beyond their husbands.[29]

David Riesman acknowledged this spatial redistribution of gendered power in his 1950 best-selling sociological analysis, *The Lonely Crowd*. "Uneasiness" caused by the recent wartime liberation of women, Riesman argued, was "one source of the current attempts to reprivatize women by redefining their roles in some comfortable domestic and traditional way" in the booming American suburbs. Scholars of the "new suburban history" have shown that mid-century American suburbs were much more complex and troubled than the uniform representations of happy, heterosexual, nuclear families on television might indicate. At the time, acknowledgment of this complexity was often articulated through the fears of "momarchy" in the suburban American home.[30]

In 1954, Philip Wylie was asked to write a new introduction for the twentieth printing of *Generation of Vipers*. He took the opportunity to double down on momism, warning that Mom's reach had spread and noting that researchers had recently discovered the "Cinderella in the suburbs," who hides her "rat-warren" of a mind underneath a thin veneer of attractive conformity and security. The much-studied soullessness of the American suburbs, then, was her deliberate doing.[31]

Despite the heavy cultural embrace of the traditional roles of male breadwinner and female homemaker, the mid-century American suburbs hosted unanticipated problems of gender, especially the perceived "loss of male authority, oppression, and subordination of man in the modern family." This dysfunction generated a series of bestsellers concerned with the so-called "crisis in masculinity" engendered by the feminizing forces of the socioeconomic changes that accompanied suburbanization. David Riesman, in *The Lonely Crowd*, contrasted the "inner direction" of the nineteenth-century self-made man with the feminized "other direction" of mid-century corporate commuters and conformists who emulated mass culture. In 1956, William H. Whyte extended Riesman's argument, arguing that corporate America's "social ethic" reached into the monotonous suburbs, which he deemed the "dormitory" of the soulless "organization man." Sloan Wilson's *The Man in the Gray Flannel Suit* (1955) depicted the upwardly mobile despair of the middle-class suburbs, symbolized on the first page of the novel by the question mark-shaped crack in the living room wall, left there by a vase thrown by the main character, Tom Rath, in a fit over money problems. Tom and his wife Betsy do not dwell on the symbolism of the crack, although Wilson tells readers on the following page that "without talking about it much, they both began to think of the house as a trap, and they no more enjoyed refurbishing it than a prisoner would delight in shining up the bars of his cell."[32]

The organization man's problems thus reached far beyond the corporate office. Like the question mark on the wall of the Raths' suburban ranch house, the so-called "crack in the picture window"—the title of John Keats's sarcastic take on the problems plaguing the suburbs—was a prescient metaphor that indicated mid-century matriarchal fears. Looming over the entire plot of *The Man in the Gray Flannel Suit* is Tom's grandmother, the matriarch who secured him a corporate job in the first place. Grandmother presides over the family from her "dwarfed castle." She is an "imperious" Mom whose son, Tom's father, was the type of character that had so concerned Dr. Strecker during World War II: he had a nervous breakdown, was removed from military service, and possibly committed suicide. Tom grows up "lusting" after Grandmother's money, and his wife Betsy is heir to her seat as family matriarch. Almost as soon as Grandmother dies, Betsy argues with Tom over her mansion and land, challenging his masculinity and calling him a coward. Concluding that Tom has "*no guts*," Betsy takes charge, inaugurating a "new regime," dictating Tom's diet and recreational habits, and literally taking the wheel to drive him to catch the train for work. The film based on the novel, released the same year as *The Organization Man* (1956), eliminates Grandmother (she is already dead when the plot begins), but Betsy is Mom from the opening scene, when she is shown driving Tom home from work and then berating him for having "lost [his] guts" a few minutes later. Tom is restless, wanting desperately to "do something" to make Betsy "proud" as she henpecks him throughout the film. In this popular film, Betsy exemplifies the "family-oriented matriarchs" of the Cold War–era suburbs. Because, as historians have shown, the suburban home was the locus of security against the "terrors of the atomic age," the perceived inversion of gender roles represented by women who ruled their communities during the day sans men prompted this new concern about momism.[33]

As with the original theory of momism, the suburban matriarchy received an academic boost from Leonard J. Duhl, a psychiatrist from the National Institute of Mental Health, who identified three warning signs in the suburbs: "That it is becoming a woman's society—and only a 'bedroom community' for men. That its residents are segregated from a normal variety of living experiences. That it offers mental health hazards to children (and women as well) through its conformity and its matriarchal set-up." Duhl here identified dual crises—conformity and masculinity—with matriarchy as a common denominator of each. He explained, "Father races out of the house early in the morning on his way to work, not to return till late at night, and leaves mother not only to care for the home, but to be the ruler of daytime suburbia," and this situation resulted in a "matriarchal society, with children who know men only as nighttime residents and weekend guests." Duhl made it his mission to "save the mental health of suburban 'matriarchal societies.'" In the "socially and economically segregated suburbs," Duhl argued, the "almost exclusive" rule of women "may leave an imprint on the minds and the health of men." He continued: "Suburbia has this absence of fathers in part, which may tend to yield results similar to what we had during the war. We have a segregated, one socio-economic level, matriarchal society that offers limited experience to the growing child."[34]

Duhl was not alone in his assessment of the matriarchal dangers of the suburbs. Media reports alleged that the lack of privacy and individuality in suburban homes would stunt male emotional growth, as suburban children "live[d] in a woman's world, both at home and at school." The solution was to combat the dual forces—dominant women and collective conformity—that were allegedly softening American manhood through the integration of more men into the suburbs and the broader integration of suburban people with other types of neighborhoods to break up the conformity of the "standardized community."[35]

The fears of the change represented by suburbanization spawned an entire body of literature in the late 1950s devoted to detailing its dangers. According to these texts, the chain reaction began something like this: conformity at work combined with conformity in suburban home life to deplete the personality of and emasculate the white, middle-class, American male. Writer John Keats explained in 1956:

> In any one of these new neighborhoods, be it in Hartford or Philadel-phia, you can be certain all other houses will be precisely like yours, inhabited by people whose age, income, number of children, problems, habits, conversation, dress, possessions and perhaps even blood type are precisely like yours. . . . In short, ladies and gentlemen, we offer here for your inspection facts relative to today's housing developments— developments conceived in error, nurtured by greed, corroding every-thing they touch. They destroyed established cities and trade patterns, and actually drive mad myriads of housewives shut up in them.

Keats goes on to describe the various details of *The Crack in the Picture Window*—his metaphor for the dark side of suburbanization—by following the lives of the fictitious Drone family. The dysfunction of the suburbs, the "stifling monotony" from which "there was no escape," in Keats's account and others, is heavily gendered; the Drones, in fact, end up in the suburb of Roll-ing Knolls by virtue of an ultimatum from the screaming, glaring young house-wife, Mary Drone. Once settled in the suburbs, the Drones are accosted by local matriarchs in the form of citizens' associations. Quoting Harold Mendelsohn of American University's Bureau of Social Research, Keats explains that the lack of privacy in the suburbs dictates that the "women become involved in one another's emotional problems," joining community organizations to resist social ostracism and loneliness.[36]

Keats's suburbs are a female world. A regular daily scene involves Mary Drone taking her children out to play on the "tiny lawn," when "at precisely the same moment Mary stepped out of her door on our sample Tuesday, Gladys Fecund, Henrietta Spleen, Maryann Faint, Jane Amiable, and Eve Wild emerged from their houses with their children" to do exactly the same thing. The women communicate in an endless loop of the same complaints, and they convene daily to list the various crimes against them. As their children played, "The good ladies of Rolling Knolls hotted the fire higher and higher, lashed themselves into a perfect frenzy against the men who'd betrayed them into matrimony." After spending the days collectively bashing their offensive partners, the women are angry, almost feral: "By the time they went their several ways to put their get to bed, the ladies' eyes were snapping, their pulses racing; their lips were icy slits. If any fool of a husband had showed himself in that neighborhood at that time, his life wouldn't have been worth a Roosevelt dollar." Although Mary Drone tries to set herself apart from her neighbors, even to the point of taking a ceramics course to get out of the house at night, the dynamic in her household is no different. Keats ironically refers to John Drone as "master of all he surveyed" just before he is cowed by his wife's frustrated shrieking about the inadequacy of their household appliances.[37]

The women of the suburbs rage and plot together during the day, and they nag and silence their husbands at night. In their crushing boredom, these "development women" turn their attention to every parenting "fad," "experiment[ing] in How To with their children," with the potential consequence of becoming the Moms who spawned various dangers ranging from homosexuality, to delinquency, to communism. Even when the Drones escape by upgrading to a bigger house in a different suburb, they remain part of this monotonous gendered system. Mary Drone, at first pleased with their escape to new surroundings, is thunderstruck to discover that "everywhere she looked, she saw houses exactly like her own, row on row of them, the same, the same, the same." Like clockwork, Mary is accosted by a neighbor from the Beleaguered Women community organization, and the process of indoctrination into the local matriarchy begins again. According to Keats, across the country each evening, suburban husbands relinquished any remnants of patriarchal control upon setting foot in their neighborhoods, whereupon the emasculation of the organization man was complete, finished off by the suburban momarchy.[38]

By 1958, these cultural concerns were widespread enough that *Look* magazine collected them in *The Decline of the American Male*. The collection offered the usual warnings about male conformity, beginning with an essay by J. Robert Moskin entitled "Why Do Women Dominate Him?" On the first page, beneath an illustration of a hulking woman towering over a tiny man, Moskin argues that "scientists who study human behavior fear that the American male is now dominated by the American female." No longer the "masculine, strong-minded man who pioneered the continent and built America's greatness," the American man, defeated by the dual threats of Momism and the "developing emancipation of the female," had become fatigued, passive, anxiety-ridden, and impotent. Citing life span, labor, consumer, and voting statistics, Moskin argues that American women had the means to take over society. He concludes: "It is certain that, as women grow even more numerous and more dominant, we will have to invent new meanings and myths for maleness in America, because, as psychiatrist Dr. Irene Josselyn warns, 'we are drifting toward a social structure made up of he-women and she-men."[39]

As belief in this new social system grew, the suburban matriarchy found its way into popular culture in various ways, as did opposition to it. Each evening, Americans were treated to soothing visions of the passive, white, middle-class American mother on popular sitcoms like *The Donna Reed Show* (1958–1966), *Leave It to Beaver* (1957–1963), and *Ozzie and Harriet* (1952–1966). The very title *Father Knows Best* denotes that the prime-time mother was no matriarch, even if she sometimes seemed to have an undue influence over her children while her husband was away at work each day. The breadwinners of these shows were almost never shown at work, which underscored fatherhood as their major role and avoided the airing of any anxieties about the soullessness of the mid-century males' middle-class occupations or the corresponding female dominance in the suburbs. These nuclear family models served as counterpart to the equally stereotypical figures that populated the most popular television shows of the 1950s and 1960s, Westerns, which, like Buffalo Bill's Wild West Show, "extolled male adventurism," "naturalized female drudgery," and promoted a patriarchal vision of "John Wayne's America." Matriarchal fears were further tempered after 1956, the centennial anniversary of L. Frank Baum's birth, when the network CBS first acquired the television rights to *The Wizard of Oz*. American viewers were treated annually to feminist matriarchalism as a "bad dream," to use Dorothy's characterization, in their own living rooms. The major networks competed to show the film, hosted by a celebrity in commercial prime time, each winter after 1959.[40]

June Cleaver et al. served as the solution to the cautionary tale provided by the bad matriarchs of daytime television, because if perfect mothers ruled prime time, soap opera representations were a different story. John Crosby of the *Washington Post* noted in 1953 that "motherhood, as practiced on TV soaps, is an absolutely agonizing experience either for the mother or the child or both." He cites "triple momism"—three Wylie-esque "mom" characters—on one soap opera, "double momism" on another, and ambitious "stage" momism on a third. Even on the one soap opera on which there were fewer mother characters, he argued that "momism is dormant; a female character has a "bad mother complex," and "while it isn't causing any trouble at the moment," Crosby predicted, "some instinct tells me, it will, it will." A "great man short-age" had daytime television's female characters "claw[ing] each other's eyes out," so that even those women who were not destructive moms were engaged in "savage contests" and catfights." He concluded: "Between motherhood and love, life isn't worth living in this jungle." Here we see the long reach of matri-archalist evolutionism: these daytime stars were the primitive matriarchs of the kill-or-be-eaten "savage" stage of human social development.[41]

These barbaric Amazons contrasted perfectly with the number-one day-time show of the late 1950s and early 1960s, Disney's *Queen For a Day*, on which depressed and desperate housewives competed for the ultimate solu-tions to their problems: jewelry or appliances. Thus, matriarchs were fun on soap operas, but they were poor role models who always suffered in the end, while real American women were self-sacrificing martyrs whose only respite was a game show appearance. "Queen" here denoted consumerist domesticity, not the much-feared socioeconomic power of suburban moms.[42]

These varied small-screen representations notwithstanding, the mid-century matriarchy had its most memorable roles in the literature and films of the 1950s. Fears of the matriarchy undergirded the mid-'50s paranoia over juvenile delinquency, most famously in *Rebel Without a Cause*. Based on the 1944 book of the same name by Robert M. Lindner, the film features James Dean as Jim Stark, a deviant but sensitive teen who defies his overbearing mother and ineffectual father. From the opening shot, young Jim is depicted as troubled and immature, as he lies drunkenly on the ground playing with a toy, curling into the fetal position as sirens sound. Momism enters in the second scene, when Mrs. Stark storms the police department screeching at Jim. Described in the book as the "over-solicitous" and "overprotective" mother of a "criminal psychopath," the film version of Mrs. Stark is an anxious maternal martyr who constantly interrogates Jim about where he's been; she peppers her interrogations with guilt-trips about her many sacrifices, including direct references to how she "almost died giving birth to" Jim. This family features a case of double momism, as Mr. Stark's mother henpecks both her son and his wife. Viewers understand this to be a multigenerational problem; when Jim refuses breakfast on his first day of school, Mr. Stark says, cheerily and cluelessly, "My first day of school, Mother made me eat so much I couldn't even swallow until recess." Of his grandmother, Jim jokes, "Somebody ought to put poison in her Epsom salts."[43]

If Jim is the rebel, Mr. Stark is the underdog in this matriarchy, cowering in a frilly apron and at one point even being confused by Jim for "Mom." Wylie wrote at length about the role of the weak father, who allows his wife to "thrust her oar into the very guts of man—and while she has made him think she is operating a gondola through the tunnels of love, and even believes it herself, she is actually taking tickets for the one-way ferry ride across the Styx." Dr. Strecker agreed with this assessment, arguing that "when an emotionally immature man marries a mature woman," the pair can merge to foment a kind of double momism: "sometimes and often, 'Pop' is mom." Accordingly, although he directs his pleas for help to his father, Jim is coded as a mama's boy—frequently gulping milk straight from the bottle throughout the film—who is trying desperately to cut the "silver cord." Removed from his family for a private talk with a police officer, Jim begs to be locked up, because he cannot endure his family dynamic. "She eats him alive and he takes it," he explains to the officer. "If he had the guts to knock Mom cold once, then maybe she'd be happy and she'd stop picking on him—'cause they make mush out of him, you know?" Lindner explains in the book that "characteristically, retribution is directed against the father," and in the film, Jim challenges his father to "stand up" for him, at one point even yanking him to his feet and attempting to choke him. He then kicks a portrait of his mother and storms out of the house to create his own imaginary family.[44]

According to *Rebel Without a Cause*, the terrible consequences of momism include juvenile delinquency and broken homes. But the film does offer solutions. Jim breaks free of his parents by forming his own partnership with Judy, played by Natalie Wood, and they serve as parental stand-ins to young Plato

(Sal Mineo), whose parents are nowhere to be found. The imaginary family experiences great tragedy when the unbalanced Plato is shot and killed by the police; Jim and Judy hover over his corpse like grieving parents, fixing his jacket and shoes. This tragedy, however, strengthens the Stark men. As Jim walks off screen with Judy, his father promises to be "strong," and Mrs. Stark is, for the first time, completely silent. The cure for momism here is to "man up" and to act the part of teenaged patriarch to show the effeminate father and domineering mother how it's done. This proved to be a popular message, as *Rebel Without a Cause* was nominated for three Oscars, tapped into the new teen market of moviegoers, and thereafter served as a "blueprint for all youth rebellion films."[45]

Mom and her accompanying specter, the weak American father, were also blamed for lifelong problems such as alcoholism. Strecker scripted this diagnosis in his first article on momism, in which he argued that "alcohol is a mom that can be poured into a glass." One oft-quoted priest who worked with alcoholics argued that "most of the alcoholics" he knew were "spoiled or frustrated" as children; this lecture was covered under the headline "Priest Sees Alcoholism Caused by 'Momism.'" Although the links between momism and addiction were debunked by Harvard's "cradle-to-compulsion" study in the late 1950s, and a 1960 longitudinal study of 650 boys in suburban Cambridge argued that "inadequate or nonfunctioning fathers," rather than "overprotective mothers," played a role in the adult onset of alcoholism in their sons, according to popular culture, Mom was responsible for all psychological and behavioral ills.[46]

As late as 1966, Mom was blamed for numerous social problems, as well, including the dropout rate in the Peace Corps. In fact, according to one Yale study, deprivation could be preferable to momism, as motherless monkeys raised in "stimulating environments" with toys and playmates functioned better than those raised in "deprived environments" alone with their mothers. Dubbed the "Momism Experiment" in the popular press, the study was widely quoted as one indicating the "problems of overmothering." Antimatriarchalism in the mid-century guise of momism thus proved to be extraordinarily malleable in its applicability to the social problem du jour.[47]

In the "momarchy," women's domestic power over children, husbands, and neighborhoods spilled into socioeconomic power; as consumers and local leaders, these suburban matriarchs thus dominated the postwar American landscape. According to their critics, their rule presaged a devolution of society, as they produced emasculated, delinquent men and Cinderella, or Mom-clone, daughters. The decline predicted by these critics ranged from the comical, as in Keats's descriptions of covens of neighborhood women screeching about and at their hapless husbands, to the dangerous, as in the cold-blooded murders and near-coup in *The Manchurian Candidate*. Each representation rested upon the original, sexist, antimatriarchalist premise of evolutionism and antisuffragism: female power entailed a savage, uncivilized society that could only be rescued by a return to traditional masculinity, as when Raymond assassinates his mother in *The Manchurian Candidate* and Jim forms his own makeshift, heterosexual, nuclear family in *Rebel Without a Cause*.

But in the early 1960s, one journalist famously flipped the script, depicting momism as the dysfunctional result of patriarchy. Betty Friedan's *The Feminine Mystique* (1963) is a major feminist critique of the mid-twentieth century suburban cult of domesticity, and her version of this cult featured miserable moms that in some ways conformed to the caricatures of Wylie and Keats. Friedan wrote: "If an able American woman does not use her human energy and ability in some meaningful pursuit, she will fritter away her energy in neurotic symptoms, or unproductive exercise, or destructive 'love.'" To Friedan, this momism was a result of, rather than a challenge to, the systematic organization of male dominance, and significantly, these Moms, although they conformed to the matriarchalist stereotype that had graced pop culture for two decades, did not experience their roles as powerful.[48]

Friedan's interviewees expressed their feelings of powerlessness in dire terms. "I feel as if I don't exist," said one. Explained another: "I'm desperate. I begin to feel I have no personality. I'm a server of food and a putter-on of pants and a bedmaker, somebody who can be called on when you want something." They reported feeling like objects, and being defined only in relation to their families: "The problem is always being the children's mommy, or the minister's wife and never being myself." Friedan described various symptoms, from extreme and prolonged fatigue to "a childlike kind of dependence." Unlike the suburban shrews of Keats's *The Crack in the Picture Window*, who spent their days storing pent-up rage that they then used to emasculate their husbands and take over local politics, Friedan's housewives suffered in isolated silence, confiding only in their psychiatrists. Friedan quoted Levy's *Maternal Overprotection* and especially Strecker's *Their Mothers' Sons* at length as evidence that the mid-century cult of domesticity was dangerous for women. Although the prevailing antimatriarchal paranoia was overly concerned with the effects of momism on sons, not daughters, as was the majority of expert advice on parenting, Friedan was prescient in her indication that American mothers would do well to pay attention to their daughters, who were, by the early 1960s, forming their own beliefs about matriarchal power.[49]

Pop culture informed white suburban daughters that their mothers were alternately contented housewives or power-hungry shrews whose takeover of middle-class neighborhoods was part and parcel of their plan to dominate American society. But what these girls saw at home was often at odds with these representations. Even if they were not the miserable, "quietly desperate" housewives offered by Friedan, their mothers were generally not the domestic goddesses or mad matriarchs that pop culture made them out to be. These stereotypes—the "happy housewife heroine," the neurotic mom, the suburban matriarch—all "flattened" the historical experiences of white, middle-class women (not to mention all women who did not fit these racial and economic categories), but they were productive in unintended ways. Scholars have long pointed out that this dissonance between these messages and women's experiences set the context for the rebirth of organized feminism in the 1960s and 1970s. Specifically, this contradiction between the cultural message about the suburban matriarchy and the experiences of girls and women who exercised little, if any, socioeconomic or political power, was a source of the women's liberation movement of the 1960s and 1970s.[50]

But even after Friedan's much-cited exposure of the suburban matriarchy as a myth, mid-century matriarchal fears did not disappear. In 1964, just after the publication of *The Feminine Mystique* and a full twenty years after the publication of *Generation of Vipers*, momism so permeated American culture that filmmaker Stanley Shapiro descried the "blatantly matriarchal type of comedy that now dominates American movies and television." Situational comedies featuring the "shrewd, Machiavellian wife" indicated, to Shapiro, the blatant "matriarchal tendencies in our society." Even Wonder Woman herself was not safe. Part of the reactionary pop cultural response to the perceived presence of multiple forms of matriarchy involved taming the Amazing Amazon. Wonder Woman changed quite a bit after Marston's death under the direction of Robert Kanigher. In 1968, DC fired Kanigher and replaced him with a Denny O'Neil, a much younger writer who was fairly new to the comics. Under O'Neil's direction, Wonder Woman became plain old Diana Prince, a "normal human" who rejected her Amazonian birthright and relinquished her superpowers in order to save Steve Trevor. A princess no more, she opened a women's clothing boutique in New York and centered her life around Trevor.[51]

In 1967, the popularity of the *Batman* television show prompted the production of a short pilot for a potential *Wonder Woman* show—the first live-action appearance of the superheroine onscreen. In it, Diana, frumpy in ill-fitting clothes and large glasses, upsets her mother by falling out of her chair and refusing to eat dinner. Her mother nags her about eating, finding a husband, and wearing her galoshes, all in one five-minute argument. She fakes "pains" for attention, and refuses Diana's request that she see a doctor. "You don't know how it feels to be the mother of an unmarried daughter!," she cries, collapsing into a chair and clutching her heart. Wonder Woman became a clumsy old maid, while her mother, an Amazonian queen no more, became that fearsome maternal staple of mid-century popular culture: Mom.[52]

By the late 1960s, then, antimatriarchalism reigned in American popular culture, featuring misogynist, essentialist notions of women as controlling mothers. Although Friedan targeted momism as a perverted product of patriarchy, there were few accompanying traces of feminist matriarchalism at mid-century. While Baum's Oz series was always popular with children, Wonder Woman was, well, wonderful no more, and the works of Gage and Gilman were out of print, virtually lost to history until their rediscovery in the 1970s. When the scholars and activists of the women's liberation movement reclaimed the feminist matriarchalism of the postwar era, ameliorating this potently sexist discourse to their own ends, they thus did so with little knowledge that they were repeating history.

8

GODDESSES, EARTH MOTHERS, AND FEMALE MEN

The Matriarchies of the Women's Liberation Movement

> She had not had subservience bred into her for untold generations.
> She was one of the Others; a newer, younger breed, more vital, more
> dynamic, not controlled by hidebound traditions from a brain that was
> nearly all memory. . . . She could accept the new, shape it to her will,
> forge it into ideas undreamed by the Clan, and, in nature's way, her
> kind was destined to supplant the ancient, dying race. . . . Ayla was
> more than a threat to his masculinity, she was a threat to his existence.
> —JEAN M. AUEL, *Clan of the Cave Bear*, 1980

I N the spring of 1972, Elizabeth Holloway Marston, then in her seven-
ties, flew to New York to visit the offices of the fledgling feminist magazine *Ms.* She had gotten word that the editors planned to feature Wonder
Woman on the cover of the first issue, and, given the many changes in the
character over the years, she felt she had to check out this new incarnation
for herself. She later wrote to Marjorie Wilkes Huntley that she supported the
magazine's mission "100%," which prompted Huntley to subscribe immediately via money order. A few months later, *Ms.* debuted with a larger-than-life
cover. Under the heading "WONDER WOMAN FOR PRESIDENT," the Amazing Amazon strode over a half-urban, half-devastated landscape meant to
signify the United States and Vietnam. The issue featured a pullout comic
of Wonder Woman's introduction from the December 1941 issue of *All-Star
Comics*—the story in which the matriarchal society of Paradise Island was first
juxtaposed against the violence and corruption of "Man's World."[1]

Ms. quickly became a mouthpiece of the women's liberation movement
of the 1970s, which advocated for many things, including equal access to
rights and opportunities, true democracy, and a revolution in gender roles—
all of which were characteristics of feminist matriarchalism, as well. Within
the context of the women's liberation movement, matriarchalism flourished
throughout the 1970s, although it took two very different forms. In her book
about the academic wing of this new era of matriarchal mythology, Cynthia

Eller lists its three major premises: prehistory featured female power in reproduction, religion, economics, and politics; the transition to patriarchal social
systems destroyed prehistoric matriarchy as it was then known; and, finally,
an awareness of the "true" matriarchal history that would help to bring about
a future featuring "peace, ecological balance, and harmony between the sexes,
with women either recovering their past ascendancy, or at last establishing a
truly egalitarian society under the aegis of the goddess."[2]

Eller argues that the matriarchal myth "house of cards" does not withstand
scrutiny, that it "fails completely on historical grounds," and that challenging
this myth through evidence is "like shooting fish in a barrel," which she proceeds to do throughout *The Myth of Matriarchal Prehistory*. As with my discussion in Chapter 1 of the development of anthropological matriarchalism in the
nineteenth century, my goal here is not to prove or disprove the veracity of
the matriarchal theory of prehistory (those who are interested in that question
would do well to read both of Eller's books on the subject). Rather, the point of
this chapter is to explore the resurgence and redevelopment of feminist matriarchalism in the final decades of the twentieth century and to understand the
cultural purposes that it served. The new forms of matriarchalism recalled the
universal prehistoric matriarchies of Gage, the fantastical utopia of Baum, the
all-female society of Gilman, and the unique female powers of Marston's superheroine. But one of the new versions also went beyond its forebears, finally
severing the link between matriarchalism and gender essentialism via radical
feminist science fiction.[3]

As the feminist movement developed in reaction to conservative Cold
War culture and out of women's experiences in the other social movements of
the 1960s—the civil rights movement, the student movement, the New Left,
the antiwar movement—the "central problematic of opposition to male supremacy" was not the only conflict addressed by feminists. While there were
many types of popular feminism in the 1970s, two in particular influenced
the development of feminist matriarchalism. "Cultural feminism" accepted
and promoted sex differences—some of which have traditionally been used
to subjugate women—as sources of uniquely female power that could be used
to correct the ills of patriarchy and remake society. This kind of feminism
echoed the white feminism that characterized the Progressive era and maternalist claims to power. Some contemporaries criticized cultural feminists
as separatist and apolitical because of their advocacy of alternate institutions
for women, while others contended that the cultural feminist emphasis on

women's uniformity—their sameness as women—silenced the experiences of women of color, lesbians, and those feminists who did not fit the mainstream, white, middle-class image of the movement.[4]

"Radical feminism," on the other hand, insisted upon the oppressive socio-political functions of sex and gender roles within existing systems of power. The idea that women are naturally more collaborative, cooperative, and empathetic because of their capacity to reproduce is, for radical feminism, part of the social construction of womanhood that shores up patriarchy. Historian Alice Echols explains the differences between cultural and radical feminism this way: "radical feminism was a political movement dedicated to eliminating the sex-class system, whereas cultural feminism was a countercultural movement aimed at reversing the cultural valuation of the male and the devaluation of the female." Radical feminism, then, is necessarily political, based on the premise that "sexuality, family life, and the relations between men and women were not simply matters of individual choice, or even of social custom, but involved the exercise of personal and institutional power and raised vital questions of public policy." The "internecine conflicts" between cultural and radical feminism in the 1970s were ultimately self-defeating, and cultural feminism won out, as it were, due to its emphasis on some of the traditionally feminine qualities that, much to cultural feminists' horror, dovetailed with the coordinated backlash against women's liberation in the 1980s. But in at least one way, this conflict was productive, and the question of essentialism, and specifically of maternalism as a claim to female power, pushed some writers to produce a new form of feminist matriarchalism via the genre of science fiction. This new version encapsulated the struggles between the cultural and radical feminist theoretical positions.[5]

The feminist matriarchalism of the 1960s and 1970s was initially premised upon a familiar theoretical standpoint. In 1972, Gloria Steinem resurrected the most popular form of American matriarchalism in an edited volume of original *Wonder Woman* comics, all of which were written by Marston in the 1940s. These early issues provided for Steinem a "passable version of the truisms" of sex equality, sisterhood, and peace that women were rediscovering via the rebirth of feminist organizing in the 1960s and 1970s. In her introductory essay, Steinem targets Wonder Woman's post-Marston evolution, which occurred just as she herself entered adolescence; she laments, "both Wonder Woman and I fell into some very hard times in the '50s." Steinem criticizes the biological essentialism of Marston's *Wonder Woman*; assuming female superiority based on the allegedly innate female quality of love both replicated stereotypes and, worse, "might accomplish nothing more than changing places with men in the hierarchy," instead of accomplishing the feminist goal of destroying that hierarchy. But the Amazing Amazon, she argues, could play a key role in the development of feminism among "heroine-starved" girls and women: "If we had all read more about Wonder Woman and less about Dick and Jane, the new wave of the feminist revolution might have happened less painfully and sooner."[6]

Citing new archaeological research that offered evidence that Amazons were more than a historical "figment of the imagination," Steinem spins her own story of "Amazonia," describing a "gynocratic" age in which "women were worshiped" because of the "mystery" of reproduction. "Men," she explains, "were on the periphery—an interchangeable body of workers for, and worshippers of, the female center, the principle of life." These matriarchies were destroyed by the discovery of paternity, which ushered in "male ownership of children," primogeniture, and sexual restriction of women through marriage. These societies were suppressed, destroyed, and erased by patriarchy, but, Steinem argues, modern archaeologists and anthropologists had recently begun to revise and rethink sex and gender in human history. In a nod to Bachofen, she cites mythology as a potential "collective human memory" that provides hints of the matriarchal past. If this is the case, she concludes, "Wonder Woman becomes just one small, isolated outcropping of a larger human memory, and the girl children who love her are responding to one small echo of dreams and capabilities in their own forgotten past."[7]

Wonder Woman became a popular symbol of the resurgence of interest in and advocacy for female equality and social, economic, and political power. As women of the various social movements of the 1960s began to critique their experiences within these movements and to connect them with sexism in the broader society, a keen interest in female power in general, and female-run societies in particular, began to develop. Anthropologist Micaela di Leonardo argues that much of the burgeoning feminist scholarship of the 1970s rested upon the premise that there is a shared "women's culture, which represents the Ur-form of women's nature and has the same characteristics across time and space," including "moral superiority to men, cooperative rather than competitive social relations, selfless maternality, and benevolent sexuality." This "Ur-form" undergirded much of the early matriarchalism of the women's liberation movement. One of the first to articulate this was Jane Alpert of the Weather Underground, who described the awareness among members of women's groups that they shared a "culture and a consciousness that was common to us as women." "Just what," she asks in a feminist manifesto, "is the powerful source of this consciousness?" Her answer relies upon prehistoric matriarchalism; she argues that the "root of this idea lies perhaps buried in history."[8]

Alpert argues that recent feminist scholarship made a persuasive case for "ancient gynocracies" across Asia, North Africa, the Arabic world, and the Mediterranean that featured powerful women in the home, in industry, and "also in the tribe or clan at large." Although these societies worshiped female deities, Alpert contends that this power was not merely symbolic, as women made decisions about families, agriculture, warfare, property rights, and clan disputes. Like Gage, Alpert sees in the god of Judaism and Christianity a deliberate patriarchal attempt to suppress female power. The qualities stemming from reproductive capacity, coded as weakness in patriarchal society, were in fact the defining aspects of female power: "empathy, intuitiveness, adaptability, awareness of growth as a process rather than as goal-ended, inventiveness, protective feelings toward others, and a capacity to respond emotionally as well as rationally."[9]

Thus, ancient matriarchies, whether historical fact or feminist myth, could be, Alpert argues, a blueprint for the women's liberation movement: "If matriarchy means a society in which these are the qualities all human beings admire and strive to embody, a society in which the paradigm for social relationships is the relationship of a healthy and secure mother to her child, then matriarchy means nothing less than the end of oppression." Like some of the other matriarchalists examined herein, Alpert sees matriarchy as a kind of silver bullet that would resolve other social problems. Because maternal capacity united women of all races, ethnicities, nations, classes, and sexualities, Alpert argues that a matriarchal setup centered around motherhood would eliminate discrimination and oppression based on these categories. She endorses the activism of the women's liberation movement, but, she argues, it was not enough to achieve the revolutionary goals of the end of all kinds of oppression against women: "It *is* the uprising of women that will presage the end of oppression, but this uprising must be based on more than opposition to oppression and the definition of Woman as Other. *It must be an affirmation of the power of female consciousness, of the Mother.*"[10]

Alpert's essay was published in various feminist papers and magazines, including *Ms., off our backs,* and *Big Mama Rag.* The significance of this piece, beyond the obvious issues of pointing to sexism within the leftist movements and delineating splits within the feminist movement, was that she provided the most explicit manifesto of the early feminist matriarchalism that developed within popular culture in the 1970s. At the same time, the academic context of the development of Women's Studies as a field combined with the vital output of feminist writers to spark a renewed interest in the possibility and potential of prehistoric matriarchal societies. Much like Gage in the 1890s, the feminist matriarchalists of the 1970s targeted the relatively young historical age of patriarchy: its late entry to world history meant that systematic male dominance could be a phase, a "blip on the radar screen" that could be overturned in the future. Much like Baum and Gilman, these scholars posited that matriarchal sociopolitical organization entailed true equality and democracy. And like French Sheldon, Gilman, and Marston, many of the feminist matriarchalists of the 1970s believed in the innate power of women, including those traits that have traditionally served patriarchal interests, such as the belief in female nurturance, compassion, and empathy that has historically accompanied restrictive stereotypes of motherhood.[11]

As we have seen, matriarchalism was dismissed as an academic theory by the early 1900s. In the twentieth century prior to the late 1960s, it was "anthropological dogma," even among those scholars who identified as feminists, that male dominance accurately described the stages of social evolution. But by the late 1960s, matriarchalism began to develop again in academic circles, influenced by the feminist movement. Specifically, this renewal of matriarchalism was heavily influenced by the feminist spirituality movement, which can be loosely defined as pan-cultural goddess worship and/or a celebration of the feminine characteristics—reproduction, nurturance, healing powers—presumably shared by the natural environment and the female body. A primary concern of feminist spirituality was to understand the destruction of universal, prehistoric matriarchies, by asking, as Merlin Stone did at the beginning of her influential text, *When God Was a Woman* (1976): "How did it actually happen? How did men initially gain the control that now allows them to regulate the world in matters as vastly diverse as deciding which wars will be fought when to what time dinner should be served?"[12]

Feminist spirituality differs across communities and cultures, but they all share a belief in the myth of matriarchal prehistory, so much so that Eller deems the myth "foundational" to all feminist spiritualism. As an offshoot or subset of the women's liberation movement, feminist spirituality's proponents shared the historical interpretation of universal, prehistoric matriarchies; the presentist critique of patriarchal, organized religions; and the future-oriented feminist belief that, as one put it, patriarchy's days are clearly numbered. This should sound familiar; as we saw in Chapter 2, Gage's feminist matriarchalism developed directly out of a rejection of organized religion in the 1880s and 1890s.[13]

Unlike the academic matriarchalism of the late nineteenth century, the similar works of the 1960s and 1970s found their way to popular audiences, largely by virtue of their connection to the ongoing feminist movement. Psychologist Phyllis Chesler investigated "The Amazon Legacy" in her 1972 essay, which prefaced Gloria Steinem's compilation of World War II–era *Wonder Woman* comics. Chesler relied upon mythological evidence to outline the probable contours of matriarchal societies, including the primacy of mother-daughter relationships, female control of production and reproduction, and a religion based around a "Great Mother Goddess." The evidence, Chesler argued, was persuasive not because it was written down or proven by artifacts, but because it was passed down through men "who wrote, traveled, fought, and painted in fiercely patriarchal culture"—men who would have had a stake in denying the existence of powerful female societies. She argued unequivocally that matriarchal and gynocratic societies existed at key points in history, "without question" and "on all continents."[14]

Other scholars were simultaneously arriving at the same conclusions. The archaeologist who was most responsible for the academic legitimization and popular dissemination of the matriarchal myth in the United States in the 1970s and 1980s was Marija Gimbutas, who taught at the University of California at Los Angeles from 1963–1989. By the late 1960s, Gimbutas's "encyclopedic knowledge" of European archaeology led her to propose the existence of a widespread Neolithic European culture that was matrilineal, egalitarian, organized around the worship of a central goddess, and highly developed. In her archaeological digs, Gimbutas unearthed hundreds of figurines, and she found thousands of others in "museums all over Europe," in storage rooms, "lying there, not understood at all." Over time, she came to believe that this figure was female, and that it represented women's central role in the religious, cultural, and social life of Old Europe, or southern and eastern Europe between 6500 and 3500 BCE.[15]

As she developed these interpretations, Gimbutas became the first scholar of her generation to distinguish between matriarchal Old Europe and the patriarchal European societies that were more familiar to archaeologists, although, as we have seen, she was following closely in the footsteps of the nineteenth-century matriarchalists. In homage to Bachofen, whose discussion about the high status of Etruscan women she cited, Gimbutas inaugurated the interdisciplinary field of archaeomythology, in which she used "sacred symbols and metaphors" as tools to interpret Neolithic European artifacts. And like the feminist matriarchalists of the late Victorian era, Gimbutas challenged the concept of civilization itself, arguing that the prehistoric societies so often dismissed as primitive by archaeologists had civilized features, such as coherent social organization, organized religion, artistic production, and language. In a series of books, Gimbutas argued that 95 percent of the figures depicting humans that she found were female, representing life-giving and sustenance, and there was no evidence at all of male gods before the Bronze Age.[16]

Although one reviewer generously deemed the academic response to Gimbutas's work from archaeologists "reserved," on the whole, the reaction was negative, even vitriolic. Gimbutas's colleagues argued that she was "tainted by modern feminism," and they accused her of being a missionary for "the modern revival movement of Goddess worship." The "nasty, unprofessional tone" of many reviewers determined that Gimbutas's hypotheses would not be widely accepted within her chosen field, even as scholars from other fields offered additional evidence for some of her claims.[17]

On the other hand, "women, artists, mythologists, and others" applauded her work. Gimbutas is frequently described as a "revolutionary" by feminist scholars for her pioneering work on the significance of female roles and especially symbolism in Neolithic societies, work which challenged the "conservative, androcentric milieu" of the field of archaeology. Gimbutas's timing was significant, as her work was easily incorporated into the stream of popular culture featuring feminist and ecofeminist revisions of history and culture (a response that she reportedly found surprising, immersed as she was in academia).[18]

In 1980, Gimbutas's matriarchalist ideas became popular via the best-selling *Clan of the Cave Bear,* the first of six novels collectively known as the *Earth's Children* series by author Jean M. Auel. Auel's primary protagonist is a "Cro-Magnon wonder woman," Ayla, who makes "an astonishing number of species-altering discoveries." Readers meet Ayla as an orphaned Cro-Magnon child who is adopted by Neanderthals. As she grows, so do her accomplish-

ments: she is an impressive tracker and hunter; she is a quick study as a medicine woman; she slays rodents and mammoths with equal skill using slings
and spears; she invents the sewing needle; she domesticates a horse, a wolf,
and a lion; she discovers how to use flint to make fire; she develops an early
form of surgical stitches; and she determines the process of conception (a
major question that plagued matriarchalist theory). Because of her capability
and intelligence, there is constant conflict among the Neanderthals over Ayla's
transgression of gender norms. After she is exiled because of this conflict, she
survives on her own for several years. During her exile, which she voluntarily
extends as she begins to thrive on her own, Ayla ably represents cultural feminism, capitalizing on the allegedly natural sex differences that serve as her
empowering connection to the environment.[19]

Thus, like the separatist Amazons of *Herland* or *Wonder Woman*, Ayla's position as an oppressed woman becomes one of strength, as she draws upon her
innate abilities in the absence of men, male dominance, and patriarchal culture. As a Cro-Magnon raised by Neanderthals, Ayla is an evolutionary "transitional figure." She exists successfully as a society of one, with a few animals in
tow, until she meets Jondalar, a Cro-Magnon hero straight out of a Harlequin
novel. Together, Ayla and her partner represent the transition from barbarism to civilization. In the vein of classic anthropological matriarchalism, Auel
makes an evolutionist argument, as she carefully contrasts the Neanderthals,
who represented prehuman societies, with the Cro-Magnons, through a clear
focus on the sexist, and at times misogynist, culture of the Neanderthals versus the reverence for women found in Cro-Magnon tribes.[20]

As in other texts in which gender essentialism is a key component of matriarchalism, motherhood plays an important role in the series. "Mother" is,
in fact, the first word spoken in *Clan of the Cave Bear,* and a plaintive cry of
"Mama!" is the last. In Clan society, the very act of conception is seen as a
struggle between the sexes, and this conflict translates into outright violence
when men beat women to subdue their spirits so that they will conceive. Pregnancy, labor, and delivery are not signs of female power so much as signs of
the triumph of the totems representing various men in the Clan. But women,
including Ayla, very much value maternity. During her own pregnancy, Ayla
is so "wrapped in a warm glow of anticipation" that she no longer minds the
constant violent assaults of one of the males.[21]

By contrast, the maternalist egalitarianism of Cro-Magnon societies stems
directly from the power of the motherly myths, symbols, and deities of their

religion. Collectively, the Cro-Magnon tribes are known as "Earth's Children," which is to say that they all stem from the same Mother, although her name differs according to the language of the tribe. The Earth Mother, or "Doni," is the creator, sustainer, and destroyer of all life. As a representation of the primacy of the female, Jondalar carries with him an image inspired by Gimbutas's research: an icon of Doni, a "small stone figurine of an obese female" with "huge breasts," "large protruding stomach," and "more than ample buttocks and thighs." The arms and legs of this figurine were "insignificant," as it was "the Mother aspects that were important."[22]

As a Cro-Magnon among Neanderthals, Ayla alone is adaptable and capable of change, growth, and innovation, and once she joins Cro-Magnon society, she surpasses even the female leaders in her intuition, inventions, and discoveries. Her role as a transitional figure between societies sets up gendered comparisons, but it is also a racialized position. We have seen how various American matriarchalists have struggled with the issue of race and perpetuated racism in their quests to make a compelling case for female power. This struggle plays out in Auel's matriarchalist fiction in complicated ways. In one sense, *Earth's Children* is all about race. The series charts the conflicts between Neanderthal and Cro-Magnon societies. Racial difference is stark here, as is the racism perpetrated by the Cro-Magnons against the Neanderthals, whom they call "flatheads." Auel denounces explicit racism, but although she attempts to humanize the Neanderthals, it is clear that the Cro-Magnons are the preferred race in this fictional world. Auel emphasizes Ayla's blonde beauty throughout the series, describing her blue eyes, golden locks, perfect figure, and long legs in great detail. In the character list at the outset of the series, Ayla is described as "tall, blond, slender, and smarter than the rest," while Brun, the Clan Leader, is "chinless, bearded, bowlegged, and barrel-chested." In general, the Clan men are described as "round" and "barrel-shaped," in contrast to Cro Magnon Jondalar's bronze skin, tall lean body, and blue eyes (Auel never misses a chance to describe his eyes, which were "so blue it was hard to believe they were real"). Interracial sex between Neanderthals and Cro-Magnons is "an abomination," according to both societies. Although Ayla's biracial son, Durc (the product of rape), appears to be normal, the other Neanderthal–Cro-Magnon child in the series is fragile and weak, indicating the apparent perils of race-mixing.[23]

The "racial memory" of the Clan ensures that they maintain survival, but they fail to adapt, and thus will die out as the more innovative and clever

Cro-Magnons build their societies. In the context of the history of American matriarchalism, the racial politics here are troubling. The evolutionist teleology in which prehistoric matriarchies gave way to patriarchal social systems is also, according to some matriarchalists, a racial teleology in which matriarchal societies of color—like the depictions of the Dahomey "Amazons" at the World's Fair—represent savagery on the evolutionary scale. In Auel's work, the darker, less evolved race is sexist, incapable of change, and inevitably left behind. This message about gender equity and social progress was well received by readers, but these racial implications echo the racism and xenophobia of imperial matriarchalism early in the century.[24]

Likewise, Auel's chronology of prehistory over the course of the series follows, wittingly or not, the time line laid out by the anthropological matriarchalists of the Victorian era. In the final book of the series, *The Land of Painted Caves* (2011), Ayla joins the ranks of the Cro-Magnon spiritual power structure as a "zelandoni," or a medicine woman and healer, taking a formal place within the matriarchal power structure. But her intuition and skills also lead Ayla to discover the male role in reproduction. The series ends with a weak Ayla recovering from a grave illness, reaffirming traditional monogamy, and planning to "start a baby" with Jondalar as soon as she is well. In the final scene, Jondalar and Ayla, secure in their heterosexual family, consider paternity, the "new Gift of Knowledge," and how it is destined to "change the world." Auel ends with these words, but matriarchalist anthropologists have long made the argument that the discovery of paternity prompted the beginning of the transition to patriarchy. In short, Ayla's legacy is presumed to sow the seeds of patriarchy, as she is responsible for the discovery that purportedly destroyed the matriarchal structures that characterized prehistoric social systems.[25]

Whether one viewed Ayla as a sort of Cro-Magnon superheroine or Eve who ruined the feminist Eden, she sold very well. The *Earth's Children* series was the first prehistoric fiction that garnered a majority female audience, although Auel had many male fans, as well. The initial books in the series were enormously popular; *Clan of the Cave Bear* went through four printings during its first year of publication and was on the bestseller lists off and on from 1980 to 1985. *Time* praised its "campy charm," lauding Auel for somehow combining "The Flintstones, Dynasty, and the story of Mme. Curie." *Valley of the Horses* similarly sold so well that *The Mammoth Hunters*, the third book in the series, had an "unprecedented" first printing of 1.1 million hard cover copies. By that point, Auel's fiction had been translated into many languages and published in over a dozen countries. Thereafter, however, the popularity dwindled; the *Washington Post* called the fourth book in the series "awful, repetitious, ponderous, [and] diabolically inept," and many other critics derided the plot as becoming more like that of a stereotypical romance novel over time. These criticisms, however, missed the point. *Earth's Children* was meant to be *both* escapist popular literature and feminist vision.[26]

Auel's version of prehistory relies upon the basic essentialism undergirding the cultural feminism that was popular when she began writing the *Earth's Children* series. Gimbutas was often criticized for being universalist in her assumption that all Old European communities and societies worshiped the same goddess, an assumption that Auel explicitly and uncritically promotes in her fiction. In the Earth Mother–worshiping Cro-Magnon communities that Auel depicts, women are naturally superior because they are a part of the bounty provided by the goddess. Women are thus objectified as part of nature, and the ability to reproduce is considered the primary source of their power, the ultimate blessing of Doni—a maternalist argument that continues to resurface in American matriarchalism. At the same time, however, a radical response was developing that offered a revolutionary form of matriarchalism to combat, as Ellen Willis dismissively put it, the cultural feminist "fantasies of benevolent matriarchies."[27]

The context for this reformulation of feminist matriarchalism was science fiction. Scholars have long noted that science fiction is "naturally compatible" with feminism via its "speculative techniques" and encouragement of envisioning alternative societies and futures. In the 1940s, many female and feminist authors began publishing within this genre. Author and editor Judith Merril, who became known as the "little mother of science fiction," explained that it was "virtually the only vehicle of political dissent" available to artists like herself during the conservative decades of the Cold War. By the 1970s, female authors were using the genre to explore matriarchal social organization and attempt to sever it from gender essentialism. In particular, fictional matriarchies set in the future—not in the distant past or the remote present, as in other matriarchalist fiction—allow feminist science fiction writers to explore "the issue of the future [as] a way of trying to write beyond the ending, especially as it has functioned in the classic novel: as closure of historical movement and therefore as the end of development."[28]

These writers tapped into the radical feminism of the era, which sought women's liberation from patriarchal oppression—which radical feminists saw as the source of all other oppressions—beyond the basic extension of rights to women within the existing system. In the "Manifesto" of the Redstockings, a radical feminist group formed in 1969, the authors explained their core premise that "women are an oppressed class":

> Because we have lived so intimately with our oppressors, in isolation from each other, we have been kept from seeing our personal sufferings as a political condition. This creates the illusion that a woman's relationship to her man is a matter of interplay between two unique personalities, and can be worked out individually. In reality, every such relationship is a *class* relationship, and the conflicts between individual men and women are *political* conflicts that can only be solved collectively.

Ti-Grace Atkinson and others pinpointed the enduring dilemma of essentialism within feminism. In an attempt to define radical feminism in 1969, Atkinson argued that, rather than a "sex," or people grouped together by virtue of reproductive function and presumed attendant characteristics, women were a "political class characterized by sexual function." She explained that political classes, unlike biologically defined groups, are *"artificial"* categorizations that "define persons *with* certain capacities *by* that capacity, changing the contingent to the necessary, thereby appropriating the *capacity* of an individual as a *function* of society."[29]

In her materialist analysis of patriarchy, *The Dialectic of Sex*, Shulamith Firestone extended this analysis of essentialism to social institutions, arguing that "unless revolution uproots the basic social organization, the biological family—the vinculum through which the psychology of power can always be smuggled—the tapeworm of exploitation will never be annihilated." We have seen how previous matriarchalists revised the oppressive institutions of the patriarchal family and motherhood by reconceptualizing motherhood as a powerful social tool. The radical feminists of the 1970s attacked these problems anew by seeking to understand maternity and other allegedly natural female experiences as sex roles and socioeconomic institutions.[30]

As opposed to cultural feminism, which tended to rely upon women's reproductive capacities as a means of reclaiming female power, radical feminism sought to sever sex from sex roles, or to destroy the correlation between biology and gendered functions in society. As the genre dedicated to explaining, exploring, and challenging the sociocultural roles and implications of science and technology, science fiction was an ideal lens through which to envision the separation of the institution of motherhood from the biological reality of female reproduction. In the course of this exploration in the 1970s, feminist science fiction writers moved from the traditional maternalism of predecessors like *Herland* to the development of an entirely new form of radical feminist matriarchalism.

The first signs of the development of this new form came from, not surprisingly, a female author well versed in the original methodology of the theory. The matriarchalism of Ursula Kroeber Le Guin has a complex genealogy, as she can trace personal influences back to some of the original fin de siècle anthropologists who explicitly rejected the ethnocentrism and racism that characterized evolutionist interpretations of indigenous societies and cultures. Le Guin's father, Alfred Kroeber, was a famed anthropologist mentored by Franz Boas. Although Boas participated in the evolutionist endeavor of the Chicago World's Fair of 1893 as the assistant to Frederick Putnam, head of the Ethnology Department, he later played a major role in the "antievolutionary reaction" within anthropology in the early twentieth century. Like his mentor, Kroeber rejected the evolutionist doctrine of racial difference and the idea that cultures were governed by universal laws and proceeded teleologically through ordered stages of civilization. Ursula Kroeber Le Guin cited her father's academic work as an influence on her own. She later explained that while he studied cultures, she created them, as when she became a professional author, science fiction was her chosen genre.[31]

Le Guin's work served as a complicated inspiration for matriarchalist science fiction in the 1970s. *The Tombs of Atuan* (1970), Le Guin's venture into matriarchalism, takes place in a distant land ruled by women within the fictional Earthsea geography. True to the basic feminist vision of uniting the public and private, and consequently the sex roles associated with these spheres, Atuan society is organized as a multigenerational family with women at its head. The various levels of priestesses are related to each other as mothers, daughters, aunts, and grandmothers, and all girls are cared for and educated by this community of adult women.[32]

The Tombs of Atuan, however, is different from previous matriarchalist fiction in the United States. Atuan is decidedly not a utopia. It is a dark place overseen by violent gods known as the Nameless Ones, and the women function as the priestesses who serve them. In this novel, peace and prosperity are not the natural outcomes of female rule, which is petty and corrupt. The crux of the plot is the prolonged encounter between Tenar, a High Priestess of Atuan, and Ged, a powerful sorcerer from Earthsea. Initially, Tenar assumes a nurturing role, providing Ged with water and food while he is trapped in a labyrinth and hiding him from danger at great risk to her own power and position. But her brief stint as his caretaker ends when Ged takes control of the narrative by naming her and restoring her true identity.[33]

Ged's naming liberates her, but despite her newfound identity, Tenar's power is completely subsumed by Ged, who lifts her "like a child" and explains that she is now free of the evil gods. Ged carries with him half of a powerful, ancient ring, and Tenar alone has access to the other half. When the ring is reconstructed, it becomes a bracelet that fits Tenar, not Ged. This singular fit is misleading, however; rather than a source of power for Tenar, the ring functions as a mechanism of control. When Ged commands, "By the bond you wear I bid you come, Tenar," the once-High Priestess, dazed and staggering, mutely obeys. There is a price to her "liberation": a woman may be safe from danger or she may be powerful, but she cannot be both.[34]

In the end, the narrative follows a traditional progression, and the main characters eventually conform to the tenets of masculine power and feminine weakness. Tenar turns out to be part of Ged's classic heroic quest, and she chooses to join the more traditional, medieval patriarchy of the other lands of Earthsea as a "beautiful" princess. Tenar is thus considered by some critics to be a "failed feminist" hero, as her self-actualization occurs only in competition with other women and under the scrutiny of Ged. In Le Guin's novel, the transition from matriarchy to patriarchy—that evolution that so troubled academic matriarchalists—was gradual, and patriarchy prevailed when the Tombs of Atuan destroyed themselves via earthquake and Tenar fled to Ged's homeland, "holding his hand, like a child coming home" (a phrase that echoes Gilman's fictional narrator Van describing the maternal social structure of Herland, although it is unlikely that Le Guin had read Herland, as it had not yet been published as a novel and was thus only available in fifty-year-old back issues of The Forerunner). This act is replicated in Tehanu (1990), the fourth book in the series, when Tenar gives up her power again by leaving her apprenticeship to a wizard to become a typical farmwife and mother.[35]

Le Guin's foray into matriarchalism, then, did not conform to the tenets of the fictional models offered by previous feminists, in which female power denoted utopia. Yet just a few years before, in the late 1960s, Le Guin had begun to question conventional dynamics of gender, sexuality, and power. Out of this thinking came *The Left Hand of Darkness* (1969), her best-known and most celebrated work of fiction. In this novel, a black man from Earth, Genly Ai, ventures to a distant planet, where he finds an androgynous culture among the Gethenians. Although the planet is not a matriarchy, it has many of the essentialist qualities of fictional matriarchies. For Le Guin, "balance" between the "female principle," which she describes as "basically anarchic"—"it values order without constraint, rule by custom not by force"—and the masculine drive to order and force, was the key question. When Gethenians "leaned toward the 'feminine,'" which featured the "valuing of patience, ripeness, practicality, liveableness" in their sociopolitical organization, peace reigned. In a later essay, Le Guin cited indigenous American cultures as her model, "though not those hierarchical and imperialistic ones approvingly termed, by our hierarchical and imperialistic standards, 'high.'"[36]

Le Guin's admittedly flawed early feminist science fiction is instructive here, for several reasons. One, with her exploration of the sociopolitical and economic "balance" between masculine and feminine, she clearly sides with previous feminist matriarchalists when she indicates that Gethen is more peaceful and prosperous when it "leans feminine." Secondly, she introduced the young, male readers of science fiction who were unlikely to encounter it elsewhere to this concept—kind of a matriarchalism-lite. Third and most significantly, the novel sparked vocal feminist criticism, which turned out to be productive. In his exploration of the role of gender in science fiction, historian Brian Attebury confesses: "Whereas many early male readers (including me) found [*The Left Hand of Darkness*] profoundly challenging to their notions of sexual difference and social organization, some women readers testify that they found it unconvincing." Some critics gave it "limited approval" as "feminism for men," and this criticism sparked conversation between authors.[37]

Scholars of science fiction have long noted the genre's "collaborative nature"; that is, new ideas in science fiction "will immediately be taken up by other writers as a challenge to find alternative outcomes, unexamined implications, parodic inversions, connections, and counterexamples." Specifically, *The Left Hand of Darkness* sparked the publication of more feminist science fiction. In a later essay, Le Guin cited this legacy: "Men were inclined to be satisfied with the book which allowed them a safe trip into androgyny and back, from a conventionally male viewpoint. But many women wanted to go further, to

dare more." Even as the original feminist matriarchalist texts were in the process of being rediscovered at the time—*Mizora* was republished in 1975, Sal-
ley Roesch Wagner explored Matilda Joslyn Gage's life and works in her 1978
dissertation, and Gilman's *Herland* was republished as a novel in 1979 by Pantheon Books—one of the ways in which women writers followed Le Guin's
diagnosis of wanting to "go further" and "dare more" in the 1970s was through
the development of a new matriarchalist tradition in feminist science fiction.[38]

Although the genre featured hundreds of works by female authors in
the middle decades of the twentieth century, they tended to write in the
"galactic suburban mode," featuring women in stereotypical roles even as
the characters embodied social criticism. In 1971, science fiction was still
male-dominated enough for author Joanna Russ to complain, with some va-
lidity, "There are plenty of images of women in science fiction. There are
hardly any women." Moreover, she continued, "speculation about the innate
personality differences between men and women, about family structure,
about sex, in short about gender roles, does not exist at all." But by the mid-
1970s, although writers and readers were still mostly men, science fiction was
a genre that provided a ripe context for the exploration of sex, gender, and
power. Writer Suzy McKee Charnas recalls the "intense" conversations about
feminism as she worked on her first science fiction series: "It was like a big
consciousness-raising group of fans and writers. And we just talked ourselves
blue." A major participant in these conversations, Joanna Russ, confessed to
fellow writer James Tiptree Jr. that in order to "learn to write at all," she had to
start by "thinking of [her]self as a sort of fake man." Tiptree was an interesting
audience for this confession, as he was a "fake man"—or rather, James Tiptree
Jr. was the pseudonym used by writer Alice Sheldon, who would go on to write
a major work of feminist science fictional matriarchalism in the mid-1970s.[39]

Sheldon's early experiences in some ways echoed those of May French
Sheldon (with whom she also coincidentally shared a last name), although
her mother, the socialite, writer, explorer, and "amateur anthropologist" Mary
Hastings Bradley, was more like the turn-of-the-century imperial matriarchal-
ist than her daughter. In 1921, Alice Bradley became known as the "Youngest
Explorer of Darkest Africa" after she traveled north from Cape Town to the
Belgian Congo, along with her parents, some family friends, and two hundred
porters. Following this adventurous childhood and a stint in boarding school,
Sheldon had a lifelong series of interesting, even at times unbelievable, occu-
pations. She was, chronologically, a painter, a captain in the Women's Army

Corps that Wonder Woman so frequently promoted to young readers during World War II, an air force intelligence officer, a poultry farmer, a CIA analyst, a researcher in experimental psychology (in which she earned a PhD in her fifties), and finally, a science fiction writer. Sheldon was well-read in feminist theory, and her dismay at the developing gender conservatism of the immediate postwar period prompted her to write a scathing critique of momism, that staple of matriarchalism in Cold War culture. In "The Woman-Haters," Sheldon charged that if "Mom" existed, she was a monster of man's creation, "cheated" as she was by the false god of traditional masculinity. The essay did not sell, but Sheldon continued to hone her analysis of gender roles, reading Hannah Arendt and Simone de Beauvoir and careening haphazardly in her own writing between arguing for gender essentialism—positing innately female characteristics—and social constructionism—critiquing gender roles as pretensions meant to shore up patriarchy.[40]

This oscillation between positions on the natures of and links between sex and gender became a running theme once Sheldon began to write science fiction in earnest in her fifties. She assumed the *nom de guerre* James Tiptree Jr. offhandedly as a means of separating her writing hobby from her scholarly career, and through the assumption of this "double life," Sheldon/ Tiptree was able to challenge gendered conventions in both life and literature. Tiptree's penpals affectionately called her "Tip," with no knowledge that, like Tip/Ozma in the *Oz* series, who was turned temporarily into a boy to hide from the patriarchal forces of the Wizard, Tiptree used the name and persona to hide the true identity, and therefore the biological sex, of Alice Sheldon. Sheldon's biographer writes that this name and the "manly voice" in Tiptree's narratives made Sheldon's "ideas seem a bit less subversive." While this is speculation, it is the case that younger writers like Ursula K. Le Guin and Joanna Russ initially struggled to write science fiction about, for, and in the voice of women. Because Sheldon kept the ruse up for almost a decade (1967–1976) and communicated with other science fiction authors solely via letters, this correspondence serves as a sort of case study of gendered assumptions within the science fiction community, and Sheldon's published works both reiterated and challenged those assumptions.[41]

Sheldon's foray into matriarchalism is something of a bridge between the early attempts by Le Guin and the deliberate destruction of gender essentialism in feminist science fiction in the late 1970s, which we will examine shortly. In *Houston, Houston, Do You Read?* (1976), Sheldon revises the conventional colonial narrative while relying upon the traditional trope of the male narrator that Gilman employed in *Herland*. Male anxiety opens *Houston, Houston, Do You Read?*, as Lorimer, the narrator, and two other astronauts have somehow breached the time-space dimension while flying behind the sun. Finding themselves three hundred years in the future, they encounter a spaceship "manned" entirely by women. Lorimer feels emasculated by both the women and his fellow astronauts, the "authentic," "alpha" males whom he fears sense his "beta bile" underneath his thin scientific exterior.[42]

As in other fictional works of matriarchalism, the predominance of women in the human population in Sheldon's work is due to a devastating natural disaster, in this case an epidemic that affected the Y chromosome, sterilized men, and significantly reduced male births. Violence followed the plague, the global population rapidly reduced from eight million to two million, and those who remained gathered in the southern part of the United States, where they could grow crops for consumption. They developed a method of cloning via in vitro fertilization; because the male population decreased precipitously, the genetic material is female, although they sometimes incorporate "androgen treatments" to create an "andy," or a woman with male body strength, to provide the "muscle power" for certain jobs.[43]

Although the society is technologically advanced, it is also simple. Five industries—farming, communications, transport, space, and factories—comprise the entire economy. These industries make up the loose structure of the government, which is ruled by consensus; one of the intruding males, Bud, considers them "ungoverned," in a sort of "permanent frontier" state, yet the entire structure of society is organized around technology that makes their lives productive and stable, so that no citizens are hungry, poor, unemployed, or otherwise unhappy. In a clear break with previous pop cultural versions of matriarchalism, Sheldon's matriarchs span races and ethnicities. While the men deem their society "primitive," the women protest that they have simply slowed the process of evolution down to improve upon it.[44]

These improvements are both political and personal. Although they have some family bonds, the concept of the heterosexual nuclear family no longer exists, and in a nod to Marston's DISC theory, the women have done away with the "dominance-submission structure" of male relations. Female reproduction via cloning is crucial for the maintenance of the species, but Sheldon does not offer any actual examples of mothering in the novel. As in every other matriarchalist work examined herein, the women of *Houston, Houston,*

Do You Read? have also eliminated organized religion, specifically Christianity. This especially concerns Dave, the alpha male astronaut whose beard lends him a "patriarchal gravity" that Lorimer both respects and fears. He is shocked by the women's confession that they have never seen a Christian Bible, and he assumes they "have lost all faith." When one woman protests that, to the contrary, they have faith in themselves, Dave retorts that if she were his daughter, she'd receive a spanking for this kind of sacrilege.[45]

This exchange makes it clear that Dave is the superego of the male trio, and he is, in fact, driven mad by the women's defiance of patriarchal order. Bud is the id; much like Terry in Gilman's *Herland,* he sees the predominance of women as an opportunity to get laid. He jokes that he and his comrades are "cavemen," and by the time the ship returns to Earth, all the "space chickies" on board will be "preggers." Recognizing this danger, the women drug the men to bring them on board the ship to return to Earth. As in *Herland,* however, Bud's animal instincts lead him to sexual assault, an act which sends Dave retreating into traditional patriarchal authority as he unsuccessfully tries to take command of the ship "in the name of the United States of America and God." The women subdue Bud and Dave, and as the last man standing, Lorimer weakly protests that the men were responsible for civilization and for protecting the women who had now turned on them. To this, one of the women replies gently, "As I understand it, what you protected people from was largely other males, wasn't it? We've just had an extraordinary demonstration. You have brought history to life for us." Sheldon thus taps into the revision of evolutionism that characterizes feminist matriarchalism: patriarchy and conflict represent a dystopian past, while matriarchy and peace are the future.[46]

Sheldon later explained that she wanted to compare this "relaxed, cheery, and practical future" with the "tense, macho-constricted, sex-and-dominance-obsessed atmosphere of the little all-male 'world.'" Yet this world, though peaceful, is not uniformly desirable; it is constricted and has to be carefully maintained, through violence if necessary. Sheldon called it a "cautionary tale, an if-this-goes-on warning about what would happen if the sexes continued to war with each other." *Houston* reflected the author's classic dilemma about sex and gender, and although not every character in the novella is a gendered stereotype, they represent what Sheldon later called the "two sexes": "men and mothers." Colleagues protested—in response to a letter spelling out this argument, Russ replied: "WASH YOUR MOUTH OUT WITH SOAP, JAMES TIPTREE!," and popular science fiction writer David Gerrold complained to Sheldon about the politically simplistic character-driven plot in which the good women must kill the bad men in order to survive.[47]

Sheldon was undeterred, and she even doubled down when she produced an essay for a science fiction symposium elaborating on this gender essentialism, resorting to evolutionary biology to prove her point. In a nod to classical anthropological matriarchalism, she argued that the maternal "bond created can be very lasting; it is now speculated that the permanent alliance of mothers and daughters and granddaughters may be the true origin of society." While her colleagues were "baffled" by this essay, her fiction was enormously popular, and *Houston* won the Nebula and the Hugo Awards for best novella in 1977.[48]

The future matriarchy in *Houston* is essentialist—female rule is characterized by allegedly innate, sex-based qualities—but it is not maternalist, per se. Reproduction is important, but mothering as an institution is not; the babies are raised in communal creches and the society is not organized according to maternal principles as in *Herland*. The novella is thus a telling example of matriarchalist thinking in the mid-1970s. By the time Sheldon published the novella, matriarchalism was straying from cultural feminism and growing more radical. In 1975, Joanna Russ, one of Sheldon's best epistolary friends and a vocal critic of Le Guin's *The Left Hand of Darkness,* published a novel she had first written in 1969, *The Female Man,* which still stands as one of the most famous works of feminist science fiction, a status which also makes it one of the most famous works of feminist matriarchalism. In a letter to Russ, Sheldon compared the two authors, joking that if Ursula K. Le Guin was the Martin Luther King of feminist science fiction, Russ was the Malcolm X. In response to Sheldon's usual confusion reconciling gender essentialism and social constructionism, in which she mused that the world is divided into "lambs and lions," Russ once responded: "Really none of us are lambs, are we? We're just smaller lions." Jokes aside, however, Russ struggled with creating matriarchs in her fiction that eschewed the stereotypical traits of both genders, including the maternalist gender essentialism that plagues matriarchalism as well as its opposite, the masculine aggression that characterizes patriarchal power.[49]

This tension is the crux of *The Female Man,* in which Russ uses the characters of four women to contrast four worlds, three of which are dystopias: Jeannine lives in the patriarchal United States in 1969, reconfigured here so that the Great Depression never ended and the social movements of the 1960s did not occur; Joanna lives in the present-day United States, which features exaggerated masculine stereotypes for both sexes in the workplace and traditional feminine submission in the home; Jael comes from a bloody future in which men and women are at war; and Janet comes from the isolated matriarchal world of Whileaway. Jeannine and Joanna represent the dystopian past and present, while Janet represents the utopian, techno-matriarchal future in which no men have existed for centuries. Jael, from the violent future of Womanlanders warring with Manlanders, is an aggressive, man-hating feminist stereotype who brings the characters together, indicating that they are counter-selves who have been thoroughly altered by their drastically different environments.[50]

The emphasis on socio-environmental influences is the primary premise of this fictional manifesto about the destruction of gender roles and the sociopolitical system that created them. In the novel's dystopian present, characters consult actual rule books on gender norms, while in the future, Whileaway is a peaceful, anarchist, high-tech society. Following the "Catastrophe," or a plague that affected all men, Whileaway evolved into a self-reproducing, all-female world over the course of several centuries. This single-sex society is not in any way essentialist. Russ's utopian characters have a range of "unfeminine" emotions, including aggression and anger. The goddess statue on Whileaway, for instance, is an "outsized female figure as awful as Zeus," a "constantly changing contradiction" that is "in turn gentle, terrifying, hateful, loving, 'stupid' (or 'dead') and finally indescribable." Russ thus offers readers an analysis of differences within, not simply between, genders.[51]

As the Whileawayans have done away with gender, they do not idealize motherhood. Via a process of gene-splicing, each woman has one baby or twins (depending on "demographic pressures") at the age of thirty, followed by a five-year "vacation." After those five years, the mothers go back to work, and the daughters are sent to regional schools, where they receive an athletic and industrial education that sounds much like Marston's Amazon training in *Wonder Woman.* By the age of 22, "the typical Whileawayan girl is able to do any job on the planet, except for specialties and extremely dangerous work." At sixty, Whileawayan women chose "sedentary jobs" so as to have "time for [themselves] again." Russ thus posits a path to women's liberation that eschews the supposed naturalness of female difference. A Whileawayan philosopher famously declared that "humanity is unnatural!," and so, in Russ's alternate future, technology has freed women so that they are so thoroughly integrated with machines and computers as to be able to perform any task without need of men.[52]

Russ contrasts the many worlds of *The Female Man* in order to satirize the construction and institutional maintenance of gender roles. Joanna explains in a monologue:

'Do you enjoy playing with other people's children—for ten minutes? Good! This reveals that you have Maternal Instinct and you will be forever wretched if you do not have a baby of your own (or three or four) and take care of that unfortunate victimized object twenty-four hours a day, seven days a week, fifty-two weeks a year, for eighteen years, all by yourself. (Don't expect much help). Are you lonely? Good! This shows that you have Feminine Incompleteness; get married and do all your husband's personal services . . .

Yet Russ, like other radical feminists of the time, indicates that women, as well, are complicit in their own oppression. In the chapter "The Great Happiness Contest," several women compare their "darling children," husbands, and domestic responsibilities, leading one to conclude, "I really feel like I'm expressing myself best when I make a custard or a meringue or decorate the basement." When one of the main characters calls them "miserable nits" and retorts that she has "a Nobel Peace Prize, fourteen published novels, six lovers, a town house, a box at the Metropolitan Opera," and that she can "fly a plane," repair a car, and "do eighteen pushups before breakfast," the happy housewives chant in unison: "Kill, kill, kill, kill, kill, kill." The social construction of these feminine roles is deliberate and intense. Joanna details how she became a woman, a process of muting and morphing the self that included "the vanity training, the obedience training, the self-effacement training, the deference training, the dependency training, the passivity training, the rivalry training, the stupidity training, the placation training." In her rejection of this role, she becomes the titular "female man," a process Russ describes through the metaphor of communion with a violent goddess: "take in your bare right hand one naked, severed end of a high-tension wire. Take the other in your left hand. Stand in a puddle. . . . When She roars down in high voltage and high amperage both, She is after your marrow-bones; you are making yourself a conduit for holy terror and the ecstasy of Hell."[53]

Janet's arrival in the United States makes apparent how unhappy Joanna is within her circumscribed role. Before Janet, she explains, she did everything to please "The Man." Contrast this to Whileaway, where there is "no being *out too late,"* or *"up too early,* or *in the wrong part of town,* or *unescorted."* The removal of sexual aggression enables humans in Whileaway to evolve along with technology to reinvent an ecologically sound world. Technology in *The Female Man* does have its negative consequences, however. Jael, a violent cyborg with steel teeth and claws, is an example of this. Her actions, including the murder of "Boss-Man," suggest that stereotypically masculine violence might be necessary to destroy patriarchy, although not all of the primary characters endorse these actions.[54]

Jael also exemplifies the thorough disconnect between femininity and nature in the futures of Womanland and Whileaway. In the latter, femaleness is superior in that women survived the Catastrophe, but Russ does not rely upon supposedly innate feminine traits like nurturing and service to make her case for matriarchy. Russ's *The Female Man* is thus representative of the future-oriented matriarchalist science fiction of the 1970s that sought to separate women from the essentialism that characterized the matriarchalist fiction of previous generations, with an eye toward the liberation of women and toward women's liberationists as readers.

Like *Houston, Houston, Do You Read?*, *The Female Man* featured successful liberation from patriarchy, but the price was separatism. Russ explored this problem in a 1981 essay, "Recent Feminist Utopias," in which she wrote: "I believe the separatism is primary, and . . . the authors are not subtle in their reasons for creating separatist utopias: if men are kept out of these societies, it is because men are dangerous." Russ argued that these separatist matriarchal societies were a way for authors to show, by virtue of comparison, how the problems of patriarchy permeated contemporary society. By emphasizing the "positive values" of isolated matriarchies, the social, economic, political, and personal destruction wrought by male dominance was thrown into high relief. As a feminist thought experiment, Russ's matriarchy is instructive of a different kind of female power. In her letters to Tiptree, Russ was open about her struggle to depict a kind of powerful womanhood that wholly destroyed traditional female stereotypes without replicating traditional male stereotypes. "Womanhood as power, sex as power, violence as power," she wrote. "And it's all power-over. . . . It's a total role-reversal, but exactly the same game. . . . I reject it utterly—with so much vehemence, so much bitterness."[55]

In her analysis of feminist science fiction, Marleen Barr argues that this subgenre offers "the possibility of real-world change" by offering "revisionary power fantasies for women." As potential blueprints for matriarchal power

specifically or even the feminist revisioning of oppressive systems more generally, however, these worlds can be troubling, if only due to the thorny question
of origins. Like *Herland,* like Wonder Woman's Paradise Island, like all of the
separatist matriarchies examined herein, these science fiction feminist utopias
have violent beginnings: natural disasters, plagues, revolutions, and warfare
are the circumstances of their births. And conflict necessarily undergirds their
interactions with men on their home turf, although in earlier matriarchalist
fiction, the violence is sanitized. In *Herland,* for instance, the subjugation of
men by women, as seen through the eyes of narrator Van, is humiliating, but
it is not depicted as violent, even though the women physically subdue and
imprison them. In *Wonder Woman,* violent interactions are relegated only to
"Man's World," and in Le Guin's *The Tombs of Atuan,* the punishment for male
interloping in the female-controlled tombs is supposed to be death, although
Tenar spares Ged.[56]

But as feminist matriarchalism branched off from cultural feminism in
the late 1970s, it began to feature more violence. In Sheldon's *Houston,* the
male interlopers are its source—that is, until the very end, when Lorimer
and his cohort drink the "antidote," which tastes "something like peace and
freedom," but also like "death." While Sheldon later denied killing off the men
at the end of the novella—she explained that the men did not die, but rather
they were put into "polite, kind isolation, like a zoo"—the novella ends on
the cusp of this action. Whatever happens to the men, it is dark. One of the
matriarchs clearly states the dilemma of coexistence to Lorimer, who protests
"elegiacally": "We can hardly turn you loose on Earth. And we simply have no
facilities for people with your emotional problems." Similarly, the utopia of
Whileaway, Russ implies, is only achievable after massive bloodshed. "That
'plague' you talk of is a lie," Jael explains to Janet. "I, I, I, I am the plague. . . .
I and the war I fought built your world for you, I and those like me, we gave
you a thousand years of peace and love and the Whileawayan flowers nour-
ish themselves on the bones of the men we have slain." The violence of these
books, whether out of the frame or in the distant past, is often, as Russ noted
in an essay, "directed *by women against men*" (her emphasis). Rather than the
ascendance of maternal instinct applied as "social housekeeping," matriarchalism here is the hard-won result of a world war between the sexes.[57]

Within the context of this vibrant conversation about gender and sex in
science fiction in the 1970s, however, a series developed that sought to fully
address some of these tensions within feminist matriarchalism. These novels

combine the proposed characteristics of ancient female-led societies in an epic tale of extreme patriarchy contrasted with several forms of matriarchies. In *The Holdfast Chronicles,* a four-novel series published between 1974 and 1999, Suzy McKee Charnas takes on the various tenets of matriarchalism, challenging both gender essentialism and sex warfare by making the anger of the oppressed women, and, indeed, the violence of female characters like Russ's Jael, the primary plot driver.[58]

The first installment in the series, *Walk to the End of the World* (1974), opens after a holocaust known as "the Wasting" in Holdfast, a dystopia of extreme patriarchy characterized by the enslavement, for labor and breeding, of women. One of these women, Alldera, a "tough dam" hardened by slavery, escapes at the end of the novel, and the second installment in the series, *Motherlines* (1978), opens with Alldera, now a pregnant runaway slave, being captured on the plains outside of Holdfast by the Riding Women, who are modeled after the Amazons of mythology. These multiethnic, expert horse handlers live in an all-female society organized around clans, or "motherlines," described as "whole strings of blood relations" consisting of "women who looked like older and younger versions of each other." Scientific experimentation has enabled the women to reproduce without men, and although many women serve in some sort of maternal capacity, motherhood is not idealized among these Amazons. It is of no consequence to the Riding Women that Alldera has no interest in the child she bears upon joining them; in their society, the "bloodmother" of each child is but one of the "sharemothers" who watch over the child until it is old enough to join the "child pack," a mass of children who run wild among the camps until puberty. There are racial, ethnic, and clan differences between the women, but there is no meaning attached to those differences—they do not entail differential behavior, treatment, or power within this Amazon society. Alldera explains, "They have no positions, only relations. You don't need a position when you have kindred." Decisions are reached by discussions in the "chief tent" that last until the women reach consensus. After a life of exploitation, Alldera weeps at the sheer "physical fact of their liberty."[59]

Like Russ, Charnas rejects the feminine essentialism inherent in other matriarchalist fiction. While conflict is resolved nonviolently among the Riding Women, they are a decidedly aggressive group, especially in their official policies regarding Holdfasters, both men and women. Men who stray too far beyond Holdfast boundaries are killed on sight, while escaped women like Alldera usually join the small, segregated colony of "free fems" living in the grass-lands. Although there is no hierarchy within the Riding Women camps, there is conflict, and the women quarrel over matters both trivial and political—a direct challenge to the uniform feminine harmony of the all-female societies of matriarchalist texts of previous generations. Indeed, Alldera recoils from their frequent "brutality" and despairs that although she "wanted the women to be perfect," they simply "were not."[60]

In *Motherlines,* the greatest conflict consists of the outright, mutual racism between the free fems and the Riding Women. The two female societies view each other as debased and animalistic. Like Auel's Ayla, who lived uneasily among both Neanderthal and Cro-Magnon societies, Alldera is a liminal figure who does not quite fit in with either the Riding Women or the escaped free fems. Charnas uses the latter group to indicate the lasting trauma of patriar-chal social organization. The escaped slaves are "incapable of decolonizing their minds," and their all-female society mimics the patriarchy of Holdfast through the recapitulation of power dynamics, a class structure, and interper-sonal violence as a means of control.[61]

In the first two novels of the series, Charnas sets up three models of soci-ety: the extremely violent patriarchy of Holdfast, the Amazonian matriarchy of the Riding Women, and the all-female imitative patriarchy of the free fems, who represent the women of the "patriarchal bargain" seen in other matriar-chalist texts. With these three models clearly juxtaposed, Charnas proceeds to use Alldera to lead readers through a remix of Bachofen's stages of matriarchal social development in the following two books, *The Furies* (1994) and *The Conqueror's Child* (1999). In the 1860s, Bachofen used mythology, including the stories of the Greek Amazons, to chart the five stages of human social evolu-tion. The first, "unregulated hetaerism," was a violent patriarchal society, a la Holdfast. The following stages are characterized by evolving forms of gynecoc-racy, and the violence and vengefulness that Bachofen posited are imagined in bloody detail in *The Furies,* which Charnas opens by quoting the angry words of a matriarchalist forebear, Elizabeth Cady Stanton: "When I think of all the wrongs that have been heaped upon womankind, I am ashamed that I am not forever in a condition of chronic wrath, stark mad, skin and bone, my eyes a fountain of tears, my lips overflowing with curses, and my hand against every man and brother!"[62]

In this installment, when Alldera leads the free fems, who have been trained to ride and fight by the Riding Women, in the conquest of Holdfast, she ushers in what Bachofen deemed the "unnatural exaggerated matriarchies" of the ancient world. In this violent, female-ruled society, Alldera, the free fems, and the "unslaves"—the women they free from Holdfaster slavery—represent an overcorrection in power relations in which they recapitulate much of what they had fled, including indiscriminate sexist violence and using men as breeders, bound laborers, and prisoners. For Bachofen, this Amazonian brutality necessarily brought about the final destruction of matriarchy, as, in their zealous attempts to forestall male rebellion, the powerful women instigated the very thing that their oppression was meant to prevent. Bachofen deemed this necessary social progress, as the male uprising reinstated patriarchy and inaugurated the rise of "civilization" as he and his Victorian colleagues understood it.[63]

Tellingly, *The Holdfast Chronicles* are set in the distant future, an implicit warning that the ancient cycle of gendered history as presented by matriarchalists like Bachofen is not necessarily something humans have transcended. Charnas, having already severed the link between matriarchalism and gender essentialism in the first three books of the series, and in stark contrast to both the original matriarchalism of Bachofen and the feminist matriarchalism of writers like Gilman, Marston, and Auel, uses the final book in her series to address the problem of separatism. That is, Charnas, unlike so many of the feminist matriarchalists examined herein, is able to offer readers a positive kind of matriarchalism that does not rely upon either the elimination of men or the emulation of corrupt male power.[64]

Before the conquest, Alldera proclaims that she wants "to see the free fems break out of the old order, not make it all over again." Accordingly, by the end of *The Conqueror's Child,* Holdfast is in the process of being rebuilt through compromise between the slaves-turned-Amazons and the patriarchs-turned-slaves, not because compromise and compassion are the essential traits of women in power, but out of necessity. The New Holdfast is postmatriarchal, a multicultural society that allows for a full range of human emotions and behaviors, rather than the harmonious, bland, and "androgynous utopias" of Gilman, Marston, or Sheldon. Although much bloodshed preceded the establishment of the New Holdfast, the final social model in this series is one based on mutual "respect," as the women and the men both forcibly discard their damaging beliefs about "how men really *are* or how women really *are*" and attempt to construct a society based on participatory democracy. The success of the New Holdfast would rely upon both sexes. Alldera concludes, "It's going to take everybody to come up with some answers," to destroy the old brutality, and to raise the younger generations in "better ways." In this series, then, Charnas writes her way out of the repetitive paradox of matriarchalism—the trap in which visions of female power either entail essentialism and separatism, or they simply re-create contemporary versions of male power.[65]

The women's liberation movement thus produced both cultural and radical feminism, and with them, both essentialist and radical matriarchalism. Classic feminist matriarchalism, along the lines of Gilman or Marston, holds that matriarchies feature peace, equality, and prosperity not because of external forces like plagues that wiped out patriarchal problems, but rather because of the exertion of power by the internal forces of femininity—the innately female characteristics of nurturing, fairness, and service to the family and community. Matriarchalist fiction about prehistory, heavily indebted to the feminist spirituality movement and to the new wave of matriarchalist archaeology, replicated these claims.

At the same time, science fiction writers like Le Guin and Sheldon offered new forms of matriarchalism that struggled openly with questions of sex and gender, only slightly refracting the traditional essentialism that characterized contemporary cultural feminism. Others, like Russ and Charnas, were more successful in their attempts to revise matriarchalism. Charnas once proclaimed that "closed systems kill," and the juxtaposition of various social forms—patriarchal oppression, matriarchal liberation, constant warfare between the sexes, and female-led cooperation between the sexes to create a new kind of society—in *The Female Man* and *The Holdfast Chronicles* offers a new form of feminist matriarchalism that does away with essentialism to envision worlds without the restrictions of gender. In this way, like Baum in an earlier era, they represent the radical feminist wing of matriarchalist texts. As such, they present two challenges to traditional interpretations of the split between cultural and radical feminism. While many feminists and scholars, most notably Alice Echols and Ellen Willis, have argued that radical feminism ended in the mid-1970s, the continued publication of radical feminist matriarchalism in science fiction, which spanned the mid-1970s to the late 1990s in terms of publication dates, indicates a longer lifespan. Moreover, although cultural feminism was often criticized by radical feminists as separatist and apolitical, in radical feminist matriarchalism, revolutionary politics and separatism are not opposed; rather, they are interdependent and intertwined.[66]

Outside of the genre of science fiction, radical feminism was subsumed by cultural feminism by the late 1970s, and the radical texts of Russ and Charnas did not revolutionize American matriarchalism. They and others did change the landscape within the genre, however; after what Russ deemed a "mini-boom of feminist utopias" in the 1970s, it was "virtually impossible for an SF writer to take gender for granted anymore." While their works were widely read within and received many awards from the science fiction community, there was not a broad audience for them. Instead, by the end of the century, essentialist, cultural feminism came to permeate both academic and popular matriarchalism. Feminist science fiction remained a niche market, and while works like *The Female Man* went through numerous printings, Auel's essentialist *Earth's Children* series sold by the millions (to date, 45 million) as the feminist spirituality movement continued to grow; one scholar found, and annotated, over one thousand publications about the feminist spirituality movement between 1980 and 1992.[67]

Although these were niche genres, matriarchalism was widely available in the 1970s. The Amazon Princess Diana, always a hit in the comics, came to television in *Wonder Woman,* which hit the small screen as a prime-time show in the late 1970s. Starring former beauty queen Lynda Carter as the Amazing Amazon, the show followed Marston's original comic closely, featuring Paradise Island in the first episode as a lush, Greek utopia inhabited by athletic, democratically minded Amazons clad in brief, pastel nightgowns. The show ran for three seasons, eventually leaving World War II behind so that Wonder Woman could fight crime in the present. American viewers were thus treated with a hefty dose of classic feminist matriarchalism each week during the second half of the 1970s via this popular television show. The repackaged Marston-era message that the superheroine's essence was to teach women loving power reflected contemporary cultural feminism, and radical feminists charged that celebrating an individual superhero was anathema to the movement's emphasis on collective experiences of sexism. Historian Jill Lepore summed up the critique: "Who needs consciousness-raising and equal pay when you're an Amazon with an invisible plane?" The maternalist matriarchalism of Auel and the cultural feminism of *Wonder Woman* enjoyed wider audiences than feminist science fiction, and by the 1980s, in the context of the Reagan-era rise of conservative politics, neoliberal economics, and antifeminist social policies, radical feminist science fiction was not likely to take root within mainstream popular culture.[68]

In short, even as the separatist female institutions of cultural feminism proved to be important spaces during antifeminist times, aspects of cultural feminism, like mother-worship, dovetailed well with the developing backlash against organized feminism in the 1980s. One scholar indicates the pitfalls of locating female power within gendered characteristics identified with maternity: "The tendency to identify women with innocence, purity, and nonviolence results in an idealization that at the very least calls into question the practicality of this kind of theorizing as a basis for social action." In the cultural context of the 1980s and 1990s, feminism suffered under a coordinated, conservative counterassault, and a neotraditional emphasis on motherhood ascended in popular culture. Scholars Susan Douglas and Meredith Michaels coined the phrase the "new momism" to describe the overwhelming idealization of motherhood in American culture in the 1980s and 1990s. A direct reference to Wylie's antimatriarchalism of the 1940s, the "new momism" was "the insistence that no woman is truly complete or fulfilled unless she has kids, that women remain the best primary caretakers of children, and that to be a remotely decent mother, a woman has to devote her entire physical, psychological, emotional and intellectual being, 24/7, to her children." The new momism was widely promoted through social mores, the media, and even legislation, as many scholars of recent history have shown. There was, however, a key difference between the old and the new: even in popular culture celebrating women as mothers in the 1980s and 1990s, they were never afforded the kind of matriarchal power that characterized Wylie's Cold War momism. The new momism, then, was just a new form of repackaged sociocultural and economic pressures that supported patriarchal gender roles.[69]

The popular feminist matriarchalism represented alternately by archaeomythology, prehistoric fiction, and science fiction of the 1970s was thus subsumed by the constant cultural promotion of the renewed idealization of motherhood in the 1980s and 1990s. Relying as it did upon both the promotion of motherhood among middle-class women and the denigration of those mothers to whom the practice of intensive mothering was either undesirable or unavailable, the new momism played a key role in the resurrection, exaggeration, and popularization of another form of antimatriarchalism in the late twentieth-century United States. In 1989, psychoanalyst Nancy Chodorow identified the two opposing sides, claiming that "blame and idealization of mothers have become our cultural ideology." In short, as pronatalism reached its peak, so, too, did mother-blaming. A range of women fell under criticism for nonconformity to the ideal, and foremost among these heavily scrutinized women were single or divorced mothers, poor mothers, and women of color. This condemnation gave rise to a constellation of images that echoed the racism and evolutionism of Gilman's feminist utopias and French Sheldon's imperial matriarchalism. In the next chapter, I will unpack the mythology of the "black matriarch," an imagined subject of concern that developed over many decades to become the most well-known form of antimatriarchalism in the past generation. Through the figure of the "black matriarch," American matriarchalism's consistent and enduring struggle with racism was renewed and reinvigorated for the twenty-first century.[70]

9

MAMMIES, MATRIARCHS, AND WELFARE QUEENS
Racist Matriarchalism

> Sapphire. Mammy. Tragic mulatto wench. Workhorse, can swing an
> ax, lift a load, pick cotton with any man. A wonderful housekeeper.
> Excellent with children . . . She's always had more opportunities than
> the black man because she was no threat to the white man so he made
> it easy for her. But curiously enough, she frequently ends up on wel-
> fare. Nevertheless, she is more educated and makes more money than
> the black man . . . She is hard on and unsupportive of black men, dom-
> ineering, castrating. She tends to wear the pants around her house.
> Very strong. Sorrow rolls right off her brow like so much rain. Tough,
> unfeminine.
>
> —MICHELLE WALLACE, *Black Macho and the Myth of the Superwoman*

N 1961, American moviegoers were introduced to three generations of the
Younger family in the award-winning film *A Raisin in the Sun*. Mama Lena
Younger's heavy-handed ministrations over each of the beings in her care,
including one sad, sun-starved potted plant, prompt reactions from her
family ranging from eye rolls to door-slamming exits. Her thirty-five-year-old
son complains that he lives in "the world's most backwards nation of women"
in which his wife henpecks him and his mother "butchers" his big plans by
refusing him money. Lena is a long-suffering, Lord-worshiping, exhausted matriarch whose only dream is for her wayward son to assume his rightful role as
head of the house so that she can just "sit this body down and let it rest—just
let it rest from here on in."[1]

Mama Lena is a combination of black character types familiar to American
audiences. She is the nurturing Mammy and the strong Matriarch. As such,
she can be both loving and fearsome; for every hug she bestows upon her
beloved grandchild, there is a glowering look at her ineffectual son. In this
chapter, I discuss these two images as part of the constant pop cultural presence of the so-called black matriarchy over the second half of the twentieth
century. As the supposedly content servant in white households, the Mammy

figure was meant to tame the perceived threat of matriarchy, or the "dominating, emasculating" stereotype of black womanhood. A salve for white anxiety, Mammy reigned as the premier black female character in mid-century popular culture, although the Black Matriarch loomed subtextually. But with the rightward sociopolitical turn against the general consensus that characterized the New Deal and civil rights eras, the Black Matriarch was defined by her "rejection of willing subjugation" to white, middle-class, nuclear-family norms. A "failed Mammy," the Black Matriarch became, by the end of the twentieth century, a popular figure of derision known as the "welfare queen."[2]

Mammy and the Matriarch are thus codependent stereotypes, and each would come to have a host of personae in pop culture. In 1982, scholar Trudier Harris wrote, these personae were "called Matriarch, Emasculator and Hot Momma. Sometimes Sister, Pretty Baby, Auntie, Mammy and Girl. Called Unwed Mother, Welfare Recipient and Inner City Consumer." These representations of the Black Matriarch are what Patricia Hill Collins has labeled "controlling images," meant to maintain and justify the oppression of African American women by making "racism, sexism, poverty, and other forms of social injustice appear to be natural, normal, and inevitable parts of everyday life." In the final decades of the twentieth century, the controlling image of the Black Matriarch became the reigning manifestation of antimatriarchalism in US popular culture.[3]

The mythology of the Black Matriarch has its roots in slavery as an image used to justify various exploitative and torturous practices. Imagining slave women as inhumanly strong justified hard labor, sexual assault, forced breeding, and the breakup of slave families through sales, and the usefulness of this stereotype for the purposes of labor exploitation lived on through Reconstruction and Jim Crow. During the 1930s, this mythology made inroads into academic discourse via sociology, as experts researched the folkways of American subcultures by studying small-town southerners and comparing rural and urban black communities. In 1937, John Dollard posited that African American women's growing economic independence fostered a "weak, mother-centered family" that disempowered black men. Dollard's description of emasculated men and sexualized, domineering women was set firmly in the Jim Crow era, but it called back heavily to the sexual stereotypes of slavery.[4]

This image continued its academic ascendance two years later, when Harvard sociologist E. Franklin Frazier published *The Negro Family in the United States*. Frazier bridged the various matriarchalist discourses, deftly combining antimatriarchalism with what would come to be known as momism just a few years later. As his editor Ernest W. Burgess explained, using classic evo-lutionist language, the mother-based family systems Frazier analyzed were based on "a pattern of familial human relations more primordial and more 'natural' in the sense of being less influenced by convention and tradition than those of any so-called 'primitive' peoples studied by the anthropologist." In Part II of *The Negro Family*, "In the House of the Mother," Frazier described the "matriarchate" of "unfettered motherhood" that replaced enslaved fam-ily systems post-Emancipation. This alleged matriarchy was characterized by a lack of birth control, multiple sexual partners, laxity about both marriage and divorce, illegitimate children, and an apparent preference on the part of African American women to live without men, often in multigenerational households headed by their own mothers. Positing a link between the gender dynamics of slavery and freedom, Frazier explained that the "self-reliance" and "self-sufficiency" that slave women had to learn meant that for freed women, "neither economic necessity nor tradition had instilled in her the spirit of sub-ordination to masculine authority."[5]

Although he listed some instances of forced family disorganization during the transition from slavery to emancipation, Frazier argued that the matriar-chal family was a voluntarily chosen social form, citing one African American widow who refused to marry the father of her youngest child because "she did not 'want to be bothered with a husband' and was glad that her first hus-band died." Frazier expressed repeated surprise at the women's lack of rec-ognition that they might be violating social mores. At the same time, they loved their children dearly and held motherhood in high esteem; this brand of matriarchal motherhood entailed "intense emotional interdependence be-tween mother and child," including extended breastfeeding, overfeeding, and a preference for maternal care when their children fell ill. The mothers "show equally strong attachment for their grown sons and daughters," such that the sons, when drafted into World War I, "often complained in the manner of chil-dren of being torn from their mothers." Daughters tended to follow the exam-ple of their mothers, so that by 1930, more black families than white families were headed by women in both rural and urban areas.[6]

Frazier expressed a begrudging admiration for many of the women he in-terviewed. He idealized the black mother of the rural South, but when she joined African American migrants from the South as they integrated into the nation's major cities, she became a social problem. Frazier's gravest concern was with the role of this family form in urban America: "As the women in these rural communities move about and come into contact with the outside world, illegitimacy loses its harmless character in becoming divorced from the folkways of these simple peasants. It becomes a part of the general disorganization of family life, in which the satisfaction of undisciplined impulses results in disease and in children who are unwanted and uncared for."

The family organization broke down in the cities, where "poverty, ignorance, and color force them to seek homes in deteriorated slum areas from which practically all institutional life has disappeared." Frazier explained: "During the course of their migration to the city, family ties are broken, and the restraints which once held in check immoral sex conduct lose their force. However, in some cases where the rural folkways concerning unmarried motherhood are in conflict with the legal requirements of the city, the persistence of these folkways in the urban environment will create social problems." The rural "Matriarchate" thus became the pathologically promiscuous "Outlawed Motherhood" in the cities.[7]

According to Frazier, "internal cohesion" and "communal institutions" were lost in the urban environment. In response to this chaos, the matriarch featured a complex and often confusing combination of maternal traits, ranging from overweening to indifference and even neglect. This change of context was key for Frazier, as it entailed widespread, rather than individual, disintegration: African American mothers were a threat to society because the matriarchal system they perpetuated resulted in socioeconomic discord. The imbalance of strong womanhood and unhealthy masculinity yielded directionless, "drifting masses" of "roving men," "homeless women," and "rebellious youth," an argument that preceded the white, middle-class fear of juvenile delinquency by several years.[8]

Praised as an "important contribution," Frazier's work was awarded the Anisfield-Wolf Award for its contributions to the understanding of racism and race relations, and it had an immediate and significant influence on the treatment of single motherhood by social workers, who came to see the "matriarchal system" in black communities as "dangerously dysfunctional" by the 1940s. Fears of the black "matriarchate" took a circuitous route from Frazier's academic warning to popular culture. This can partially be accounted for simply because of racism, or more specifically, because of segregation—the dearth of African Americans in popular culture, with the exception of music, can help explain the lack of "black momism" in mid-century media. This is not to say,

however, that images of the matriarchal black female were not carefully commodified and created for white consumption during the era of Cold War momism. When African American women did appear in mid-century pop culture,
they were depicted in one primary way: as Mammy, or the domestic worker
who existed solely to comfort the white family for whom she worked.[9]

If the Matriarch was the representation of the black mother within the
black home, the Mammy was the representation of the black mother within
the white home. Mammy's occupation reflected the reality of black domestic service in white households, but her character in popular culture denoted
something else entirely. She was depicted as a happy servant, at her best when
serving white folks, devoid of her own familial and cultural connections except her her domineering relationship with other African American servants.
In 1938, Jessie Parkhurst listed her traits: "She was considered self-respecting,
independent, loyal, forward, gentle, captious, affectionate, true, strong, just,
warm-hearted, compassionate-hearted, fearless, popular, brace, good, pious,
quick-witted, capable, thrifty, proud, regal, courageous, superior, skillful, tender, queenly, dignified, neat, quick, tender, competent, possessed with a temper, trustworthy, faithful, patient, tyrannical, sensible, discreet, efficient, careful, harsh, devoted, truthful, neither apish nor servile."

Although she hardly ever lived in the "big house" with her white employers
and she often had to eat alone in the kitchen, the Mammy was "like one of the
family." Generically named ("Mammy") or symbolically adopted ("Auntie"),
the African American mother was removed from the context of her power—
black households and communities—and summarily defused. Her authority
was clearly constrained: it was only over the white children for whom she was
employed to care, and even then final authority rested with their biological
parents. Mammy clearly represented nostalgia for the "Lost Cause" of the Old
South, but she also represented a timely containment of black women's desta-
bilizing potential in white homes. Large, asexual, nurturing, and always smiling in the white kitchen, her alleged contentedness was a comfort to white
audiences during decades of violent segregation.[10]

In a nod to matriarchal evolutionism, Mammy's "subhuman" qualities, a
holdover from racist perspectives of female slaves, contrasted starkly with
those of the white women for whom she worked: she was large and strong,
she rarely ate and never slept, and she had no apparent need for human contact beyond her white charges. This subtle positioning of Mammy as somehow less-than-human and definitely less-than-white-woman belied her place

within the history of American matriarchalism. Mammy represented docile near-savagery, but, with the aid of her white employers, she could be uplifted to semi-civilized status. Mammy was, in essence, the "white woman's burden" of evolutionist matriarchalism within the home.[11]

In keeping with Frazier's contextual argument, Mammy was always represented in a controlled context. Just as Frazier argued that black matriarchy was a positive, even useful, system in rural, isolated areas and a dangerous one in urban settings, the Mammy figure's dominance was a force for social good in specific contexts—i.e., the white home, where she could be surveilled and contained. These representations often ignored or minimized the Mammy's relationship with her biological children, because severing the Black Matriarch from her offspring symbolically destroyed the source of her power. When Mammy's own children were mentioned, it was assumed that she "had done a better job of raising her white children than she had done with her own" children, who were often "disappointing" at best and criminal at worst. Thus, the Mammy image was an attempt to "influence Black maternal behavior," as African American domestic workers could use their experiences in their employers' homes to teach their own children "their assigned place in White power structures" and to train them in the ways of white civilization.[12]

The timing of Mammy's popularity as a character in film and on television indicates her role as a salve for white anxiety. Mammy preexisted Frazier's academic study by a long shot, but she proved to be extraordinarily durable, a frequent fixture of popular culture by the 1930s. The increase in Mammy representations indicates white concern about several trends: the Great Migration, or the mass movement of African Americans out of the South; the inability of white employers to control and fully exploit black domestic laborers; and the increase of white women, especially married white women, in the labor force by the 1940s. Mammy was something of a staple of interwar popular culture, often played on film by the same few actors. Louise Beavers made a career out of the role of the black domestic, training herself in Hollywood's version of working-class, southern "black dialect" and force-feeding herself throughout her career to maintain the heavy weight required of Mammy. But Mammy's most famous turn on screen was Hattie McDaniel's Oscar-winning performance in *Gone With the Wind* (1939), which came out the same year as Frazier's sociological study. The novel and the film span the Civil War, from slavery to freedom, but Mammy's role as "Miss Scarlett's" maid never changes, indicating her transhistorical devotion to her white charge. McDaniel, like

Beavers, made a career out of playing the character in films, on the radio, and, at the end of her life, on television.[13]

As scholars have noted, Mammy was much more complicated than her caricature. One of Hattie McDaniel's biographers argues that "not too far beneath the smiling and nurturing surface lay a simmering rage with the white people that she loyally but often grudgingly served." In *Soul on Ice* (1968), Eldridge Cleaver explained that "[the white man] turned the black women into a strong self-reliant Amazon and deposited her into his kitchen—that's the secret of Aunt Jemima's bandana." Cleaver is, of course, not to be held up as an unimpeachable authority on black women, but his metaphor here is instructive. As the Combahee River Collective reiterated in their foundational "Black Feminist Statement," African American women have "always embodied, if only in their physical manifestation, an adversary stance to white male rule and have actively resisted its inroads upon them and their communities in both dramatic and subtle ways." Mammy's smile in response to white labor exploitation did nothing to diminish this significant community function; in fact, her cheerful demeanor may have served as a valuable cover. Domestic work could be more exploitive than other labor due to the shared private space and sometimes intense personal relationships between domestic laborers and their employers. Deference and submission were rewarded, as was silence. Yet domestic labor in white homes also, according to Patricia Hill Collins, "created the conditions for distinctively Black and female forms of resistance." These "outsider-within" conditions allowed for the formation of political critique and economic solidarity. Mammy's bandana or the "help's" apron—accessories meant to denote inferior racial and class status—could mask personal politics and the potential for resistance. By the 1960s, a new form of matriarchalism developed that acknowledged this potential, and depictions of Mammy in film and literature became accordingly more complex.[14]

Mama Lena Younger of *A Raisin in the Sun* (1962), as we have seen, was a combination of archetypes. Bosomy and maternal, she was Mammy, but the setting is a crucial departure for the stereotype: her story takes place in her family's home, away from the control of white employers. In this space, Mama Lena is in charge of her three-room, five-person household. With the exception of *Time*, which tellingly deemed Mama Lena "a mean old man in a wig," critics hailed her as the "most realistic portrait" to date of a black female character. As the Black Matriarch, Mama Lena rules the household, emasculating her son, annoying her daughter, and training her daughter-in-law in her tactics. Her years of back-breaking work are eclipsed by the chronic sadness she feels for the impotent Walter, her son who believes himself to be too good for his chauffeur job. For all of Lena's strength, she wants nothing more than to abdicate her position to Walter. She relies upon her strong will to get the family to the point of this transfer of power, inflicting psychological pain—and physical pain, as she slaps her daughter at one point and later towers over a cowering Walter as she raises her hand to strike him—on the entire family, including herself. Although she proudly asserts at the end that Walter finally "came into his manhood," like "the rainbow after the storm," his ascendance is, in fact, bought and paid for by Lena.[15]

Other pop culture of the 1960s featured strong black female characters who revealed the Mammy-Matriarch's life away from controlling white eyes. Calpurnia, of Harper Lee's *To Kill A Mockingbird* (1960), signals an obvious change in the representation of Mammy. Although she fits the usual stereotype of caretaker, cook, and "one of the family," Calpurnia has a nickname, Cal, that is not based on her status as a servant, although she is not given a last name in the novel. She is not large and round, signifying soft maternity; rather, she is "all angles and bones," and she can be a threatening figure when the children disobey. Lee refers to her as a "tyrannical presence" while at work caretaking for Scout and Jem Finch.[16]

Significantly, Calpurnia has a family and complicated life of her own outside of the white Finch household. Calpurnia's real life is lived outside of the white family's surveillance and control, as the young Finches learn when they attend church with her one Sunday. To make the white children presentable to her own community, she bathes them roughly, chooses their clothing carefully, and orders them to smile. At church, the children notice that Calpurnia is different; she code switches, speaks in dialect, and serves as a translator regarding the racial and sexual politics of the sexual assault case that is currently rocking the small town. The occasion prompts the children to think about Calpurnia differently. Scout muses: "That Calpurnia led a modest double life never dawned on me. The idea that she had a separate existence outside our household was a novel one, to say nothing of her having command of two languages." The children learn more about Calpurnia on this day trip to her church than they had in years of her service in their household. They knew, for instance, that she had children, but they had never considered them.[17]

Although these glimpses into Calpurnia's home life did not make it into the award-winning film version of *To Kill a Mockingbird* (1962), it seems that they were significant to the narrative, as Harper Lee emphasized the differences between the local black and white communities in an early draft of the novel, published in 2015 as *Go Set a Watchman*. In this version, which controversially features Atticus Finch recast as a white supremacist and evolutionist who argues that African Americans are in their "childhood as a people," readers get a revealing look into Calpurnia's life when Scout—here known by her formal name, Jean Louise—goes to her home. The politics of local white opposition to desegregation become personal for Calpurnia when her grandson is accused of vehicular homicide for running over a drunken white man. In her own home, Calpurnia shuns Jean Louise, avoiding eye contact, dissembling, "wearing her company manners," and putting on the "rigidly controlled public performance" of self that African American women enacted as both survival and resistance. "She sat there in front of me," thinks Jean Louise, "and she didn't see me, she saw white folks." This revelation of the subtextual dynamics of their lifelong relationship devastates Jean Louise:

> She looked into the old woman's face and she knew it was hopeless. Calpurnia was watching her, and in Calpurnia's eyes was no hint of compassion.
>
> Jean Louise rose to go. "Tell me one thing, Cal," she said, "just one thing before I go—please, I've got to know. Did you hate us?"
>
> The old woman sat silent, bearing the burden of her years. Jean Louise waited.
>
> Finally, Calpurnia shook her head.

In this original draft, Calpurnia "subverts the myth" of devotion to her white employers, directing her loyalties and love to the local black community.[18]

As these changing pop cultural representations indicate, with the vocal and visible activism of African American women that characterized the civil rights movement, the Mammy figure had become a target. Local NAACP branches across the country organized boycotts and protests of Aunt Jemima in the late 1950s, and by 1960, the national NAACP became involved as well. By the early 1960s, black women were over twice as likely as black men to find work in professional occupations, and in a 1972 sociological study, many of these women cited their strong mothers as the impetus behind their professional careers. African American women were sitting down on buses, sitting in on segregated businesses, marching in the streets, registering to vote, and taking jobs that were once unavailable to them. As one scholar put it, "Rosa Parks, Jo Ann Gibson Robinson, Coretta Scott King, and their sister activists served as flesh-and-blood reminders" that the contented caricature of Mammy "bore little resemblance" to real African American women. Integration was depicted as dangerous to the traditional American family for many reasons, not the least of which was that the Mammy would no longer smile, sing, and stay in the white folks' kitchen, and her children would no longer stay hidden. For many African Americans, this fracturing of the white supremacist containment of the Black Matriarch was heralded as liberation; but for many white people, who understood the significance of the containment of black female power to the maintenance of white supremacy, there was major cause for concern.[19]

At the same time, the move within the civil rights and black power movements toward examining the roots of poverty in black communities and the rebellions in poor, urban neighborhoods in the mid-1960s prompted a policy answer from the federal government. A flurry of academic and demographic research accompanied President Lyndon Johnson's declaration of the "war on poverty" as scholars, politicians, and activists investigated the problem. As Johnson's researchers sought to answer this question, the ensuing report they issued could have centered upon institutions and structures that maintained systemic inequality. Instead, it rested awkwardly, and very heavily, upon the shoulders of black women.[20]

In the spring of 1965, Secretary of Labor Daniel Patrick Moynihan submitted a report to Johnson on the status of black families in the United States, in which he argued that their matriarchal "family structure" was a primary source of poverty. In the report, Moynihan stated bluntly: "A fundamental fact of Negro American family life is the often reversed role of husband and wife." This "highly unstable" family structure had its roots in slavery, and, Moynihan warned in bold print, it was approaching "complete breakdown" in "urban centers," just as Frazier had warned in 1939. Moynihan relied upon Frazier's historical time line, arguing that following Emancipation, racism had in effect "forced [black families] into a matriarchal structure which, because it is so out of line with the rest of American society, seriously retards the progress of the group as a whole, and imposes a crushing burden on the Negro male and, in consequence, on a great many Negro women as well." Citing illegitimacy rates and the number of female-headed households within black communities, Moynihan explained that this family dynamic led to "low power" males, unemployment, poverty, welfare dependency, delinquency, crime, addiction to narcotics, and a generational "tangle of pathology" that perpetuated and even increased over time. Indeed, the damage was so thorough, Moynihan remarked, that the fact "that the Negro American has survived at all is extraordinary—a lesser people might simply have died out."[21]

The matriarchal structure had the effect of unmanning black men, who became demoralized by and resentful of their demotion from the provider role. Receiving welfare exacerbated this emasculation: "Consider the fact that relief investigators or caseworkers are normally women and deal with the housewife. Already suffering a loss in prestige and authority in the family because of his failure to be the chief breadwinner, the male head of the family feels deeply, this obvious transfer of planning for the family's well being to two women, one of them an outsider." Moynihan explained that because patriarchy was the dominant American institutional model, it was dangerous for any group not to follow suit: "It is clearly a disadvantage for a minority group to be operating on one principle, while the great majority of the population, and the one with the most advantages to begin with, is operating on another." The current situation was most "humiliating" for African American men, because, Moynihan argued, the "segregation and the submissiveness it exacts, is surely more destructive to the male," as the "very essence of the male animal, from the bantam rooster to the four-star general, is to strut." In addition to jobs for African American men, Moynihan suggested that training in the "utterly masculine world" of military service—a "world away from women, a world run by strong men of unquestioned authority"—would help men learn how to counteract matriarchy at home.[22]

As proof of the transformative powers of patriarchy, Moynihan pointed to the success of the black middle class, which apparently rectified any residual matriarchal proclivities by erring in the opposite direction; citing Frazier, Moynihan suggested that black middle-class families were "if anything, more patriarchal and protective of [their] children than the general run of such families." However, because of housing segregation patterns, which often lumped African American families together in urban areas regardless of class, the "stable half" of African American children—those of the middle class— were always in danger of "being drawn into" the "disturbed group," due to their constant exposure to the matriarchal pathology of their poverty-stricken neighbors. The necessary "national action," then, was to break the cycle of the "tangle of pathology" by addressing "questions of family structure." The report ended in bold print: "The policy of the United States is to bring the

Negro American to full and equal sharing in the responsibilities and rewards of citizenship. To this end, the programs of the Federal government bearing on this objective shall be designed to have the effect, directly or indirectly, of enhancing the stability and resources of the Negro American family."[23]

Although the report later helped to inspire conservative welfare reform, it was intended as a research-based, racially liberal text that squarely placed the blame not on racist biological arguments, but on cultural ones—family structures, and more specifically, on the Black Matriarch. In a policy speech cowritten by Moynihan at Howard University in June of 1965, President Johnson explained: "For Negro poverty is not white poverty. Many of its causes and many of its cures are the same but there are differences—deep, corrosive, obstinate differences radiating painful roots into the community and into the family and the nature of the individual." The governmental approach, then, would focus on families and would include employment and income assistance programs, subsidies for homes, and a White House conference to further investigate the issue.[24]

Many media outlets, as well as the Johnson administration, accepted the report uncritically, as did some civil rights leaders like Bayard Rustin, who proclaimed, "the Negro family can be reconstructed only where the Negro male is permitted to be the economic and psychological head of the family." A *Newsweek* story entitled "New Crisis: The Negro Family"—published one day before the riots in Watts began—bemoaned the "splintering Negro family," which was apparently a "germ" endemic to the race and "a constant threat to the youngsters of millions of stable, middle-class Negro families." The family "disintegration" was a "self-sustaining vicious circle" that kept all black people in danger of falling into poverty. Although many publications avoided mention of the Matriarch in favor of the vague term "families," others pinpointed her as the cause, as seen in the alliterative and unwieldy *Wall Street Journal* headline, "Family Life Breakdown in Negro Slums Sows Seeds of Race Violence—Husbandless Homes Spawn Young Hoodlums, Impede Reforms, Sociologists Say." Lloyd Shearer, Hollywood reporter for *Parade* magazine, offered celebrities Lena Horne and Eartha Kitt, both of whom were married to white men, as evidence of "the rejection of the Negro male by his own women." The page-long article included a photograph of an African American man getting arrested with the caption, "Negro male hostility, born of rejection." "The reason Negro men so frequently desert their families is that they feel inferior to their women," Shearer explained. "They feel inferior, because

they are inferior—educationally, economically, morally—and this omnipres-
ent inferiority breeds hostility."[25]

At the time, and certainly in numerous volumes ever since, African American scholars disputed Moynihan's evidence. Many challenged his numbers,
which were less profound in context; despite the renewed concern about the
Black Matriarch's increasing power, the number of female-headed households
rose only 5 percent between 1940 and 1960. Others argued that the rate of
family "deterioration" was no more alarming in black communities than it
was in white ones, and several studies published before and after the report
confirmed that black families in no way resembled matriarchies. Moreover,
policy perspectives on single motherhood were obviously racialized, as white
single mothers were seen as "neurotic" and in need of treatment, while black
single mothers were "pathological" and in need of correction. Critics charged
that Moynihan and his research team failed to take into account demographic
realities, such as the sex ratio of black men to black women, which indicate
that the number of female-headed households was a function of broad structural forces rather than racialized matriarchal tendencies. Pauli Murray, the
civil rights activist, lawyer, and frequent critic of "Jane Crow," wrote a furious,
unpublished letter to *Newsweek* condemning the censure of black women "for
their efforts to overcome a handicap not of their making and for trying to
meet the standards of the country as a whole." The National Organization for
Women, made up largely of white women, condemned the report as "pure
slander of women" meant to shore up patriarchy.[26]

Powerful women, other respondents countered, were a source of strength,
not pathology, in black communities. Moreover, "matriarchy" was a misnomer,
a "cruel hoax" in a society in which the wage gap placed African American
women substantially below both black men and white women. Angela Davis
wrote that "as is so often the case" with stereotypes, "the "reality is actually the
diametrical opposite of the myth." bell hooks stated bluntly, "No matriarchy
has ever existed in the United States." The report, then, held "Black women
responsible for power they do not possess."[27]

Moynihan's gender politics were obviously problematic, as his primary
premise seemed to be that the solution to the problem of poverty was, in short,
patriarchy. His clear emphasis was on securing jobs for African American men,
"even if this meant that some women's job had to be redesigned to enable men
to fulfill them." Although Moynihan was not explicit about the subtext of his
recommendations, scholars like Paula Giddings have spelled them out: "The

thinking seemed to be: Just make Black men the lords of their own castles and everything will be all right. To reach this utopia, of course, Black women would somehow have to slow down, become less achievement-oriented, give up much of their independence. By remaining assertive, they were ruining the family and so ruining the race." Giddings concludes: "The Moynihan Report was not so much racist as it was sexist." Moynihan, of course, did not invent this gendered framework, but the report did have the effect of reviving the specter of the Black Matriarch who had for so long been buried under Mammy's cheerful girth.[28]

Although the Moynihan Report would later fuel racialized right-wing policies, particularly those dealing with crime and welfare, at the time, the revival of the Black Matriarch at first failed to garner as much pop cultural attention as her white counterpart, the suburban Mom. The systematic exclusion of African Americans from postwar suburbanization meant that these two allegedly coexisting matriarchies had little to no contact with each other. But the fears of each were linked. As sociologist Robert Staples explained in a takedown of the Moynihan Report, those social scientists who expressed concern about both the suburban and the black matriarchies warned of a sort of downward spiral. If the solution to the latter, they argued, was to "exhort black slum dwellers to emulate the presumably more stable white middle-class, restore father to his rightful place, and build a more durable family life," then these families were double endangered by exposure to "the threat of a suburban matriarchy."[29]

The reemergence of the Black Matriarch had the effect of changing representations in popular culture. It seems that the matriarchal subtext of the Mammy apparently made her too dangerous for white consumption, especially when she began to clap back in popular culture. Mammy rebelled in the film *Hurry Sundown* (1968), in which postwar housewife-cum-southern-belle Julie tries to convince her "old colored mammy" Aunt Rose to sell her family's land to a developer. Julie and her husband Henry are convinced that Aunt Rose's family has lived on the land for generations due to the white family's benevolence, despite Aunt Rose's insistence that her family bought it from "the Yankees" at a public auction during Reconstruction. Aunt Rose, a sickly old woman who gets out of bed just once in the film to greet Julie when she comes to talk business, appears at first to be the elderly version of the sacrificial Mammy; she beams and praises the Christian God and appears to love her former white charge. Julie explains the land deal, and Rose, who already knows the details from her son, plays dumb as she rocks and sings to Julie's child. Julie persists until the smile finally vanishes from Rose's face. "No," she says flatly. "We ain't sellin.'" She rises, angry, and gives Julie a brief history lesson on the land, finally collapsing into bed and whispering to her son, "Make her leave." Although this confrontation kills Rose, on her deathbed, she talks back as no Mammy on screen had done before, explaining to her son:

> I was wrong. I was wrong. I was a white folks' nigger. I was . . . You've got to learn from my mistakes. You've got to fight. You've got to . . . You've got to . . . Swear to me. Swear. It ain't going to be easy . . . You know what I feel most of all? Anger. And hatred. Not so much at what they done to me . . . helping them do it . . . I truly grieve for this sorry thing that has been my life.

Fighting and swearing, anger and hatred: this is the stuff of white fears of black women, and it is especially dangerous when it is revealed as the true feelings of the Mammy in the kitchen. Aunt Rose's final stand, and the interracial cooperation that in the end enables her son to keep her land, prefigured a trend in black female self-representation.[30]

It may have killed her, but Aunt Rose was not alone in her resistance. African American women targeted the reigning stereotypes of the Mammy and the Matriarch, struggling to make their voices heard in the 1960s and 1970s. June Jordan, in her 1970 poem "Memo to Daniel Patrick Moynihan," addressed Moynihan, and by extension all white men, directly: "Don't you liberate me/ From my female black pathology . . . I got a simple proposition/ You take over my position/ Clean your own house, babyface." That same year, in an essay in *Sisterhood is Powerful,* Eleanor Holmes Norton, the ACLU attorney and later congresswoman, questioned the timing of the resurrection of the Black Matriarch: "Are black people to reject so many of white society's values only to accept its view of woman and of the family? At the moment when the white family is caught in a maze of neurotic contradictions, and white women are supremely frustrated with their roles?"[31]

That same year, Toni Cade published an anthology of black female voices— in the form of essays, stories, poems, and conversations—that was later deemed by bell hooks "the most notable attempt by black women to articulate their experiences, their attitudes toward woman's role in society, and the impact of sexism on their lives." Echoing activists like Sojourner Truth and Ida B.

Wells-Barnett, Cade and her contributors challenge an especially destructive use of the Black Matriarch image against African American female activists: as black feminism developed out of women's experiences in the civil rights, New Left, Black Power, and women's liberation movements, charges of matriarchy could derail and obfuscate valid critiques of sexism within these very movements. In a list of twelve pressing agenda items for African American women, Cade places "set[ting] the record straight on the matriarch and the evil Black bitch" third. Nearly every one of the pieces in *The Black Woman* speaks to stereotypes, and the Matriarch—the "folk character largely fashioned by whites out of half-truths and lies about the involuntary condition of black women"— is front and center. Moynihan inserted the Black Matriarch into national discourse, but, unlike Mammy, this stereotype was not simply a white fantasy; the authors included in *The Black Woman* target the internalization of the matriarchal mythology by African American men, who, according to one contributor, "swallowed [Moynihan's] assumptions and conclusions hook, line, and sinker." Over half of the contributors analyze the male backlash against black women, who were told to "stand aside" and let the men do the "real" work of freedom struggles while the women birthed babies for the revolution. Cade asks: "Am I to persist in the role of the Amazon workhorse and house slave?" The contributors invariably agree that the Matriarch was a powerfully racist and sexist myth that, when internalized by African Americans, exposed sexism within and helped to fracture the struggle for black liberation. These authors unpack the damage wrought by the Black Matriarch, a dialogue that continued in nonfiction writing and literature throughout the 1970s.[32]

In the early 1970s, then, critiques of the Moynihan thesis made their way into popular culture. In fact, a popular image of powerful black womanhood appeared in the comics as Nubia, Wonder Woman's black Amazon sister. Like Diana, Nubia is formed by their mother, Queen Hippolyta, out of clay. But the "proud mother of two daughters" is summarily attacked by Mars, the God of War, who kidnaps young Nubia and raises her as "an instrument of vengeance against the Amazons." Nubia is trained by the warlike forces of masculinity, and she is a worthy adversary of men and of Princess Diana herself, until Diana destroys Mars's hold over Nubia by removing his ring from her hand, whereupon she becomes an Amazonian sister and ally who plans to "lead [her] warriors into ways of peace!" Although the story line smacks of white saviorism—Nubia is a violent villain until Diana rescues her—and the sisters are initially pitted against each other, as in the famous cover of *Wonder*

Woman no. 206 in 1973, which features the Wonder Women chained to each other and facing off, swords raised, scowls blazing—the introduction of the "Black Wonder Woman" into the Amazon sisterhood, and her dominance in the popular series for the better part of a year, is noteworthy.[33]

In 1974, fictional representations of the Black Matriarch went beyond mere inclusion when some of the specific critiques voiced in Cade's *The Black Woman* found a pop cultural outlet in the John Berry film *Claudine*. *Claudine* targets negative stereotypes of African American woman- and manhood explicitly, with a keen eye on the supposedly emasculating Matriarch and her ideological offspring, who would soon come to be known as "the welfare queen." Despite her employment as a maid in a white home, the title character is not coded as a Mammy. She is shown first with her own children, and then with her female friends discussing love interests, defying the traditional representation of the black domestic worker who has no life, family, or community of her own. Claudine Price, played by Diahann Carroll, supports herself and her six children in Harlem by collecting welfare and working, but her job as a maid is illicit because her minimal paycheck would cause deductions from her public assistance check if the welfare office were to find out about it. She is thus a welfare "cheat," even though this strategy is necessary to survive and provide for her children. Claudine is well aware of this Catch-22, and she lashes out against the gender politics of poverty throughout the film. She exposes the fault line of structural inequality as she talks back to the white social worker that comes to her apartment unannounced to inspect the family's lifestyle, deducting pennies from the assistance total when she discovers that Claudine's boyfriend Rupert has bought the children soda.[34]

Although she is always straightforward, at times stern, and frequently open with her frustration, Claudine is no matriarchal ballbreaker. She worries about the "shitty neighborhood and the shitty school and the shitty world," and she is empathetic when Rupert discusses his struggles with African American masculinity and fatherhood. Together, they openly mock the governmental rules about public assistance for married couples. The cause of oppression of African American men is clear; it is not Claudine, who is herself in a powerless position, but rather, as she explains to her oldest son, "Mr. Whitey" who exploits the black man and "cuts off his manhood." The obvious villain that plagues this family is the welfare worker, and, by extension, the racist socioeconomic system. Although it is one of the main characters' goals, Moynihan's solution—the formation of a heteronormative nuclear family—is exposed as flawed in

Claudine, as she and Rupert encounter various state-sponsored obstacles to marriage. A pop cultural version of the welfare rights movement of the 1970s, *Claudine* explores the misconceptions and stereotypes of Moynihan's "pathological" subjects.[35]

Lest any viewer miss the message, the original soundtrack underscored the film's message about gender, race, class, and systemic oppression. In "Mr. Welfare Man," which plays during multiple scenes of the film, Curtis Mayfield's lyrics, ably sung by Gladys Knight and the Pips, descry the sexism, classism, and racism of the welfare system in which "Society gave us no choice, tried to silence my voice, pushing me on the welfare." "Mr. Welfare Man" plays loudly during the scenes in which Claudine and her children rush to hide things— the toaster, the iron, the coffee pot—from the social worker, for fear the white woman will think that they were somehow cheating the system through the use of basic household appliances. These various visual and aural cues make plain the overwhelming nature of state surveillance of the poor African American mother, underscoring her powerlessness against the white supremacist apparatus—which is, according to the song, a control mechanism that functions like a "private eye for the FBI" or even the KKK—and belying any dangerous matriarchal tendencies.[36]

A cleverly blunt exposé of the racialized and gendered stereotypes of poverty in the United States, *Claudine* was very popular. Diahann Carroll was nominated for the Academy Award for Best Actress that year, the soundtrack won a Golden Globe, and the film grossed an estimated $6 million. Tellingly, some reviews sought to distance the film from its messages about race, while one critic argued that the movie's positive message could speak to both black and white audiences. Not all reviews were positive, and some accused the film of trafficking in stereotypes. Many moviegoers, however, identified with Claudine's frustrations and small victories against the system. In "Remembering Claudine," writer Kristal Brent Zook recalls "cheer[ing] her ability to 'get away with it.'" *Claudine* stands as one of the only positive filmic explorations of black female motherhood in the age of the gendered politics of welfare, and it would come to seem both quaint in its optimism and revolutionary in its social critique, as Ronald Reagan's racist "welfare queen" imagery began its meteoric ascendance just two years later.[37]

African American women continued to challenge negative stereotypes throughout the 1970s, notably in Ntozake Shange's *For Colored Girls Who Have Considered Suicide/When the Rainbow is Enuf* (1975), which ran on Broadway and played to sell-out crowds on its national tour. Shange's "choreopoem" (twenty poems accompanied by movement and music) uses women wearing the individual colors of the rainbow to represent the collective experiences of the "dark phases of womanhood." "Somebody, anybody," pleads the "lady in brown," "sing a black girl's song," and so they do. Multiple oppressions— sexism, sexual assault, incest, intimate partner violence, poverty, murder— intersect in these women's lives, and they find themselves grouped as the rainbow, rising to hold each other after one woman claims, "I found God in myself and I loved her/I loved her fiercely." Shange ends, "And this is for colored girls who have considered suicide, but are moving to the ends of their own rainbows." Moynihan's "pathological" matriarchs here are instead survivors who find strength in each other.[38]

Three years later, feminist author Michele Wallace explicitly tackled the racist antimatriarchalism of the era in *Black Macho and the Myth of the Superwoman.* Black male acceptance of the Moynihan Report, she argued, helped to turn the movement for African American civil rights and liberation into a promotion of "Black Macho" and a derision of the stereotype of the strong black woman, "a woman of inordinate strength, with an ability for tolerating an unusual amount of misery and heavy, distasteful work." Wallace has been criticized for short-shrifting female resistance to the matriarchal stereotype, and her rhetoric about black male sexism is heavy-handed, even vicious at times, but her critique indicates that the Moynihan Report, at the very least, "helped shape black male attitudes" in addition to determining socioeconomic policy.[39]

Both Shange and Wallace engendered defensive reactions, notably from Robert Staples in his "Response to Angry Black Feminists." Staples interpreted these works as "attacks on black men," arguing that the authors errantly universalized black female experiences. He goes on to universalize the black male experience in his rebuttal:

> There is a curious rage festering inside black men because, like it or not, they have not been able to fulfill the roles (i.e. breadwinner, protector) society ascribes to them. . . . Some black men have nothing but their penis, an object which they use on as many women as possible. In their middle years they are deprived of even that mastery of the symbols of manhood, as the sex drive wanes and the consuming chase of women becomes debilitating.

This failure to recognize the unique and enduring pain of black men, Staples charges, results in "a collective appetite for black male blood" among the black female audience at performances of *For Colored Girls*. Exhorting African American women to love themselves, as Shange does at the end of the play, is nothing less than narcissism, according to Staples. Of Wallace, he writes that she unfairly blamed black men for abandonment and poverty; he concedes her point about sexism within the black liberation movement, although he argues that black women were complicit in this, citing a "general consensus" that black men would lead the movement because "black women had held up their men for too long and it was time for the men to take charge." Staples unwittingly proves the point of African American women challenging these stereotypes in his criticisms of *For Colored Girls* and *Black Macho and the Myth of the Superwoman,* which he lumps together derisively as the "Shange-Wallace thesis" that fails to offer "a reasonable and articulate male point of view."[40]

There was thus a tension within this new form of antimatriarchalism between the stereotypes of the Black Matriarch and the African American women who explicitly challenged it. In 1978, there was an indication of which of these sides would prevail in popular culture in the remake of *The Wonderful Wizard of Oz* known as *The Wiz* (1978). *The Wiz* started out as a Broadway musical with an all-black cast and creative team, much to the consternation of critics, many of whom initially dismissed the show. Although most avoided overt racism in their reviews, Rex Reed of the *New York Daily News* argued that the racial recasting of the original fairy tale was not just misguided, but dangerous. "The quickest way to start a race riot," he wrote, "other than bombing the White House, is for someone to tamper with an American classic like *The Wizard of Oz*." Reed proved to be wrong about the stage version of *The Wiz;* audiences, which were about 50 percent African American, ignored the critics, and the show went on to be a major commercial success. During its Broadway run, the Broadway production of *The Wiz* was "immensely popular," attracting busloads of theatergoers, garnering seven Tony Awards in 1975, and prompting Hollywood to give it the silver screen treatment.[41]

Featuring an all-star, all-black cast, including Michael Jackson as the Scarecrow, Lena Horne as Glinda, and Diana Ross as Dorothy, in an urban landscape, *The Wiz* remade the original fairyland into one that addressed contemporary issues, including middle-class aspirations, working-class despair, and the politics of uplift, from a generally conservative point of view. Although the mural featured in the opening credits promises a story about black female power—a goddess figure (who turns out to be Glinda) flanked by the sun and the moon hovers over a cityscape of black people—the film offers a tempered matriarchal message. *The Wiz* offers competing versions of the imaginary black matriarchy. There is the emasculating, oppressive matriarchy represented by Evillene, *The Wiz's* version of the Wicked Witch of the West who runs a sweatshop full of slaves that she commands, whips, and even dances upon. As queen of this industrial hell, Evillene is rotund, gaudy, and abusive, and she proceeds to emasculate Dorothy's male traveling companions one by one in short order (by sawing the Scarecrow in half, smelting the Tin Man, and hanging the Lion by his tail).[42]

A parallel to Evillene is found in the mute carnival figure of Teenie, the Tin Man's fourth wife who is responsible for his sorry state when Dorothy finds him stiff and rusting at the Coney Island amusement park. He is lodged under the hulk of the former park's laughing machine, a huge, obese—indeed, almost perfectly round—figure of a smiling black woman. Dorothy and the Scarecrow rescue the Tin Man from the "posterior prison" of the "hulking she-devil," the metal Mammy-Matriarch who had "crushed [him] in his prime," made him her "seat cushion," and rendered him impotent. Together, Evillene and Teenie are *The Wiz's* representation of dysfunctional black womanhood, responsible for the oppression of African American men and the "tangle of pathology" in this poverty-stricken landscape.[43]

As in Baum's original tales, female power in *The Wiz* is more properly used for the promotion of community good. The opening of the film firmly establishes Dorothy's stable, middle-class credentials, and she accordingly promotes a lukewarm message of uplift. Diana Ross's Dorothy is a shrinking violet compared to the original young protagonist of Baum's imagination, offering a familiarly racialized doctrine of self-help, telling the Scarecrow, for instance, that he is not a failure, but rather "just a product of some negative thinking." When the Cowardly Lion, weeping, lays his head in her lap for comfort, Dorothy comforts him with song, urging him to keep "trying, and trying, and trying." When the Wizard, a failed politician played by Richard Pryor, asks Dorothy for help, she replies that he must venture into the world and let "people see who you really are." Dorothy is no matriarch; rather, she is diminished to the role of mere facilitator, a helpmate who enables men to find their true potential, the subdued nurturer who was the subtextual solution in the Moynihan Report.[44]

If the original *Wizard of Oz* film muted the matriarchy of Gage and Baum,

The Wiz thoroughly defeated the Black Matriarch represented by Evillene and Teenie, and reduced black womanhood to a shy, beautiful young mother fig- ure who was not popular with black moviegoers. As with any film, there are many reasons why the intended audience responds in various ways, but the fact is that "Blacks did not go see" *The Wiz*. Expected to be an "unstoppable blockbuster," the $22 million production—at the time, the "most expensive movie musical ever made"—became known as one of famed director Sidney Lumet's "debacles," an "ill-fated" remake that did not break even, grossing $21 million domestically. Although some critics enjoyed the film, they were in the minority; the ambitious musical flopped, and a major opportunity to recon- ceptualize matriarchalism as a positive endorsement of black female power for a wide audience via a beloved narrative was squandered.[45]

As the essentially conservative message of *The Wiz* indicated, by the last two decades of the twentieth century, it was difficult for radical challenges to the mythology of the Black Matriarch to reach mainstream audiences, white or black. Increasingly, the matriarchal mythology of African American wom- anhood, as it developed by the end of the twentieth century, was used to serve destructive political purposes. As we have seen, Moynihan did not create the figure of the Black Matriarch, but his report reinvigorated the stereotype as a perceived social problem. Over time, the popular interpretation of the report helped to create a "tangle" of pathological images by merging the emasculat- ing matriarchal stereotype with two other stereotypes of African American women: the "breeder," or the hypersexual Jezebel image that has been used to justify sexual exploitation of African American women since slavery, and the shiftless mother. By the 1980s, these three images would famously combine to produce a new stereotype: the Welfare Queen.[46]

In his failed 1976 presidential bid, Ronald Reagan introduced the phrase "welfare queen" by detailing the corrupt (and imagined) life of a woman from Chicago's South Side with "eighty names, thirty addresses, [and] twelve So- cial Security cards" who was "collecting benefits on four deceased husbands." The matriarchalism of this ideology was a throwback to the Gilded Age, as it posited that potently negative matriarchal figures—the "queens"—were the source of all of society's ills. Wahneema Lubiano explains:

> "Welfare queen" is a phrase that describes economic dependency—the lack of a job and/or income (which equal degeneracy in the Calvin- ist United States); the presence of a child or children with no father

and/or husband (moral deviance); and, finally, a charge on the collective U.S. treasury—a human debit. . . . The welfare queen represents moral aberration and an economic drain, but the figure's problematic status becomes all the more threatening once responsibility for the destruction of the American way of life is attributed to it.

The Queen would play a central role in Reagan's presidential rhetoric and support for the rollback of governmental support for socioeconomic programs as part of the neoliberal agenda. During the final two decades of the twentieth century and into the twenty-first, the Black Matriarch became a staple of popular culture as part of the rising white panic over the dual images of the black single mother and the Welfare Queen.[47]

As in Frazier's assessment in the 1930s, class was thoroughly tied up with race in the new social concern over the figure of the black female welfare recipient. The recession of the early 1980s hit African Americans especially hard; in 1982, unemployment increased to almost 20 percent and income plummeted as more and more black Americans found themselves living in poverty. In response, the Moynihan Report was summarily dusted off and presented anew as an explanation for black poverty and as a justification for the decreased funding or defunding of federal and state programs addressing inequality and discrimination in housing, education, and employment. The neoconservative embrace of his thesis prompted Moynihan to publish a series of his Harvard lectures as *Family and Nation* (1986), in which he clung to most of his original claims. The media followed suit; one *Newsweek* headline read, "Moynihan: I Told You So," while a *Washington Post* reporter called Moynihan an "embattled prophet redeemed." Coverage of the "new" crisis of the black family featured calls for "self-help" and "personal responsibility."[48]

As the media coverage increased, so, too, did the reach of the Queen's destruction. By 1986, Reagan blamed the "welfare culture" over which she ruled for "the breakdown of the family, female and child poverty, child abandonment, horrible crimes, and deteriorating schools." That same year, CBS's television documentary *The Vanishing Family: Crisis in Black America* treated viewers to a mother-blaming festival featuring young, black women in the public housing projects of Newark. Although the documentary cites absent fathers as one cause of African American poverty, the real problem is clear from the opening shots, which show a row of young mothers and their babies being interviewed. "Are any of you married?" Bill Moyers asks off-camera, prompting a round of head shakes. "Raise your hand if you would like to be married to your baby's father," he instructs; incredulous laughter follows, and only one woman raises her hand. He presses the women, asking if they thought they'd need help with the children. "Not really," responds one woman. "My father wasn't in the home, so—really—male figures are not substantially important in the family." Many of the women are third-generation single mothers, and in this "world turned upside-down," welfare serves as both their child support and their income. As the camera pans over a line of women and children, Moyers explains: "On the first day of the month at noon, the mothers gather outside the project's mailroom, waiting for the postman to deliver their checks. . . . They call it 'Mothers' Day.'"[49]

This narrative progression—women who choose urban life over their rural roots, eschew marriage, and use state assistance to support themselves and their children—relied heavily upon both Frazier and Moynihan (without citing either), indicating the evolution of the Black Matriarch into the Welfare Queen. It is not simply her own family she would ruin; concludes one psychologist: "It won't be long before it becomes a disease that affects an entire population." Although Eleanor Holmes Norton, as part of the panel of experts that comprised the second hour of the documentary, cited systemic problems and solutions like job programs, the other panelists, all male, seemed to agree that the problem was one of morality, arguing that the "family means a husband and a wife." *Ebony* magazine marshaled its resources to present a counterargument, relying upon the authority of longtime critics of these claims in a 1986 special issue, "The Crisis of the Black Family." But it was too late. The Matriarch had morphed into the Welfare Queen, and she became a popular symbol of a host of social, economic, and political problems. The CBS documentary won a Peabody Award that year.[50]

Although some critics deemed Reagan's Queen a "weapon of class warfare," the image obviously capitalized on long-standing racial and gendered conflicts, as well. With the Black Matriarch-Welfare Queen in the spotlight, systemic causes could be ignored. A code quickly developed; the phrases "the culture of poverty," "the culture of single motherhood," and "personal responsibility" all came to denote the Black Matriarch who eschewed the patriarchal family structure, bred wantonly, and lived off of governmental "handouts."[51]

By the early 1990s, the Black Matriarch-Welfare Queen was nightly news. Lubiano notes that many themes in the media conjured up the Queen, often without ever naming her. She even made an appearance as one of the supporting female antagonists in the drama surrounding Clarence Thomas's Supreme Court nomination in 1991 when Thomas derided and discarded his sister Emma Mae Martin as a "welfare dependent." In this narrative, however, "dependence" on public assistance rhetorically denoted power, or the Matriarch's ability to abuse the system. "She gets mad when the mailman is late with her welfare check," Thomas explained to the *New York Times*. Thomas's own biography of transcending poverty to become a federal judge and then a Supreme Court Justice made him, within the mythology of the Black Matriarch and the Welfare Queen, one of the "male figures so desperately needed (and missing from) Moynihan's 'black family.'"[52]

The following year, in the summer of 1992, this racialized form of anti-matriarchalism made headlines again when Vice President Dan Quayle famously blamed the Welfare Queen for the urban violence that followed the Rodney King verdict. The "lawless social anarchy" that characterized the riots was, according to Quayle, "directly related to the breakdown of family structure, personal responsibility and social order in too many areas of our society." Quayle combined evolutionism with Moynihan's thesis when he argued that the absence of fathers and the so-called "illegitimacy rate" in many poor families underscored how "quickly civilization [could fall] apart." Bluntly, Quayle proclaimed that single mothers produced criminals: "Nature abhors a vacuum. Where there are no mature, responsible men around to teach boys how to be good men, gangs serve in their place. In fact, gangs have become a surrogate family for much of a generation of inner-city boys. . . . marriage is a moral issue that requires cultural consensus, and the use of social sanctions. Bearing babies irresponsibly is, simply, wrong." The Matriarch's destructive path thus included teen pregnancy, black male unemployment, inner-city poverty, the welfare rolls, juvenile delinquency, and urban riots by the 1990s.[53]

The uses of the Welfare Queen imagery in the Hill confirmation and the coverage of the 1992 riots were part and parcel of what one scholar deemed "ideological war by narrative means." And so, over time, it became axiomatic among politicians of either major party that the "demon that policymakers needed to exorcise" was not poverty, but welfare. Many scholars have shown that the mythology of welfare, and particularly the gendered and racialized stereotypes of welfare recipients, rather than socioeconomic realities, have guided the governmental approach to public assistance. By the 1990s, the debate over social safety nets in the United States was "reduced to a clash of moral symbols," with the undeserving Black Matriarch on one side and the "bootstraps mentality" of American meritocracy, now reconceptualized as "personal responsibility," on the other. Newt Gingrich, Republican House leader and major proponent of the so-called "Contract with America" that ushered in major welfare reform in the mid-1990s, spelled out the evolutionist threat: "No civilization can survive for long with twelve-year-olds having babies, fifteen- year-olds killing each other, seventeen-year-olds dying of AIDS, and eighteen- year-olds getting diplomas they can't read. Yet every night on the local news, you and I watch the welfare state undermining our society." The solution, of courses, was to rein in the excesses of the matriarchal Welfare Queen by denying aid to women who had children out of wedlock and women who had more children while on welfare. Without these restraints, proponents warned in classic evolutionist, antimatriarchalist language, the Black Matriarch-Welfare Queen would turn the system into a nanny state and send the nation spiraling into devolution.[54]

In 1994, this matriarchalist paranoia became legislated reality: a large portion of the proposed Republican "Contract with America," the highlight of that midterm campaign season, was devoted to welfare reform. Although politicians were generally careful not to frame the reforms within overtly racialized terms, the gendered frame was explicit. Reagan's image of the Welfare Queen became the premise of federal and state policy in the form of the Personal Responsibility and Work Opportunity Reconciliation Act, which explicitly targeted unmarried mothers who received state assistance and rewarded women who got or stayed married while on welfare. The new welfare system, Temporary Assistance to Needy Families (TANF), required paternity establishment and at least thirty hours of work outside the home per week of unmarried mothers on welfare. Married mothers, on the other hand, did not have to meet any of these requirements to qualify for assistance. The logic was simple, according to neoconservatives: "once single motherhood ceased to be subsidized by the taxpayer, poor women would settle down and marry before having kids." And this was not a narrow New Right discourse, as President Clinton enthusiastically signed the bill that fulfilled his campaign promise to "end welfare as we knew it." Indeed, Clinton initially advocated for a two-year limit on benefits, rather than the five-year limit that was signed into law.[55]

Thus was welfare reform articulated as a necessary policy reaction to the ever-growing power of the Black Matriarch. A full generation after the Moynihan Report, the pathological mother that he described, but provided very little evidence for, came to determine the allocation of public assistance in the

United States. At the same time, she moved firmly into popular culture. In the spring of 1995, American audiences were treated to a battle of good versus bad motherhood in the film drama *Losing Isaiah*. In a poster that asked plaintively in all caps, "WHO DECIDES WHAT MAKES A MOTHER?," acclaimed white actress Jessica Lange nuzzles a tiny African American baby, while black actress Halle Berry looks on from the background, eyes locked confrontationally with the camera. Berry's character Khaila—no last name—is a crack-addicted, rags-clad, apparently homeless mother who abandons her three-day-old son in a dumpster while she is high. The newborn wails as her mother retreats unsteadily down the street, finding relief as she smokes crack in the next frame; at the same time, garbage collectors find the boy, Isaiah, in the trash just in the nick of time before the compactor in the truck crushes him. He is rushed to the hospital, where he has the good fortune of being seen by Margaret Lewin, a social worker who falls in love with him immediately. The differences between Khaila and Margaret are stark. Khaila is a "crack mother," a close cousin of the Welfare Queen. She is shown coming to after a high, her face bleeding, her breasts lactating, as she rushes to the dumpster when she realizes what she has done. This scene is juxtaposed with Margaret smiling at baby Isaiah and worrying over him as he is wheeled through the hospital. She quotes the Bible—"Isaiah—And he shall be called wonderful"—as Khaila staggers through the streets and gets arrested for shoplifting at a convenience store. Khaila goes off to prison and a rehabilitation program, while Margaret goes to her upper-class home to convince her dubious husband that they should adopt Isaiah.[56]

Fast forward a few years, and Khaila is out of prison, clean, and shocked to find out from her counselor that her son is alive. The contrast between Khaila and her roommate, an ill-tempered single mother on welfare, and her nannying job for a middle-class white family are meant to indicate that she has developed some potential as a Mammy, but she is still depicted as possibly dangerous and outside the law. When she follows Isaiah and his white nanny to the playground, for instance, there is a moment in which it seems as if she is about to abandon the white child in her care to kidnap her own son. Meanwhile, Margaret is ideal motherhood incarnate: she is infinitely patient with Isaiah, who has behavioral problems (presumably due to his mother's in utero drug use), and she turns even the smallest conversation with her adopted son into a fun lesson in which he learns new words, numbers, and songs.[57]

Khaila hires an attorney to get her son back, and the ensuing custody case hinges on the question of whether "black babies belong with black mothers," as Khaila's attorney put it, regardless of class circumstances. The Lewins' attorney challenges this line of questioning as "politically correct," countering that this argument "put[s] political interest above the emotional health of these children." She paints Khaila with the classic features of the Jezebel and the Welfare Queen, asking her about her drug use in the past, about taking money for sex, and about Isaiah's father (Khaila does not know who he is). Although Khaila is awarded custody, she is the unfit mother in this narrative, and the "colorblind love" of the white savior mother will win the day. Isaiah is miserable in Khaila's care. He won't talk or eat, and he lashes out violently. Khaila wakes up one night to find him missing from his bed; the sight of him curled up, fully clothed in her stained, old bathtub, is the last straw, and Khaila calls Margaret the next day. Isaiah goes back to the Lewins, but he stays in his African American school, "with these kids just like him," as a compromise to the racial argument on which the custody case hinged. When Margaret appears at the school, her adopted son rushes to her, finally smiling again. They all sit on the floor as he builds their separate houses with blocks next to each other, and the screen fades to black, with the message: "And a little child shall lead them. Isaiah 11:6."[58]

Critics generally bashed *Losing Isaiah*, although their unanimous point of concern was in the saccharine delivery, rather than the gendered or racial politics of the message itself. Some scholars, however, called the film out for perpetuating stereotypes. Duchess Harris targeted the character of Khaila as pop cultural evidence for the damaging stereotypes undergirding the welfare reform that passed later that year. But, in keeping with the tenets of racist matriarchalism, Khaila is not coded as wholly bad or evil; rather, as a Matriarch-turned-Mammy, while on her own she is dangerous, but under the supervision of the system—prison, the rehab program, social services, her white employers, and, finally, the Lewins themselves—she is depicted as having potential as the white woman's helper. In an echo of the imperial matriarchalism, she is the dysfunctional Matriarch brought safely under state and white control.[59]

By the 1990s, then, matriarchalism had been downgraded into a racialized duel between good white mothers and bad Black Matriarchs. Like May French Sheldon, Margaret Lewin would embody proper, maternal, female power for Khaila, the "savage" who was educable but could not be trusted unsurveilled. A century of American pop cultural matriarchalism thus ended very close to where it began at the World's Columbian Exposition in 1893, as a racialized discourse of good versus bad matriarchs. More broadly, most popular matriarchalist texts, such as the Oz series and *Wonder Woman*, almost always represent positive matriarchs—peaceful, benevolent, democratic—as white, with the notable exception of Nubia's later appearances in the comics. Not all white matriarchs are represented positively, as the prevalent mid-century discourse of momism indicates; on the other hand, however, almost all dark-skinned matriarchs are represented negatively, as in the long-standing fear of the Black Matriarch, from the Dahomey Amazons, to Frazier's "outlaw" mothers, to Moynihan's pathological poverty, to the Welfare Queen, to Khaila the crack mother. Instead of a progressive evolution or even a paradigm shift indicating the cumulative effects of over one hundred years of matriarchalist theory, American matriarchalism at the end of the century had come full circle, echoing many of the problematic premises of its predecessors.

EPILOGUE

MADEAS AND THE MANOSPHERE

American Matriarchalism in the Early Twenty-First Century

> Re-vision—the act of looking back, of seeing with fresh eyes, of enter-
> ing an old text from a new critical direction—is for women more than
> a chapter in cultural history: it is an act of survival.
> —ADRIENNE RICH, "Writing as Re-Vision," 1971

A s we have seen, matriarchalism has been an enduring and evolving theme in American popular culture over the course of the
twentieth century. Nearly all of these manifestations remain
in some form or fashion, but the historical trajectory has been
buried, hidden within the muted history of matriarchalism as a theory. This
history illuminates the complex connections between the various Amazons,
witches, Black Matriarchs, and superheroines of American popular culture in
the early twenty-first century.

Although the figure of the Welfare Queen was the most potent matriarchal
symbol at the turn of the twentieth century, at the same time that she was a
popular figure of derision, American television viewers formed a cult following around the reimagined figures of the Greek Amazons. Soon after it debuted as a spin-off of *Hercules* in 1995, the show *Xena: Warrior Princess* gained
a loyal, even obsessive, audience. Xena, played by actress Lucy Lawless, is a
former warlord; once known as the "Destroyer of Nations," she repudiates her
dark past, and the series follows her attempts to restore good to the world. The
opening credits describe her as "a mighty princess forged in the heat of battle"
in a "land in turmoil crying out for a hero." Xena is beautiful, strong, sarcastic,
and skilled as she ably handles horses, swords, lassos, crossbows, diplomacy,
military strategy, and political leadership. In each episode, she is recognized
as a formidable foe by gods, kings, and men alike, and although Xena fights
brutally when necessary, she prefers to make peace between warring factions
and to bring justice to those who have been wronged.[1]

Despite her appearance, gender politics, leadership, and combat skills, the
titular character is not an Amazon, although she very briefly becomes their

leader after winning a Royal Challenge against an Amazon queen. When the matriarchal Amazons appear on the show, Xena often teams up with them, and they always fight as valiantly and capably as Xena herself. Although at least one scholar dismisses this televised version of the Amazons as simple "display[s]" of "gyrations of scantily-clad female bodies" to cater to the male gaze (and there is, to be fair, quite a bit of bikini-clad Amazon kickboxing during fight scenes), *Xena* offers viewers something never seen before on television: an army of strong women warriors who live in a fully developed, settled, matriarchal society that is less barbaric than those of their warring male neighbors. Moreover, these matriarchalist characters eschew essentialism and maternalism—although children are shown playing in the Amazon villages, motherhood is not the source of their strength nor a focus of their society. The Amazon Nation on *Xena* is a diverse one, featuring women of different races and ethnicities, although the queens, including the blonde, blue-eyed Gabrielle, are usually white. *Xena,* then, both challenges and replicates the tenets and pitfalls of previous forms of American matriarchalism.[2]

These Amazons are the televised representation of matriarchalist early history, paying particular homage to the feminist spirituality and goddess worship of the 1970s. Their frequent appearances on the series indicate that, unlike Wonder Woman in "Man's World," Xena is not a lone, anomalous feminine hero. Rather, according to *Xena's* fictional history, women were frequently powerful leaders in the ancient world. Although the Amazons only appeared in roughly one-fifth of the 134 episodes, scholars have noted that in the "Xenaverse," or the online fan community, interest in the Amazons "extends far beyond the diegetic constructions of the television series." Indeed, the all-female society from *Xena* has been "reclaimed," "reformulated," and repurposed in a "highly politicized" form of mythopoetic matriarchalism that exists solely on the internet. As with other feminist matriarchalist texts, the goal of this fan fiction is to reclaim historical female power and challenge current concepts of traditional femininity. Reflecting the political project of feminist matriarchalism, this online version offers visions of "Amazonism" in twenty-first-century society, providing extensive information about Amazonian myths, feminist spirituality, and a safe space for the "virtual tribe" of activist women, much like a women's liberation consciousness-raising session of the 1970s. "The New AmazoNation," one of the most heavily trafficked of these sites, opens with a quote echoing Marston's 1938 prediction of the "global reappearance of the Divine Feminine," in which women "will retake their power in the millennium," with "Amazons" at the "forefront of this movement." In scholar Sara Jones's study of the overlap between the Xenaverse and the Amazonist online community, she concludes that the "postmodern mythopoesis" of marginalized—female, lesbian, feminist—Xena fans "functions as a strategy of resistance whereby the complexities of the present are addressed through imaginative reformulations of identities, agency, relations, and outcomes in self-consciously fabulous or speculative narratives."[3]

It seems, then, that pop cultural consumers at the turn of the twenty-first century were reinventing the past to envision female power in the present, a recurring project of feminist matriarchalism. In addition to online Amazonism, which catered to the same kind of niche audience that characterized the popular matriarchalism of the women's liberation movement, the first few decades of the twenty-first century featured a mix of matriarchalist forms, including reformulations of older pop cultural texts, like *The Wizard of Oz* and *Wonder Woman*. Antimatriarchalism ascended, as well, especially the racist forms exemplified by films like *The Help* and the *Madea* franchise, and in a new form of cyber-antimatriarchalism that has become a virulent, misogynist movement known as men's rights activism.[4]

Recycled versions of matriarchalism, such as the Amazonism of *Xena*, proved to be very popular in the late 1990s and early 2000s. One of the better-known examples is the revamped version of *The Wizard of Oz* series that began with Gregory Maguire's novel *Wicked: The Life and Times of the Wicked Witch of the West* (1995). Maguire was inspired by Baum's children's literature, which he deemed "part of the foundation myth of our culture," to revision the fantastical world of Oz a century after the originals. By foundational, Maguire apparently meant not the value of home, as the 1939 film implied. Rather, the mythology he explores in the *Wicked* series (1995–2011) is, in fact, matriarchalism.[5]

In Maguire's Oz, the much-maligned Wicked Witch of the West (known here as Elphaba, a derivation of L. Frank Baum's initials) is a troubled teen turned revolutionary freedom fighter and animal rights activist who opposes the tyrannical dictator Wizard. Maguire stays true to Baum's intent; indeed, the events that set the series in motion are motivated by none other than Madame Blavatsky, the famed Theosophist. According to Maguire's tales, Blavatsky used her crystal ball to find the Grimmerie, an "ancient manuscript of magic" in Oz, whereupon the Wizard traveled to Oz to retrieve it, thus inaugurating the oppressive regime against which Elphaba fought. Maguire ironically deploys negative stereotypes of matriarchs throughout his novels. *Wicked* opens with some well-known characters speculating about the Wicked Witch of the West, employing every epithet hurled at the suffragists of Baum's era. "She was castrated at birth," explains the Tin Woodman. "She was born hermaphroditic, or maybe entirely male" (one birthing attendant did confuse Elphaba for a "willful boy" at first). The Lion argues that she was unloved and abused as a child, and an addict besides. The Scarecrow chimes in that she is a lesbian, prompting additional speculation that Elphaba is either "the spurned lover of a married man" or, perhaps, "she *is* a married man." Whatever she is, she is powerful, as the Lion concludes that she is both a "despot" and a "dangerous tyrant." The mysterious power of women is thus the subtext of the entire series.[6]

Elphaba's power is obvious from the moment she is born emerald green. Elphaba's parents valiantly attempted to make her a normal child, even organizing an exorcism as if she were one of Gage's historical witches. Despite her appearance—by the time she heads to college, Elphaba is a "hatchet-faced girl with putrescent green skin and long, foreign-looking black hair"—she, not the young farm girl Dorothy and not the beautiful Glinda, is the primary heroine of this fairy tale. Like so many feminist matriarchalist heroines before her, Elphaba is a "half-breed, a new breed," a "dangerous anomaly," and a revolutionary threat to the patriarchal tyranny of the Wizard. Her narrative role is to help return the land to its matriarchal origins, as over the course of the four books in the series her actions help to orchestrate the return of the Princess Ozma. In Maguire's telling, Oz was originally a matrilineal society, with political power descending through the female line of the "House of Ozma." At the outset of the series, there had been three centuries of Ozmas, followed by only forty years of the Wizard—a shortened version of Elizabeth Cady Stanton's estimation of the matriarchal time line of world history.[7]

Elphaba is, like Gage and Baum, an avowed atheist who fights fiercely against racism and the Wizard's expansionist program of expropriation, environmental wreckage, and "systematic marginalizing of populations" through "pogroms" and "purges." An "Avenging Angle of Justice," she fights for "a land where injustice and common cruelty and despotic rule and the beggaring fist of drought didn't work together to hold everyone by the neck." In Maguire's interpretation, then, Elphaba, a powerful woman of color, critiques, avenges, and corrects the racial supremacy of old Oz, a reformulation of matriarchalism that combats the problem of racism that has long plagued the theory. Although

Elphaba is gone by the end of *Wicked*, disappeared, as in Baum's original, by Dorothy's bucket of water, Maguire leaves her exit in question, and her haunting of the subsequent novels and one brief, murky reappearance reflect the task of academic matriarchalism: using vague clues from history, mythology, and archaeology to unearth the woman-centered ancient past.[8]

Wicked received mixed reviews and was generally misunderstood by reviewers to be "far removed in spirit from the Baum books." Even in positive reviews, *The Wicked Years* series are deemed simply "revisionist fairy tales." Despite the negative book reviews, in 2003, *Wicked* became a popular Broadway play. The stage musical has won over one hundred awards, including a Grammy and ten Tonys. As of 2016, it has grossed over $1 billion in the United States and over $4 billion globally. Maguire has said he "believes" that *Out of Oz* is his last book on Oz, but, citing another matriarchalist series, Le Guin's *Earthsea Trilogy*, to which she returned decades after writing the first book, he has acknowledged the possibility that he will write another. The much-anticipated film version of *Wicked* is scheduled for a 2019 release.[9]

Like the matriarchs of Oz, the Amazing Amazon has undergone many revisions, including the low points of the Cold War–era, romance-obsessed Wonder Woman and the Diana Prince era (1968–1972), in which she was merely human. Although she gave up her Amazon birthright, and the last vestiges of Marston's matriarchalism, during this era, Wonder Woman recovered both on the television show in the late 1970s and then again in the comic with the advent of George Pérez as her primary writer in 1987. Pérez's origin story for Wonder Woman began with the Greek goddesses inaugurating a new race of women, the Amazons, to set an example for warring men. According to this new creation myth, the goddesses released the souls of women who had been murdered by men from Hades, and they emerged as Amazons. Hippolyte, their queen, is a reincarnation of a woman killed by her husband, and Diana is the daughter she molds from clay, the first born on Paradise Island. As in the Marston era, Pérez's Wonder Woman had a host of female helpers. In addition to her Amazon sisters, Wonder Woman's best friend was a new character, Julia Kapatelis, a Harvard archaeologist and historian—perhaps Perez's homage to the contemporary matriarchalist trend among feminist academics.[10]

This was a short-lived feminist revision of the superheroine, however. When Pérez left the comic in 1992, as after Marston's death in 1947, *Wonder Woman*'s matriarchalism again stagnated and all but disappeared, and the 1990s featured Diana's temporary loss of her powers, a hypersexualized version of the Amazons, and general misogyny and violence against female comic characters. In the twenty-first century, though, Wonder Woman began to enjoy a renaissance. Writer Gail Simone helped Princess Diana recover her former powers in *Wonder Woman, Volume 3* (2006), and in the thorough 2011 revamp of DC superheroes known collectively as "The New 52," Wonder Woman, revised as the offspring of the god Zeus and the warrior queen Hippolyte, achieved demigoddess status. As Wonder Woman became more powerful in the pages of the comics, in homage to the iconic "Wonder Woman for President" cover of their founding issue in 1972, the editors of *Ms.* Magazine again featured the Amazing Amazon on the cover of the fortieth anniversary issue in 2012. This time, a larger-than-life Princess Diana is shown storming through Washington, DC, with the Capitol Building behind her and her arm outstretched toward women holding political signs that read "STOP the War on Women" and "Vote as if your life depends on it."[11]

In 2016, at the age of 75, Wonder Woman, along with the other DC superheroes, was rebooted in the comics yet again. DC's *Rebirth* series combined Marston's matriarchalism with early twenty-first-century feminism, retaining both her 1940s origin story and Pérez's mythology of the Amazonian reincarnation of the souls of slain women. Significantly, Wonder Woman finally appeared on the silver screen in 2016, albeit as a backup superheroine to Batman and Superman. Although she is at first depicted as a sexual object of interest to Batman for her looks alone, and she is not revealed as Wonder Woman until a whopping two hours into the film, actress Gal Gadot as Diana more than holds her own, wielding her bracelets, sword, and lasso to help defeat the monstrous villain. This is not a matriarchalist film by any means, although Marston might agree with its depiction of the wreckage that results from male jealousy, ego, competition, and violence. Diana acknowledges as much when she explains why she walked away from the "century of horrors" in what Marston called "Man's World" at the end of the film.[12]

But Wonder Woman returned to promote matriarchy (and to stoke fears of it, in the case of the theater chain that was condemned by some men online when it announced "women-only" screenings) when she finally got her own live-action film in June of 2017. The filmic Diana is an amalgamation of her previous incarnations, as she harkens back to some of Marston's original intentions while discarding others. Her flashback to her Themiscyra/Paradise Island takes up over one-fifth of the film, which means that over the first half-hour, audiences are treated to a matriarchalist setup featuring a stern Amazon queen and her fierce senators, advisors, and warriors in an Elysian setting. The Amazons are skilled and shrewd, and although they have not come into contact with the corruption of Man's World in many centuries, they continually hone their impressive combat abilities with swords, bows, lassos, and horses. These warrior women form a loyal and brilliant sisterhood in which they are all athletic, combat-ready, intelligent, and multilingual. However, while the Amazons are ethnically diverse, the first woman of color the audience sees in the film is chasing after a wayward young Diana. Her narrative function is to show that the princess is strong-willed and keen to learn the core Amazon skills of combat, but this was regrettable casting, at best; one critic responded incredulously, "They have Mammies on Paradise Island, too? Whose paradise is this exactly?" While Amazons of color abound in Themiscyra, as warriors, senators, and advisors, the inclusion of the black female domestic archetype in the very first of these scenes recycles the racism of previous versions of matriarchalism.[13]

This film version of Paradise Island generally sticks closely to Marston's original intention, save one major exception: the Amazons' origin story. In the film, the history of Themiscyra is shorn of its relationship to the goddesses as well as the Amazons' enslavement by Hercules. Instead, Zeus hid the women on the island to protect them from Ares, the God of War who killed the other gods in a rampage. Hippolyta sculpted Diana from clay, as in the original comic, but then she "begged Zeus to give [her] life," which makes the princess a demigoddess, as in the twenty-first-century comic reboot, but also writes the goddesses Aphrodite and Athena—who watched over Wonder Woman's original narratives like worried mothers—completely out of the story. Moreover, the story of Hercules is significant to the matriarchalism of the original Wonder Woman, in which the Amazons fled the human world to escape male violence with the help of the goddesses; female rule, for Marston, was the only effective antidote to war and conflict, not simply a defensive position against male abuse and invasion.[14]

Likewise, although the sisterhood on Paradise Island is strong, it is left behind when Diana sails away with Steve Trevor. Etta Candy is a sassy suffragette in London—perhaps a winking nod to some of Marston's original influences—but her function is to provide office support and comic relief, and the Holliday Girls, Etta's sorority/army of capable, human women, are nowhere to be found. While Wonder Woman wields a golden lasso and speaks of love as a conquering force, this is the only representation of Marston's original theories of dominance and submission. There is no sense of Marston's "coming matriarchy" in the film; Wonder Woman and her band of misfit, adoring men, rather than the Amazon and her sisters-in-arms, save the day. She does so heroically, of course—she leaps from the trenches and strides confidently (and metaphorically) alone across No Man's Land, fending off an entire German battalion and saving a village before, in a lengthy, CGI-heavy battle, she defeats Ares and ends World War I. In the final scene, Wonder Woman concludes that "only love can truly save the world," but she is alone, without the Allied army, her new human friends, or her Amazon sisters. This ending reduces matriarchalist arguments regarding the natural power of all women to the singular power of one superheroine, alone on a tower. *Wonder Woman* was enormously successful, leading to a surge in the popularity of the comic book character. It is likely that she will get her own film franchise, and representations of her character may well become more nuanced over time: DC Comics confirmed that she is bisexual in September of 2017, the same month that a film loosely based on the origins of Wonder Woman—in particular, the polyamorous relationship of Marston, Holloway, and Byrne—appeared in theaters to enthusiastic reviews but low profits.[15]

The themes, and often the original characters, of previous versions of matriarchalism thus weave through more recent pop cultural texts, and many matriarchalist works have been revised and recycled in the early twenty-first century. Unfortunately, this is true of the themes and characters of antimatriarchalism, as well. Mammy, the panacea of the Black Matriarch stereotype, enjoyed renewed popularity with Katherine Stockett's novel *The Help* (2009) and the award-winning film based on it (2011). In the novel, a young white woman interviews the domestic workers of Jackson, Mississippi, in the early 1960s to tell their stories and win herself a book contract. The African American women who represent "the help" in Jackson are a quiet, dissembling bunch, with the exception of Minny, played by Octavia Spencer in an Oscar-winning turn. Minny, known among the white women for her "sass mouth," defies her employer's mandate regarding in-home segregated bathrooms, and bakes her a famously "Terrible Awful" pie so that she literally "eats [her] shit." Skeeter, the white savior journalist who was raised by her own Mammy on a cotton plantation, gives the domestic servants of the town a voice in her writing because, as she protests, "Nobody ever asked Mammy in *Gone With the Wind* how she felt about it." When Skeeter drives off into the sunset at the end of the film, triumphant, she leaves "the help" behind her to suffer the fallout. Recently fired housekeeper Aibilene says she feels "free" after "telling the truth" about what it felt like to be "the help," but in the novel and the popular film based on it, this ending is ambiguous, and readers know that the violent clashes of the 1960s are ahead. In a statement on *The Help*, the Association of Black Women Historians applauded the performances of the African American actresses, condemned the inaccurate and insulting portrayal of southern black culture, and concluded that it was simply a "coming-of-age story of a white protagonist who uses myths about the lives of black women to make sense of her own." This detailed peak under Aunt Jemima's bandanna notwithstanding, the white supremacist domestic matriarchy of Jackson remains intact in the film as Skeeter leaves for New York, and Aibilene, now jobless but still in her maid's uniform, walks alone down a tree-lined Mississippi street.[16]

Lee Daniels directed *The Help* just after he brought the Black Matriarch to the big screen in *Precious, Based on the Novel 'Push' by Sapphire*. Precious, a 16-year-old who is pregnant with her second child, the product of rape by her own father (as was her first child), lives in Harlem with her mother Mary, who is likely the most fearsome Black Matriarch American audiences have ever seen on screen. Mary is terrifying; when she is not screaming at or attacking Precious, she is scarily calm and quiet, which always portends violence. She smokes, eats, and watches television constantly, preening and complaining in her nightdress and marabou slippers, and she only leaves the apartment to "play her numbers." She is a welfare cheat, collecting checks for herself, Precious, and Precious's first child, who lives with her grandmother. Mary allowed her husband to rape her daughter repeatedly throughout her childhood, and she is emotionally, physically, and sexually abusive to Precious herself. She is the destructive Black Matriarch incarnate.[17]

As she begins to break out of her hellish home life, Precious finds herself at an alternative school, where she learns to read and, with the help of her teacher, applies for welfare, moves into a halfway house with her new baby, and, at the end of the film, gets custody of her first child, as well. She is ambitious and imaginative, and she wants, among other goals, to be a good mother. In the novel, her social worker believes that Precious "seems to envision social services, AFDC, as taking care of her forever," but this is not the case; Precious adamantly insists that she wants to get her G.E.D., a job, an independent living situation, and, eventually, a college education. Welfare is thus a stop-gap measure while Precious gets an education so that she can support her family. The film version, however, ends with Precious going from her social worker's office to legal aid services, indicating that she is seeking additional assistance from the state and perhaps will stay on welfare "forever."[18]

Thus, the novel *Push* and the film *Precious* offer two generations of potential Welfare Queens in Mary and Precious, but the premises of each are very different. In both, Mary is the stuff of right-wing nightmares, while Precious fights against every possible hardship to achieve the American dream, which she fantasizes about in technicolor frequently throughout the film. But in the novel, Sapphire, as part of the long resistance tradition of black women writers, offers a challenge to "respectability politics," as the solution is not a patriarchal family model, but an empowered, individual woman who takes charge of her own destiny, with some temporary help from the state. In the novel, Precious's teacher, Ms. Rain, a dark-skinned woman with braids, is her model of black female empowerment. But in the film, Ms. Rain is a light-skinned model of middle-class aspirations, from her hairstyle, to her clothing, to the scene in which she plays Scrabble with Precious and they exchange Christmas gifts in her home.[19]

More significantly, although the novel *Push* emphasizes that, in addition to her family, numerous social institutions—schools, hospitals, the local welfare apparatus—have completely failed her, the film *Precious* represents these institutions as ones that work to help her against all odds. The novel ends with Precious alone, reading to her child, writing her own next chapter. In the film, the hands-on teaching at the alternative school, the excellent care she gets in the hospital when she has her second baby, and the empathy of her social worker essentially save her, so that in the end, Precious walks out on a welfare meeting with her mother, visits a legal aid and service organization, and strolls happily down the street in Harlem with her two children. In short, for director Lee Daniels, the problem here is the Black Matriarch/Welfare Queen; she alone is the villain who ruins lives, while systemic problems that link race, poverty, and violence, as well as the structural racism that infects policies and organizations that are meant to address these issues, remain unexplored. As if to underscore the value placed on this enduring matriarchal myth, Mo'Nique was awarded an Oscar for her portrayal of this matriarchal monster, and screenwriter Geoffrey Fletcher won for his adapted screenplay. Scholars argue that Daniels works within "cinematic trends that have been re-developing over the last few decades," resulting in "caricatured options" for major characters, and this trend will apparently continue: Daniels is reportedly now working on a biopic about Linda Taylor, the woman Ronald Reagan described in the speech in which he coined the label "welfare queen," which will complete Daniels's cinematic trilogy from Mammy, to Matriarch, to Welfare Queen.[20]

Additionally, as a staple of American film, the Black Matriarch has also become a wildly popular comedic figure. Tyler Perry's creation Mabel "Madea" Simmons is a brassy composite character reportedly based on his mother and his aunt. Perry, arguably the "premier black American producer, director, and playwright of the twenty-first century," is a prolific screenwriter and director, and his films traffic heavily in racial caricatures, or what filmmaker Spike Lee derided as Perry's "coonery and buffoonery." Madea has been criticized as another "big-breasted, mammy-style" character, but more specifically, she is the Black Matriarch rebranded for comic effect.[21]

In character as Madea, Perry literally embodies antimatriarchalist fears of gender inversion as a black man in women's clothing. Everything about Madea is hyperbolic; rarely a scene goes by without her threatening violence and/or wildly waving her handgun, which she keeps in her purse. Perry has argued that Madea gives him a freedom that he otherwise would not have:

> As Madea, whose melon-sized breasts flop energetically over her waist, Mr. Perry ladles out wit and indignation as potentially scathing as the grits on his stove . . . They are the zingers that, out of costume, Mr. Perry . . . is loath to speak. "I hate all the makeup and the wigs that come with the character," [Perry] said last week at his studio in Atlanta. "But the freedom to be able to say whatever I want, that's pretty cool."

Perry-as-Madea exercises a kind of male privilege in the many films in which Madea talks back to and even seeks revenge upon errant men, most obviously in *Diary of a Mad Black Woman,* in which she takes a chainsaw to her granddaughter's abusive husband's furniture. Other black female characters in the films are usually more passive, and the solution to their plights, more often than not, is to "settle" down into marriage with a "good man," as in the primer on taming the Black Matriarch, *I Can Do Bad All By Myself,* which ends with the church wedding of the sexy nightclub singer. This solution mirrors the logic of both the Progressive era emphasis on white, middle-class institutions as the key to racial "uplift," the Moynihan Report's patriarchal prescription, and the more recent "personal responsibility" welfare policies of the 1990s, which posited that heterosexual marriage could solve the problem of poverty.

In Perry's version of matriarchalism, those Matriarchs that are unable to be tamed are punished.[22]

In addition to the matriarchalist Madea franchise, in 2010, Tyler Perry directed *For Colored Girls*, the first film version of the famed 1975 choreopoem. In place of Shange's colors of representation that gave voice to multiple collective experiences, Perry created characters that limited audience interpretation. Despite the difference in tone, as in his other films, the women in Perry's *For Colored Girls* are a mélange of stereotypes—Mammy, Matriarch, Jezebel, Sapphire—and they are all bad or failed mothers. Removed from both the original text and context, Perry's version is muddled at best and self-defeating at worst. Black feminist critics have argued that in direct contradiction to Shange's intentions, the film "created controlling images where none existed" in order to blame black women for violence and dysfunction in their communities.[23]

By the second decade of the twenty-first century, then, matriarchalist images continued to permeate popular culture, calling upon many of the incarnations examined herein. But by the 2010s, one version of the theory came to drown out all others in a concerted sexist campaign reminiscent of antisuffragism a century before. In the early twenty-first century, the debate over the "end of men" spanned the political spectrum, from self-described feminists to misogynist ideologues. Visually, twenty-first-century musings on matriarchalism echoed some of the images of the antisuffrage campaign, in which women were enlarged and intimidating, while men were cowering and often infantilized. Perhaps the most oft-seen antimatriarchalist imagery is that of a woman, usually in a business suit and heels, stepping on a man, who is more often than not rendered very small.[24]

The most extreme form of twenty-first-century antimatriarchalism is found within the men's rights movement. Almost a century after women got the vote, internet users who read Paul Elam's oft-reposted "How to Build a Man Bomb" could be forgiven for thinking that the matriarchal nightmare of antisuffragists had been realized. According to Elam (who blogs under this pseudonym, "male" spelled backwards), by the end of the twentieth century, instead of gender and sexual equality, American women had achieved what they had secretly wanted all along: female supremacy over men. This rise to supremacy began with suffrage, and it proceeded unabated to the end of the century, permeating society via antimale legislation like Title IX, the Violence Against Women Act, child support mandates, the bias against men in family court cases, the "phony statistics" on the gendered wage gap, and intimate partner violence. Elam, the voice of men's rights activism who posts online under the handle "TheHappyMisogynist," complains that he warned everyone, but this "wool of the matriarchal matrix being pulled over" the eyes of American men had blinded them all "until it is too late." The "misandric Zeitgeist" and "malicious matriarchy" of "feminist governance" had created a vast, ticking "man bomb" of an oppressed class, and female supremacy in employment and education would eventually spark a full-scale male revolution.[25]

Male oppression, social anarchy, governmental overreach and/or collapse: this is the enduring stuff of American fears of matriarchy. And these are just not the paranoid ravings of madmen. Elam is the face of the modern men's rights movement, creator of A Voice for Men, the movement's most popular website and a very lucrative for-profit organization, and lord of a broad online community of tens of thousands of men descrying the "misandry" in twenty-first-century America. He is men's rights activists' "rock star," their most high-profile figure and the source of much MRA funding. "If Men's Rights Activism has a Gloria Steinem, it is Paul Elam," wrote one journalist in a recent profile. At the time of publication of this book, Elam's 2010 "How to Build a Man Bomb," one of his many rants about the current matriarchy, is still frequently reposted and referenced on MRA sites.[26]

As part of the vocal opposition to organized feminism in the final decades of the twentieth century, this movement was generally unknown, and it did not expand or generate media coverage for many years. This changed after 1993, when "father of modern men's rights movement" and Elam's mentor Warren Farrell published *The Myth of Male Power*, a "foundational text" in which he argued that modern men have become the "disposable sex," powerless and oppressed like antebellum slaves. Farrell's work fed into the so-called "angry white male" vote that fueled the 1994 midterm elections, and the movement began to grow just as the internet started to become more widely available. Like Farrell himself, who was once a local leader of the New York chapter of the National Organization for Women, the men's rights movement is a mutated offshoot of the men's liberation movement, which had its roots in the feminist proposition that patriarchy harmed men via oppressive gender roles. In the 1990s, Farrell and other men's rights activists used this premise to come to an alarming set of conclusions: the cause of male suffering was not patriarchy, but feminism. As sociologist Michael Kimmel illustrates in *Angry White Men*, men's rights activists see themselves as both champions of civil rights for men and victims of women; one claims he suffers from "PMS," or "persecuted male syndrome." Just as in the antisuffrage posters of one hundred years ago, the men's rights movement feels more than threatened. Rather, its members feel victimized by what they see as the unwanted intrusion of women into the male public sphere. This intrusion is seen as an orchestrated campaign not for equality, but for the matriarchal seizure of power from men, or the "transfer of rights from guys to girls." Their points of attack include (unsuccessful) legal challenges to "ladies' nights" at bars, the Violence Against Women Act for not including men, and gender studies programs at universities. They argue that they are discriminated against in the home, in the workplace, and in politics.[27]

Journalists and academics credit the internet with the explosion of the MRM, as the medium brought together a loose coalition of men's legal causes, including intimate partner abuse, the perceived prejudice against paternal custody (also known as "fathers' rights"), and male rape. Soon other apparent injuries against men, such as the romantic rejection of men by women and allegedly false rape allegations after "regrettable" sexual encounters, found their niche within this coalition, as well, so that the movement came to house such groups as Pick-Up Artists (whose goal is to seduce women) and male separatists (who argue that women are unnecessary). Within this collective of blogs and websites, or the "manosphere," the one ideology that binds these disparate groups together is not just "their deep-seated hatred of feminism"; it is more specifically their antimatriarchalism. MRAs often target women as a group in their threats, some of which are open, explicit threats of violence. This violence is not confined to online threats, and many of the sites are listed as hate groups by the Southern Poverty Law Center.[28]

These matriarchal fears can seem fringe, belonging to the deep recesses of the internet and the comment sections of websites. But the men's rights movement is "one of the quirkiest, fastest-growing, and most frustrating civil rights movements in the Western world today." MRAs promote formal political participation, warning each other to "vote male" to combat the "hidden matriarchy." In some instances, they have gained political power. New Hampshire state representative Robert Fisher was forced to resign in May 2017 when it was discovered that he was the founder of the online discussion community, "The Red Pill," which is dedicated to antifeminism and misogyny. And more broadly, the antimatriarchalism of the MRM gained publicity with the recent presidential election.[29]

In 2016, MRAs burst out of the fringes with the rival campaigns of Hillary

Clinton and Donald Trump. Clinton was either heralded or derided, depending upon one's gender politics, as the ultimate symbol of the "rise of the matriarchy." "Men Going Their Own Way," a subset of the MRAs that vows to avoid women completely, hosted many online discussions expressing fears about the antimale policies of the impending Clinton matriarchy, including "male curfews" to prevent rape, taxes on single men, and mandatory female accompaniment of men around children. Others, echoing the medieval misogyny that Gage detailed in *Women, Church and State,* deemed Clinton a powerful "witch." These matriarchal fears prompted the *New Yorker* to jokingly publish a list of "Anticipated Changes After the Matriarchal Revolution," including equal pay, the amendment of "In God We Trust" on American dollars to add "(God Is a Woman)," "hot robots" to replace men, and vagina-shaped buildings. Jokes aside, the representations were stereotypically uniform; a stock illustration of the fears of the coming matriarchy under Clinton appeared on the cover of *Time* in early 2014. Beside the headline, "Can Anyone Stop Hillary?," there appeared an image of a woman's foot and leg, in sensible heels and suit trousers. Dangling precipitously by one hand from the heel of her shoe was a man. Again, we see that the "women's-success-crushes-men metaphor" has become the most frequent cliché of antimatriarchalism.[30]

As with the opposition to suffrage a century before, the specter of a female president would certainly be enough to stoke antimatriarchal paranoia, but these fears received an unprecedented boost from Clinton's opponent, Donald Trump. Men's rights–brand sexism has been making inroads into state-level legislative politics for several years, but with the rise of Hillary Clinton, the "alt-right," which is more aptly called the extreme right, became more vocal and, via Trump's success as a presidential candidate, men's rights has gone mainstream. To be clear, Trump does not identify as a men's rights activist, and not all MRAs supported his presidential bid. A former managing editor of A Voice for Men, however, acknowledged that while he did not support Trump, it was "nice to hear him" use rhetoric that supported the MRM: "Somebody had the guts to say that men have it tougher than women, it gives you an emotional rush." Donald Trump used the language of the men's rights movement so frequently that *New York* magazine developed a quiz, "Who Said It, Donald Trump or a Men's Rights Activist?"[31]

While Paul Elam and A Voice for Men did not explicitly endorse Trump, other men's rights sites did, including the pro-rape, "neo-masculine" Return of Kings; the founder warned his thousands of readers that Clinton's first move would be to "establish a techno-matriarchy where men are second-class citizens to any female." Clinton's "gynocentric socialism" that so worried men's rights activists was apparently too focused on addressing issues like reproductive rights, equal pay, and violence against women—issues that the feminist matriarchalist texts examined herein tackle. But Clinton deviated widely from most feminist representations of matriarchs with her "hawkish" aggression on foreign policy, and she defeated the only socialist in the race, Bernie Sanders, when she received the nomination of the Democratic Party. In other words, the Clinton matriarchy would likely have looked very little like those of feminist imaginations, but MRAs continued to rage on the internet throughout her campaign.[32]

Of course, these MRA nightmares will remain just that, for the time being anyway, because their spokesperson—or at least, the candidate who speaks their language—won, and ideas about gender and power clearly played a key role in how Americans cast their votes. Sebastian Gorka, a former Trump advisor, declared just over a month after the election that "the era of the pajama-boy is over, and the alpha males are back," and one of Trump's first acts as president-elect was to name a men's rights sympathizer as his chief strategist. Although he served less than a year in this post, Steve Bannon, formerly of Breitbart (an extremist right-wing news site that publishes articles with headlines like "The Men's Rights Movement: A Smart, Necessary Counterweight to Man-hating Feminism"), endorses and espouses many of the movement's misogynist beliefs, deriding women's liberation as just a "bunch of dykes that came from the Seven Sisters schools" and explaining that feminism makes women unattractive, even "mannish." In addition to the many other racist and bigoted arguments made by Bannon and on his news site is the charge that the United States is a "near-matriarchy" established by feminists hell-bent on taking rights from men. After the US presidential election of 2016, it seems as if we have ended up in one of Marston's comics from 1943, which pitted the virulently sexist "Man's World Party" against the matriarchalist platform of Wonder Woman—except that in the 2016 election, the Amazing Amazon did not save the day.[33]

Given the many revisions and recycling of previous versions, it seems that matriarchalism, as a set of beliefs about the origins, history, and nature of female power, is stuck in a rut, so to speak. For every film like *Claudine* or fictional series like *The Holdfast Chronicles*, there are multiple, often more popular forms of antimatriarchalism. Just as troubling is the consistent reiteration of the problematic premises of matriarchalist texts that claim to be feminist. As a branch of feminist theory, matriarchalism both challenges and reiterates several core debates within American feminism. Many iterations of matriarchalism rely upon essentialism, or what has been called at different times in recent US history "difference feminism" or "cultural feminism"—the branch of feminism that recognizes core differences between the sexes and tends to derail questions of equality. In the case of matriarchalism, the premise of woman's perceived essential "differences" of nurturance, service, and love—as well as the supporting supposition of men's natural ego, aggression, and competition—allows authors to argue that matriarchies have been or would be necessarily different from Western patriarchies, without engaging with the question of the social construction of those differences. Those texts examined herein that attempt to do away altogether with gender differences in their matriarchalist worlds often do so at the steep price of the elimination or severe decimation of men, usually through warfare, natural disaster, or epidemic. This, too, is a sidestep, as eliminating men means that the author does not have to engage with the core theoretical problem of how multiple sexes might work together in a matriarchal society.

Another problem within feminism that matriarchalism exposes is the issue of intersectionality. Many of the matriarchalist texts in US history have been written by white authors, and they tend to reiterate the dominant racial politics of each era, so much so that most African American female authors who address matriarchalism are forced to do so defensively. Racial, ethnic, and class-based hierarchies have been fundamental to the construction and maintenance of patriarchal societies, and those matriarchalist texts that rely upon such hierarchies therefore recapitulate some of the core building blocks of white patriarchy. In "The Master's Tools Will Never Dismantle the Master's House," Audre Lorde famously asked: "What does it mean when the tools of a racist patriarchy are used to examine the fruits of that same patriarchy?" Likewise, when we imagine alternatives to patriarchy by using its tools, such as racism, the "perimeters of change" are similarly "narrow." In short, white supremacy is foundational to American patriarchy, and there can be no successful matriarchalist challenge, disruption, destruction, or replacement (fictional or otherwise) of one without the other. The texts examined herein that unpack racist matriarchalism by examining the intricate intersections of gender, racial, class, and sexual politics are thus crucial to twenty-first-century feminism, as they offer historical manuals of how multiple factors, experiences, and forms of exploitation determine the politics of gender, regardless of whether men, women, or "manwomen" are in power.[34]

In *Amazons in America,* we have seen how matriarchalists across several generations have grappled with these issues. There are, in fact, only a few matriarchalist texts, or sets of texts, that successfully—without re-creating any semblance of contemporary patriarchy—address these core issues of feminist theory, gender essentialism, intersectionality, and the enduring problem of theoretical stagnation within matriarchalism due to the absence, burial, and/or manipulation of cultural memory. In a 1999 interview, Suzy McKee Charnas cited the recurring "rediscovery" of feminism because of the generational problem of constantly forgetting "the memories of what has just been achieved." She explains: "This means that [women] are unprepared to hold on to what has been given to them when the backlash rolls in to take it all away again." The paradox of matriarchalism, then, is that, from the 1860s onward, it has been buried as an evolving theory and remade anew each generation, condemning itself to a cyclical history. In her excellent biography of William Moulton Marston, historian Jill Lepore writes that one of the great tragedies of "feminism in the twentieth century was the way its history seemed to be forever disappearing," and this is especially true of matriarchalism.[35]

Indeed, my most disappointing finding as I pieced together the unbroken trajectory of this branch of feminist theory was how little so many of its proponents seemed to know about each other, with the obvious exception of the clear familial connection between Matilda Joslyn Gage and L. Frank Baum. Gage, Elizabeth Cady Stanton, and Lester Frank Ward moved within the same circles in the 1880s, yet they do not cite each other in their discussions of matriarchalism. Charlotte Perkins Gilman cites Ward, not Gage, although the racism that serves as the unacknowledged spine of her matriarchalism would have vastly benefited from a thorough reading of Gage. A younger contemporary, Marston, obviously read Inez Haynes Gillmore's matriarchalist novel *Angel Island,* which came out at the same time as Gilman's *Herland,* but he cites neither, even after lifting a scene straight out of Gillmore's novel and depositing it into his comic book. Gillmore, Gilman, and Margaret Sanger, the illustrious aunt of Marston's long-time lover Olive Byrne, shared a social context, and, for a while at least, membership in the same women's club, in the 1910s and 1920s, yet again, their shared belief in matriarchalism was unacknowledged.

So many of the early feminist texts either went out of publication and gathered dust, or were not recognized as such (in the case of Baum and Marston) in the ensuing decades, that the feminist matriarchalists of the women's liberation movement had to retread theoretical and historiographical ground that had already been covered, especially by Gage and Gilman, both of whom were rediscovered and restored to history as part of the wave of new feminist scholarship in the 1970s. At the same time, the racism of antimatriarchalism ascended as opponents of the so-called Black Matriarch manipulated statistics, shored up traditional gender norms, and encoded stereotypes with little apparent knowledge of their ideological forebears, who supported imperialist matriarchalism at the turn of the twentieth century and momism at mid-century by using the very same sexist and racist foundations upon which they relied. As Trump supporters and men's rights activists, two groups that share a sizable proportion of their self-identified members, shrug off their fears of presidential matriarchy and temporarily suspend their calls to "#repealthe19th," we seem to have come full circle from Weir's 1895 antimatriarchal diatribe about female suffrage, although few MRAs seem to realize that they are echoing, not inaugurating, age-old misogynist critiques. Moreover, the sizable proportion of white female voters who helped to elect Trump represent two antimatriarchalist themes: the complicity of women who buy into the "patriarchal bargain," and, significantly, the continued power that racism offers to white women, a problem that gets less press than the violent, masculine racism of the white supremacist "alt-right" but has been an enduring force in matriarchal theory and gender politics.[36]

And so the matriarchalist tradition in US popular culture has remained unexplored, because its linkages have been buried and the theory itself is thus cyclical. Historian Peggy Pascoe has defined history as "a kind of conversation between the past and the present in which we travel through time to examine the cultural assumptions—and possibilities of our society as well as the societies before us." If, as Pascoe suggests, history is a conversation, then American matriarchalists tend to repeat the same discussion over and over again. Although some texts have broken new ground, the circular evolution of this pop culture prohibits the envisioning of transformative iterations of matriarchalism—ones that embrace liberation from the intertwined constraints of patriarchy, white supremacy, and capitalism.[37]

The way forward out of the trap presented by this circular evolution is through conscientious conversations about historical memory, as when Charnas's Riding Women loudly belt out "self-songs," or their own personal histories, or when the conquering "free fems" are taught to read, write, and record history as a crucial first step in the matriarchal remaking of the New Holdfast. Taken together and examined as a historical process, matriarchalism in its many pop cultural iterations is a vital branch of feminist theory that explores the external constraints on and tensions within challenges to conventional gendered notions of power within the United States. The study of these texts can be deemed "cultural work," something that has been recognized by matriarchalists themselves. Gilman called her fiction "world-food," while Marston called his comic books "America's most popular mental vitamin." Literary scholar Brian Attebery deems fantasy literature, the most popular genre of matriarchalist popular culture, a kind of "resistance movement" that "work[s] to undermine the national faith in things-as-they-are." Thus, the study of matriarchalism as an evolving branch of feminist theory and site of popular culture can help to make plain the multiple ways in which gender has determined the unequal distribution of power within the United States and serve as inspiration to envisioning alternative states. "I think hard times are coming," Ursula Le Guin said at the National Book Awards in 2014, "when we will be wanting the voices of writers who can see alternatives to how we live now, and can see through our fear-stricken society and its obsessive technologies, to other ways of being." She concluded: "We will need writers who can remember freedom." As racialized patriarchy continues to dominate American society, politics, and economics, and twenty-first-century intersectional feminism evolves, the many ways in which various American cultural producers have considered and imagined the contours of female power over the past century and a half can help us to understand both the missteps and the potential inherent in the ideals of liberation, democracy, and equality.[38]

NOTES

INTRODUCTION

1. Associated Press, "UN Naming Wonder Woman as Honorary Ambassador Sparks Protests," *NBC News*, October 22, 2016, accessed November 24, 2017, https://www.nbcnews.com/news/us-news/un-naming-wonder-woman-honorary-ambassador-sparks-protests-n671121; Charlotte Alter, "Marchers Say They Are Going to Stay Active in Politics, *Time*, January 21, 2017, accessed November 24, 2017, http://time.com/4642488/womens-march-washington-d c-donald-trump-action/; Leah Cornish, "'Wonder Woman' Director Patty Jenkins on the Feminist Superhero," *Glamour*, May 16, 2017, accessed November 24, 2017, https://www.glamour.com/story/wonder-woman-director-patty-jenkins-on-the-feminist-superhero; Mark Hughes, "Wonder Woman Is Officially the Highest-Grossing Superhero Origin Film," *Forbes*, November 2, 2017, accessed November 24, 2017, https://www.forbes.com/sites/markhughes/2017/11/02/wonde r-woman-is-officially-the-highest-grossing-superhero-origin-film/#74986ef4ebd9; Associated Press, "Clinton Honored with Wonder Woman Award," accessed November 24, 2017, https://www.youtube.com/watch?v=iZXEdOi1I-w; John Patrick Pullen, "This Year's Hottest Halloween Costumes, According to Google's Search Data," *Fortune*, accessed November 24, 2017, http://fortune.com/2017/10/23/google-halloween-costume-2017/.

2. Cynthia Eller, *The Myth of Matriarchal Prehistory: Why an Invented Past Won't Give Women a Future* (Boston: Beacon Press, 2000), 10.

3. Sara Gwenllian Jones, "Histories, Fictions, and *Xena: Warrior Princess*," *Television and New Media* 1, no. 4 (November 2000): 403–18, 413.

4. Jane L. Donawerth and Carol A. Kolmerten, "Introduction," in *Utopian and Science Fiction by Women: Worlds of Difference*, ed. Jane A. Donawerth and Carol A. Kolmerten (Syracuse, NY: Syracuse University Press, 1994), 1.

5. Donawerth and Kolmerten, "Introduction," 1.

6. Anita M. Superson and Ann E. Cudd, eds., *Theorizing Backlash: Philosophical Reflections on the Resistance to Feminism* (Lanham, MD: Rowman & Littlefield, 2002); Sylvia Walby, "'Backlash in Historical Context," in Mary Kennedy, Cathy Lubelska, and Val Walsh, eds., *Making Connections: Women's Studies, Women's Movements, Women's Lives* (London: Taylor & Francis, 1993), 76–87; Susan Faludi, *Backlash: The Undeclared War Against American Women* (New York: Crown, 1991); Kellie Bean, *Post-Backlash Feminism and the Media Since Reagan-Bush* (Jefferson, NC: McFarland, 2007).

7. Seth Koven and Sonya Michel, "Womanly Duties: Maternalist Politics and the Origins of Welfare States in France, Germany, Great Britain, and the United States, 1880–1920," *American Historical Review* 95, no. 4 (Oct. 1990): 1079; Rebecca Jo Plant and Marian van der Klein, "Introduction," in *Maternalism Reconsidered: Motherhood, Welfare and Social Policy in the Twentieth Century*, ed. Marian van der Klein, Rebecca Jo Plant, Nichole Sanders, and Lori R. Weintraub (New York: Berghahn Books, 2012), 8 3, 4, 5. For more on the historiography of maternalism, see: Theda Skocpol, *Protecting Soldiers and Mothers: The Political Origins of Social Policy in the*

United States (Cambridge, MA: Harvard University Press, 1992); Lynn Y. Weiner, "Maternalism as Paradigm: Defining the Issues," *Journal of Women's History* 5, no. 2 (Fall 1993): 95–130; Seth Koven and Sylvia Michel, eds., *Mothers of a New World: Maternalist Politics and the Origins of Welfare States* (New York: Routledge, 1993); Molly Ladd-Taylor, *Mother-Work: Women, Child Welfare, and the State, 1890–1930* (Urbana: University of Illinois Press, 1994); Linda Gordon, *Pitied But Not Entitled: Single Mothers and the History of Welfare, 1890–1935* (New York: Free Press, 1994); Gwendolyn Mink, *The Wages of Motherhood: Inequality in the Welfare State, 1917–1942* (Ithaca, NY: Cornell University Press, 1995).

8. Elaine Tyler May, *Homeward Bound: American Families in the Cold War Era* (New York: Basic Books, 1988); Ruth Feldstein, *Motherhood in Black and White: Race and Sex in American Liberalism, 1930–1965* (Ithaca: Cornell University Press, 2000).

9. Catherine MacKinnon, *Toward a Feminist Theory of the State* (Cambridge, MA: Harvard University Press, 1991), 157; Katherine Broad, "Race, Reproduction, and the Failures of Feminism in Mary Bradley Lane's *Mizora*," *Tulsa Studies in Women's Literature* 28, no. 2 (Fall 2009): 250; Frances Bartkowski, *Feminist Utopias* (Lincoln: University of Nebraska Press, 1989), 162.

10. Eric Edwards, "Matriarchy, Mother Right, and the Vindication of the Female Principle," *Eric Edwards Collected Works,* July 7, 2013, accessed December 10, 2016, https://ericwedwards.wordpress.com/2013/07/07/matriarchy-mother-right-and-vindication-of-the-female-principle-3/; "Matriarchy," *Oxford English Dictionary,* accessed December 10, 2016, http://www.oed.com; "Matriarchy," *Merriam-Webster,* accessed December 10, 2016, https://www.merriam-webster.com/dictionary/matriarchy; *The American Heritage Dictionary of the English Language,* accessed December 10, 2016, https://ahdictionary.com/word/search.html?q=matriarchy&submit.x=45&submit.y=34; Heide Gottner-Abendroth, "Why the Term Matriarchy?," International Academy HAGIA, 2009, accessed December 10, 2016, http://www.hagia.de/en/matriarchy/why-the-term-matriarchy.html.

11. Peggy Reeves Sanday, "Matriarchal Values and World Peace: The Case of the Minangkabau," Second World Congress of Matriarchal Studies, 2005, accessed December 10, 2016, http://www.second-congress-matriarchal-studies.com/sanday.html; Sanday, *Women at the Center: Life in a Modern Matriarchy* (Ithaca, NY: Cornell University Press, 2002), xi.

12. Sanday, *Women at the Center,* x–xi, xii; "Matriarchy by Peggy Reeves Sanday: Feminism and Religion," July 29, 2011, accessed December 10, 2016, http://feminismandreligion.com/2011/07/29/matriarchy-by-peggy-reeves-sanday/.

13. Eller, *Myth of Matriarchal Prehistory,* 13.

14. Simone de Beauvoir, *The Second Sex* (New York: Penguin, 1972), 100–101; Brian Attebury, *Decoding Gender in Science Fiction* (New York: Routledge, 2002), 107, 116.

15. For more on archaeological evidence of prehistoric matriarchies, see: J. M. Adovasio, Olga Soffer, and Jake Page, *The Invisible Sex: Uncovering the True Roles of Women in Prehistory* (New York: HarperCollins, 2007), 277.

16. Claude Levi-Strauss, *The Naked Man: Mythologiques* (Chicago: University of Chicago Press, 1981), 675.

17. Eller, *Myth of Matriarchal Prehistory,* 6–7.

18. Nancy F. Cott, *The Grounding of Modern Feminism* (New Haven, CT: Yale University Press, 1989), 271.

19. Please note that I was not able to be comprehensive in this book; it was impossible to include every pop cultural text that touches upon matriarchies or matriarchalism. Instead, I have chosen the most historically significant and representative examples from each era. Apologies to fans of those pop cultural texts that did not make the cut.

CHAPTER ONE

1. Cynthia Eller, *Gentleman and Amazons: The Myth of Matriarchal Prehistory, 1861–1900* (Berkeley: University of California Press, 2011), 16; Stanley B. Alpern, *Amazons of Black Sparta: The Women Warriors of Dahomey* (New York: New York University Press, 2011), 1–11. Eller traces the development of academic matriarchalism, particularly through European anthropology, in *Gentleman and Amazons;* those looking for the more intricate details of this history than is provided in this chapter would do well to consult her work.

2. Eller, *Gentlemen and Amazons,*74.

3. Marx's letters quoted in Daniel Gasmna, *The Scientific Origins of National Socialism* (London: McDonald, 1971), 107.

4. Eller, *Gentlemen and Amazons,* 67; Adam Kuper, *The Reinvention of Primitive Society: Transformations of a Myth* (New York: Routledge, 2005), xi; Burrow quoted in Kuper, 16. Please note that "evolutionism" refers to sociocultural theories, rather than biological evolution, although proponents of the former often based their ideas, at least loosely, on the latter (George W. Stocking Jr., *Victorian Anthropology* (New York: Free Press, 1987), xv).

5. Erich Fromm, "The Theory of Mother Right and Its Relevance to Social Psychology," in *Erich Fromm: Love, Sexuality, and Matriarchy—About Gender,* ed. Rainer Funk (New York: International Publishing, 1997), 46; Bachofen quoted in Jonathan David Fishbane, *Mother-Right, Myth, and Renewal: The Thought of Johann Jakob Bachofen and Its Relationship to the Perception of Cultural Decadence in the Nineteenth Century* (PhD diss., University of Michigan, 1981), 489; Johann Jakob Bachofen, *Myth, Religion, and Mother-Right,* trans. Ralph Manheim (Princeton, NJ: Princeton University Press, 1967).

6. Fromm, *Love, Sexuality, and Matriarchy,* 4; Bachofen, *Myth, Religion, and Mother-Right,* 170, 71.

7. Bachofen, *Myth, Religion, and Mother-Right,* 93, 141; Adovasio, *The Invisible Sex,* 251; Bachofen, *Myth, Religion, and Mother-Right,* 79.

8. Bachofen, *Myth, Religion, and Mother-Right,* 143–44.

9. Bachofen, *Myth, Religion, and Mother-Right,* 101, 153.

10. Bachofen, *Myth, Religion, and Mother-Right,* 153–54, 171, 148, 149.

11. Eller, *Gentlemen and Amazons,* 46; Bachofen, *Myth, Religion, and Mother-Right,* 72, 76.

12. Bachofen, *Myth, Religion, and Mother-Right,* 186; Eller, *Gentlemen and Amazons,* 65.

13. Lionel Gossman, "Orpheus Philologus: Bachofen versus Mommsen on the Study of Antiquity," *Transactions of the American Philosophical Society* 73, no. 5 (1983): 3; Gerry Stagl, "Johann J. Bachofen," in *Theory in Social and Cultural Anthropology,* ed. R. Jon McGee and Richard L. Warms (Thousand Oaks, CA: Sage Publications, 2013), 40; Adam Kuper, *The Reinvention of Primitive Society: Transformations of a Myth* (New York: Routledge, 2005), 4; Julia Reid, "'She-who-must-be-obeyed': Anthropology and Matriarchy in H. Rider Haggard's *She,*" *Journal of*

Victorian Culture 20, no. 3 (2015): 360. A few years after *Mother-Right,* British anthropologist John Ferguson McLennan, in *Primitive Marriage* (1865), offered a dim view of what he deemed the promiscuous matrilineal stage of human societies (McLennan, *Primitive Marriage: An Inquiry into the Origin of the Form of Capture in Marriage Ceremonies* (Edinburgh: Adam and Charles Black, 1865), https://archive.org/details/Mclennan1865gg670). He did not cite Bachofen, claiming that he read *Mother-Right* in 1866, one year after publishing *Primitive Marriage* (Kuper, *Reinvention of Primitive Society,* 55).

14. Catherine Davies, Hillary Owen, and Claire Brewster, *South American Independence: Gender, Politics, Text* (Liverpool: Liverpool University Press, 2007), 132; Rosalina Diaz, "The Amazon of Matinino: A Personal Legacy of Female Empowerment in the Greater Antilles," *Journal of the Motherhood Initiative* 3, no. 2 (2012): 241; Abby Kleinbaum, *The War Against the Amazons* (New York: New Press, 1983), 79–84; Mark Raab, Jim Cassidy, Andrew Yatsko, and William J. Howard, *California Maritime Archaeology: A San Clemente Island Perspective* (Lanham, MD: Altamira Press, 2009), 68; Davies et al., *South American Independence,* 132; Miguel Leon-Portilla, "California: Land of Frontiers," in *Common Border, Uncommon Paths: Race, Culture, and National Identity in U.S.-Mexican Relations,* ed. Jaime E. Rodriguez O. and Kathryn Vincent (Wilmington: Scholarly Resources, Inc., 1997), 16; Alfredo Ruiz Islas, "Hernán Cortés y la Isla California," *Iberoamericana* no. 27 (September 2007): 42.

15. de Acuña quoted in Wolfgang Haase and Reinhold Mayer, eds., *European Images of the Americas and the Classical Tradition* (Berlin: De Gruyter, 1993), 317; de Carvajal quoted in Francesca Miller, *Latin American Women and the Search for Social Justice* (Lebanon, PA: University Press of New England, 1991), 16; Eller, *Gentlemen and Amazons,* 20.

16. Kathleen Brown, *Good Wives, Nasty Wenches, and Anxious Patriarchs: Gender, Race, and Power in Colonial Virginia* (Chapel Hill: University of North Carolina Press, 1996), 5, 45, 57.

17. Gretchen L. Green, "Gender and the Longhouse: Iroquois Women in a Changing Culture," in *Women and Freedom in Early America,* ed. Larry D. Eldridge (New York: New York University Press, 1997), 12, 9, 15; Pierre Francois Xavier de Charlevoix, "The Dilemmas of New France," in *Voices of the American Past, vol. 1,* ed. Raymond Hyser and J. Arndt (Independence, KY: Cengage Learning, 2011), 34–37; W. M. Beauchamp, "Iroquois Women," *Journal of American Folklore* 13, no. 49 (April–June 1900): 89; Arthur C. Parker, *The Life of General Ely S. Parker: The Last Grand Sachem of the Iroquois and General Grant's Military Secretary* (Buffalo, NY: Buffalo Historical Society, 1919), 45–46.

18. Christian F. Feest, "Father Lafitau as Ethnographer of the Iroquois," *Native American Studies* 15, no. 2 (2001): 21–22; David Allen Harvey, "Living Antiquity: Lafitau's *Moeurs des Sauvages Amériquains* and the Religious Roots of the Enlightenment Science of Man," *Proceedings of the Western Society for French History* 36 (2008): 75–92; James Evans, "Joseph Francois Lafitau: A Disciple of Herodotus Amongst the Iroquois," accessed December 21, 2015, http://www.academia.edu/6171003/Lafitau.

19. Joseph Francois Lafitau, *Customs of the American Indians Compared with the Customs of Primitive Indians,* ed. and trans. by William N. Fenton and Elizabeth L. Moore (Toronto: Champlain Society, 1974), 285, 72, 80; Evans, "Joseph Francois Lafitau."

20. Lafitau, *Customs of the American Indians,* 82, 69; Evans, "Joseph Francois Lafitau"; Feest,

"Father Lafitau as Ethnographer," 20; Kay Anderson, *Race and the Crisis of Humanism* (London: Routledge, 2006), 55; David L. Blaney and Naeem Inayatullah, *Savage Economics: Wealth, Poverty, and the Temporal Walls of Capitalism* (London: Routledge, 2010), 17.

21. Evans, "Joseph Francois Lafitau"; Feest, "Father Lafitau as Ethnographer," 20; James E. Seaver, *A Narrative of the Life of Mary Jemison* (1824), Project Gutenberg e-book, accessed December 21, 2015, http://www.gutenberg.org/files/6960/6960-h/6960-h.htm; Ian K. Steele, *Setting All the Captives Free: Capture, Adjustment, and Recollection in Allegheny County* (Montreal: McGill-Queen's University Press, 2013), 292; Green, "Gender and the Longhouse," 12–13; Julie Falkner, "Molly Brant, Mohawk Loyalist," *History's Women,* accessed December 21, 2015, http://www.historyswomen.com/earlyamerica/mollybrant.htm; Nancy Shoemaker, "The Rise or Fall of Iroquois Women," *Journal of Women's History* 2, no. 3 (Winter 1991): 39–57, 44.

22. Bernhard J. Stern, ed., "The Letters of Asher Wright to Lewis Henry Morgan," *American Anthropologist* (1933): 140.

23. Shoemaker, "Rise or Fall," 39.

24. Shoemaker, "Rise or Fall," 42.

25. Fenton, "Introduction" to Lewis Henry Morgan, *League of the Haudenosaunee: A Classic Study of an American Tribe with Original Illustrations* (New York: Citadel Press, 1984), v; Morgan, *League of the Haudenosaunee,* 91.

26. Lewis Henry Morgan, *Systems of Consanguinity and Affinity of the Human Family* (Washington: Smithsonian Institution, 1870); Feest, "Father Lafitau as Ethnographer," 19; Morgan, *Ancient Society, or Researches into the Lines of Human Progress From Savagery to Barbarism to Civilization,* part 3, chap. 1, "The Ancient Family."

27. Morgan, *Ancient Society,* "Preface"; Micaela di Leonardo, *Exotics at Home: Anthropologies, Others, and American Modernity* (Chicago: University of Chicago Press, 1998), 152.

28. Meyer Fortes, *Kinship and Social Order: The Legacy of Lewis Henry Morgan* (Chicago: Aldine, 1969), 36; Morgan, *Ancient Society,* "Preface."

29. Morgan, *Ancient Society,* part 1, chap. 1, "Ethnical Periods."

30. Morgan, *Ancient Society,* part 2, chap. 14, "Change of Descent from the Female to the Male Line"; part 2, chap. 3, "The Iroquois Phatry."

31. Morgan, *Ancient Society,* part 2, chap. 2, "The Iroquois Gens"; part 3, chap. 5, "The Monogamian Family"; part 4, chap. 2, "The Three Rules of Inheritance (Continued)."

32. Morgan, *Ancient Society,* part 1, chap. 1, "Ethnical Periods."

33. See Michael A. Bellisiles, *1877: America's Year of Living Violently* (New York: The New Press, 2010).

34. Kuper, *Reinvention of Primitive Society,* 58, 82. Marvin Harris, *The Rise of Anthropological Theory: A History of Theories of Culture* (Lanham, MD: AltaMira Press, 2001), 189; Eller, *Gentlemen and Amazons,* 92, 61.

35. Eller, *Gentlemen and Amazons,* 105, 106.

36. Friedrich Engels, *Origin of the Family, Private Property, and the State,* part 2: The Family, chap. 3, "The Pairing Family," accessed December 21, 2015, https://www.marxists.org/archive/marx/works/1884/origin-family/ch02c.htm.

37. Engels, *Origin of the Family,* chap. 3.

38. Eller, *Gentlemen and Amazons,* 106.

39. Ellen Carol DuBois, *Feminism and Suffrage: The Emergence of an Independent Women's Movement in America, 1848–1869* (Ithaca, NY: Cornell University Press, 1978), 60.

40. *General Laws, Memorials, and Resolutions of the Territory of Wyoming,* c. 31 (Cheyenne, WY: S. Allen Bristol, Public Printer, Tribune Office, 1869), 371; Thomas G. Alexander, "An Experiment in Progressive Legislation: The Granting of Woman Suffrage in Utah in 1870," *Utah Historical Quarterly* 38 (Winter 1970), accessed December 21, 2015, http://content.lib.utah.edu/utils/getfile/collection/USHSArchPub/id/6449/filename/6484.pdf; Leila R. Brammer, *Excluded from Suffrage History: Matilda Joslyn Gage, Nineteenth-Century American Feminist* (Westport, CT: Praeger, 2000), 10; Eleanor Flexner and Ellen Fitzpatrick, *Century of Struggle: The Woman's Rights Movement in the United States* (Cambridge, MA: Harvard University Press, 1996).

CHAPTER TWO

1. Reprinted in Ellen Carol DuBois and Richard Candida Smith, eds., *Elizabeth Cady Stanton: Feminist as Thinker* (New York: New York University Press, 2007), 264–65.

2. DuBois and Smith, *Elizabeth Cady Stanton,* 265.

3. DuBois and Smith, *Elizabeth Cady Stanton,* 270–71.

4. DuBois and Smith, *Elizabeth Cady Stanton,* 268, 270–71, 269, 265.

5. Leila R. Brammer, *Excluded from Suffrage History: Matilda Joslyn Gage, Nineteenth-Century American Feminist* (Westport, CT: Praeger, 2000), 75.

6. Sally Roesch Wagner, *Matilda Joslyn Gage: She Who Holds the Sky* (Aberdeen, SD: Sky Carrier Press, 1999); Sally Roesch Wagner, "That Word is Liberty: A Biography of Matilda Joslyn Gage" (PhD diss., University of California at Santa Cruz, 1978), 5, 161, 49, 53.

7. Wagner, "That Word Is Liberty," 100, 106, 112, 115, 113.

8. Wagner, "That Word Is Liberty," 161; Evan I. Schwartz, *Finding Oz: How L. Frank Baum Discovered the Great American Story* (New York: Houghton Mifflin Harcourt, 2009), 38; Wagner, "That Word Is Liberty," 296.

9. Wagner, "That Word Is Liberty," 467, vi.

10. Wagner, *Matilda Joslyn Gage,* 8, 21; Schwartz, *Finding Oz,* 41; Fran Capp and Frank Borzellieri, *It Happened in New York* (Guilford, CT: Globe Pequot Press, 2007), 73; Polly Kaufman, *National Parks and the Woman's Voice: A History* (Albuquerque: University of New Mexico Press, 2006), 54; Gage, "To the Daughters of 1986," in Sally Roesch Wagner, *A Time of Protest: Suffragists Challenge the Republic, 1870–1887* (Aberdeen, SD: Sky Carrier Press, 1988), 107–11.

11. Wagner, *Matilda Joslyn Gage,* 31; Nancy Tystad Koupal, "On the Road to Oz: L. Frank Baum as Editor," in *Baum's Road to Oz: The Dakota Years,* ed. Nancy Koupal (Pierre: South Dakota State Historical Society Press, 2000), 63; David B. Parker, "Oz: L. Frank Baum's Theosophical Utopia," accessed December 21, 2015, http://www.mindspring.com/~daveh47/OzFiles/wiztheos.txt.

12. Koupal, "On the Road to Oz," 63–64; Ann Taylor Allen, *Feminism and Motherhood in Western Europe, 1890–1970: The Maternal Dilemma* (New York: Palgrave Macmillan, 2005), 29; "Lectures: Ancient Egypt," *National Citizen and Ballot Box,* January 1880, http://www.accessible-archives.com/2013/03/lectures-by-matilda-joslyn-gage-1880/; Schwartz, *Finding Oz,* 105–9.

13. Wagner, "That Word Is Liberty," abstract; Gage, in *Twentieth Century*, December 25, 1890, reprinted in Susan Savion, *Quoting Matilda* (Bloomington, IN: AuthorHouse, 2014), chap. 10, "On the Vote."

14. Wagner, *Matilda Joslyn Gage*, 48; Gage, "The Dangers of the Hour," speech at the founding convention of the National Women's Liberation Union, 1890, http://www.matildajoslyngage.org/gage-home/religious-freedom-room/dangers-of-the-hour/; Brammer, *Excluded from Suffrage History*, 70; Wagner, "That Word Is Liberty," abstract.

15. Gage, *Women, Church and State: A Historical Account of the Status of Women Through the Christian Ages: with Reminiscences of the Matriarchate* (Chicago: Charles H. Kerr, 1893), Kindle e-book, dedication page.

16. Gage, *Church and State*, chap. 1, "The Matriarchate."

17. Gage, *Church and State*, chap. 1, "The Matriarchate."

18. Gage, *Church and State*, chap. 1, "The Matriarchate."

19. Kathryn Kish Sklar, "The Historical Foundations of Women's Power in the Creation of the American Welfare State, 1830–1930," in Koven and Michel, *Mothers of a New World*, 43–93, 63; Mary Ritter Beard, *Woman's Work in Municipalities* (New York: D. Appleton and Company, 1915), accessed May 9, 2017, https://archive.org/details/womansworkinmun1oobear.

20. Koven and Michel, "Womanly Duties," 1079, 1107; Suzanne M. Marilley, "Frances Willard and the Feminism of Fear," *Feminist Studies* 19, no. 1 (1993), 125.

21. Ladd-Taylor, *Mother Work*, 43.

22. Gage, *Women, Church and State*, chap. 1, "The Matriarchate."

23. Gage, *Women, Church and State*, chap. 1, "The Matriarchate."

24. Savion, *Quoting Matilda*, chap. 22, "On the Haudenosaunee"; Melissa Ann Ryan, "(Un)natural Law: Women Writers, the Indian, and the State in Nineteenth-Century America," PhD. diss., University of Arizona, 2004, 155–56. I should also note here that Gage, like her suffragist contemporaries, often viewed the federal preoccupation with Native Americans as "yet another distraction" from suffrage (156). And she was, at times during her early career as an activist, hostile to Native American citizenship rights; they seemed to be at odds with female or universal suffrage (Ryan, "(Un)natural Law," 158), which led her to characterize citizenship as the privilege of the "civilized," using language that placed her firmly within the racism of the nineteenth-century suffrage movement (Ryan, "(Un)natural Law," 160). By the late 1880s and into the 1890s, however, as she conducted more research, delved more deeply into Theosophy, spent more time among the Iroquois, and grew to understand the matriarchal structure of the Nations, Gage had discarded racist language in favor of universal rights.

25. Schwartz, *Finding Oz*, 57; Wagner, *Matilda Joslyn Gage*, 34; Schwartz, 249; Matilda Joslyn Gage to Helen Leslie Jones, December 5, 1896, "Papers of Matilda Joslyn Gage," Schlesinger Library, Harvard University; Savion, chap. 23, "On the Haudenosaunee."

26. Gage, *Women, Church and State*, chap. 10, "Past, Present, Future," and chap. 1, "The Matriarchate."

27. Gage, *Women, Church and State*, chap. 5, "Witchcraft."

28. Gage, *Women, Church and State*, chap. 5, "Witchcraft."

29. Gage, *Women, Church and State*, chap. 5, "Witchcraft," chap. 10, "Past, Present, Future," "Preface," and chap. 4, "Marquette."

30. Gage, *Women, Church and State*, "Preface."

31. Gage quoted in Karlyn Kohrs Campbell, *Women Public Speakers in the United States, 1800–1925* (Westport, CT: Greenwood Press, 1993), 280; Brammer, *Excluded from Suffrage History*, 61.

32. "Mrs. Gage's Book: Her Side of the Case," *Fayetteville Recorder*, August 23, 1894; Brammer, *Excluded from Suffrage History*, 62.

33. Naomi Jacobs, "Reviewed Works: *Mizora: A Prophecy* by Mary E. Bradley Lane and Jean Pfaelzer," *Utopian Studies* 12, no. 1 (2001): 210; Katherine Broad, "Race, Reproduction, and the Failures of Feminism in Mary Bradley Lane's *Mizora*," *Tulsa Studies in Women's Literature* 28, no. 2 (Fall 2009): 248; Mary E. Bradley Lane; *Mizora: A Prophecy. A Manuscript Found among the Papers of Princess Vera Zarovitch* (New York: G. W. Dillingham, 1989).

34. Julian Robinson, *Gynecocracy: A Narrative of the Adventures and Psychological Experiences of Julian Robinson Under Petticoat Rule, Written by Himself* (London: Locus Elm Press, 2014; reprint of 1893 edition), Kindle e-book, vol. 1, chapter 3, "Mademoiselle Hortense de Chambonnard"; chapter 4, "The Birch"; chapter 6, "A Lesson in Psychology"; vol. 3, "Epilogue."

35. Lisa Tickner, *The Spectacle of Women: Imagery of the Suffrage Campaign, 1907–1914* (Chicago: University of Chicago Press, 1988), 50; Laura L. Behling, *The Masculine Woman in America, 1890–1935* (Champaign: University of Illinois Press, 2001), 3; "Feminization of Men," Catherine H. Palczewski Suffrage Postcard Archive, University of Northern Iowa, accessed December 10, 2016, http://www.uni.edu/palczews/NEW%20postcard%20webpage/Feminine%20Men.html; Gwen Sharp, "Vintage Anti-Suffrage Postcards," *Sociological Images*, accessed December 10, 2016, https://thesocietypages.org/socimages/2012/11/08/vintage-anti-suffrage-postcards/.

36. James B. Weir, "Domesticity or Matriarchy, Which?," *The American Practitioner*, vol. 18, 419–23.

37. Bushnell quoted in Behling, 2–3; James Weir, Jr., "The Effect of Female Suffrage on Posterity," *The American Naturalist*, vo. 29, no. 345 (Sept., 1895), 817.

38. Weir, "Effect of Female Suffrage," 818, 819, 820, 822.

39. Weir, "Effect of Female Suffrage," 822, 825.

40. Wagner, *Matilda Joslyn Gage*, 60, 58; Wagner, "That Word Is Liberty," abstract; Leila R. Brammer, *Excluded from Suffrage History*, 110; William M. Fenton, "Introduction" to Lewis Henry Morgan, *League of the Haudenosaunee: A Classic Study of an American Tribe with Original Illustrations* (New York: Citadel Press), 1984, 34; Matilda Joslyn Gage to T. C. Gage, July 11, 1893, "Papers of Matilda Joslyn Gage," Schlesinger Library, Harvard.

41. Friedrich Engels, preface to the 4th edition, *Origins of the Family, Private Property, and the State*.

42. Johann Jakob Bachofen, *Myth, Religion, and Mother-Right*, trans. Ralph Manheim (Princeton, NJ: Princeton University Press), 1967, 81–82.

43. Judith R. Walkowitz, *City of Dreadful Delight: Narratives of Sexual Danger in Late-Victorian London* (Chicago: University of Chicago, 1992), 154; Adam Kuper, *The Reinvention of Primitive Society: Transformations of a Myth* (New York: Routledge, 2005); Erich Fromm, "The Theory of Mother Right and Its Relevance to Social Psychology," in *Erich Fromm: Love, Sexuality, and Matriarchy—About Gender*, ed. Rainer Funk (New York: International Publishing, 1997), 20.

CHAPTER THREE

1. "Women as Explorers," *The Inter Ocean,* Saturday, October 22, 1892 ("World's Columbian Exposition Records, 1891–1895," Special Collections Research Center, University of Chicago, Box 2, Folder 6); May French Sheldon, foreword in *Sultan to Sultan: Adventures Among the Masai and Other Tribes of East Africa* (Boston: Arena Publishing, 1892), 13, archive.org e-book, accessed May 24, 2017, https://archive.org/stream/sultantosultanadooshel#page/n8/mode/1up/search/natural+primitives.

2. Tracy Jean Boisseau, *White Queen: May French Sheldon and the Imperial Origins of American Feminism Identity* (Bloomington: Indiana University Press, 2004), Kindle e-book, "Introduction: A Tale of Imperial Feminism," chap. 2, "Self-Discovery"; Louise Michele Newman, *White Women's Rights: The Racial Origins of Feminism in the United States* (New York: Oxford University Press, 1999), 20.

3. Robert Muccigrosso, *Celebrating the New World: Chicago's Columbian Exposition of 1893* (Chicago: Ivan R. Dee, 1993), 93; Anne E. Feldman, "Women and the Press at the 1893 World's Columbian Exposition," in *World's Fair Notes: A Woman Journalist Views Chicago's 1893 Columbian Exposition,* by Marian Shaw (St. Paul, MN: Pogo Press, 1992), 83; Robert W. Rydell, *The Books of the Fairs: Materials About World's Fairs, 1834–1916, in the Smithsonian Institution Libraries* (Chicago: American Library Association, 1992), 1.

4. G. Brown Goode, *First Draft of a Classification for the World's Columbian Exposition* (Washington, DC: Government Printing Office, 1893), 654; William E. Cameron, *The World's Fair, Being a Pictorial History of the Columbian Exposition, Containing a Complete History of the World-Renowned Exposition at Chicago* (Chicago: Chicago Publication & Lithograph, 1893), 5; "Man and His Works: Ethnological Exhibits at the Fair," reprinted in *Coming of Age in Chicago: The 1893 World's Fair and the Coalescence of American Anthropology,* ed. Curtis M Hinsley and David R. Wilcox (Lincoln: University of Nebraska Press, 2016), 91–98, 91; Hinsley, "Anthropology as Education and Entertainment: Frederic Ward Putnam at the Fair," in Hinsley and Wilcox, eds., *Coming of Age in Chicago,* 47.

5. *Chicago Tribune, From Peristyle to Plaisance, with a Short History of the World's Columbian Exposition, Chicago, 1893* (Chicago: Chicago Tribune, 1893), n.p.; George W. Stocking Jr., *Victorian Anthropology* (New York: Free Press, 1987), 5;.Shaw, *World's Fair Notes,* 25.

6. Muccigrosso, *Celebrating the New World,* 93, 164; H. D. Northrop, *The World's Fair as Seen in One Hundred Days* (Philadelphia, PA: Ariel Book Co., 1893), 674; Tudor Jenks, *The Century World's Fair Book for Boys and Girls* (New York: The Century Co, 1893), 81; Julian Hawthorne, "Foreign Folk at the Fair," *Cosmopolitan* 15, no. 5, September 1893, 568 (Chicago, World's Columbian Exposition: A Collection of Articles from *Cosmopolitan, Century, Scribner's, Harper's, Atlantic Monthly* and *Munsey's Magazine*) (New York: 1892–1899), World's Fair Collection, Dibner Library Special Collections, Smithsonian Institutions).

7. Wim De Wit, James Gilbert, Robert W. Rydell, Neil Harris, and the Chicago Historical Society, *Grand Illusions: Chicago's World's Fair of 1893* (Chicago: Sewall Co., 1993), 166; *World's Fair Number, The Youth's Companion* (Boston, Thursday, May 4, 1893), "World's Columbian Exposition Records, 1891–1895," Special Collections Research Center, University of Chicago, Box 2, Folder 5,

p. 18; Barnum quoted in Bluford Adams, "'A Stupendous Mirror of Departed Empires': The Barnum Hippodrome and Circuses, 1874–1891," *American Literary History* 8, no. 1 (Spring 1996): 36; Jane Goodall, *Performance and Evolution in the Age of Darwin: Out of the Natural Order* (London: Routledge, 2002), 99; *The Dream City: A Portfolio of Views of the World's Columbian Exposition* (St. Louis: N. D. Thompson Publishing, 1893), n.p.; M. P. Handy, *World's Columbian Exposition Official Catalogue* (Chicago: W. B. Conkey Co., 1893), 21; *Picturesque World's Fair: An Elaborate Collection of Colored Views* (Chicago: W. B. Conkey Co., 1894), 34; Gertrude M. Scott, "Village Performance: Villages at the Chicago World's Columbian Exposition" (PhD diss., New York University, 1991), 183; Amy Leslie, *Amy Leslie at the Fair* (Chicago: W. B. Conkey Co., 1893), 99.

8. Claire Louise Burnham, *Sweet Clover: A Romance of the White City* (Boston: Houghton, Mifflin, 1894), 71; Leslie, *Amy Leslie at the Fair*, 99; Hawthorne, "Foreign Folk at the Fair," 570; Shaw, *World's Fair Notes*, 56; *The Chicago Record's History of the World's Fair* (Chicago Daily News Co., October 1893), 249; Denton Jacques Snider, *World's Fair Studies* (London: Forgotten Books, 2013), 300–301.

9. Gerald D. Nash, "The Census of 1890 and the Closing of the Frontier," *Pacific Northwest Quarterly* 71, no. 3 (July 1980): 98. The "Africa Question" was on the minds of many at the Fair, as observers commented upon the advance of "civilization" on the continent's "rich and fertile region[s]." "Huts in the African Wilds," *The Columbian Gallery; a Portfolio of Photographs from the World's Fair* (Chicago: The Werner Co., 1894), n.p.

10. Frederick J. Turner, "The Significance of the Frontier in American History," address to the American Historical Association, 1894, accessed December 10, 2016, http://www.historians.org/about-aha-and-membership/aha-history-and-archives/archives/the-significance-of-the-frontier-in-american-history.

11. Goodall, *Performance and Evolution*, 96; Leslie, *Amy Leslie at the Fair*, 20; Erik Larson, *The Devil in the White City: A Saga of Magic and Murder at the Fair that Changed America* (New York: Vintage, 2004), 133; "Wild West Show Advertisement," World's Columbian Exposition Collection, University of Chicago Special Collections, Box 4, Folder 6; Advertisement, *World's Fair Puck*, 2, May 15, 1893, 24; Goodall, *Performance and Evolution*, 111; G. L. Dybwad and Joy V. Bliss, eds., *White City Recollections: A Young Man's World's Fair Adventure with His Father* (Albuquerque, NM: The Book Stops Here, 2003), 133; Larson, *Devil in the White City*, 305; David R. Wilcox, "Anthropology in a Changing America: Interpreting the Chicago 'Triumph' of Frank Hamilton Cushing," in Hinsley and Wilcox, *Coming of Age in Chicago*, 170.

12. "1892 Buffalo Bill's Wild West Programme," available online in the William F. Cody Archive, accessed May 9, 2017, http://codyarchive.org/memorabilia/wfc.mem00279.html; Kim Warren, "Gender, Race, Culture, and the Mythic American Frontier," *Journal of Women's History* 19, no. 1 (Spring 2007): 235; Larson, *Devil in the White City*, 286.

13. Christopher Reed, *"All the World Is Here": The Black Presence at White City* (Bloomington: Indiana University Press, 2002), 27; Susan B. Anthony, "The Moral Leadership of the Religious Press," May 27, 1893, accessed December 11, 2016, http://ecssba.rutgers.edu/docs/sbaexpo.html#may275/27; Jeanne Madeline Weimann, *The Fair Women* (Chicago: Academy, 1981), 518; Susan B. Anthony, "Organization Among Women as an Instrument in Promoting Liberty," May 20, 1893, accessed December 11, 2016, http://ecssba.rutgers.edu/docs/sbaexpo.html#may20; *Chicago Sunday Post*, May 28, 1893, p. 11.

14. Boisseau, "Introduction," and chap. 3, "Forging a Feminine Colonial Method," in *White Queen*. Her biographer reports that French Sheldon "privately imagined herself on a par with Susan B. Anthony," citing an image she drew of Anthony's face next to "an unidentified woman's face remarkably resembling her own younger self," which, French Sheldon claimed, "had come to her in a dream" (chap. 8, "Taking Feminism on the Road," in Boisseau, *White Queen*).

15. Boisseau, "Introduction," chap. 1, "The Caravan Trek to Kilimanjaro," and chap. 2, "Self-Discovery," in *White Queen*; May French Sheldon, *Sultan to Sultan: Adventures Among the Masai and Other Tribes of East Africa* (Boston: Arena Publishing, 1892), 131–32; Newman, *White Women's Rights*, 106; Boisseau, chapter 3, "Forging a Feminine Colonial Method," in *White Queen*.

16. Boisseau, chapter 2, "Self-Discovery," in *White Queen*; Sheldon, *Sultan to Sultan*, 174–75; French Sheldon, "Customs Among the Natives of East Africa, from Teita to Kilimegalia, with Special Reference to Their Women and Children," *Journal of the Anthropological Institute of Great Britain and Ireland* 21 (1892): 359; Newman, *White Women's Rights*, 106.

17. French Sheldon, *Sultan to Sultan*, 292; Fannie C. Williams, "A 'White Queen' at the World's Fair," *Chautauquan* 18 (1893): 342; Newman, *White Women's Rights*, 15; French Sheldon, *Sultan to Sultan*, 254; Boisseau, chap. 2, "Self-Discovery," in *White Queen*.

18. Boisseau, chap. 1, "The Caravan Trek to Kilimanjaro," in *White Queen*; Melinda Stump, "'The Most Deadly Spot on the Face of the Earth': The United States and Antimodern Images of 'Darkest Africa,' 1880–1910" (Master's thesis, University of Northern Iowa, 2013), 16; Williams, "A 'White Queen at the World's Fair," 342; Hinsley, "Ambiguous Legacy: Daniel Garrison Brinton at the International Congress of Anthropology," in Hinsley and Wilcox, *Coming of Age in Chicago*, 111.

19. French Sheldon, "An African Expedition," reprinted in *The Congress of Women: Held in the Women's Building, World's Columbian Exposition, Chicago, U.S.A., 1893* (Chicago: Monarch Book Co., 1894), 131–34.

20. Williams, "A 'White Queen,'" 342, 343.

21. French Sheldon, *Sultan to Sultan,* 136.

22. Northrop, *The World's Fair*, xi; "Women of the Fair Meet," *Chicago Daily News*, July 5, 1893; Micaela di Leonardo, *Exotics at Home: Anthropologies, Others, and American Modernity* (Chicago: University of Chicago Press, 1998), 11. The murals are available for viewing online at "Women's Public Art and Architecture," http://arcadiasystems.org/academia/cassatt5.html.

23. "World's Columbian Exposition Records, 1891–1895," Folder 1, Box 9, Special Collections Research Center, University of Chicago; *World's Fair Puck*, vol. 4, May 29, 1893, 42–43; *World's Fair Puck*, vol. 9, July 3, 1893, 102–3.

24. *World's Fair Puck*, vol. 25, October 23, 1893, cover.

25. Robert Rydell, "'Darkest Africa': African Shows at America's World's Fairs, 1893–1940," in *Africans on Stage: Studies in Ethnological Show Business*, ed. Bernth Lindfors (Bloomington: Indiana University Press, 1999), 140; Scott, "Village Performance," 283; Hinsley, "Anthropology as Education and Entertainment," 62, 63. One observer wrote that the traveling group was made up of five different tribal groups (Scott, "Village Performance," 289), but historian Christopher Robert Reed argues that the villagers were of the Fon linguistic and cultural group of West Africa (Reed, *"All the World Is Here,"* 144).

26. Rydell, "'Darkest Africa,'" 140; Scott, "Village Performance," 284. Anne McClintock

coined the phrase *commodity racism* in *Imperial Leather: Race, Gender, and Sexuality in the Colonial Context* (New York: Routledge, 1995), 33.

27. "Dahomeyans Revel in Cruelty," *Chicago Tribune*, June 13, 1892.

28. Richard Burton, *A Mission to Gelele, King of Dahome* (London: Tylston and Edwards, 1863), xi, 112, 214. The first Western mention of Dahomeyan women was by Archibald Dalzel, the British colonialist, in 1793, exactly a century before the World's Columbian Exposition (Dalzel, *The History of Dahomey, An Inland Kingdom of Africa* [self-published, 1793], x–xi, accessed May 11, 2017, https://archive.org/details/historydahomyanoodalzgoog.)

29. Stanley B. Alpern, *Amazons of Black Sparta: The Women Warriors of Dahomey* (New York: New York University Press, 2011), 195–97, 201–2.

30. "The Amazon Troops of Dahomey," *Chicago Tribune*, May 22, 1892; Scott, "Village Performance," 295; *Dream City*, n.p.; "Dahomey Cannibals," *The Magic City: A Portfolio of Original Photographic Views of the Great World's Fair and Its Treasures of Art*, Historical Fine Arts Series, vol. 1, no. 2, Jan. 22, 1894 (Philadelphia: H. S. Smith and C. R. Graham for Historical Publishing, 1894), n.p.

31. Putnam, "Introduction," *Oriental and Occidental Northern and Southern Portrait Types of the Midway Plaisance* (St. Louis: N. D. Putnam Publishing, 1894), n.p.; *Conkey's Complete Guide to the World's Columbian Exposition, May 1 to October 30, 1893* (Chicago: W. B. Conkey Co., 1893), 26; Leslie, *Amy Leslie at the Fair*, 99; "Dahomey Village, X. Pene, Concessionaire," *Official Catalogue of Exhibits on the Midway Plaisance: Department M-Ethnology, Group 176: isolated exhibits, Midway Plaisance*, no. 37, accessed December 11, 2016, http://scholarship.rice.edu/jsp/xml/1911/22074/1/aa00144.tei.html#div1037; Shaw, *World's Fair Notes*, 59; *Chicago Standard*, June 8, 1893 and May 25, 1893 ("*Chicago Standard* World's Columbian Exposition Clippings," "World's Columbian Exposition Records, 1891–1895," Special Collections Research Center, University of Chicago, Box 2, Folder 8). At least one visitor was rendered speechless; in a diary in which she painstakingly recorded minute details of other exhibits, Mary E. Chase was unable to fill out the many blank lines that she left herself in her notebook to describe the Dahomey Village (Mary E. Chase, Diary, 1893, Special Collections, Newberry Library).

32. John J. Flinn, *Official Guide to the Midway Plaisance* (Chicago: The Columbian Guide Co., 1893), 30; "Exposition Sketches," *Chicago Standard* Clippings, June 22, 1893; Jenks, *Century World's Fair Book*, 223. References to the alleged cannibalistic habits of the Africans and Samoans on display abounded in guides to the Fair: Trumbull White, *The World's Columbian Exposition, Chicago, 1893* (Chicago: International Publishing, 1893), 583; "A Group of Dahomeyans," *Midway Types and Scènes*, n.p.; *World's Fair Puck*, #23, October 9, 1893, 267; *Picturesque World's Fair*, 106; Muccigrosso, *Celebrating the New World*, 164; "Art Series #13, March 5, 1894, and Art Series #16, March 26, 1894, *Portfolio of Photographs of the World's Fair* (Chicago: Werner Co., 1893); "Good bye Samoans," *Columbus Portfolio of Midway Types* (Chicago: American Engraving Co., 1893), n.p.; "Samoan Girls!," *The Magic City*.

33. No. 30, *Official Guide to Midway Plaisance* (Chicago: The Columbian Guide Co., , n.p., e-book accessed June 22, 2017, http://archive.org/stream/officialguidetomooflin/officialguidetomooflin_djvu.txt); Northrop, *The World's Fair*, 281; Hubert Howe Bancroft, *The Book of the Fair: An Historical and Descriptive Presentation of the World's Science, Art, and Industry* (Chicago: The Bancroft Co., 1893), 878; "Black Continentals in Their Scarce Regimentals," *Midway Types and Scenes*.

34. "Black Continentals in Their Scarce Regimentals," *Midway Types and Scenes*; *Chicago Record's History of the World's Fair*, 247; Goodall, *Performance and Evolution*, 103; "Fire in the Dahomey Village," *Chicago Tribune*, June 8, 1893; "Four Amazons," *Midway Types and Scenes*.

35. Reed, *"All the World Is Here,"* 164.

36. Siobhan B. Somerville, *Queering the Color Line: Race and the Invention of Homosexuality in American Culture* (Durham, NC: Duke University Press, 2000), 26; Sadiah Qureshi, "Displaying Sara Baartman, 'The Hottentot Venus,'" *History of Science* 43 (2004): 237; Rachel Holmes, *The Hottentot Venus: The Life and Death of Saartjie Baartman* (London: Bloomsbury, 2007), chap. 5, "Venus Rising."

37. "World's Fair Notes," March 23, 1892, "World's Columbian Exposition Records, 1891–1895," Special Collections Research Center, University of Chicago, Box 2, Folder 4, n.p. .

38. *The Columbian Gallery; a Portfolio of Photographs from the World's Fair* (Chicago: Werner Co., 1894), n.p.; C. D. Arnold and H. D. Higginbotham, *Official Views of the World's Columbian Exposition, Issued by the Department of Photography* (Chicago: Photo-Gravure Co., 1893), Plate 92; *The Photographic World's Fair and Midway Plaisance* (Chicago: Monarch Book Co., 1894), 196; *The Dream City*, n.p.; Northrop, *The World's Fair*, 670; Leslie, *Amy Leslie at the Fair*, 66; *Picturesque World's Fair*, 97, 108; "Boushareens," *Midway Types and Scenes*, n.p.; *The Photographic World's Fair and Midway Plaisance*, 217.

39. Leslie, *Amy Leslie at the Fair*, 81; "Samoan Girls," *The Wonders of the World's Fair: Only the Most Superb Views* (Chicago: W. B. Conkey Co., 1894), Newberry Library General Collection, n.p.; Leslie, *Amy Leslie at the Fair*, 38; di Leonardo, *Exotics at Home*, 199, 161.

40. Somerville, *Queering the Color Line*, 27; *Picturesque World's Fair*, 106; Hawthorne, "Foreign Folk at the Fair," 572; *World's Fair Number, The Youth's Companion*, 18; di Leonardo, *Exotics at Home*, 7.

41. Newman, *White Women's Rights*, 16; *World's Fair Puck*, vol. 23, October 9, 1893, 267; Larson, *Devil in the White City*, 31–312; Leslie, *Amy Leslie at the Fair*, 38; "The Ball of the Midway Freaks," *Chicago Tribune*, August 11, 1893; Leslie, *Amy Leslie at the Fair*, 81.

42. Leslie, *Amy Leslie at the Fair*, 80, 81; Scott, 348, 350, 354, 351.

43. Leslie, *Amy Leslie at the Fair*, 80–81; Larson, 313–14; Louis S. Warren, *Buffalo Bill's America: William Cody and the Wild West Show* (New York: Random House, 2007), 420; *Chicago Record's History of the World's Fair*, 44.

44. *Dedicatory and Opening Ceremonies of the World's Columbian Exposition* (Chicago: Stone, Kastle, and Painter, 1893), 43; *Chicago Standard* Clippings, May 18, 1893, and June 22, 1893.

45. Alpern, *Amazons of Black Sparta*, 202–6.

46. *Official History of the California Midwinter International Exposition* (H. S. Crocker Co., 1894), 11; *San Francisco Chronicle, Midwinter Fair and the Golden State: Art Views*, n.p.; *In Remembrance of the Midwinter International Exposition, San Francisco, California* (San Francisco: California Midwinter International Exposition, 1894), n.p.; *Official Guide to the Midwinter Exposition in Golden Gate Park* (San Francisco: G. Spaulding & Co., 1894), 115; Taliesen Evans, *All about the Midwinter Fair, San Francisco*, 2nd edition (San Francisco: W. B. Bancroft & Co., 1894), 149.

47. *Official History of the California Midwinter International Exposition*, n.p.; *Los Angeles Herald*, October 25, 1893.

48. *Official History of the California Midwinter International Exposition*, n.p.; Rydell, "Darkest

Africa," 140; Arthur Chandler and Marvin R. Nathan, *The Fantastic Fair: The Story of the California Midwinter International Exposition, Golden Gate Park, San Francisco, 1894* (San Francisco: Pogo Press, 1993), 19.

49. *Official History of the California International Exposition*, 142, 150, 155, 164, 190, 227; *Midway Types and Scenes*, n.p.; Hinsley, "Anthropology as Education and Entertainment," 62; Killingray and Henderson, "Bata Kindai Amgoza Ibn LoBagola and the Making of *An African Savage's Own Story*," in Lindfors, *Africans on Stage*, 238, 228–65. Although it was likely the "most photographed exposition of the nineteenth century," there were few official photographs of the Dahomeyan women from Chicago. Ira Jacknis, "Refracting Images: Anthropological Display at the Chicago World's Fair, 1893," in *Coming of Age in Chicago: The 1893 World's Fair and the Coalescence of American Anthropology*, ed. Curtis M. Hinsley and David R. Wilcox (Lincoln: University of Nebraska Press, 2016), 323. Many guides to the Chicago Fair featured photographs of every other "Midway" type except the Dahomeyans. Perhaps the African women's absence from photographic retrospectives can be explained by their toplessness, although that did not stop some guides from distributing their image. In *Midway Types and Scenes*, for instance, the "Group of Dahomeyans" are flanked by two bare-breasted women, staring resolutely at the camera ("A Group of Dahomeyans," *Midway Types and Scenes*). When the African Amazons did appear in print, they were more likely to be covered up, as in the ill-fitting, painted-on drapery in the photographs "Four Amazons" and "Black Continentals and Their Scarce Regimentals" (*Midway Types and Scenes*; also see Reed's comparison of two images from the collections of the Chicago Public Library and the Chicago Historical Society, 162–63). The toplessness of the Dahomey women was an aesthetic, Orientalist choice made by organizers; as warriors and members of the king's court in Dahomey, the women usually wore the same uniforms as men. Peggy Reeves Sanday, *Female Power and Male Dominance: On the Origins of Sexual Inequality* (Cambridge: Cambridge University Press, 1981), 87.

50. Taliesin Evans, *All About the Midwinter Fair, San Francisco, and Interesting Facts Concerning California* (San Francisco: W. B. Bancroft, 1894), 121; Caille F. Forbes, *Introducing Bert Williams: Burnt Cork, Broadway, and the Story of America's First Black Star* (New York: Basic Books, 2008), 31, 27, 30.

51. Caille F. Forbes, *Introducing Bert Williams: Burnt Cork, Broadway, and the Story of America's First Black Star* (New York: Basic Books, 2008), 32; Karen Sotiropoulos, *Staging Race: Black Performers in Turn-of-the-Century America* (Cambridge, MA: Harvard University Press, 2006), 26; Thomas Riis, ed., *The Music and Scripts of In Dahomey* (Madison: A-R Editions, 1996), xviii, lxvii, and Script, Act III, Scene 1 stage directions; Daphne A. Brooks, *Bodies in Dissent: Spectacular Performances of Race and Freedom, 1850–1910* (Durham, NC: Duke University Press, 2006), 277.

CHAPTER FOUR

1. Nancy Tystad Koupal, "Introduction," in *Baum's Road to Oz: The Dakota Years*, ed. Nancy Koupal (Pierre: South Dakota State Historical Society Press, 2000), 6, 29, 20–21, 16, 42.

2. Koupal, *Baum's Road to Oz*, 66, 71, 74, 85–90.

3. Nancy Tystad Koupal, "From the Land of Oz," in Koupal, *Baum's Road to Oz*, 49; Baum to

Thomas Clarkson Gage, July 3, 1888, quoted in Michael Patrick Hearn, "The Wizard Behind the Plate," in Koupal, *Baum's Road to Oz*, 7; Evan I. Schwartz, *Finding Oz: How L. Frank Baum Discovered the Great American Story* (New York: Houghton Mifflin Harcourt, 2009), 141–42.

4. Hearn, "The Wizard Behind the Plate," 41; Koupal, "From the Land of Oz," 48; *Aberdeen Saturday Pioneer*, January 25, 1890; Koupal, "From the Land of Oz," 57.

5. Koupal, "From the Land of Oz," 48, 84; Nancy Tystad Koupal, ed., *Our Landlady* (Lincoln: University of Nebraska Press, 1999), 11–12; L. Frank Baum, "Our Landlady," March 8, 1890; Baum, "Our Landlady," *Aberdeen Saturday Pioneer*, March 15, 1890.

6. Koupal, *Our Landlady*, 12; Schwartz, *Finding Oz*, 156; Baum, *Aberdeen Saturday Pioneer*, March 15, 1890.

7. Schwartz, *Finding Oz*, 178–79; Koupal, "From the Land of Oz," 90.

8. Koupal, "From the Land of Oz," 92; Baum, *Aberdeen Saturday Pioneer*, November 29, 1890.

9. Koupal, *Our Landlady*, 143; Baum, *Aberdeen Saturday Pioneer*, Nov 29, 1890.

10. Schwartz, *Finding Oz*, 182; Baum, *Aberdeen Saturday Pioneer*, Dec 20, 1890.

11. Koupal, "From the Land of Oz," 94; Marty Gitlin, *Wounded Knee Massacre* (Denver: Greenwood Press, 2011), 149–50; Koupal, *Our Landlady*, 147; Gretchen Ritter, "Silver Slippers and a Golden Cap: L. Frank Baum's *The Wonderful Wizard of Oz* and Historical Memory in American Politics," *Journal of American Studies* 31, no. 2 (August 1997): 186.

12. Baum, "Our Landlady," *Aberdeen Saturday Pioneer*, December 6, 1890.

13. Koupal, "From the Land of Oz," 66, 72; Baum, *Aberdeen Saturday Pioneer*, January 25, 1890; Baum, *Aberdeen Saturday Pioneer*, October 18, 1890; Baum, *Aberdeen Saturday Pioneer*, December 6, 1890.

14. Baum, *Aberdeen Saturday Pioneer*, February 22, 1890; Koupal, "From the Land of Oz," 55, 63, 69; Julia Reid, "'She-who-must-be-obeyed': Anthropology and Matriarchy in H. Rider Haggard's *She*," *Journal of Victorian Culture* 20, no. 3 (2015): 362.

15. Koupal, *Our Landlady*, 23; Koupal, "From the Land of Oz," 104, 106.

16. Schwartz, *Finding Oz*, 201–2.

17. Schwartz, *Finding Oz*, 209–10; M. P. Handy, *World's Columbian Exposition Official Catalogue* (Chicago: W. B. Conkey Co., 1893), 13; Gary Laderman and Luis Leon, eds., *Religion and American Cultures: Tradition, Diversity, and Popular Expression,vol. 1* (Santa Barbara, CA: ABC-CLIO Press, 2003), 1386.

18. Kaveh Askari, Scott Curtis, Frank Gray, Louis Pelletier, Tami Williams, and Joshua Yumibe, *Performing New Media, 1890–1915* (Bloomington: Indiana University Press, 2015), 145; Northrop, *The World's Fair as Seen in One Hundred Days* (Philadelphia: Ariel Book Co., 1893), 674. Indeed, argues one scholar, *The Wonderful Wizard of Oz* can be read as "the surreal adventure of a child lost at the exposition." Michael O'Neal Riley, *Oz and Beyond: The Fantasy World of L. Frank Baum* (Lawrence: University Press of Kansas, 1997), 57.

19. Schwartz, *Finding Oz*, 245, 251, 252; Gage to Helen Leslie Gage, February 11, 1895, Matilda Joslyn Gage Papers, Schlesinger Library.

20. Schwartz, *Finding Oz*, 252; Katherine M. Rogers, *L. Frank Baum, Creator of Oz* (New York: St. Martin's Press, 2002), 54.

21. Schwartz, *Finding Oz*, 260.

22. Schwartz, *Finding Oz*, 262, 263–64.

23. Schwartz, *Finding Oz*, xii.

24. Baum, "The Cyclone" and "The Girl in the Chicken Coop," in *Wizard of Oz*.

25. Baum, "How Dorothy Saved the Scarecrow," "The Road Through the Forest," and "How Dorothy Saved the Scarecrow," in *Wizard of Oz*.

26. Baum, "The Rescue of the Tin Woodman" and "The Cowardly Lion," in *Wizard of Oz*.

27. Baum, "The Guardian of the Gate" and "The Wonderful City of Oz" in *Wizard of Oz*.

28. Baum, "The Search for the Wicked Witch," in *Wizard of Oz*. Scholars, including Matilda Joslyn Gage, have long noted the symbolism of the water in the history of the identification and execution of witches, its function as a purifying and baptismal agent, and its role as a "symbol of household drudgery" (Celia Anderson, "The Comedians of Oz," *Studies in American Humor,* Winter 1986–1987). In *Women, Church and State,* Gage discusses the method of throwing women into water to determine if they were witches (235, 237), as well as the early modern method of boiling "heretics and malefactors," including witches, alive in water (267).

29. Baum, "The Discovery of Oz, the Great and Terrible" and "Glinda the Good Witch Grants Dorothy's Wish" in *Wizard of Oz*; Schwartz, *Finding Oz*, 221–22.

30. Baum, "The Scarecrow Appeals to Glinda the Good" and "Princess Ozma of Oz" in *Marvelous Land of Oz*.

31. Baum, "Tip Makes an Experiment in Magic," "The Flight of the Fugitives," "The Awakening of the Saw-Horse," "A Highly Magnified History," and "Princess Ozma of Oz" in *Marvelous Land of Oz*; Tison Pugh, "'There lived in the Land of Oz two queerly made men': Queer Utopianism and Antisocial Eroticism in L. Frank Baum's Oz Series," *Marvels and Tales: Journal of Fairy-Tale Studies* 22, no. 2 (2008): 221; Baum, "Ozma Uses the Magic Belt," in *Dorothy and the Wizard in Oz*.

32. Baum, "The Riches of Content"; Baum, "The Truth Pond" *Road to Oz*; Baum, "How Ozma Looked into the Magic Picture" and "How Ozma Granted Dorothy's Request" in *Emerald City of Oz*.

33. Baum, "Ozma of Oz to the Rescue" in *Ozma of Oz*; Baum, "The Trial of Eureka the Kitten" in *Dorothy and the Wizard in Oz*; Cameron, William E. *The World's Fair, Being a Pictorial History of the Columbian Exposition, containing a Complete History of the World-Renowned Exposition at Chicago,* ... (Chicago: Chicago Publication & Lithograph Co., 1893), 654.

34. Baum, "Dorothy Picks the Princess" in *Dorothy and the Wizard in Oz*; Baum, "Shaggy Seeks his Stray Brother" in *Tik-Tok of Oz*; Baum, "A Terrible Loss" in *The Lost Princess of Oz*; Osmond Beckwith, "The Oddness of Oz," in *L. Frank Baum: The Wizard of Oz,* ed. Michael Patrick Hearn (New York: Schocken, 1983), 236; Baum, "Gen. Jinjur's Army of Revolt" in *Marvelous Land of Oz*.

35. Baum, "General Jinjur's Army of Revolt," "The Scarecrow Plans an Escape," and "The Prisoners of the Queen" in *Marvelous Land of Oz*.

36. Baum, "The Prisoners of the Queen" and "The Riches of Content" in *Marvelous Land of Oz*.

37. Ritter, "Silver Slippers and a Golden Cap," 178; Marius Bewley, "The Land of Oz: America's Great Good Place," in Hearn, ed., *L. Frank Baum: The Wizard of Oz,* 203; Koupal, "Wonderful Wizard of the West," 210; Baum, "The Emerald City," in *Ozma of Oz*.

38. Baum, *Wizard of Oz*, "The Search for the Wicked Witch."

39. Deniz Kandiyoti, "Bargaining with Patriarchy," *Gender and Society* 2, no. 3 (Sept. 1988):

275, 280–82; Immanuel Ness, *Encyclopedia of American Social Movements* (London: Routledge, 2004), 274. Gage echoed this sentiment in *Women, Church and State*: "The most degraded slave of olden time was the one content in his slavery" (Gage, *Women, Church and State,* 536).

40. Baum, "The Council with the Munchkins," in *Wizard of Oz.*

41. Baum, "King Dox" and "The Shaggy Man's Transformation," in *Road to Oz.*

42. Baum, "The Scarecrow Appeals to Glinda the Good," in *Marvelous Land of Oz;* Baum, "Glinda the Good Witch Grants Dorothy's Wish," in *Wizard of Oz;* Baum, "The Call to Duty," "The Alarm Bell," and "The Call to Duty," in *Glinda of Oz;* Schwartz, *Finding Oz,* 274.

43. Baum, "The Scarecrow Appeals to Glinda the Good," in *Marvelous Land of Oz;* Baum, "The Alarm Bell," in *Glinda of Oz;* Baum, "How Ozma Refused to Fight for Her Kingdom," in *The Emerald City of Oz.*

44. Ritter, "Silver Slippers and a Golden Cap," 173.

45. Baum, "The Scarecrow Takes Time to Think," in *Marvelous World of Oz;* Baum, "Toto Loses Something," in *Lost Princess of Oz;* Baum, "The Forest of Gugu," in *Magic of Oz;* Baum, "How They Matched the Fuddles," in *Emerald City of Oz.*

46. Pugh, "'There lived in the Land of Oz,'" 218, citing Harry M. Benshoff and Sean Griffin, *Queer Images: A History of Gay and Lesbian Film in America* (Lanham, MD: Rowman & Littlefield, 2006), 68; Fred Erisman, "L. Frank Baum and the Progressive Dilemma," *American Quarterly* 20, no. 3 (Autumn 1968): 618; Raylyn Moore, *Wonderful Wizard, Marvelous Land* (Bowling Green, KY: Bowling Green University Press, 1974), 17; W. H. Kirby, "The Universal Brotherhood of Humanity," *The Theosophic Messenger* 12, no. 6 (March 1911): 344–45.

47. Sally Roesch Wagner, *Matilda Joslyn Gage: She Who Holds the Sky* (Aberdeen, SD: Sky Carrier Press, 1999), 48; Daniel E. Saros, *Labor, Industry, and Regulation During the Progressive Era* (London: Routledge, 2008), 59; Ira Kipnis, *The American Socialist Movement, 1897–1912* (Chicago: Haymarket Books, 2005), 364; Saros, *Labor, Industry, and Regulation,* 60; Regin Schmidt, *Red Scare: FBI and the Origins of Anticommunism in the United States, 1919–1943* (Copenhagen: Museum Tusculanum Press, 2000), 26. Although his feminism is overt in Oz, the series is a complicated example of Baum's politics, which has sparked a scholarly debate; see Henry M. Littlefield, "The Wizard of Oz: Parable on Populism," *American Quarterly* 16, no. 1 (Spring 1964): 49; Ranjit S. Dighe, *The Historian's Wizard of Oz: Reading L. Frank Baum's Classic as a Political and Monetary Allegory* (Praeger, 2002), x; Baum, *Aberdeen Saturday Pioneer,* July 12, 1890). David B. Parker charts the fifty-year evolution of political analysis of the series in "The Rise and Fall of *The Wonderful Wizard of Oz* as a 'Parable on Populism,'" *Journal of the Georgia Association of Historians* 15 (1994): 49–64.

48. Baum, *Aberdeen Saturday Pioneer,* January 24, 1891; Koupal, "On the Road to Oz," 77; Riley, *Oz and Beyond,* 24.

49. Koupal, "On the Road to Oz," 80; S. J. Sackett, "The Utopia of Oz," in Hearn, ed., *L. Frank Baum: The Wizard of Oz,* 208; Russell B. Nye, "An Appreciation," in Hearn, *The Wizard of Oz,* 170; Baum, "The Emperor's Tin Castle" and "The Emerald City," in *Road to Oz;* Baum, "How Ozma Granted Dorothy's Request," in *Emerald City of Oz.*

50. Baum, "How Ozma Granted Dorothy's Request," in *Emerald City of Oz;* Baum, "The Road Through the Forest," in *Wizard of Oz;* Baum, "How Ozma Refused to Fight for Her Kingdom," in *Emerald City of Oz.*

51. Pugh, "'There Lived in the Land of Oz," 219; Nye, "An Appreciation," 166.

52. Edward Wagenknecht, "Utopia Americana," in Hearn, ed., *The Wizard of Oz*, 248; Maud Baum quoted in Attebury, "Oz," 83; James Thurber, "The Wizard of Chittenango," in Hearn, ed., *The Wizard of Oz*, 161; Ritter, 171, 176; "A New Book for Children," *New York Times*, September 8, 1900, p. 605; Baum, "Author's Note," in *Marvelous Land of Oz*; Baum, "Author's Note," in *Ozma of Oz*; Baum, "Author's Note," in *Dorothy and the Wizard in O*; Baum, "How the Story of Oz Came to an End, in *The Emerald City of Oz*"; Baum, "Prologue," in *The Patchwork Girl of Oz*.

53. Schwartz, *Finding Oz*, 296–97; Moore, *Wonderful Wizard*, 64–66.

54. Wagenknecht, "Utopia Americana," 147.

CHAPTER FIVE

1. Judith A. Allen, *The Feminism of Charlotte Perkins Gilman: Sexualities, History, Progressivism* (Chicago: University of Chicago Press, 2009), 2; Ann J. Lane, *To Herland and Beyond: The Life and Works of Charlotte Perkins Gilman* (New York: Pantheon, 1990), 8; Allen, *Feminism of Charlotte Perkins Gilman*, 7; Alys Eve Weinbaum, "Writing Feminist Genealogy: Charlotte Perkins Gilman, Racial Nationalism, and the Reproduction of Maternalist Feminism," *Feminist Studies* 27, no. 2 (Summer 2001): 274; Carol Farley Kessler, *Charlotte Perkins Gilman: Her Progress Toward Utopia with Selected Writings* (Syracuse, NY: Syracuse University Press, 1995), 13.

2. Charlotte Perkins Gilman, *The Living of Charlotte Perkins Gilman: An Autobiography* (Madison: University of Wisconsin Press, 2014), 5; Lane, *To Herland and Beyond*, 34, 38; Allen, *Feminism of Charlotte Perkins Gilman*, 89.

3. Gilman, *Living*, 80, 81, 82, 87; Allen, *Feminism of Charlotte Perkins Gilman*, 37; Gilman, *Living*, 87–88; Allen, *Feminism of Charlotte Perkins Gilman*, 42.

4. Gilman, *Living*, 89, 91, 93–95.

5. Ibid, 95, 96; Gilman, *The Yellow Wallpaper* (New York: Bedford/St. Martin's, 1998), 4.

6. Gilman, *Living*, 163, 96, 98; Allen, *Feminism of Charlotte Perkins Gilman*, 14.

7. Gilman, *Living*, 119, 121; Gilman, *Yellow Wallpaper*, 48; Gilman, "Why I Wrote 'The Yellow Wallpaper," *Forerunner* 4, no. 10 (October 1913): 271. Gilman sent Mitchell a copy of the story; he never responded, but she later wrote that "many years later, I met some one who knew close friends of Dr. Mitchell's who said he had told them that he had changed his treatment of nervous prostration since reading 'The Yellow Wallpaper.' If this is a fact, I have not lived in vain" (Gilman, *Living*, 121).

8. Gilman, *In This Our World* (Oakland, CA: McCombs & Vaughan, 1893), 99.

9. Lane, *To Herland and Beyond*, 161.

10. Karl Marx and Friedrich Engels, *The Communist Manifesto*, Section III, accessed December 11, 2016, http://www.historyguide.org/intellect/manifesto.html; Engels, "Socialism: Utopian and Scientific," 1880, accessed December 11, 2016, https://www.marxists.org/archive/marx/works/1880/soc-utop/; Mari Jo Buhle, *Women and American Socialism, 1870–1920* (Urbana: University of Illinois Press, 1981), 74; Laura E. Donaldson, "The Eve of De-Struction: Charlotte Perkins Gilman and the Feminist Re-Creation of Paradise," *Women's Studies* 16 (1989): 377; Jean Pfaelzer, *The Utopian Novel in America, 1886–1896* (Pittsburgh: University of Pittsburgh Press,

1985), 316; Lane, *To Herland and Beyond*, 161–62; Gilman, *Living*, 129; Allen, *Feminism of Charlotte Perkins Gilman*, 5.

11. "Lester Frank Ward," American Sociological Association, accessed December 11, 2016, http://www.asanet.org/about/presidents/Lester_Ward.cfm; Gilman, *Living*, 187.

12. Edward C. Rafferty, *Apostle of Human Progress: Lester Frank Ward and American Political Thought, 1841–1913* (New York: Rowman & Littlefield, 2003), 172; Lester Frank Ward, "Our Better Halves," *Forum* (November 1888), 275; Louise Michele Newman, *White Women's Rights: The Racial Origins of Feminism in the United States* (New York: Oxford University Press, 1999), 50; Allen, *Feminism of Charlotte Perkins Gilman*, 82.

13. Ward, *Pure Sociology: A Treatise on the Origin and Spontaneous Development of Society* (New York: Macmillan, 1903), 300.

14. Ward, *Pure Sociology*, 323, 302; Newman, *White Women's Rights*, 50.

15. Rafferty, *Apostle of Human Progress*, 172; Buhle, *Women and American Socialism*, 79.

16. Allen, *Feminism of Charlotte Perkins Gilman*, 76; Bernice L. Hausman, "Sex Before Gender: Charlotte Perkins Gilman and the Evolutionary Paradigm of Utopia," *Feminist Studies* 24, no. 3 (Autumn 1998): 491; Allen, *Feminism of Charlotte Perkins Gilman*, 96.

17. Allen, *Feminism of Charlotte Perkins Gilman*, 98, 99; Gilman, *Women and Economics: A Study of the Economic Relation Between Men and Women as a Factor in Social Evolution* (Boston: Small, Maynard, 1898), 31; Gilman, *The Man-Made World: Or, Our Androcentric Culture* (New York: Charlton Co., 1911), Kindle e-book, chap. 10, "Law and Government"; Gilman, *Women and Economics*, 31.

18. Gilman, *Women and Economics*, 12, 9, 48.

19. Gilman, *Women and Economics*, 35, 37.

20. Gilman, *Women and Economics*, 145, 167.

21. Allen, *Feminism of Charlotte Perkins Gilman*, 88, 100.

22. Judith Schwarz, *Radical Feminists of Heterodoxy, Greenwich Village, 1912–1940* (Norwich, VT: New Victoria Publishers, 1986), 1; Gilman, *Living*, 313; Schwarz, *Radical Feminists*, 40; Lisa A. Long, "*With Her in Ourland*: Herland Meets Heterodoxy," in *Charlotte Perkins Gilman and Her Contemporaries: Literary and Intellectual Contexts*, ed. Cynthia J. Davis and Denise D. Knight (Tuscaloosa: University of Alabama Press, 2004), 192.

23. Lane, *To Herland and Beyond*, 4; Gilman, *The Man-Made World*, chap. 5, "Masculine Literature."

24. Gilman, *Moving the Mountain*, in Gilman, *The Herland Trilogy* (New York: Start Publishing, 2012), chap. 1; Cynthia Davis, *Charlotte Perkins Gilman: A Biography* (Stanford, CA: Stanford University Press, 2010), 298.

25. Gilman, *Moving the Mountain*, chap. 1, 2.

26. Gilman, *Moving the Mountain*, chap. 2, 5, 4.

27. Gilman, *Moving the Mountain*, chap. 2, 4, 5.

28. Gilman, *Moving the Mountain*, chap. 11, 7, 5, 6, 7, 3; Alisa Klaus, "Depopulation and Race Suicide: Maternalism and Pronatalist Ideologies in France and the United States," in Koven and Michel, *Mothers of a New World*, 203–4.

29. Bartkowski, 23; Gilman, "A Not Unnatural Enterprise" and "Rash Advances" in *Herland*, in *The Herland Trilogy*.

30. Donaldson, "The Eve of De-Struction," 380; Gilman, "A Peculiar Imprisonment" and "A Unique History," in *Herland*.

31. Gilman, "A Unique History," in *Herland*.

32. Gilman, "A Unique History" and "Our Relations and Theirs," in *Herland*; Carol Farley Kessler, "Consider Her Ways: The Cultural Work of Charlotte Perkins Gilman's Pragmatopian Stories," in *Utopian and Science Fiction by Women: Worlds of Difference*, ed. Jane A. Donawerth and Carol A. Kolmerten, 1–14 (Syracuse, NY: Syracuse University Press, 1994), 130.

33. Gilman, "A Unique History," "Their Religions and Our Marriages," and "Expelled," in *Herland*,; Eric Leif Davin, *Partners in Wonder: Women and the Birth of Science Fiction, 1926–1965* (New York: Lexington Books, 2006), 229.

34. Gilman, *The Home*, 56; Jane Addams, "Woman's Conscience and Social Amelioration," accessed June 22, 2017, http://hullhouse.uic.edu/hull/urbanexp/main.cgi?file=new/show_doc.ptt&doc=341&chap=87; Addams quoted in Lucy Delap, *The Feminist Avant-Garde: Transatlantic Encounters of the Early Twentieth Century* (Cambridge: Cambridge University Press, 2007), 148. Molly Ladd-Taylor analyzes Gilman's conflicted maternalism in *Mother-Work: Women, Child Welfare, and the State, 1890–1930* (Urbana: University of Illinois Press, 1994), 107–12.

35. Charlotte Perkins Gilman, "New Mothers of a New World," in Larry Ceplair, ed., *Charlotte Perkins Gilman: A Nonfiction Reader* (New York: Columbia University Press, 1991), 249; Kenneth Florey, "Suffrage Postcards," accessed May 11, 2017, WomanSuffrageMemorabilia.com, http://womansuffragememorabilia.com/woman-suffrage-memorabilia/post-cards/; "Official Program, Woman Suffrage Procession, 1913," reprinted in *American Feminism: Key Source Documents, 1848–1920, vol. 1: Suffrage*, ed. Janet Beer and Katherine Joslin (New York: Routledge, 2002), 365.

36. Gilman, "Our Growing Modesty," "A Unique History," "A Not Unnatural Enterprise," and "Rash Advances," in *Herland*.

37. Gilman, "Our Growing Modesty," "Our Relations and Theirs," and "Their Relations and Our Marriages," in *Herland*.

38. Allen, *Feminism of Charlotte Perkins Gilman*, 339. Gilman very clearly subscribed to notions of white racial superiority. In *Women and Economics*, she lauded "Anglo-Saxon blood" as "the most powerful expression of the latest current of fresh racial life from the North," she described the peoples of Africa and Asia as evolutionarily retarded, and there is no evidence that she strayed from these views in subsequent writing (Gilman, *Women and Economics*, 73).

39. Lane, *To Herland and Beyond*, 102, 100–101, 164; Weinbaum, "Writing Feminist Genealogy," 62.

40. Gilman, "A Unique History," "Comparisons Are Odious," and "Our Growing Modesty," in *Herland*; Alys Eve Weinbaum, *Wayward Reproductions: Genealogies of Race and Nation in Transatlantic Modern Thought* (Durham, NC: Duke University Press, 2004), 64.

41. Angelika Bammer, *Partial Visions: Feminism and Utopianism in the 1970s* (New York: Routledge, 1991), 39; Gilman, "Our Difficulties," "Expelled," and "Comparisons Are Odious," in *Herland*,; Pfaelzer, *The Utopian Novel*, 325.

42. Gilman, "Expelled," in *Herland*.

43. Susan S. Lanser, "Feminist Criticism, 'The Yellow Wallpaper,' and the Politics of Color in America," *Feminist Studies* 15, no. 3 (Autumn 1989), 433.

44. Gilman, "The Return," "War," and "A Journey of Inspection," in *With Her in Ourland* (in *The Herland Trilogy*); Georgia Johnston, "Three Men in *Herland*: Why They Enter the Text," *Utopian Studies*, no. 4 (1991): 55–59; Allen, *Feminism of Charlotte Parkins Gilman*, xiv, 80.

45. Gilman, "My Country," "War," and "Race and Religion," in *With Her in Ourland*.

46. Gilman, "In Our Homes" and "More Diagnosis," in *With Her in Ourland*; Kessler, "Consider Her Ways," 128.

47. Gilman, "Nearing Home" and "My Country," in *With Her in Ourland*.

48. Gilman, "The Diagnosis," in *With Her in Ourland*; Hausman, "Sex Before Gender," 499.

49. Jennifer Hudak, "The 'Social Inventor': Charlotte Perkins Gilman and the (Re)Production of Perfection," *Women's Studies* 32 (2003): 471; Gilman, "Comparisons Are Odious," in *Herland*; Gilman, "Feminism and the Woman's Movement," in *With Her in Ourland*.

50. Gilman, "Conclusion," in *With Her in Ourland*.

51. Davis, *Charlotte Perkins Gilman*, 306, 292, 287; George Ritzer and Jeffrey Stepnisky, eds., *The Wiley-Blackwell Companion to Major Social Theorists* (Hoboken, NJ: Wiley-Blackwell, 2011), 295.

52. Davis, *Charlotte Perkins Gilman*, 312; Correa Moylan Walsh, *Feminism* (New York: Sturgis and Walton, 1917), 74, 81–82, 83, 174; Allen, *Feminism of Charlotte Perkins Gilman*, 199, 197.

53. Gilman, *Living*, 310.

54. Susan Faludi, *Backlash: The Undeclared War Against American Women* (New York: Crown, 1991), 64–65; Nancy F. Cott, *The Grounding of Modern Feminism* (New Haven, CT: Yale University Press, 1989), 260; Joan M. Jensen, "All Pink Sisters: The War Department and the Feminist Movement in the 1920s," in *Decades of Discontent: The Women's Movement, 1920–1940*, ed. Lois Scharf and Joan M. Jensen (Boston: Northeastern University Press, 1987), 199–222; "Gentlemen, Make Way for the 'Matriarchy,'" *The Woman Patriot* 4, no. 8 (February 21, 1920); Rayna Rapp and Ellen Ross, "The 1920s: Feminism, Consumerism, and Political Backlash in the United States," in *Women in Culture and Politics: A Century of Change*, ed. Judith Friedlander, Blanche Wiesen Cook, Alice Kessler-Harris, and Carroll Smith-Rosenberg (Bloomington: Indiana University Press, 1986), 54; Gilman, *Living*, 334.

55. Stevens quoted in Cheryl Black, *Women of Provincetown: 1915–1922* (Tuscaloosa: University of Alabama Press, 2002), 135; Kathleen Margaret Lant, "The Rape of the Text: Charlotte Gilman's Violation of Herland," *Tulsa Studies in Women's Literature*, 9, no. 2 (Autumn 1990): 295; Allen, *Feminism of Charlotte Perkins Gilman*, 290, 303, 323; Weinbaum, "Writing Feminist Genealogy," 279–81; Kessler, *Charlotte Perkins Gilman*, 39.

56. Gilman, *Unpunished: A Mystery* (New York: Feminist Press at CUNY, 1998); Gilman, *Living*, xviii, 334; Kessler, *Charlotte Perkins Gilman*, 40.

57. Allen, *Feminism of Charlotte Perkins Gilman*, 8; Catherine J. Golden, "Looking Backward: Rereading Gilman in the Early Twenty-First Century," in *Charlotte Perkins Gilman: New Texts, New Contexts*, ed. Jennifer S. Tuttle and Carol Farley Kessler (Columbus: Ohio State University Press, 2011), 50; Weinbaum, "Writing Feminist Genealogy," 282; Dorothy Berkson, "'So We All Became Mothers': Harriet Beecher Stowe, Charlotte Perkins Gilman, and the New World of Women's Culture," in *Feminism, Utopia, and Narrative*, ed. Libby Falk Jones and Sarah Webster Goodwin (Knoxville: University of Tennessee Press, 1990), 110.

58. Gilman, "A Unique History," "Expelled," and "Our Difficulties," in *Herland*.

CHAPTER SIX

1. Judith Schwarz, *Radical Feminists of Heterodoxy, Greenwich Village, 1912–1940* (Norwich, VT: New Victoria Publishers, 1986), 20, 61.

2. Inez Haynes Gillmore, *Angel Island* (Project Gutenberg e-book), 13, 73, 94, 151, accessed June 22, 2017, http://www.gutenberg.org/files/4637/4637-h/4637-h.htm.

3. Gillmore. *Angel Island*, 215, 189, 214, 196, 220, 232, 231. *Angel Island* was published before *Herland*, and the similarities indicate that Gilman likely read it, or was at least familiar with the narrative.

4. Jill Lepore, *The Secret History of Wonder Woman* (New York: Vintage, 2014), 4–5, 15.

5. Lepore, *Secret History*, 29, 35.

6. Lepore, *Secret History*, 41, 44, 61, 74–75; Les Daniels, *Wonder Woman: The Complete History* (New York: Chronicle Books, 2004), 12. The decision in the murder trial mandated that scientific evidence had to have general acceptance to be admissible in court; the lie detector test did not survive that scientific scrutiny (*Secret History*, 72).

7. Lepore, *Secret History*, 110, 81, 112.

8. Lepore, *Secret History*, 117, 118.

9. Daniels, *Wonder Woman*, 18; Lepore, *Secret History*, 120–22, 126, 128, 131.

10. Lepore, *Secret History*, 173; Marston, *Try Living!* (New York: Thomas Y. Crowell, 1937), 2–3; Daniels, *Wonder Woman*, 43, 31.

11. Lepore, *Secret History*, 118–19.

12. Lepore, *Secret History*, 119.

13. Margaret Sanger, chap. 13, "Battalions of Unwanted Babies: The Cause of War," and chap. 14, "Woman and the New Morality," in *Women and the New Race* (Library of Alexandria e-book).

14. Sanger, chap. 4, "Two Classes of Women," chap. 1, "Woman's Error and Her Debt," chap. 8, "Birth Control—A Parents' Problem or Woman's?," chap. 2, "Woman's Struggle for Freedom," and chap. 14, "Woman and the New Morality," in *Women and the New Race*.

15. Sanger, chap. 15, "Legislating Woman's Morals," in *Women and the New Race*; Lepore, *Secret History*, 103.

16. Lepore, *Secret History*, 138; Daniels, *Wonder Woman*, 18; Lepore, *Secret History*, 146.

17. Marston, *Emotions of Normal People* (New York: Harcourt, Brace, 1928), 258, 391, 113, 135, 136.

18. Marston, *Emotions*, 258–59, 394.

19. Marston, *Emotions*, 391, 394, 394, 396, 395; Margaret Sanger, *Happiness in Marriage* (Oxford: Pergamon, 1926), 139–40.

20. F. Aveling, "*Emotions of Normal People* (Review)", *Philosophy* 4, no. 13 (1929): 140; Joseph Jastrow, "The Pathology of Emotion," *Saturday Review*, May 4, 1929, 978, accessed December 12, 2016, http://www.unz.org/Pub/SaturdayRev-1929may04–00978a03?View=PDF; *Mind* 38, no. 150 (April 1929), back matter; Olive Byrne Richards, "*Emotions of Normal People* (Review)," *Journal of Abnormal and Social Psychology* 24, (April 1929): 135, 138.

21. Lepore, *Secret History*, 148; Daniels, *Wonder Woman*, 17.

22. Marston, *Venus With Us: A Tale of the Caesar* (New York: Sears Publishing, 1932), 349, 375, 377.

23. Lepore, *Secret History*, 250; Daniels, *Wonder Woman*, 28, 18, 17.

24. Marston, *Try Living*, title page, 53, 95; Marston, *March On!* (New York: Doubleday, Doran, 1939), 128.

25. *The Wizard of Oz*, directed by Victor Fleming, George Cukor, Mervyn LeRoy, Norman Taurog, and King Vidor (Warner Bros., 1939).

26. Daniels, *Wonder Woman*, 11; Lepore, *Secret History*, 145.

27. Inez Haynes Irwin, *Amazons and Angels* (New York: Doubleday, Doran, 1933), 422–23, 439; Susan Ware, *Beyond Suffrage: Women in the New Deal* (Cambridge, MA: Harvard University Press, 1981); June Melby Benowitz, *Days of Discontent: Women and Right-Wing Politics*, 1933–1945 (DeKalb: Northern Illinois University Press, 2002).

28. Lepore, *Secret History*, 171–72.

29. "Marston Advises 3 L's for Success," *New York Times*, November 11, 1937; "Neglected Amazons to Rule Men in 1,000 Years, Says Psychologist," *Washington Post*, November 11, 1937.

30. Marston's biographer, the Harvard historian Jill Lepore, argues simply that "Wonder Woman is Margaret Sanger," although it's clear that Marston was influenced by many other women, including the two mothers of his children ("Historian on Wonder Woman's Origin Story and Ties to Feminism," *Here and Now*, wbur.org, June 5, 2017, accessed June 6, 2017, http://www.wbur.org/hereandnow/2017/06/05/wonder-woman-jill-lepore-feminism).

31. Olive Richards, "Don't Laugh at the Comics," *Family Circle*, October 25, 1940, 10–12; Lepore, *Secret History*, 184; Daniels, *Wonder Woman*, 20, 22; Bradford W. Wright, *Comic Book Nation: The Transformation of Youth Culture in America* (Baltimore: Johns Hopkins University Press, 2003), 33.

32. Marston, "Why 100,000,000 Americans Read Comics," *American Scholar* 13, no. 1 (Winter 1943–1944): 42–43; Daniels, *Wonder Woman*, 23.

33. Marston, letter to Mayer, February 23, 1941 ("Wonder Woman: Selected Letters, 1941–1945," Dibner Library, Smithsonian Institution).

34. Gardner Fox, "Justice Society—Two New Members Win Their Spurs," *All-Star Comics* 1, no. 8 (December 1941).

35. Marston, "Script 1A," *Wonder Woman, Selected Continuities*," Dibner Library, Smithsonian Institution.

36. Marston, Script 1A; "Justice Society—Two New Members Win Their Spurs."

37. Marston, "Women: Servants for Civilization," *Tomorrow*, February 1924, 42–45.

38. "Noted Psychologist Revealed as Author of Best-Selling 'Wonder Woman' Children's Comic," n.d., Marston, Selected Letters, 1941–1945, Dibner Library; Marston, "Why 100,000,000," 44; Marston to Colton Waugh, March 5, 1945, Marston, Selected Letters; "A Wife for Superman," *Hartford Journal*, September 28, 1942; Marston, "The Invisible Invader," *Comic Cavalcade* no. 3 (Summer 1943); Daniels, *Wonder Woman*, 33.

39. Marston, Script 1A. Marston probably wrote some of the "Wonder Women of History," as did Dorothy Roubicek (Lepore, *Secret History*, 222–23).

40. Fox, "Justice Society: Two New Members Win Their Spurs"; Marston, "The God of War," *Wonder Woman* 1, no. 2 (September 1942).

41. Marston, "Wonder Woman Arrives in Man's World," *Sensation Comics* no. 1 (January

1942); Marston, Script 1C, "Wonder Woman: Selected Continuities," Dibner Library, Smithsonian Institution; Marston, "Wonder Woman and the Winged Maidens of Venus," *Wonder Woman* 1, no. 12 (March 1945).

42. Marston, "The Menace of Doctor Poison," *Sensation Comics* 1, no. 2 (February 1942); Marston, "The Return of Diana Prince," *Sensation Comics* 1, no. 9 (September 1942); Marston, "The First Test of Aphrodite," *Wonder Woman* 1, no. 4 (May 1943); Marston, "Wonder Woman Versus the Saboteurs," *Sensation Comics* 1, no. 5 (May 1942); Marston, Script 1A; Fox, "Justice Society—Two New Members Win Their Spurs"; Marston, "The Menace of Doctor Poison"; *Comic Cavalcade* 1, no. 26, no title, typewritten script, Hummel papers, Dibner Library.

43. Marston, "The Adventures of the Pilotless Plane," *Sensation Comics* 1, no. 24 (December 1943).

44. Marston, "The Menace of Doctor Poison"; Marston, "The Invisible Invader," *Comic Cavalcade* 1, no. 3 (June 1943); Marston, "The Million Dollar Tennis Game," *Sensation Comics* 1, no. 61 (January 1947); Marston, "The Severed Bracelets," *Comic Cavalcade* 1, no. 14 (April 1946); Marston, "Wonder Woman: The Underwater Follies," *Comic Cavalcade* 1, no. 13 (December 1946). Jennifer K. Stuller has noted in her work on female superheroes that they tend to work in teams, "reject[ing] the 'lone wolf' model of heroism." See Stuller, "What Is a Female Superhero?," in *What Is a Superhero?*, ed. Robin S. Rosenberg and Peter Coogan (New York: Oxford University Press, 2013); also see Stuller's book on the subject, *Ink-Stained Amazons and Cinematic Warriors: Superwomen in Modern Mythology* (London: I. B. Tauris, 2010).

45. Marston, "The Adventures of the Pilotless Plane"; Marston, "The Adventure of the Life Vitamin," *Wonder Woman* 1, no. 7 (December 1943); Marston, "Wonder Woman: The Valkyries' Prey," *Comic Cavalcade* 1, no. 17 (October 1946); Marston, "Wonder Woman: The Masquerader," *Sensation Comics* 1, no. 26 (February 1944).

46. Marston, *Try Living*, 175, 176, 179; Marston, "The Unconquerable Women of Cochabamba," *Sensation Comics* 1, no. 70 (October 1947); Marston, "The Witches' Trials," *Sensation Comics* 1, no. 73 (January 1948).

47. Marston, *Try Living*, 3.

48. Marston, letter to Mayer, April 16, 1942 ("Wonder Woman: Selected Continuities"); Marston, Script 1A; Marston, "The God of War," *Wonder Woman* 1, no. 2 (September 1942); Marston, (no title), *Wonder Woman* 1, no. 3 (February 1943); Marston, "Wonder Woman: The Milk Swindle," *Sensation Comics* 1, no. 7 (July 1942).

49. Marston, "The Milk Swindle"; Lepore, *Secret History*, 211–12.

50. Marston, "Department Store Perfidy," *Sensation Comics* 1, no. 8 (August 1942).

51. Joye Murchison, "Rebellion on Paradise Island," *Comic Cavalcade* 1, no. 12 (Fall 1945); Marston, "The Severed Bracelets," *Comic Cavalcade* 1, no. 14 (April–May 1946).

52. Marston, "The Menace of Doctor Poison," *Sensation Comics* 1, no. 2 (February 1942). Noah Berlatsky thoroughly examines the sexual subtext of Wonder Woman in *Wonder Woman: Bondage and Feminism in the Marston/Peter Comics, 1941–1948* (New Brunswick, NJ: Rutgers University Press, 2015).

53. Julian Robinson, *Gynecocracy: A Narrative of the Adventures and Psychological Experiences of Julian Robinson Under Petticoat Rule, Written by Himself* (London: Locus Elm Press, 2014, first published 1893), vol. 2, chap. 1, "Retrospection." Kindle e-book.

54. Marston, "The Battle of Desires," *Comic Cavalcade* 1, no. 16 (August 1946).

55. Marston, "School for Spies," *Sensation Comics* 1, no. 4 (April 1942); Marston, "Summons to Paradise," *Sensation Comics* 1, no. 6 (June 1942); Robert Kanigher, "Deception's Daughter," *Comic Cavalcade* 1, no. 26 (April 1948); Marston, "The Crime Combine," *Sensation Comics* 1, no. 32 (August 1944); Marston, "The Fun Foundation," *Sensation Comics* 1, no. 27 (March 1944); Joye Murchison, "The Cheetah Returns," *Comic Cavalcade* 1, no. 11 (Summer 1945); Robert Kanigher, "The Mysterious Prisoners of Anglonia," *Sensation Comics* 1, no. 62 (February 1947).

56. Marston, "Wonder Woman Arrives in Man's World," *Sensation Comics* 1, no. 1 (January 1942); Marston, "Department Store Perfidy"; Marston, "Wonder Woman Versus the Saboteurs"; Marston, "The Lawbreakers' League," *Sensation Comics* 1, no. 46 (October 1945).

57. Marston, "Wonder Woman Arrives in Man's World"; Marston, "Victory at Sea," *Sensation Comics* 1, no. 15 (March 1943); Marston, "The Crime of Boss Brekel," *Sensation Comics* 1, no. 51 (March 1946); untitled newspaper comic strip, in "Wonder Woman: Selected Continuities (Magazine, Wonder Woman Newspaper Strip, King Features)," Dibner Library.

58. Marston, "The Buddha Wishing Ring," *Comic Cavalcade* 1, no. 20 (April 1947); Marston, "The Adventure of the Pilotless Plane," *Sensation Comics* 1, no. 24; Wright, *Comic Book Nation*, 45; Robert Kanigher, "Treachery in the Arctic," *Sensation Comics* 1, no. 65 (May 1947); Marston, "The First Test of Aphrodite," *Wonder Woman* 1, no. 4 (May 1943); Joye Murchison, "The Winds of Time," *Wonder Woman* 1, no. 17 (May 1946); Joye Murchison, "Invisible Terror," *Wonder Woman* 1, no. 19 (September 1946); Marston, "Grown-Down Land," *Sensation Comics* 1, no. 31 (July 1944).

59. Lepore, *Secret History*, 209, 246; Marston, "The Menace of Doctor Poison."

60. Daniels, *Wonder Woman*, 61.

61. Josette Frank to Gaines, February 17, 1943, "Wonder Woman: Selected Letters, 1941–1945," Dibner Library, Smithsonian Institution; Dorothy Roubicek, memo to Charley Gaines, February 19, 1943, "Wonder Woman: Selected Letters, 1941–1945," Dibner Library, Smithsonian Institution; Gaines to Marston, no date, "Wonder Woman: Selected Letters, 1941–1945," Dibner Library, Smithsonian Institution; Marston to Gaines, February 20, 1943, "Wonder Woman: Selected Letters, 1941–1945," Dibner Library, Smithsonian Institution.

62. Roubicek, memo to Gaines, March 12, 1943 "Wonder Woman: Selected Letters, 1941–1945," Dibner Library, Smithsonian Institution.

63. Frank to Gaines, February 29, 1944, "Wonder Woman: Selected Letters, 1941–1945," Dibner Library, Smithsonian Institution; Sgt. John D. Jacobs to Charles Moulton, September 9, 1943, "Wonder Woman: Selected Letters, 1941–1945," Dibner Library, Smithsonian Institution; Marston to Gaines, February 20, 1943; Frank to Gaines, February 29, 1944; Lepore, *Secret History*, 245.

64. Sones to Gaines, March 15, 1943, "Wonder Woman: Selected Letters, 1941–1945," Dibner Library, Smithsonian Institution; Marston to Sones, March 20, 1943, "Wonder Woman: Selected Letters, 1941–1945," Dibner Library, Smithsonian Institution.

65. "The Press: Are the Comics Fascist?," *Time*, October 22, 1945, 67–68; Ong, "Comics and the Super State," *Arizona Quarterly* 1 (1945): 34–48.

66. Marston, letter to Gaines, February 1, 1944, "Wonder Woman: Selected Letters, 1941–1945," Dibner Library, Smithsonian Institution.

67. Lepore, *Secret History*, 246–47; Hummel papers, May 31, 2014.

68. Lepore, *Secret History,* 253, 258; Hummel papers, May 31, 2014; Hummel Account Journals, 1945–1946, in Joye Hummel Papers, Dibner Library, Smithsonian Institution.

69. Hummel papers, May 31, 2014; Marston, "Villainy, Incorporated," *Wonder Woman* 1, no. 28 (April 1948).

70. "Obituaries: Dr. W. M. Marston, Psychologist, 53," *New York Times,* May 3, 1947, p. 17; Lepore, *Secret History,* 259.

71. Daniels, *Wonder Woman,* 74, 76; Hummel papers, May 31, 2014; Lepore, *Secret History,* 289, 273.

72. Wright, *Comic Book Nation,* 57, 58; Craig This, "Containing Wonder Woman: Frederic Wertham's Battle Against the Mighty Amazon," in *The Ages of Wonder Woman: Essays on the Amazon Princess in Changing Times,* ed. Joseph Darowski (Jefferson, NC: McFarland, 2013), 37; Tim Hanley, *Wonder Woman Unbound: The Curious History of the World's Most Famous Superheroine* (Chicago: Chicago Review Press, 2014), Kindle e-book, "Interlude 1: *Wonder Woman's* Extra Features."

73. Robert Kanigher, "I Married a Monster!," *Wonder Woman* 1, no. 155 (July 1965); Robert Kanigher, "Planet of the Giants," *Wonder Woman* 1, no. 90 (May 1957); Robert Kanigher, "S.O.S. Wonder Woman," *Sensation Comics* 1, no. 94 (October 1949); Joan Ormrod, "Cold War Fantasies: Testing the Limits of the Familial Body," in Darowski, ed., *The Ages of Wonder Woman,* 52–65.

CHAPTER SEVEN

1. Judith Crist, "Horror in the Nursery," *Collier's Magazine,* March 27, 1948; Frederic Wertham, "The Comics . . . Very Funny!," *The Saturday Review of Literature,* May 29, 1948, 6–7.

2. Frederic Wertham, *Seduction of the Innocent* (London: Museum Press Limited), 33–34.

3. Frank Nickell, "The Burning of the Comic Books," National Public Radio, March 1, 2016, http://krcu.org/post/burning-comic-books#stream/0.

4. Joe Botsford, "Troubled Times for Teens: 'Momism' Viewed as Family Peril," *Milwaukee Sentinel,* February 8, 1960; Ethan Thompson, *Parody and Taste in American Television Culture* (New York: Routledge, 2011).

5. *The Silver Cord,* directed by John Cromwell (RKO Radio Pictures, 1933); Sidney Howard, *The Silver Cord: A Comedy in Three Acts* (New York: Samuel French, 1926), 24, 53.

6. Philip Wylie, *Generation of Vipers* (Normal, IL: Dalkey Archive Press, 1996), 204; Rebecca Jo Plant, *The Repeal of Mother Love: Momism and the Construction of Motherhood in Philip Wylie's America* (PhD diss., Johns Hopkins University, 2001), 29, 25, 43, 38, 57; Wylie, *Generation of Vipers,* xi; Rebecca Jo Plant, *Mom: The Transformation of Motherhood in Modern America* (Chicago: University of Chicago Press, 2010), 2.

7. David M. Levy, *Maternal Overprotection* (New York: Columbia University Press, 1943), 163, 168, 171, 182.

8. Wylie, *Generation of Vipers,* 3, 21, 8, 198.

9. Wylie, *Generation of Vipers,* 47, 49, 51; Plant, *Repeal of Mother Love,* 86; Wylie, *Generation of Vipers,* 199, 52, 53, 194.

10. Wylie, *Generation of Vipers,* 210, 198, 197, 198, 200, 65, 201.

11. Wylie, *Generation of Vipers*, 215, 203, 213, 201, 212, 207, 208, 207, 213, 216, 215, 216, 215–16.

12. Plant, *Repeal of Mother Love*, 1–3.

13. Plant, *Repeal of Mother Love*, 4, 13, 47, 48, 90; Lewis Nichols, "Talk with Philip Wylie," *New York Times Book Review*, February 21, 1954.

14. Amram Scheinfeld, "Are American Moms a Menace?," *Ladies Home Journal*, November 1945.

15. "Mom Denounced as Peril to Nation," *New York Times*, April 28, 1945; "1945 Peace 'Wreck' Laid to 'Momism,'" *Washington Post*, December 25, 1950.

16. Kyle A. Cuordileone, *Manhood and American Political Culture in the Cold War* (New York: Routledge, 2005), 516; Eugene Meyer, "Foreword," in *Their Mother's Sons: The Psychiatrist Examines an American Problem*, by Edward Strecker (Philadelphia: Lippincott, 1946), 5.

17. Strecker, "Motherhood and Momism: Effect on the Nation," *University of West Ontario Medical Journal* (March 1946), 61, 64.

18. "Unconscious Freighted with Nameless Fear, Guilt," *Washington Post*, March 25, 1953, 26; Strecker, "Motherhood and Momism," 13, 21, 25, 30.

19. Strecker, "Motherhood and Momism," 160, 219, 133, 234; "Unconscious Freighted with Nameless Fear, Guilt."

20. Plant, *Mom*, 102; "The Habit of 'Momism,'" *New York Times*, December 8, 1946. Also see Roel van den Oever, *Mama's Boy: Momism and Homophobia in Postwar American Culture* (New York: Palgrave Macmillan, 2012).

21. Leland Stowe, "What's Wrong with American Women?," *Reader's Digest*, October 1949, 49–51; Ferdinand Lundberg and Marynia F. Farnham, *Modern Woman: The Lost Sex* (New York: Grosset and Dunlap, 1947), 235–36; Malvina Lindsay, "Society's Scapegoat: In Defense of 'Mom,'" *Washington Post*, January 18, 1947.

22. Nora Sayre, *Running Time: Films of the Cold War* (New York: Doubleday, 1982), 102; *Cinderella*, directed by Clyde Geronimi and Wilfred Jackson (Walt Disney Productions, 1950); *Snow White and the Seven Dwarfs*, directed by William Cottrell, David Hand, Wilfred Jackson, Larry Morey, Perce Pearce, and Ben Sharpsteen (Walt Disney Productions, 1937); *Sleeping Beauty*, directed by Glyde Geronimi (Walt Disney Productions, 1959).

23. Robert Bloch, *Psycho: A Novel* (New York: Overlook Press, 2010, first published 1959), 12, 13, 15, 16; Strecker, "Motherhood and Momism," 30–31; Strecker, "Motherhood and Momism," 70; *Psycho*, directed by Alfred Hitchcock (Shamley Productions, 1960).

24. Strecker, "Motherhood and Momism," 73; *Psycho*; Hans Sebald, *Momism: The Silent Disease of America* (Chicago: Nelson-Hall, 1976), 127.

25. *Notorious*, directed by Alfred Hitchcock (RKO Radio Pictures, 1946).

26. *My Son John*, directed by Leo McCarey (Rainbow Productions, 1952); Stephen J. Whitfield, *The Culture of the Cold War* (Baltimore: Johns Hopkins University Press, 1996), 127; Sayre, *Running Time*, 95–96.

27. *My Son John*.

28. Whitfield, *Culture of the Cold War*, 212; *The Manchurian Candidate*, directed by John Frankenheimer (M. C. Productions, 1962).

29. Sayre, *Running Time*, 126; Kenneth T. Jackson, *Crabgrass Frontier: The Suburbanization of*

America (New York: Oxford University Press, 1985), 232; Wini Breines, *Young, White, and Miserable: Growing Up Female in the Fifties* (Boston: Beacon Press, 1992), 51; Jackson, *Crabgrass Frontier,* 243; Frank, "Gender Trouble in Paradise: Suburbia Reconsidered," in *Gender in an Urban World,* ed. Judith N. DeSana (Bingley, UK: Emerald Group Publishing, 2008), 127; Jackson, *Crabgrass Frontier,* 244.

30. David Riesman, *The Lonely Crowd: A Study of the Changing American Character* (New Haven, CT: Yale University Press, 1950), 331; see Martin Dines' and Timotheus Vermeulen's historiographical essay, "Introduction: New Suburban Stories," in *New Suburban Stories,* ed. Dines and Vermeulen (London: Bloomsbury, 2013), 1–16.

31. Wylie, *Generation of Vipers,* 196–97, 53–55.

32. Elaine Tyler May, *Homeward Bound: American Families in the Cold War Era* (New York: Basic Books, 1988), 5; Susanne Frank, "Gender Trouble in Paradise: Suburbia Reconsidered," in *Gender in an Urban World,* ed. Judith N. DeSana (Bingley, UK: Emerald Group Publishing, 2008), 133; James Gilbert, *Men in the Middle: Searching for Masculinity in the 1950s* (Chicago: University of Chicago Press, 2005); William H. Whyte, *The Organization Man* (New York: Simon and Schuster, 1956), 6, 10; Sloan Wilson, *The Man in the Gray Flannel Suit* (New York: Four Walls Eight Windows, 1955), 1–2, 3.

33. Wilson, *The Man in the Gray Flannel Suit,* 16, 18, 49, 52–53, 21, 60, 64, 65–67; *The Man in the Gray Flannel Suit,* directed by Nunnally Johnson (Twentieth Century Fox, 1956); Frank, "Gender Trouble in Paradise," 133; May, *Homeward Bound,* 14, 23.

34. Lindsay, "Feminine Suburbia: Mental Health Risk," *Washington Post,* October 3, 1955; Cuordileone, *Manhood and American Political Culture,* 523; John Keats, *The Crack in the Picture Window* (Boston: Houghton Mifflin, 1957), 144–45.

35. Eugene Griffin, "Cites Danger of Matriarchy in Suburbia," *Chicago Daily Tribune,* September 29, 1955; Cuordileone, 523; Lindsay, "Feminine Suburbia."

36. Robert C. Wood, *Suburbia: Its People and Their Politics* (Boston: Houghton Mifflin, 1958); Keats, *The Crack,* xi–xii, 57, 2, 6, 22–23, 58.

37. Keats, *The Crack,* 51, 72, 55, 95, 43.

38. Keats, *The Crack,* 61, 61, 67, 85, 138, 149–150.

39. J. Robert Moskin, "Why Do Women Dominate Him?," in *The Decline of the American Male,* by *Look* magazine (New York: Random House, 1958), 3, 5, 11, 12, 18–19, 20, 24.

40. Susan Douglas, *Where the Girls Are* (New York: Three Rivers Press, 1995), 26, 43; May, *Homeward Bound,* 146; Gilbert, *Men in the Middle,* 1; Raylyn Moore, *Wonderful Wizard, Marvelous Land* (Bowling Green, KY: Bowling Green University Press, 1974), 2; "The Oz Bowl Game," *Time,* January 15, 1965.

41. Crosby, "Momism Running Rampant on Televised Soap Opera," *Washington Post,* September 2, 1953.

42. Douglas, *Where the Girls Are,* 32–33.

43. *Rebel Without a Cause,* directed by Nicholas Ray (Warner Brothers, 1955); Robert M. Lindner, *Rebel Without a Cause: The Hypnoanalysis of a Criminal Psychopath* (New York: Grove Press, 1944), 26.

44. *Rebel Without a Cause*; Wylie, *Generation of Vipers,* 209; Plant, *Mom,* 186; Strecker, "Moth-

erhood and Momism," 71; Lindner, 76. The "gender inversion" in the film anticipated a 1957 *New York Times* article about a conference on "The Man in the Family" entitled, "Trousered Mothers and Dishwashing Dads" (Dorothy Barclay, *New York Times Magazine*, April 28, 1957, 48); *Rebel Without a Cause*; Lindner, 56.

45. *Rebel Without a Cause*; Plant, *Mom*, 71, 28; Emanuel Levy, "*Rebel Without a Cause*: Critical Vs. Popular Response," accessed June 22, 2017, emanuellevy.com, http://emanuellevy.com/review/rebel-without-a-cause-is-50brcritical-vs-popular-response-1/.

46. Strecker, "Motherhood and Momism," 73; "Priest Sees Alcoholism Caused by 'Momism,'" *Washington Post and Times Herald*, December 31, 1957; "Study Clears 'Momism' in Drunk's Past," *Washington Post and Times Herald*, January 16, 1960.

47. "Momism Isn't Dead," *Los Angeles Times*, October 2, 1966; "Motherless Monkeys Often Prove Happier," *Los Angeles Times*, December 29, 1964.

48. Betty Friedan, *The Feminine Mystique* (New York: Laurel, 1963), 374.

49. Friedan, 20, 21, 28, 44, 198, 190–92.

50. Joanne Meyerowitz, *Not June Cleaver: Women and Gender in Postwar America, 1954–1960* (Philadelphia: Temple University Press, 1994), 2. Also see: Breines, *Young, White, and Miserable*; Susan Douglas, *Where the Girls Are*; May, *Homeward Bound*.

51. Peter Bart, "Momism in Films Gets a New Twist," *New York Times*, August 13, 1964; "Lack of Love Blamed for Youth Problems," *Chicago Daily Defender*, August 24, 1968; Tim Hanley, *Wonder Woman Unbound: The Curious History of the World's Most Famous Superheroine* (Chicago: Chicago Review Press, 2014), chap. 7, "Wonder Woman No More"; Dennis O'Neill, "Wonder Woman's Last Battle," *Wonder Woman* 1, no. 179 (December 1968).

52. Pilot. The plan for the series was discarded before an entire pilot was made (Hanley, *Wonder Woman Unbound*, 3340).

CHAPTER EIGHT

1. Jill Lepore, *The Secret History of Wonder Woman* (New York: Vintage, 2014), 283; *Ms. Magazine*, January 1972. At the time, the Amazing Amazon was recovering from her superpower-less stint as boutique owner Diana Prince, and her writers were struggling with including feminism in the comic; in the "Special Women's Lib" issue, Diana claims that she does not even "like women," and she questions the radical tactics of female department store workers who strike for minimum wages and equal pay (Lepore, *Secret History*, 288; "The Grandee Caper," *Wonder Woman* 1, vol. 203, December 1, 1972).

2. Cynthia Eller, *The Myth of Matriarchal Prehistory: Why an Invented Past Won't Give Women a Future* (Boston: Beacon Press, 2000), 3.

3. Eller, *Myth*, 180, 81, 5. Readers should be aware that in this chapter, I have not tried to be comprehensive, but rather strategic, in my choice of matriarchalist fiction in the 1970s–1980s. There are other popular works from this era that feature matriarchies, like, for instance, Marion Zimmer Bradley's *Darkover* series (see the Marion Zimmer Bradley Literary Works Trust's list: http://www.mzbworks.com/darkover.htm), or Sally Gearhart's *The Wanderground: Stories of the*

Hill Women. I have chosen the works herein to emphasize two things: the problem of gender essentialism and the evolution from feminist matriarchalism to radical feminist matriarchalism in science fiction.

4. Denise Thompson, *Radical Feminism Today* (London: SAGE Publications, 2001), 1; Williams, "The Retreat to Cultural Feminism," in *Feminist Revolution,* ed. Redstockings of the Women's Liberation Movement (New York: Random House, 1978); Alice Echols, *Daring to Be Bad: Radical Feminism in America, 1967–1975* (Minneapolis: University of Minnesota Press, 1989), 244. To be fair, radical feminism has also been accused of silencing or ignorance around issues of race and class. Ellen Willis explains that the singular focus on gender and sex often precluded "other forms of social domination," so that when radical feminists of the working class charged classism, "the movement had no agreed-upon politics of class that we could refer to, beyond the assumption that class hierarchy was oppressive" (Willis, "Radical Feminism and Feminist Radicalism," *Social Text,* no. 9/10 (Spring–Summer 1984), 95–96).

5. Echols, *Daring to Be Bad,* 6; Willis, "Preface," in Echols, *Daring to be Bad,* ix; Echols, 243.

6. Gloria Steinem, "Introduction," in *Wonder Woman,* ed. and with essays by Gloria Steinem and Phyllis Chesler (New York: Outlet, 1972), 1, 4, 3, 5.

7. Steinem, "Introduction," 5–6.

8. Micaela di Leonardo, *Exotics at Home: Anthropologies, Others, and American Modernity* (Chicago: University of Chicago Press, 1998), 98; Echols, *Daring to Be Bad,* 248; Jane Alpert, "Mother Right: A New Feminist Theory," Atlanta Lesbian Feminist Alliance Archives, Duke University Library, accessed December 16, 2016, http://library.duke.edu/digitalcollections/wlmpc_wlmms01022/, 6, 7.

9. Alpert, "Mother Right," 8.

10. Alpert, "Mother Right," 8, 9, 10.

11. Echols, *Daring to be Bad,* 351; Eller, *Myth,* 20, 65.

12. Eller, *Myth,* 35; Merlin Stone, *When God Was a Woman* (New York: Harcourt Brace Jovanovich, 1976), xi.

13. Eller, *Myth,* 36; Mary Zeiss Stange, "The Once and Future Heroine: Paleolithic Goddesses and the Popular Imagination," *Women's Studies Quarterly* 21, no. 1 (Spring 1993): 55.

14. "Indian Women," *off our backs* 4, no. 8 (July 1974): 28; Brigitte Berger, "Introduction," in *Mothers and Amazons* (New York: Doubleday, 1973); Phyllis Chesler, "The 'Amazon Legacy,'" in *Wonder Woman,* ed. Gloria Steinem and Phyllis Chesler, n.p. (New York: Holt, Rinehart and Winston, 1972).

15. Ernestine S. Elster, "Marija Gimbutas, 1921–1994," *American Journal of Archaeology* 98, no. 4 (October 1994): 756; Eller, *Myth,* 90; Joan Marler, "The Life and Work of Marija Gimbutas," *Journal of Feminist Studies in Religion* 12, no. 2 (Fall 1996): 42, 44.

16. Marsha Aileen Hewitt, *Critical Theory of Religion: A Feminist Analysis* (Minneapolis: Fortress Press, 1995), 192; Charlene Spretnak, "Beyond the Backlash: An Appreciation of the Work of Marija Gimbutas," *Journal of Feminist Studies in Religion* 12, no. 2 (Fall 1996): 96; Iain Gow, "Review, *From the Realm of the Ancestors,*" *Canadian Journal of Political Science* 31, no. 4 (December 1998): 837–39, 837; Marija Gimbutas, *The Goddesses and Gods of Old Europe, 6500–3500 B.C.: Myths and Cult Images* (Berkeley: University of California Press, 2007, first published 1974); Marija Gimbutas, *The Language of the Goddess* (London: Thames and Hudson, 1989); Marija Gimbu-

tas, *The Civilization of the Goddess: The World of Old Europe* (San Francisco: Harper San Francisco, 1991); Marija Gimbutas, *The Living Goddesses* (Berkeley: University of California Press, 2001).

17. Marler, "Life and Work," 46; Carol P. Christ, "Reading Marija Gimbutas," *NWSA Journal* 12, no. 1 (Spring 2000): 170; Valerie Abrahamsen, "Essays in Honor of Marija Gimbutas: A Response," *Journal of Feminist Studies in Religion* 13, no. 2 (Fall 1997): 69–74, 70; "Beyond the Backlash," 91.

18. Carol P. Christ, "Introduction: The Legacy of Marija Gimbutas," *Journal of Feminist Studies in Religion* 12, no. 2 (Fall 1996): 31–35, 33; Christ, "A Different World: The Challenge of the Work of Marija Gimbutas to the Dominant World-View of Western Cultures," *Journal of Feminist Studies in Religion* 12, no. 2 (Fall 1996): 55; Spretnak, "Beyond the Backlash," 91, 92; Christ, "Introduction," 33; Christ, "Reading," 173.

19. Ken Ringle, "Jean M. Auel: The Smashing Saga of the 'Cave' Woman," *Washington Post*, February 21, 1986; Robin McKinley, "Meanwhile Back in the Ice Age," *Washington Post*, November 4, 1990, K6; Jean M. Auel, *The Clan of the Cave Bear* (New York: Bantam Books, 1980).

20. Auel, *Valley of the Horses* (New York: Crown, 1982); Stange, "Once and Future Heroine," 56.

21. Auel, *Clan*, 2, 2, 502, 325.

22. Auel, *Valley*, 33.

23. Auel, *Valley*, 24; Auel, *Clan*, character list, n.p.; Auel, *The Mammoth Hunters* (New York: Crown, 1985), 25.

24. Auel, *Clan*, 29.

25. Auel, *The Land of Painted Caves* (New York: Crown, 2011), 733, 660, 757.

26. Nicholas Ruddick, *The Fire in the Stone: Prehistoric Fiction from Charles Darwin to Jean M. Auel* (Middletown, CT: Wesleyan University Press, 2009), 87; Ken Ringle, "Jean M. Auel: The Smashing Saga of the Cave Woman," *Washington Post*, February 21, 1986; *Time* quoted in Ringle; Robin McKinley, "Meanwhile Back in the Ice Age," *Washington Post*, November 4, 1990; Clyde Wilcox, "The Not-so-Failed Feminism of Jean Auel," *Journal of Popular Culture* 28, no. 3 (Winter 1994): 63.

27. Willis, "Radical Feminism," 105.

28. Lisa Yaszek, "Feminism," in *The Oxford Handbook of Science Fiction*, ed. Rob Latham (New York: Oxford University Press, 2014), 537; Judith Merril, *Better to Have Loved: The Life of Judith Merril* (Toronto: Between the Lines, 2002), 105; Lisa Yaszek, *Galactic Suburbia: Recovering Women's Science Fiction* (Columbus: Ohio State University Press, 2008), 3; Rachel Blau DuPlessis, "The Feminist Apologues of Lessing, Piercy, and Russ," *Frontiers* 4 (Spring 1979): 2. Also see Yaszek, "Stories 'That Only a Mother' Could Write: Midcentury Peace Activism, Maternalist Politics, and Judith Merril's Early Fiction," *NWSA Journal* 16, no. 4 (Summer 2004): 70–97.

29. Barbara A. Crow, "Introduction," in *Radical Feminism: A Documentary Reader*, ed. Barbara A. Crow (New York: New York University Press, 2000), 2; "Redstockings Manifesto," in Crow, *Radical Feminism*, 223; Ti-Grace Atkinson, "Radical Feminism," in Crow, 85.

30. Shulamith Firestone, "The Dialectic of Sex," in Crow, 95–96.

31. Stephen K. Sanderson, *Evolutionism and Its Critics: Deconstructing and Reconstructing as Evolutionary Interpretation of Human Society* (Boulder: Paradigm Publishers, 2007), 35; Eugene N. Cohen and Edwin Eames, *Cultural Anthropology* (Little, Brown, 1982); Theodora Kroeber, *Alfred Kroeber: A Personal Configuration* (Berkeley: University of California Press, 1970), 65; Theo-

dora Kroeber, *Ishi in Two Worlds: A Biography of the Last Wild Indian in North America* (Berkeley: University of California Press, 1961); Theodora Kroeber, *Alfred Kroeber: A Personal Configuration* (Berkeley: University of California Press, 1970), 190; John Wray, "Ursula K. Le Guin, The Art of Nonfiction no. 221," *Paris Review,* accessed June 24, 2017, https://www.theparisreview.org/interviews/6253/ursula-k-le-guin-the-art-of-fiction-no-221-ursula-k-le-guin. Boas was the primary representative of the generation of anthropologists who preferred "particularist histories of ethnic groups" (Kuper, *Reinvention of Primitive Society,* 115, 117), and he explicitly rejected evolutionism (di Leonardo, *Exotics at Home,* 161). One of his mentees, Melville J. Herskovits, was responsible for correcting the racist anthropological view of the Fon civilization of Dahomey (Christopher Reed, *"All the World Is Here": The Black Presence at White City* (Bloomington: Indiana University Press, 2002) 154–55).

32. Ursula Le Guin, *The Tombs of Atuan,* in *The Earthsea Quartet* (New York: Penguin Books, 1992).

33. Le Guin, *Tombs,* 175–205, 271; Le Guin, *A Wizard of Earthsea,* in *The Earthsea Quartet* (New York: Penguin Books, 1992), 50.

34. Le Guin, *Tombs,* 258, 266; Le Guin, *Wizard of Earthsea,* 16; Le Guin, *Tombs,* 280, 272.

35. Le Guin, *Tombs,* 195, 300; Le Guin, *Tehanu,* in *The Earthsea Quartet,* 509.

36. Lisa Hammond Rashley, "Revisioning Gender: Inventing Women in Ursula K. Le Guin's Nonfiction," *Biography* 20, no. 1 (Winter 2007): 22; John Wray, "Ursula K. Le Guin, The Art of Nonfiction no. 221," *Paris Review*; Le Guin, "Is Gender Necessary?" (1976) and "Is Gender Necessary Redux" (1988), 163, 164–65, accessed June 24, 2017, https://americanfuturesiup.files.wordpress.com/2013/01/is-gender-necessary.pdf; Le Guin, *The Left Hand of Darkness* (New York: Ace Books, 1987, first published 1969).

37. Attebury, *Decoding Gender,* 131; Craig Barrow and Diana Barrow, *"The Left Hand of Darkness*: Feminism for Men," *Mosaic: An Interdisciplinary Critical Journal* 20, no. 1 (Winter 1987), 83.

38. Attebury and Hollinger, "Introduction," ix; Le Guin, "Is Gender Necessary Redux"; Naomi Jacobs, "*Mizora: A Prophecy* (Review)," *Utopian Studies* 12, no. 1 (2001): 210.

39. Russ, *The Image of Women in Science Fiction* (Andover, MA: Warner Modular Publications, 1973), 91, 79–80; Julie Phillips, *James Tiptree Jr.: The Double Life of Alice B. Sheldon* (New York: St. Martin's, 2006), 330, 223. Russ coined the phrase "galactic suburbia" in *The Image of Women in Science Fiction* (88). Also see Jane Donawerth, *Frankenstein's Daughters: Women Writing Science Fiction* (Syracuse, NY: Syracuse University Press, 1997), 177.

40. Phillips, *James Tiptree Jr.,* 21, 15, 7, 140, 151, 120, 109, 147, 152, 155.

41. Phillips, *James Tiptree Jr.,* 215, 219.

42. Phillips, *James Tiptree Jr.,* 29; James K. Tiptree Jr., *Houston, Houston, Do You Read?* (New York: Doubleday, 1996), 1, 41, 10–11.

43. Tiptree, *Houston,* 94–95, 96, 112–13.

44. Tiptree, *Houston,* 55, 59, 96, 97, 82, 115.

45. Tiptree, *Houston,* 37, 39, 9, 49.

46. Tiptree, *Houston,* 63, 8, 132, 141, 146, 147. That same year, Marge Piercy published *Woman on the Edge of Time* (1976), a novel that bridged the present of the 1970s and the future of 2137. *Woman on the Edge of Time* is something of an expanded, updated version of Gilman's *The Yellow Wallpaper,* which was rediscovered by feminist scholars and republished as a stand-alone volume

in the 1970s (Beth Sutton-Ramspeck, "Shot Out of the Canon: Mary Ward and the Claims of Conflicting Feminism," in Nicola Diana Thompson, ed., *Victorian Women Writers and the Woman Question* (Cambridge: Cambridge University Press, 1999), 204–22, 220n49). In Piercy's revision, the abuses of the patriarchal system are overt and systemic, not limited to one man, as in *The Yellow Wallpaper.* But instead of descending into solitary insanity during her incarceration in a mental hospital, the protagonist transcends time to visit a future in which gender roles have been abolished. While it is not a full-fledged matriarchy—power is not concentrated in the hands of women—Mattapoisett is based on many of the matriarchalist principles examined herein: pacifism, freedom of labor, anticapitalism, shared domestic duties, and childrearing (Marge Piercy, *Woman on the Edge of Time* (New York: Knopf, 1976)).

47. Phillips, *James Tiptree Jr.,* 310, 312, 334, 312.

48. Inez van der Spek, *Alien Plots: Female Subjectivity and the Divine in the Light of James Tiptree's "A Momentary Taste of Being"* (Liverpool: Liverpool University Press, 2000), 94; Phillips, *James Tiptree Jr.,* 336, 367, 324, 325. In homage to the feminist tension within and about Sheldon's body of work, the James Tiptree Jr. Award was created in the early 1990s to reward works that "encourag[es] the exploration and expansion of gender" within science fiction ("James Tiptree Jr. Literary Award," https://tiptree.org).

49. Phillips, *James Tiptree Jr.,* 331, 304.

50. Joanna Russ, *The Female Man* (Boston: Beacon Press, 2000).

51. Russ, *Female Man,* 108; Attebury, *Decoding Gender,* 124; Russ, *Female Man,* 103.

52. Russ, *Female Man,* 49–50, 52, 15, 12.

53. Russ, *Female Man,* 151–52, 116–17, 151, 138–39.

54. Russ, *Female Man,* 29, 81. Donna Haraway argues that cyborg characters in feminist SF offer "transgressed boundaries, potent fusions, and dangerous possibilities which progressive people might explore as one part of needed political work" (Haraway, "A Manifesto for Cyborgs: Science, Technology, and Socialist Feminism in the 1980s," in *Coming to Terms: Feminism, Theory, Politics,* ed. Elizabeth Weed (New York: Routledge, 2013), 178).

55. Russ, "Recent Feminist Utopias," in *Future Females: A Critical Anthology,* ed. Marleen S. Barr (Bowling Green, KY: Bowling Green University Press, 1981), 77, 81; Phillips, *James Tiptree Jr., ,*332.

56. Marleen Barr, *Feminist Fabulation: Space/Postmodern Fiction* (Iowa City: University of Iowa Press, 1992), xxvii, 3.

57. Tiptree, *Houston,* 150; Phillips, *James Tiptree Jr.,* 312; Tiptree, *Houston,* 146–47; Russ, *Female Man,* 211; Russ, "Recent Feminist Utopias," 81.

58. Suzy McKee Charnas, *Walk to the End of the World* (New York: Berkeley, 1976); Charnas, *Motherlines* (New York: Berkeley, 1978); Suzy McKee Charnas, *The Furies* (New York: Tor Books, 1994); Suzy McKee Charnas, *The Conqueror's Child* (New York: Tor Books, 1999). Charnas dedicated *Motherlines,* the second book in the series which focuses on two opposing matriarchal societies, to Joanna Russ.

59. Charnas, *Walk to the End of the World,* 3; Charnas, *Motherlines,* 18, 60, 70, 101, 88, 29, 40, 46, 63, 64, 182, 60, 86, 47.

60. Charnas, *Motherlines,* 44, 99.

61. Charnas, *Motherlines,* 70; Dunja M. Mohr, "Parity, with Differences: Suzy McKee Char-

nas Concludes the Holdfast Series," *Science Fiction Studies* 26 (1999): 469; Charnas, *Motherlines* 51, 56; Charnas, *The Furies*, 54, 38.

62. Elizabeth Cady Stanton, "Epigraph," in Charnas, *The Furies*.

63. Charnas, *Motherlines*, 238; Charnas, *The Furies*, 58.

64. Charnas, *Motherlines*, 158.

65. Mohr, "Parity, with Differences," 471; Charnas, *The Conqueror's Child*, 395, 406.

66. Charnas, interview, http://www.depauw.edu/sfs/interviews/charnasinterview.htm. Willis dates the end of radical feminism to 1975 (foreword in Echols, *Daring to be Bad*, vii; Willis, "Radical Feminism," 92), while Echols dates it to 1973 (244).

67. Russ, "Recent Feminist Utopias," 71; Attebury, *Decoding Gender*, 6; "About Jean Auel," accessed June 25, 2017, JeanAuel.com, http://www.jeanauel.com/about.php.

68. Episode 1, Season 1, *The New Original Wonder Woman*, created by William Moulton Marston and Stanley Ralph Ross (Bruce Lansbury Productions, 1976); Lepore, *Secret History*, 293.

69. Echols, *Daring to be Bad*, 245; Stange, "Once and Future Heroine," 61; Susan Douglas and Meredith Michaels, *The Mommy Myth: The Idealization of Motherhood and How It Has Undermined All Women* (New York: Free Press, 2004),, 4, 5–6. Also see Susan Faludi, *Backlash: The Undeclared War Against American Women* (New York: Crown, 1991),

and Williams, *Gendered Politics in the Modern South* (Baton Rouge: Louisiana State University Press, 2012). Margaret Atwood masterfully encapsulated the dangers of the backlash in *The Handmaid's Tale* conservatism; see Atwood, *The Handmaid's Tale* (Toronto: McClelland and Stewart, 1985).

70. Nancy Chodorow, *Feminism and Psychoanalytic Theory* (New Haven, CT: Yale University Press, 1989), 90.

CHAPTER NINE

1. *A Raisin in the Sun*, directed by Daniel Petrie (Columbia Pictures, 1961).

2. Patricia Bell Scott, "Debunking Sapphire: Toward a Non-Racist and Non-Sexist Social Science," in Akasha Gloria Hull, Patricia Bell Scott, and Barbara Smith, eds., *All the Women Are White, All the Blacks Are Men, But Some of Us Are Brave* (New York: Feminist Press, 1982); Robin M. Boylorn and Mark C. Hopson, "Learning to Conquer Metaphysical Dilemmas: Womanist and Masculinist Perspectives on Tyler Perry's *For Colored Girls*," in *Black Women and Popular Culture: The Conversation Continues*, ed. Adria Y. Goldman, VaNatta S. Ford, Alexa A. Harris, and Natasha R. Howard (London: Lexington Books, 2014), 94.

3. Trudier Harris, *From Mammies to Militants: Domestics in Black American Literature*. (Philadelphia: Temple University Press, 1982), 4; Patricia Hill Collins, *Black Feminist Thought: Knowledge, Consciousness, and Empowerment*, 2nd edition (New York: Routledge, 2000), 69.

4. John Dollard, *Caste and Class in a Southern Town* (Madison: University of Wisconsin Press, 1988), 153, 144.

5. E. Franklin Frazier, *The Negro Family in the United States* (Chicago: University of Chicago Press, 1939), x, 107, 123, 133, 109, 142, 124.

6. Frazier, *The Negro Family*, 114, 115, 143, 143, 144, 118, 126.

7. Franklin, *The Negro Family*, 357, 122, 342.

8. Franklin, *The Negro Family*, 340, 95, 271, 358.

9. Thomas A. Parham, Adisa Ajamu, and Joseph L. White, *Psychology of Blacks: Centering Our Perspectives in the African Consciousness* (New York: Psychology Press, 2010), 52; Harris, *From Mammies to Militants*, 1.

10. Collins, *Black Feminist Thought*, 75, 72; Jessie W. Parkhurst, "The Role of the Black Mammy in the Plantation Household," *Journal of Negro History* (1938), 352–53; Kimberly Wallace-Sanders, *Mammy: A Century of Race, Gender, and Southern Memory* (Ann Arbor: University of Michigan Press, 2008), 7, 118.

11. Harris, *From Mammies to Militants*, 3.

12. Cheryl Thurber, "The Development of Mammy Image and Mythology," in *Southern Women: Histories and Identities*, ed. Virginia Bernhard, Betty Brandon, Elizabeth Fox-Genovese, and Theda Perdue (Columbia: University of Missouri Press, 1992), 87–108; Collins, *Black Feminist Thought*, 73.

13. Bogle, *A Raisin in the Sun*, 62, 63; *Gone With the Wind*, directed by Victor Fleming, George Cukor, and Sam Wood (Selznick International Pictures, 1939).

14. Jill Watts, *Hattie McDaniel: Black Ambition, White Hollywood* (New York: Amistad, 2007), 173; Eldridge Cleaver, *Soul on Ice* (New York: Random House, 1968), 191; The Combahee River Collective, "A Black Feminist Statement," in Hull, Scott, and Smith, eds., *All the Women Are White*; Collins, *Black Feminist Thought*, 56–57, 10, 11.

15. Bogle, *A Raisin in the Sun*, 198; Harris, *From Mammies to Militants*, 21, 38.

16. Harper Lee, *To Kill a Mockingbird* (New York: HarperCollins, 1960), 209, 6.

17. Lee, *To Kill a Mockingbird*, 15, 156, 164, 166, 165; *To Kill a Mockingbird*, directed by Robert Mulligan (Universal International Pictures, 1962).

18. Harper Lee, *Go Set a Watchman* (New York: HarperCollins, 2015), 264, 161, 159–60; Melissa Harris-Perry, *Sister Citizen: Shame, Stereotypes, and Black Women in America* (New Haven, CT: Yale University Press, 2011), 82.

19. Maurice M. Manring, *Slave in a Box: The Strange Career of Aunt Jemima* (Charlottesville: University of Virginia Press, 1998), 168; Paula Giddings, *When and Where I Enter: The Impact of Black Women on Race and Sex in America* (New York: W. Morrow, 1996), 329, 333.

20. Giddings, *When and Where I Enter*, 325; Harris-Perry, *Sister Citizen*, 95.

21. Carl Ginsburg, *Race and Media: The Enduring Life of the Moynihan Report* (New York: Institute for Media Analysis, 1989), 5–6; Office of Policy Planning and Research, US Department of Labor, chap. 4: "The Tangle of Pathology," and chap. 2: "The Negro American Family," in "The Negro Family: The Case for National Action," March 1965, accessed June 25, 2017, http://www.blackpast.org/primary/moynihan-report-1965.

22. "The Negro Family," chap. 4, and chap. 3: "The Roots of the Problem."

23. "The Negro Family," chap. 4, chap. 5.

24. Daniel Geary, *Beyond Civil Rights: The Moynihan Report and Its Legacy* (Philadelphia: University of Pennsylvania Press, 2015), 3; Dionne Bensonsmith, "Jezebels, Matriarchs, and Welfare Queens: The Moynihan Report of 1965 and the Social Construction of African-American Women in Welfare Policy," in *Deserved and Entitled: Social Constructions and Public Policy*, ed. Anne L. Schneider and Helen M. Ingram (Albany: State University of New York Press, 2005), 245; Lyndon Baines Johnson, "To Fulfill These Rights: Commencement Address at Howard University,"

June 4, 1965, accessed June 25, 2017, http://www.presidency.ucsb.edu/ws/?pid=27021; Lee Rainwater and William L. Yancey, *The Moynihan Report and the Politics of Controversy* (Boston: MIT Press, 1967), 131.

25. Geary, *Beyond Civil Rights*, 140; "New Crisis: The Negro Family," *Newsweek*, August 9, 1965, 32–25; "Family Life Breakdown in Negro Slums Sows Seeds of Race Violence—Husbandless Homes Spawn Young Hoodlums, Impede Reforms, Sociologists Say," *Wall Street Journal*, August 16, 1965; Lloyd Shearer, "Negro Problem: Women Rule the Roost," *Parade*, August 20, 1967, 4.

26. Robert Staples, "The Myth of the Black Matriarchy," *Black Scholar* (November–December 1981), 30; Giddings, *When and Where I Enter*, 326; Willie and Reddick, *A New Look at Black Families* (Lanham, MD: Rowman & Littlefield, 2010), 101–10; Bensonsmith, "Jezebels, Matriarchs, and Welfare Queens," 252; Regina Kunzel, "White Neurosis, Black Pathology: Constructing Out of Wedlock Pregnancy in the Wartime and Postwar United States," in Meyerowitz, *Not June Cleaver*, 304; Jacquelyne Jackson, "Black Women in a Racist Society," in *Racism and Mental Health*, ed. Charles Willie, Bernard Kramer, and Bentram Brown (Pittsburgh: University of Pittsburgh Press, 1972), 185–268; Geary, *Beyond Civil Rights*, 142, 145.

27. Robert Staples, "Myth of the Black Matriarchy," 26; Angela Davis, *Women, Race and Class*, 5; bell hooks, *Ain't I a Woman: Black Women and Feminism* (New York: Routledge, 2015), 72; Harris-Perry, *Sister Citizen*, 93.

28. Giddings, *When and Where I Enter*, 328; Rainwater and Yancey, *Moynihan Report*, 29; Giddings, *When and Where I Enter*, 328–29.

29. May, *Homeward Bound*, 13; Staples, "Myth of the Black Matriarchy," 33.

30. *Hurry Sundown*, directed by Otto Preminger (Otto Preminger Films, 1967).

31. June Jordan, "Memo to Daniel Patrick Moynihan," in Jordan, *New Days: Poems of Exile and Return* (New York: Emerson Hall, 1974), 6; Norton, "For Sadie and Maude," in Robin Morgan, ed., *Sisterhood is Powerful: An Anthology of Writings from the Women's Liberation Movement* (New York: Random House, 1970), 357.

32. Toni Cade, "Preface," in *The Black Woman: An Anthology* (New York: Washington Square Press, 2010), Kindle e-book; and the following, all in Toni Cade, ed., *The Black Woman:* Jean Carey Bond and Patricia Peery, "Is the Black Male Castrated"; Kay Lindsey, "Poem"; Paule Marshall, "Reena"; Joanna Clark, "Motherhood"; Fran Sanders, "Dear Black Man"; Abbey Lincoln, "To Whom Will She Cry Rape?"; Toni Cade, "On the Issue of Roles"; Toni Cade, "The Pill: Genocide or Liberation?"

33. Robert Kanigher, "The Second Life of the Original Wonder Woman," *Wonder Woman* 1, no. 204 (January–February 1973); Robert Kanigher, "Target Wonder Woman," *Wonder Woman* 1, no. 205 (March–April 1973); Cary Bates, "War of the Wonder Women," *Wonder Woman* 1, no. 206 (June–July 1973). Nubia played a bit part in other DC comic narratives, including Cary Bates, "The Super-Amazon!," *Supergirl* 1, no. 9 (December–January 1974), "The Boy Who Hated the Legion," *Superboy and the Legion of Super-Heroes* 1, no. 216 (May 1976); "Puppets of the Overlord," *Super-Friends* no. 25 (October 1979). Nubia is resurrected as Nu'Bia in "The Thin Gold Line," *Wonder Woman Annual* 2, no. 8 (September 1999), and appears in two later issues: "Three Hearts," *Wonder Woman* 2, no. 154 (March 2000), and "Three Hearts Part Two: Lies," *Wonder Woman* 2, no. 155 (April 2000). Just as Nubia entered the comics, Paradise Island was quietly

desegregated; the disastrous *Wonder Woman* television movie, starring a blonde Cathy Lee Crosby as a spy with no superpowers, briefly featured—without commentary or spoken lines—one black Amazon, played by Beverly Gill (*Wonder Woman,* directed by Vincent McEveety, Warner Bros. Television, 1974).

34. *Claudine,* directed by John Berry (Twentieth Century Fox, 1974).

35. *Claudine.*

36. *Claudine.*

37. Brenda Cossman, *Sexual Citizens: The Legal and Cultural Regulation of Sex and Belonging* (Stanford, CA: Stanford University Press, 2007), 116; "Box Office/Business for *Claudine* (1974), accessed June 7, 2017, IMDB,com http://www.imdb.com/title/tt0071334/business; untitled *Claudine* review, *The New Republic,* May 25, 1974; untitled *Claudine* review, *Product Digest,* March 8, 1974; Richard Schickel, "Fried Chicken Romance," *Time,* May 20, 1974; "Remembering *Claudine*: A Granddaughter Remembers Welfare without Judgment," *Savoy,* April 2001, 67; untitled *Claudine* review, *The New Ingenue,* May 1974.

38. Robert Staples, "The Myth of Black Macho: A Response to Angry Black Feminists," *Black Scholar* 10, no. 6/7 (March/April 1979), 25; Ntozake Shange, *for colored girls who have considered suicide/when the rainbow is enuf* (New York: Scribner, 2010; repr. 1975, New York: Macmillan).

39. Michele Wallace, *Black Macho and the Myth of the Superwoman* (New York: Verso, 1990; repr. 1979, New York: Dial Press), 107; hooks, *Ain't I a Woman?,* 183; Giddings, *When and Where I Enter,* 329.

40. Staples, "Myth of Black Macho," 24–33, 26, 27, 31, 26.

41. Peter Bailey, "Music Plus Magic Equals Money," *Black Enterprise* 6, no. 6, January 1976, 43, 44, 45, Carlyle C. Douglas, "The Whiz Behind 'The Wiz,'" *Ebony,* October 1, 1975; John Hurst, "If Ever Oh Ever a 'Wiz' There Was—This 'Wiz' Surely Is," *Sacramento Bee,* April 25, 1974.

42. *The Wiz,* directed by Sidney Lumet (Universal Pictures, 1978).

43. *The Wiz.*

44. *The Wiz.*

45. Spike Lee in Audrey T. McCluskey, "Telling Truth and Taking Names: An Interview with Spike Lee," *Black Camera* 19, no. 1 (Spring/Summer 2004): 1–2, 9–11, 9; Bill Higgins, "In 1978, Wiz Went from Broadway to Bust," *Hollywood Reporter,* December 11, 2015; Roger Ebert, "The Wiz," October 24, 1978, accessed December 16, 2016, http://www.rogerebert.com/reviews/ the-wiz-1978; Phillip Lopate, "Sidney Lumet, or the Necessity for Compromise," *Film Comment* 33, no. 4 (July–August 1997): 50–53, 50; Michael Webb, "The City in Film," *Design Quarterly* no. 136 (1987): 3–32, 19; "Diana Ross in 'The Wiz,'" *Ebony,* November 1, 1978, 115–18.

46. Collins, *Black Feminist Thought,* 78.

47. Susan Douglas and Meredith Michaels, *The Mommy Myth: The Idealization of Motherhood and How It Has Undermined All Women* (New York: Free Press, 2004), 185; Wahneema Lubiano, "Black Ladies, Welfare Queens, and State Minstrels: Ideological War by Narrative Means," in *Race-ing Justice, En-gendering Power: Essays on Anita Hill, Clarence Thomas, and the Construction of Social Reality,* ed. Toni Morrison (New York: Pantheon Books, 1992), 337–38.

48. *Economic Report of the President* (Washington, DC: US Government Printing Office, February 1988), 299; Ginsburg, *Race and Media,* vii; Moynihan, *Family and Nation: The Godkin Lectures, Harvard University* (San Diego: Harcourt Brace, 1986); *Newsweek,* April 22, 1985, 30; David

Remnick, "The Family Crusader, Belying Labels, Drawing Crowds, and Loving It All," *Washington Post*, July 16, 1986; "New Theme: Save Yourselves," *Los Angeles Times*, March 8, 1986; "A Whole Generation is Self-Destructing," *USA Today*, April 20, 1989; "Blacks Debating a Greater Stress on Self-Reliance Instead of Aid," *New York Times*, June 15, 1986.

49. Reagan quoted in Valerie Polakow, *Lives on the Edge: Single Mothers and Their Children in the Other America* (Chicago: University of Chicago Press, 1993), 59; "CBS Reports: The Vanishing Family—Crisis in Black America," CBS, January 26, 1986.

50. *CBS Reports*; "Special Issue: The Crisis of the Black Family," *Ebony*, August 1986; "CBS Reports: The Vanishing Family—Crisis in Black America," PeabodyAwards.com, accessed June 15, 2017, http://www.peabodyawards.com/award-profile/cbs-reports-the-vanishing-family-crisis-in-black-america.

51. Kevin Sack, "The New, Volatile Politics of Welfare," *New York Times*, March 15, 1992.

52. Lubiano, *Black Ladies*, 332–33, 336; *New York Times*, July 7, 1991; Lubiano, *Black Ladies*, 334.

53. Dan Quayle, "Address to the Commonwealth Club of California," May 19, 1992, accessed June 7, 2017, http://www.vicepresidentdanquayle.com/speeches_StandingFirm_CCC_3.html.

54. Lubiano, *Black Ladies*, 350; Anonymous, "Dethroning the Welfare Queen: The Rhetoric of Reform," *Harvard Law Review* 107, no. 8 (June 1994): 2013, 2016; Harris-Perry, *Sister Citizen*, 209; Gingrich, *To Renew America*, 8–9; United States House of Representatives, "Contract with America (1994)," National Center for Public Policy Research, accessed June 7, 2017, http://www.nationalcenter.org/ContractwithAmerica.html.

55. Rosalee A. Clawson and Yakuya Trice, "Poverty as We Know It: Media Portrayals of the Poor," *Public Opinion Quarterly* 64 (2000): 53–64; Sanford F. Shcram and Jose Soss, "Success Stories: Welfare Reform, Policy Discourse, and the Politics of Research, *Annals, The American Academy of Political and Social Science* 577 (2001): 49–65; Katha Pollitt, "What Ever Happened to Welfare Mothers?," *The Nation*, May 13, 2010; Anonymous, "Dethroning the Welfare Queen," 2013.

56. *Losing Isaiah*, directed by Stephen Gyllenhaal (Paramount Pictures, 1995).

57. Soren Anderson, "Review: *Losing Isaiah* Can't Find Emotional Power Its Title Implies," Tacoma *News Tribune*, March 17, 1995, SL5.

58. *Losing Isaiah*.

59. Anderson, "Review"; Duchess Harris, "More than Memorabilia? Khaila as Jezebel, Mammy, and Sapphire in *Losing Isaiah*," *COLORS: Opinion & the Arts in Communities of Color* (1995), quoted in Sandra Patton, *Birthmarks: Transracial Adoption in Contemporary America* (New York: New York University Press, 2000), 135.

EPILOGUE

1. Opening credits, *Xena: Warrior Princess*, created by Sam Raimi, John Schulian, and R. J. Stewart (Renaissance Pictures, 1995–2001).

2. "Hooves and Harlots," *Xena: Warrior Princess*, season 1, episode 10, directed by Jace Alexander (Renaissance Pictures, 1995); "The Gauntlet," *Hercules: The Legendary Journeys*, season 1,

episode 12, directed by Jack Perez (Renaissance Pictures, 1995); "Endgame," *Xena: Warrior Princess,* season 4, episode 20, directed by Garth Maxwell (Renaissance Pictures, 1999); "To Helicon and Back," *Xena: Warrior Princess,* season 6, episode 15, directed by Michael Hurst (Renaissance Pictures, 2001); David Fillingim, "By the Gods—Or Not: Religious Plurality in *Xena: Warrior Princess,*" *Journal of Religion and Popular Culture* 21, no. 3 (Fall 2009): n.p. For a full list of the episodes on which the Amazons appear, see "The Amazon Episodes of *Xena: Warrior Princess,*" accessed June 15, 2017, http://www.reneeoconnorfan.pixe151.com/xenaera/amazons/episodes .html.

3. Sara Gwenllian Jones, "Histories, Fictions, and *Xena: Warrior Princess.*" *Television and New Media* 1, no. 4 (November 2000), 411, 410, 413, 415; "The New AmazoNation," accessed June 15, 2017, http://www.amazonation.com.

4. *TV Guide* hailed *Xena* as one of the top "cult shows" in 2004, and when the magazine revisited the list three years later, *Xena* remained in the top ten alongside the likes of *Star Trek* and *Buffy the Vampire Slayer* ("TV Guide Names the Top Cult Shows Ever," June 29, 2007, accessed June 15, 2017, http://www.tvguide.com/news/top-cult-shows-40239/).

5. John Fleming, "'Wicked' Good Fortune," *St. Petersburg Times,* January 15, 2006; Gregory Maguire, *Wicked: The Life and Times of the Wicked Witch of the West* (New York: William Morrow, 1996); Gregory Maguire, *Son of a Witch* (New York: HarperCollins, 2005); Gregory Maguire, *A Lion Among Men* (New York: William Morrow, 2008); Gregory Maguire, *Out of Oz* (New York: HarperCollins, 2011).

6. Kerry Lengel, "Q & A: Gregory Maguire on *Out of Oz,* last in *Wicked* series," *Arizona Republic,* November 12, 2011, accessed June 6, 2017, http://archive.azcentral.com/arizonarepublic/ae/ articles/20111109gregory-maguire-interview-out-oz-wicked-book-signing-tempe.html; Maguire, *Wicked,* 428, 426; Maguire, *A Lion Among Men,* 294, 2; Maguire, *Wicked,* 369, 22, 1.

7. Maguire, *Wicked,* 23; Maguire, *Son of a Witch,* 128; Maguire, *Wicked,* 64, 29, 53, 412, 34, 84, 453; Maguire, *A Lion Among Men,* 2, 136; Maguire, *Wicked,* 363; Maguire, *Out of Oz,* 507; Maguire, *Wicked,* 174, 361; Maguire, *Son of a Witch,* 189; Maguire, *Wicked,* 77; Maguire, *A Lion Among Men,* 2; Maguire, *Wicked,* 50.

8. Maguire, *Wicked,* 167, 434, 134, 137, 434, 164; Maguire, *Son of a Witch,* 47, 66; Maguire, *Wicked,* 447, 183; Maguire, *Son of a Witch,* 249, 259, 282, 304, 326; Maguire, *A Lion Among Men,* 80; Maguire, *Out of Oz,* 277; Maguire, *Son of a Witch,* 303, 315; Maguire; *Out of Oz,* 557.

9. Douglas Smith, "Review, *Wicked,*" PublishersWeekly.com, http://www.publishersweekly. com/978–0-06–039144–7); Greg Cook, "In 'Maleficent,' A New Kind of Disney Princess— Dark, Sexy, Wicked Good," WBUR.org, May 30, 2014, http://www.wbur.org/artery/2014/05/30/ maleficent-disney-princess; "Broadway Blockbuster 'Wicked' Returns to Phillips Center," ICFlorida.com, October 26, 2016, http://www.icflorida.com/entertainment/entertainment-headlines/ broadway-blockbuster-wicked-returns-to-dr-phillips-center/460835698; "Awards," Tickets-Wicked.org, accessed November 7, 2016, http://ticketswicked.org/awards; Kerry Lengel, "Q & A: Gregory Maguire on 'Out of Oz,' last in 'Wicked' Series," *Arizona Republic,* November 12, 2011, http://archive.azcentral.com/thingstodo/stage/articles/2011/11/09/20111109gregory-maguire-inte rview-out-oz-wicked-book-signing-tempe.html); Tufayel Ahmed, "Exclusive: Stephen Daldry Offers Update on *Wicked* Movie Adaptation," *Newsweek,* October 28, 2016, http://www.newsweek. com/exclusive-stephen-daldry-offers-update-wicked-movie-514434).

10. "The Princess and the Power," *Wonder Woman* 2, no. 1, February 1987; "Deadly Arrival," *Wonder Woman* 2, no. 3, April 1987.

11. "Forced Entry," *Green Lantern* 3, no. 54, August 1994; Gail Simone, "Women in Refrigerators," accessed June 6, 2017, http://www.lby3.com/wir/; "The Hawkeye Initiative," accessed June 6, 2017, http://thehawkeyeinitiative.com; *Wonder Woman* 4, November 2011–July 2016; Kathy Spillar, "*Ms.* Turns 40—And Wonder Woman's Back On Our Cover," Msmagazine.com, October 1, 2012, accessed June 6, 2017, http://msmagazine.com/blog/2012/10/01/ms-turns-40-and-wonder-womans-back-on-our-cover/.

12. "Wonder Woman: Rebirth," *Wonder Woman,* June 2016; "Year One, Part One," *Wonder Woman,* July 2016; *Batman vs. Superman: Dawn of Justice,* directed by Zack Snyder (Warner Bros., 2016).

13. *Wonder Woman,* directed by Patty Jenkins (Atlas Entertainment, 2017); Valerie Complex and Robert Jones Jr., "My Soul Looks Back and Wonders: A Critical Examination of the *Wonder Woman* Movie," Medium.com, accessed June 6, 2017, https://medium.com/@Sonof-Baldwin/my-soul-looks-back-and-wonders-a-critical-examination-of-the-wonder-woman-movie-10ba3bfd71f0. In an analysis of the role of race in the film, Hari Ziyad, writing for Afropunk.com, critiqued the film's imperial matriarchalism, arguing that "the success of *Wonder Woman* proves white liberals are OK with imperialism as long as it is led by a (white) woman," accessed June 6, 2017, http://www.afropunk.com/m/blogpost?id=2059274%3ABlogPost%3A1480976).

14. *Wonder Woman* (film).

15. *Wonder Women,* Jenkins; "Exclusive Interview: Greg Rucka on Queer Narrative and Wonder Woman," Comicosity.com, September 28, 2017; *Professor Marston and the Wonder Woman,* directed by Angela Robinson, Opposite Field Productions, 2017; Manohla Dargis, "Review: *Professor Marston,* With Kinks! Pleasure! Female Power!," *New York Times,* October 12, 2017.

16. Alice Randall, *The Wind Done Gone* (New York: Houghton Mifflin Harcourt, 2001); Katherine Stockett, *The Help* (New York: Penguin Books, 2009); *The Help,* directed by Tate Taylor (Dreamworks, 2011); Association of Black Women Historians, "An Open Statement to the Fans of *The Help,*" accessed June 6, 2017, http://aalbc.com/reviews/the_help_historical_context.html.

17. *Precious,* directed by Lee Daniels (Lionsgate, 2009).

18. *Precious;* Sapphire, *Push* (New York: Vintage, 1996), 120.

19. *Precious;* Sapphire, 39–40; Susana M. Morris, chap. 4: "The Language of Family: Talking Back to Narratives of Black Pathology in Sapphire's *Push,*" in *Close Kin and Distant Relatives: The Paradox of Respectability in Black Women's Literature* (Charlottesville: University of Virginia Press, 2014), Google e-book.

20. *Precious;* Benjamin Lee, "Lee Daniels to Make True Story of Welfare Queen Criminal," the *Guardian,* November 24, 2015, accessed June 15, 2017, https://www.theguardian.com/film/2015/nov/24/lee-daniels-the-welfare-queen-criminal-biopic; Chistopher Burrell and James Wermers, "Why Does *Precious* Have to Lighten Up or Shuffle? Teaching with Lee Daniels's 'Adaptation,'" in *Sapphire's Literary Breakthrough: Erotic Literacies, Feminist Pedagogies, Environmental Justice Perspectives,* ed. Elizabeth McNeil, Neal A. Lester, DoVeanna S. Fulton, and Lynette D. Myles (New York: Palgrave Macmillan, 2012).

21. Eng, "Tyler Perry's Mother, Inspiration for Madea, Dies," TVGuide.com, December 9, 2009, accessed June 6, 2017, *http://www.tvguide.com/news/tyler-perrys-mother-1012984/*; Tamura A.

Lomax and LeRhonda Manigault-Bryant, "Introduction," in *Womanist and Black Feminist Responses to Tyler Perry's Productions*, ed. LeRhonda Manigault-Bryant, Tamura A. Lomax, and Carol B. Duncan (Palgrave Macmillan, 2014), 2; Keith Josef Adkins, "Spike Lee Blasts a Hole Into Tyler Perry," accessed June 6, 2017, TheRoot.com, http://www.theroot.com/blog/on-the-dig/spike_lee_blasts_a_hole_into_tyler_perry/; Whitney Peoples, "(Re)Mediating Black Womanhood: Tyler Perry, Black Feminist Cultural Criticism, and the Politics of Legitimation," in Manigault-Bryant et al., *Womanist and Black Feminist Responses to Tyler Perry's Productions*, 151.

22. Peoples, 151, 150; *Diary of a Mad Black Woman*, directed by Tyler Perry (Lionsgate, 2005); *Why Did I Get Married Too?*, directed by Tyler Perry (Lionsgate, 2010).

23. *For Colored Girls*, directed by Tyler Perry (Lionsgate, 2010); Robin M. Boylorn and Mark C. Hopson. "Learning to Conquer Metaphysical Dilemmas: Womanist and Masculinist Perspectives on Tyler Perry's *For Colored Girls*," in *Black Women and Popular Culture: The Conversation Continues*, ed. Adria Y. Goldman, VaNatta S. Ford, Alexa A. Harris, and Natasha R. Howard, 89–108 (London: Lexington Books, 2014), 95.

24. Maureen Dowd, *Are Men Necessary? When Sexes Collide* (New York: G. P. Putnam's Sons, 2005); Rauch, "The Coming American Matriarchy," reason.com, January 15, 2008, accessed June 6, 2017, http://reason.com/archives/2008/01/15/the-coming-american-matriarchy/1; Sheelah Kolhatkar, "Book Review: 'The End of Men,' by Hanna Rosin," *Bloomberg*, September 13, 2012, accessed June 6, 2017, http://www.bloomberg.com/news/articles/2012–09–13/book-review-the-end-of-men-by-hanna-rosin; Jennifer Homans, "A Woman's Place: 'The End of Men,'" by Hanna Rosin, *New York Times*, September 13, 2012, accessed June 6, 2017, http://www.nytimes.com/2012/09/16/books/review/the-end-of-men-by-hanna-rosin.html. Also see "Women's Heels Conquering Tiny Men: Feminism According to Stock Photography," *New York Magazine*, accessed June 6, 2017, http://nymag.com/thecut/2013/11/feminism-according-to-stock-photography/slideshow/2013/11/22/feminism_accordingtostockphotography/heels-3/.

25. Elam, "How to Build a Man Bomb," *Spearhead*, May 13, 2010, accessed June 6, 2017, http://archive.is/8BS9J.

26. Adam Serwer and Katie J. M. Baker, "How Men's Rights Leader Paul Elam Turned Being a Deadbeat Dad into a Moneymaking Movement," Buzzfeed.com, February 5, 2015, accessed June 7, 2017, https://www.buzzfeed.com/adamserwer/how-mens-rights-leader-paul-elam-turned-being-a-deadbeat-dad?utm_term=.plp2rp6J1#.tiMnkMRNw; R. Tod Kelly, "The Masculine Mystique: Inside the Men's Rights Movement (MRM)," *Daily Beast*, October 20, 2013, accessed June 7, 2017, http://www.thedailybeast.com/the-masculine-mystique-inside-the-mens-rights-movement-mrm; Emmett Rensin, "The Internet Is Full of Men Who Hate Feminism. Here's What They're Like in Person," *Vox*, August 18, 2015, accessed June 18, 2017, https://www.vox.com/2015/2/5/7942623/mens-rights-movement.

27. Jaclyn Friedman, "A Look Inside the 'Men's Rights' Movement that Helped Fuel California Alleged Killer Elliot Rodger," *American Prospect*, October 24, 2013, accessed June 7, 2017, http://prospect.org/article/look-inside-mens-rights-movement-helped-fuel-california-alleged-killer-elliot-rodger; Mariah Blake, "Mad Men: Inside the Men's Rights Movement—and the Army of Misogynists and Trolls It Spawned," *Mother Jones*, January/February 2015, accessed June 7, 2015, http://www.motherjones.com/politics/2015/01/warren-farrell-mens-rights-movement-feminism-misogyny-trolls; Warren Farrell, "The Myth of Male Power: Why Men

Are the Disposable Sex," excerpt in *New Male Studies: An International Journal* 1, no. 2 (2012): 4; Michael Kimmel, *Angry White Men: American Masculinity at the End of an Era* (New York: Nation Books, 2013), 110; Blake, "Mad Men"; Kimmel, *Angry White Men*, 106, 99, 100, 102, 100–101.

28. Gary Costanza, "An Open Letter to Senator Kirsten Gillibrand," A Voice for Men, October 10, 2014, accessed June 7, 2017, http://www.avoiceformen.com/gynarchy/an-open-letter-to-senator-kirsten-gillibrand/; Kimmel, *Angry White Men*, 113; Kelly, "The Masculine Mystique"; "Big Manosphere Reveal: Matt Forney Was Ferdinand Bardamu," We Hunted the Mammoth, April 27, 2013, accessed June 7, 2017, http://www.wehuntedthemammoth.com/2013/04/27/big-manosphere-reveal-matt-forney-was-ferdinand-bardamu/; Blake, "Mad Men"; Southern Poverty Law Center, "Misogyny: The Sites," *The Intelligence Report*, March 1, 2012, https://www.splcenter.org/fighting-hate/intelligence-report/2012/misogyny-sites. For examples of advocacy of violence and acts of physical violence by MRAs, see: "Ferdinand Bardamu: 'Women Should Be Terrorized by Their Men,'" wehuntedthemammoth.com, August 15, 2012, accessed June 7, 2017, http://www.wehuntedthemammoth.com/2012/08/15/ferdinand-bardamu-women-should-be-terrorized-by-their-men-its-the-only-thing-that-makes-them-behave-better-than-chimps/; Blake, "Mad Men"; and Anna Theriault, "The Men's Rights Movement Taught Elliott Rodger Everything He Needed to Know," *Huffington Post*, May 25, 2014, accessed June 7, 2017, http://www.huffingtonpost.ca/anne-theriault/elliot-rodger-shooting_b_5386818.html.

29. Olga Khazan, "The Dark Psychology of the Sexist Internet Commenter," *Atlantic*, January 14, 2015, accessed June 7, 2017, http://www.theatlantic.com/technology/archive/2015/01/the-dark-psychology-of-the-sexist-internet-commenter/384497/; Kelly, "Masculine Mystique" Blake, "Mad Men"; Masculist Man, "Not So Hidden Matriarchy," June 2, 2010, accessed June 7, 2017, http://mensrightsboard.blogspot.com/2010/06/not-so-hidden-matriarchy.html; Ruth Graham, "How did a Men's Right's Supporter End Up in New Hampshire's Woman-Friendly Legislature?," April 27, 2017, Slate.com, accessed June 7, 2017, http://www.slate.com/blogs/xx_factor/2017/04/27/how_did_robert_fischer_of_men_s_rights_reddit_the_red_pill_end_up_in_new.html.

30. Claire Landsbaum, "Men's Rights Activists Are Finding a New Home with the Alt-Right," TheCut.com, December 4, 2016, accessed June 6, 2017, https://www.thecut.com/2016/12/mens-rights-activists-are-flocking-to-the-alt-right.html; Mike Robinson, "Clinton Symbolizes the Rise of the Matriarchy," *Troy Media*, October 2, 2016, accessed June 7, 2017, http://www.troymedia.com/2016/10/02/clinton-rise-matriarchy-trump-decline-patriarchy/; Mack Lamourex, "This Group of Straight Men Is Swearing Off Women," Vice.com, September 24, 2015, accessed June 7, 2017, http://www.vice.com/read/inside-the-global-collective-of-straight-male-separatists; Eyes on the Right, "MGTOWers are Ready for Hillary Clinton's Matriarchal Tyranny," Angrywhitemen.org, February 22, 2015, accessed June 7, 2017, https://angrywhitemen.org/2015/02/22/mgtowers-are-ready-for-hillary-clintons-matriarchal-tyranny/; Blythe Roberson, "Some Anticipated Changes After the Matriarchal Revolution," *New Yorker*, July 25, 2016; Amanda Marcotte, "Time Cover Pushes Sexist Women's-Success-Crushes-Men Metaphor," Talking Points Memo, January 16, 2014, accessed June 7, 2017, http://talkingpointsmemo.com/cafe/time-cover-pushes-sexist-women-s-success-crushes-men-metaphor. Examples abound; for instance, the popular podcast How Stuff Works, in their exploration of matriarchal societies, included a stock photograph on

their website of a pant-suited woman stepping on a man's head with her red, high-heeled shoe. The caption read: "Does a matriarchal society have to look like this? Perhaps not . . ." (Jessika Toothman, "What does a society run by women look like?," HowStuffWorks.com, http://science. howstuffworks.com/life/evolution/society-run-by-women.htm).

31. Barbarossaaaa, "Is the Right Sympathetic to the MRA?," AVoiceforMen.com, June 3, 2012, accessed June 7, 2017, http://www.avoiceformen.com/misandry/is-the-right-sympathetic-t o-the-mra/; Amanda Marcotte, "The Creepy Misogynist Movement that's Making Conservatives Even More Sexist," Alternet.org, December 24, 2014, accessed June 7, 2017, http://www.alternet. org/gender/creepy-misogynist-movement-thats-making-conservatives-even-more-sexist?pag ing=off&current_page=1#bookmark; Hannah Levintova, "Even Some Men's Rights Activists Are Worried About a Trump Presidency," *Mother Jones,* May 20, 2016, accessed June 7, 2017, http:// www.motherjones.com/politics/2016/05/mens-rights-movement-donald-trump-presidency; "Quiz: Who Said It, Donald Trump or a Men's Rights Activist?," TheCut.com, May 11, 2016, accessed June 7, 2017, http://nymag.com/thecut/2016/05/who-said-it-donald-trump-or-an-mra. html.

32. "Why Donald Trump's Veterans' Rally in Des Moines Was a Resounding Success," accessed June 7, 2017, returnofkings.com, http://www.returnofkings.com/78972/why-donal d-trumps-veterans-rally-in-des-moines-was-a-resounding-success; "Roosh: Hillary Will Usher in a Techno-Matriarchy and Ban Talking to Women in Public," wehuntedthemammoth.com, August 14, 2016, accessed June 7, 2017, http://www.wehuntedthemammoth.com/2016/08/14/ roosh-hillary-will-usher-in-a-techno-matriarchy-and-ban-talking-to-women-in-public/; Costanza, "Open Letter to Senator Kirsten Gillibrand"; Mark Landler, "How Hillary Clinton Became a Hawk," *New York Times,* April 21, 2016, accessed June 7, 2017, http://www.nytimes. com/2016/04/24/magazine/how-hillary-clinton-became-a-hawk.html.

33. "Gorka: The Alpha Males Are Back," Foxnews.com, accessed June 7, 2017, http://video. foxnews.com/v/5251654900001/?#sp=show-clips; Jack Hadfield, "The Men's Rights Movement: A Smart, Necessary Counterweight to Man-hating Feminism," Breitbart.com, August 2, 2016, http://www.breitbart.com/tech/2016/08/02/mens-rights-counterweight-feminism/; Claire Landsbaum, "Here's What Donald Trump's New Chief Strategist Thinks of Women and Minority Groups," *The Cut,* November 14, 2016, http://nymag.com/thecut/2016/11/what-steve-banno n-thinks-of-women-and-minority-groups.html; Andrew Kaczynski and Nathaniel Meyersohn, "Trump Campaign CEO Once Blasted 'Bunch of Dykes' from the 'Seven Sisters Schools,'" Buzzfeed News, August 29, 2016, https://www.buzzfeed.com/andrewkaczynski/trump-campaign-ce o-once-blasted-bunch-of-dykes-from-the-seve?utm_term=.ybPQWaAj8#.vmjrJEmbp; Milo, "Does Feminism Make Women Ugly?," Breitbart, Jly 26, 2015, http://www.breitbart.com/ big-government/2015/07/26/does-feminism-make-women-ugly/; Jamelle Bouie, "White Nationalism in the White House," Slate.com, November 14, 2017, http://www.slate.com/articles/news_ and_politics/politics/2016/11/donald_trump_s_pick_of_stephen_bannon_means_white_nationalism_is_coming.html; Claire Landsbaum, "Here's What Donald Trump's New Chief Strategist Thinks of Women and Minority Groups," TheCut.com, November 14, 2016, accessed June 7, 2017, http://nymag.com/thecut/2016/11/what-steve-bannon-thinks-of-women-and-minority-groups. html.

34. Audre Lorde, "The Master's Tools Will Never Dismantle the Master's House," in *This Bridge Called My Back: Writings By Radical Women of Color*, ed. Cherrie Moraga and Gloria Anzaldua (New York: Kitchen Table Press, 1983), 94.

35. Joan Gordon and Suzy McKee Charnas, "Closed Systems Kill: An Interview with Suzy McKee Charnas," *Science Fiction Studies* 26, no. 3 (November 1999), 461; Jill Lepore, *The Secret History of Wonder Woman* (New York: Vintage, 2014), 293.

36. Sophia Tesfaye, "#RepealThe19th: Donald Trump Supporters Tweet New Anthem After Nate Silver's Poll Shows He'd Win if Only men Voted," *Salon.com*, October 12, 2016, http://www.salon.com/2016/10/12/repealthe19th-donald-trump-supporters-tweet-new-anthem-after-nate-silvers-poll-shows-hed-win-if-only-men-voted/; 'Hey, fellas! Let's just take away their right to vote!," *WeHuntedtheMammoth.com,* September 18, 2010, http://www.wehuntedthemammoth.com/2010/09/18/hey-fellas-lets-just-take-away-their-right-to-vote/; Alec Tyson and Shiva Maniam, "Behind Trump's Victory: Divisions by Race, Gender, and Education," November 9, 2016, pewresearch.org, http://www.pewresearch.org/fact-tank/2016/11/09/behind-trumps-victory-divisions-by-race-gender-education/.

37. Pascoe, *Relations of Rescue: The Search for Female Moral Authority in the American West* (New York: Oxford University Press, 1990), xxiii.

38. Suzy McKee Charnas, *Motherlines* (New York: Berkeley, 1978), 79; Suzy McKee Charnas, *The Conqueror's Child* (New York: Tor Books, 1999), 45; Carol Farley Kessler, "Consider Her Ways: The Cultural Work of Charlotte Perkins Gilman's Pragmatopian Stories," in *Utopian and Science Fiction by Women: Worlds of Difference*, ed. Jane L. Donawerth and Carol A. Kolmerten, 126–36 (Syracuse, NY: Syracuse University Press, 1994), 127; Charlotte Perkins Gilman, *The Man-Made World: Or, Our Androcentric Culture* (New York: Charlton Co., 1911), e-book location 638; William Moulton Marston, "Why 100,000,000 Americans Read Comics," *American Scholar* 13, no. 1 (Winter 1943): 44; Brian Attebury, *The Fantasy Tradition in American Literature: From Irving to Le Guin* (Bloomington: Indiana University Press, 1980), vii, http://www.vogue.com/13301055/ursula-le-guin-steering-the-craft/.

BIBLIOGRAPHY

ARCHIVES

Gage, Matilda Joslyn. Papers. Schlesinger Library, Harvard University.

General Collection. Dibner Library Special Collections, Smithsonian Institutions.

General Collections. Newberry Library.

Library of Congress.

Palczewski, Catherine H. Suffrage Postcard Archive. University of Northern Iowa.

Special Collections. Newberry Library.

World's Columbian Exposition Records, 1891–1895. Special Collections Research Center, University of Chicago.

World's Fair Collection. Dibner Library Special Collections, Smithsonian Institutions.

COMIC BOOKS, MAGAZINES, AND NEWSPAPERS

Aberdeen Saturday Pioneer (SD)

All-Star Comics

American Prospect

Arizona Republic

The Atlantic

Black Enterprise

Bloomberg News

Chicago Daily Defender

Chicago Record

Chicago Standard

Chicago Tribune

Collier's

Comic Cavalcade

Design Quarterly

Ebony

Family Circle

Fayetteville Recorder (NY)

Fifth Estate

Film Comment

The Forerunner

Green Lantern

Hartford Journal (CT)
Hollywood Reporter
Inter Ocean (Chicago)
Ladies' Home Journal
Los Angeles Times
Milwaukee Sentinel
Mother Jones
Ms.
National Citizen and Ballot Box
The New Ingenue
The New Republic
Newsweek
The New Yorker
New York Times
New York Times Book Review
New York Times Magazine
off our backs
Parade
Paris Review
Product Digest
Reader's Digest
Sacramento Bee
San Francisco Pioneer
Saturday Review of Literature
Savoy
Sensation Comics
St. Petersburg Times (FL)
Superboy and the Legion of Super-heroes
Super-Friends
Supergirl
Time
TV Guide
USA Today
Vogue
The Wall Street Journal
Washington Post
Washington Post and Times Herald
The Woman Patriot
Wonder Woman
World's Fair Puck

FILMS AND TELEVISION SHOWS

Attack of the Fifty-Foot Woman. Directed by Nathan Juran. Woolner Brothers Pictures Inc., 1958.

Batman vs. Superman: Dawn of Justice. Directed by Zack Snyder. Warner Bros., 2016.

Cinderella. Directed by Clyde Geronimi and Wilfred Jackson. Walt Disney Productions, 1950.

Claudine. Directed by John Berry. Twentieth Century Fox, 1974.

Diary of a Mad Black Woman. Directed by Tyler Perry. Lionsgate, 2010.

For Colored Girls. Directed by Tyler Perry. Lionsgate, 2010.

Gone With the Wind. Directed by Victor Fleming, George Cukor, and Sam Wood. Warner Brothers, 1939.

The Help. Directed by Tate Taylor. Dreamworks, 2011.

Hurry Sundown. Directed by Otto Preminger. Otto Preminger Films, 1967.

I Can Do Bad All By Myself. Directed by Tyler Perry. Lionsgate, 2009.

Losing Isaiah. Directed by Stephen Gyllenhaal. Paramount Pictures, 1995.

The Manchurian Candidate. Directed by John Frankenheimer. M. C. Productions, 1962.

The Man in the Gray Flannel Suit. Directed by Nunnally Johnson. Twentieth Century Fox, 1955.

My Son John. Directed by Leo McCarey. Rainbow Productions, 1952.

The New Original Wonder Woman (series). Created by William Moulton Marston and Stanley Ralph Ross. Bruce Lansbury Productions, 1976–1979.

Notorious. Directed by Alfred Hitchcock. RKO Radio Pictures, 1946.

Precious. Directed by Lee Daniels. Lionsgate, 2009.

Psycho. Directed by Alfred Hitchcock. Shamley Productions, 1960.

A Raisin in the Sun. Directed by Daniel Petrie. Columbia Pictures, 1961.

Rebel Without a Cause. Directed by Nicholas Ray. Warner Brothers, 1955.

She. Directed by Robert Day. Associated British Picture Association, 1965.

The Silver Cord. Directed by John Cromwell. RKO Radio Pictures, 1933.

Sleeping Beauty. Directed by Clyde Geronimi. Walt Disney Productions, 1959.

Snow White and the Seven Dwarfs. Directed by William Cottrell, David Hand, Wilfred Jackson, Larry Morey, Perce Pearce, and Ben Sharpsteen. Walt Disney Productions, 1937.

To Kill a Mockingbird. Directed by Robert Mulligan. Universal International Pictures, 1962.

Vengeance of She. Directed by Cliff Owen. Hammer Films, 1968.

Why Did I Get Married Too? Directed by Tyler Perry. Lionsgate, 2010.

The Wiz. Directed by Sidney Lumet. Universal Pictures, 1978.

The Wizard of Oz. Directed by Victor Fleming, George Cukor, Mervyn LeRoy, Norman Taurog, and King Vidor. Warner Bros., 1939.

Wonder Woman. Directed by Patty Jenkins. Atlas Entertainment, 2017.

Wonder Woman. Directed by Vincent McEveety. Warner Bros. Television, 1974.

Xena: Warrior Princess (series). Created by Sam Raimi, John Schulian, and R. J. Stewart. Renaissance Pictures, 1995–2001.

PUBLISHED SOURCES

Abrahamsen, Valerie. "Essay in Honor of Marija Gimbutas: A Response." *Journal of Feminist Studies in Religion* 13, no. 2 (Fall 1997): 69–74.

Adams, Bluford. "'A Stupendous Mirror of Departed Empires': The Barnum Hippodrome and Circuses, 1874–1891." *American Literary History* 8, no. 1 (Spring 1996): 34–56.

Adovasio, J. M., Olga Soffer, and Jake Page. *The Invisible Sex: Uncovering the True Roles of Women in Prehistory.* New York: HarperCollins, 2007.

Alexander, Thomas G. "An Experiment in Progressive Legislation: The Granting of Woman Suffrage in Utah in 1870." *Utah Historical Quarterly* 38 (Winter 1970), accessed December 11, 2016. http://content.lib.utah.edu/utils/getfile/collection/USHSArchPub/id/6449/filename/6484.pdf.

Allen, Ann Taylor. *Feminism and Motherhood in Western Europe, 1890–1970: The Maternal Dilemma.* New York: Palgrave Macmillan, 2005.

Allen, Judith A. *The Feminism of Charlotte Perkins Gilman: Sexualities, History, Progressivism.* Chicago: University of Chicago Press, 2009.

Alpern, Stanley B. *Amazons of Black Sparta: The Women Warriors of Dahomey.* New York: New York University Press, 2011.

Alpert, Jane. "Mother Right: A New Feminist Theory." Atlanta Lesbian Feminist Alliance Archives, Duke University Library, accessed December 16, 2016. http://library.duke.edu/digitalcollections/wlmpc_wlmms01022/.

Anderson, Celia. "The Comedians of Oz." *Studies in American Humor* (Winter 1986–1987): 229–42.

Anderson, Kay. *Race and the Crisis of Humanism.* London: Routledge, 2006.

Anonymous, "Dethroning the Welfare Queen: The Rhetoric of Reform." *Harvard Law Review* 107, no. 8 (June 1994): 2013–30.

Anthony, Susan B. "The Moral Leadership of the Religious Press." Speech to the World's Congress of Representative Women, World's Columbian Exposition, May 27, 1893, accessed December 11, 2016. http://ecssba.rutgers.edu/docs/sbaexpo.html#may275/27.

———. "Organization Among Women as an Instrument in Promoting Liberty." Speech to the World's Congress of Representative Women, World's Columbian Exposi-

tion, May 20, 1893, accessed December 11, 2016. http://ecssba.rutgers.edu/docs/
sbaexpo.html#may20.

Arnold, C. D., and H. D. Higginbotham. *Official Views of the World's Columbian Exposition, Issued by the Department of Photography.* Chicago: Photo-Gravure Co., 1893.

Askari, Kaveh, Scott Curtis, Frank Gray, Louis Pelletier, Tami Williams, and Joshua Yumibe. *Performing New Media, 1890–1915.* Bloomington: Indiana University Press, 2015.

Association of Black Women Historians. "An Open Statement to the Fans of *The Help.*" Accessed December 19, 2016. http://aalbc.com/reviews/the_help_historical_context.html.

Atkinson, Ti-Grace. "Radical Feminism." In *Radical Feminism: A Documentary Reader.* Edited by Barbara A. Crow, 82–89. New York: New York University Press, 2000.

Attebury, Brian. *Decoding Gender in Science Fiction.* New York: Routledge, 2002.

———. *The Fantasy Tradition in American Literature: From Irving to Le Guin.* Bloomington: Indiana University Press, 1980.

———. "Oz." In *L. Frank Baum: The Wizard of Oz.* Edited by Michael Patrick Hearn, 278–304. New York: Schocken, 1983.

Attebury, Brian, and Veronica Hollinger. "Parabolas of Science Fiction." In *Parabolas of Science Fiction.* Edited by Brian Attebury and Veronica Hollinger, vii–xv. Middletown, CT: Wesleyan University Press, 2013.

Atwood, Margaret. *The Handmaid's Tale.* Toronto: McClelland and Stewart, 1985.

Auel, Jean M. *The Clan of the Cave Bear.* New York: Bantam Books, 1980.

———. *The Land of Painted Caves.* New York: Crown, 2011.

———. *The Mammoth Hunters.* New York: Crown, 1985.

———. *The Plains of Passage.* New York: Crown, 1990.

———. *The Shelters of Stone.* New York: Crown, 2002.

———. *The Valley of the Horses.* New York: Crown, 1982.

Aveling, F. "*Emotions of Normal People* (Review)." *Philosophy* 4, no. 13 (1929): 138–41.

Bachofen, Johann Jakob. *Myth, Religion, and Mother-Right.* Translated by Ralph Manheim. Princeton, NJ: Princeton University Press, 1967.

Ballard, Barbara J. "A People Without a Nation." *Chicago History* (Summer 1999), accessed December 11, 2016. http://www.chicagohs.org/documents/chicago-history-magazine/ChicagoHistory_Vo128No1_Ballard.pdf.

Bambara, Toni Cade. *The Salt-Eaters.* New York: Knopf, 2011.

Bammer, Angelika. *Partial Visions: Feminism and Utopianism in the 1970s.* New York: Routledge, 1991.

Bancroft, Hubert Howe. *The Book of the Fair: An Historical and Descriptive Presentation of the World's Science, Art, and Industry, as Viewed through the Columbian Exposition at Chicago in 1893.* Chicago: The Bancroft Co., Publishers, 1893.

Barr, Marleen. *Feminist Fabulation: Space/Postmodern Fiction.* Iowa City: University of Iowa Press, 1992.

Barrow, Craig and Diana Barrow. "*The Left Hand of Darkness*: Feminism for Men." *Mosaic: An Interdisciplinary Critical Journal* 20, no. 1 (Winter 1987): 83–96.

Bartkowski, Frances. *Feminist Utopias.* Lincoln: University of Nebraska Press, 1989.

Baum, L. Frank. *Dorothy and the Wizard in Oz* (1908). Oz: The Complete Collection. Maplewood Books, 2013. Kindle e-book.

———. *The Emerald City of Oz* (1910). Oz: The Complete Collection. Maplewood Books, 2013. Kindle e-book.

———. *Glinda of Oz* (1920). Oz: The Complete Collection. Maplewood Books, 2013. Kindle e-book.

———. *The Lost Princess of Oz* (1917). Oz: The Complete Collection. Maplewood Books, 2013. Kindle e-book.

———. *Marvelous Land of Oz* (1904). Oz: The Complete Collection. Maplewood Books, 2013. Kindle e-book.

———. *Ozma of Oz* (1907). Oz: The Complete Collection. Maplewood Books, 2013. Kindle e-book.

———. *The Patchwork Girl of Oz* (1913). Oz: The Complete Collection. Maplewood Books, 2013. Kindle e-book.

———. *The Road to Oz* (1909). Oz: The Complete Collection. Maplewood Books, 2013. Kindle e-book.

———. *Tik-Tok of Oz* (1914). Oz: The Complete Collection. Maplewood Books, 2013. Kindle e-book.

———. *Wizard of Oz* (1900). Oz: The Complete Collection. Maplewood Books, 2013. Kindle e-book.

———. "Yesterday at the Exposition." In *The Short Stories of L. Frank Baum,* 12–16. Victorville, CA: Wizard of Baum Publishing, 2013).

Bean, Kellie. *Post-Backlash Feminism and the Media Since Reagan-Bush.* Jefferson: McFarland, 2007.

Beard, Mary Ritter. *Woman's Work in Municipalities.* New York: D. Appleton, 1915. E-book accessed May 9, 2017, https://archive.org/details/womansworkinmunioobear.

Beauchamp, W. M. "Iroquois Women." *Journal of American Folklore* 13, no. 49 (April–June 1900): 81–91.

de Beauvoir, Simone. *The Second Sex.* New York: Penguin, 1972.

Beckwith, Osmond. "The Oddness of Oz." In *L. Frank Baum: The Wizard of Oz,* ed. Michael Patrick Hearn. New York: Schocken, 1983, 233–47.

Bederman, Gail. *Manliness and Civilization: A Cultural History of Gender and Race in the United States, 1880–1917.* Chicago: University of Chicago Press, 1996.

Beer, Janet, and Katherine Joslin, eds. *American Feminism: Key Source Documents, 1848–1920. Vol. 1: Suffrage.* New York: Routledge, 2002.

Behling, Laura L. *The Masculine Woman in America, 1890–1935*. Champaign: University of Illinois Press, 2001.

Bellisiles, Michael A. *1877: America's Year of Living Violently*. New York: New Press, 2010.

Benowitz, June Melby. *Days of Discontent: Women and Right-Wing Politics, 1933–1945*. DeKalb: Northern Illinois University Press, 2002.

Benshoff, Harry M., and Sean Griffin. *Queer Images: A History of Gay and Lesbian Film in America*. Lanham, MD: Rowman & Littlefield, 2006.

Bensonsmith, Dionne. "Jezebels, Matriarchs, and Welfare Queens: The Moynihan Report of 1965 and the Social Construction of African-American Women in Welfare Policy." In *Deserved and Entitled: Social Constructions and Public Policy*. Edited by Anne L. Schneider and Helen M. Ingram, 243–60. Albany: State University of New York Press, 2005.

Berger, Brigitte. "Introduction." *Mothers and Amazons*. New York: Doubleday, 1973.

Berkson, Dorothy. "'So We All Became Mothers': Harriet Beecher Stowe, Charlotte Perkins Gilman, and the New World of Women's Culture." In *Feminism, Utopia, and Narrative*. Edited by Libby Falk Jones and Sarah Webster Goodwin, 100–15. Knoxville: University of Tennessee Press, 1990.

Berlatsky, Noah. *Wonder Woman: Bondage and Feminism in the Marston/Peter Comics, 1941–1948*. New Brunswick, NJ: Rutgers University Press, 2015.

Bewley, Marius. "The Land of Oz: America's Great Good Place." In *L. Frank Baum: The Wizard of Oz*. Edited by Michael Patrick Hearn, 199–207. New York: Schocken, 1983.

Black, Cheryl. *Women of Provincetown: 1915–1922*. Tuscaloosa: University of Alabama Press, 2002.

Blaney, David L., and Naeem Inayatullah. *Savage Economics: Wealth, Poverty, and the Temporal Walls of Capitalism*. London: Routledge, 2010.

Bloch, Robert. *Psycho: A Novel*. New York: Overlook Press, 2010.

Bogle, Donald. *Toms, Coons, Mammies, Mulattoes, and Bucks*. New York: Bloomsbury Academic, 1973.

Boisseau, Tracy Jean. *White Queen: May French Sheldon and the Imperial Origins of American Feminist Identity*. Bloomington: Indiana University Press, 2004.

Bond, Jean Carey, and Patricia Peery. "Is the Black Male Castrated?" In *The Black Woman: An Anthology*. New York: New American Library, 1970. Kindle e-book.

Boylorn, Robin M., and Mark C. Hopson. "Learning to Conquer Metaphysical Dilemmas: Womanist and Masculinist Perspectives on Tyler Perry's *For Colored Girls*." In *Black Women and Popular Culture: The Conversation Continues*. Edited by Adria Y. Goldman, VaNatta S. Ford, Alexa A. Harris, and Natasha R. Howard, 89–108. London: Lexington Books, 2014.

Brammer, Leila R. *Excluded from Suffrage History: Matilda Joslyn Gage, Nineteenth-Century American Feminist*. Westport, CT: Praeger, 2000.

Breines, Wini. *Young, White, and Miserable: Growing Up Female in the Fifties.* Boston: Beacon, 1992.

Broad, Katherine. "Race, Reproduction, and the Failures of Feminism in Mary Bradley Lane's *Mizora.*" *Tulsa Studies in Women's Literature* 28, no. 2 (Fall 2009): 247–66.

Brooks, Daphne A. *Bodies in Dissent: Spectacular Performances of Race and Freedom, 1850–1910.* Durham, NC: Duke University Press, 2006.

Brown, Kathleen. *Good Wives, Nasty Wenches, and Anxious Patriarchs: Gender, Race, and Power in Colonial Virginia.* Chapel Hill: University of North Carolina Press, 1996.

Brown, Rita Mae. "Roxanne Dunbar: How a Female Heterosexual Serves the Interests of Male Supremacy." In *Radical Feminism: A Documentary Reader.* Edited by Barbara A. Crow, 395–400. New York: New York University Press, 2000.

Buhle, Mary Jo. *Women and American Socialism, 1870–1920.* Urbana: University of Illinois Press, 1981.

Burnham, Claire Louise. *Sweet Clover: A Romance of the White City.* Boston: Houghton, Mifflin, 1894.

Burrell, Christopher, and James Wermers. "Why Does *Precious* Have to Lighten Up or Shuffle? Teaching with Lee Daniels's 'Adaptation.'" In *Sapphire's Literary Breakthrough: Erotic Literacies, Feminist Pedagogies, Environmental Justice Perspectives.* Edited by Elizabeth McNeil, Neal A. Lester, DoVeanna S. Fulton, and Lynette D. Myles, 211–24. New York: Palgrave Macmillan, 2012.

Burton, Richard. *A Mission to Gelele, King of Dahome, with Notices of the So-Called Amazons, the Grand Customs, the Yearly Customs, the Human Sacrifices, the Present State of the Slave Trade, and the Negro's Place in Nature.* London: Tylston and Edwards, 1863.

Cade, Toni, ed. "On the Issue of Roles." In *The Black Woman: An Anthology.* New York: New American Library, 1970. Kindle e-book.

———. "The Pill: Genocide or Liberation?" In *The Black Woman: An Anthology.* New York: New American Library, 1970. Kindle e-book.

———. "Preface." In *The Black Woman: An Anthology.* New York: New American Library, 1970. Kindle e-book.

Cameron, William E. *The World's Fair, Being a Pictorial History of the Columbian Exposition, containing a Complete History of the World-Renowned Exposition at Chicago; Captivating Descriptions of the Magnificent Buildings and Marvelous Exhibits, such as Works of Art, Textile Fabrics, Machinery, Natural Products, the Latest Inventions, Discoveries, Etc., Etc.* Chicago: Chicago Publication & Lithograph Co., 1893.

Campbell, Karlyn Kohrs. *Women Public Speakers in the United States, 1800–1925.* Westport, CT: Greenwood Press, 1993.

Capp, Fran, and Frank Borzellieri. *It Happened in New York.* Guilford, CT: Globe Pequot Press, 2007.

Ceplair, Larry, ed. *Charlotte Perkins Gilman: A Nonfiction Reader.* New York: Columbia University Press, 1991.

Chandler, Arthur, and Marvin R. Nathan. *The Fantastic Fair: The Story of the California Midwinter International Exposition, Golden Gate Park, San Francisco, 1894.* San Francisco: Pogo Press, 1993.

Charnas, Suzy McKee. *The Conqueror's Child.* New York: Tor Books, 1999.

———. *The Furies.* New York: Tor Books, 1994.

———. *Motherlines.* New York: Berkeley, 1978.

———. *Walk to the End of the World.* New York: Berkeley, 1976.

Chesler, Phyllis. "The 'Amazon Legacy.'" In *Wonder Woman.* Edited by Gloria Steinem and Phyllis Chesler, n.p. New York: Holt, Rinehart and Winston, 1972.

The Chicago Record's History of the World's Fair. Chicago Daily News Co., October 1893.

Chicago Tribune. From Peristyle to Plaisance, with a Short History of the World's Columbian Exposition, Chicago, 1893. Chicago: *Chicago Tribune,* 1893.

Chodorow, Nancy. *Feminism and Psychoanalytic Theory.* New Haven, CT: Yale University Press, 1989.

Christ, Carol P. A Different World: The Challenge of the Work of Marija Gimbutas to the Dominant World-View of Western Cultures." *Journal of Feminist Studies in Religion* 12, no. 2 (Fall 1996): 53–66.

———. "Introduction: The Legacy of Marija Gimbutas." *Journal of Feminist Studies in Religion* 12, no. 2 (Fall 1996): 31–35.

———. "Reading Marija Gimbutas." *NWSA Journal* 12, no. 1 (Spring 2000): 169–73.

Clark, Joanna. "Motherhood." In *The Black Woman: An Anthology.* New York: New American Library, 1970. Kindle e-book.

Clawson, Rosalee A., and Yakuya Trice. "Poverty as We Know It: Media Portrayals of the Poor." *Public Opinion Quarterly* 64 (2000): 53–64.

Cleaver, Eldridge. *Soul on Ice.* New York: Random House, 1968.

Cohen, Eugene N., and Eames, Edwin. *Cultural Anthropology.* Little, Brown, 1982.

Collection of Watercolor Prints of the World's Columbian Exposition, Special Collections. Newberry Library, Chicago.

Collins, Patricia Hill. *Black Feminist Thought: Knowledge, Consciousness, and Empowerment.* 2nd edition. New York: Routledge, 2000.

The Columbian Gallery; a Portfolio of Photographs from the World's Fair, including the Chief Palaces, Interiors, Statuary, Architectural and Scenic Groups, Characters, Typical Exhibits, and Marvels of the Midway Plaisance. Chicago: Werner Co., 1894.

Columbus Portfolio of Midway Types. Chicago: American Engraving Co., 1893.

Combahee River Collective. "A Black Feminist Statement." In *All the Women Are White, All the Blacks Are Men, But Some of Us Are Brave.* Edited by Akasha Gloria Hull, Patricia Bell Scott, and Barbara Smith. New York: Feminist Press, 1982. Kindle e-book.

Cossman, Brenda. *Sexual Citizens: The Legal and Cultural Regulation of Sex and Belonging.* Stanford, CA: Stanford University Press, 2007.

Cott, Nancy. *The Grounding of Modern Feminism*. New Haven, CT: Yale University Press, 1989.

Crew, Danny O., ed. *Suffragist Sheet Music: An Illustrated Catalogue of Published Music Associated with the Women's Rights and Suffrage Movement in America, 1795–1921, with Complete Lyrics*. Jefferson, NC: McFarland, 2002.

Crow, Barbara A. "Introduction." In *Radical Feminism: A Documentary Reader*. Edited by Barbara A. Crow, 1–10. New York: New York University Press, 2000.

Cuordileone, Kyle A. *Manhood and American Political Culture in the Cold War*. New York: Routledge, 2005.

Dalzell, Archibald. *The History of Dahomy, an Inland Kingdom of Africa*. London, 1793. E-book. https://archive.org/details/historydahomyanoodalzgoog.

Daniels, Les. *Wonder Woman: The Complete History*. New York: Chronicle Books, 2004.

Davies, Catherine Hillary Owen, and Claire Brewster. *South American Independence: Gender, Politics, Text*. Liverpool: Liverpool University Press, 2007.

Davin, Eric Leif. *Partners in Wonder: Women and the Birth of Science Fiction, 1926–1965*. New York: Lexington Books, 2006.

Davis, Angela. *Women, Race and Class*. New York: Vintage Books, 2011.

Davis, Cynthia. *Charlotte Perkins Gilman: A Biography*. Stanford, CA: Stanford University Press, 2010.

de Charlevoix, Pierre Francois Xavier. "The Dilemmas of New France." In *Voices of the American Past. Vol. 1*. Edited by Raymond Hyser and J. Arndt, 34–37. Belmont, CA: Wadsworth Publishing, 2011.

Dedicatory and Opening Ceremonies of the World's Columbian Exposition. Chicago: Stone, Kastle, and Painter, 1893.

Delap, Lucy. *The Feminist Avant-Garde: Transatlantic Encounters of the Early Twentieth Century*. Cambridge: Cambridge University Press, 2007.

De Wit, Wim, James Gilbert, Robert W. Rydell, Neil Harris, and the Chicago Historical Society. *Grand Illusions: Chicago's World's Fair of 1893*. Chicago: Sewall Co., 1993.

Diaz, Rosalina. "The Amazon of Matinino: A Personal Legacy of Female Empowerment in the Greater Antilles." *Journal of the Motherhood Initiative* 3, no. 2 (2012): 241–48.

Dighe, Ranjit S. *The Historian's Wizard of Oz: Reading L. Frank Baum's Classic as a Political and Monetary Allegory*. Santa Barbara, CA: Praeger, 2002.

Dines, Martin, and Timotheus Vermeulen. "Introduction: New Suburban Stories." In *New Suburban Stories*. Edited by Dines and Vermeulen, 1–16. London: Bloomsbury, 2013.

Dollard, John. *Caste and Class in a Southern Town*. Madison: University of Wisconsin Press, 1988.

Donaldson, Laura E. "The Eve of De-Struction: Charlotte Perkins Gilman and the Feminist Re-Creation of Paradise." *Women's Studies* 16 (1989): 373–87.

Donawerth, Jane. *Frankenstein's Daughters: Women Writing Science Fiction.* Syracuse, NY: Syracuse University Press, 1997.

Donawerth, Jane, and Carol A. Kolmerten. "Introduction." In *Utopian and Science Fiction by Women: Worlds of Difference.* Edited by Jane A. Donawerth and Carol A. Kolmerten, 1–14. Syracuse, NY: Syracuse University Press, 1994.

Douglas, Susan. *Where the Girls Are.* New York: Three Rivers Press, 1995.

Douglas, Susan, and Meredith Michaels. *The Mommy Myth: The Idealization of Motherhood and How It Has Undermined All Women.* New York: Free Press, 2004.

Dowd, Maureen. *Are Men Necessary? When Sexes Collide.* New York: G. P. Putnam's Sons, 2005.

The Dream City: A Portfolio of Views of the WCE, Comprising its marvelous architectural, sculptural, artistic, mechanical, agricultural, industrial, archaeological, ethnological, historical and scenic attractions. St. Louis: N. D. Thompson Publishing, 1893.

DuBois, Ellen Carol. *Feminism and Suffrage: The Emergence of an Independent Women's Movement in America, 1848–1869.* Ithaca, NY: Cornell University Press, 1978.

DuBois, Ellen Carol, and Richard Candida Smith, eds. *Elizabeth Cady Stanton: Feminist as Thinker.* New York: New York University Press, 2007.

DuPlessis, Rachel Blau. "The Feminist Apologues of Lessing, Piercy, and Russ." *Frontiers* 4, no. 1 (Spring 1979): 1–8.

Dybwad, G. L., and Joy V. Bliss, eds. *White City Recollections: A Young Man's World's Fair Adventure with His Father.* Albuquerque: The Book Stops Here, 2003.

Echols, Alice. *Daring to Be Bad: Radical Feminism in America, 1967–1975.* Minneapolis: University of Minnesota Press, 1989.

Economic Report of the President. Washington: US Government Printing Office, February 1988.

Edwards, Eric. "Matriarchy, Mother Right, and the Vindication of the Female Principle." In *Eric Edwards Collected Works,* July 7, 2013, accessed December 10, 2016. https://ericwedwards.wordpress.com/2013/07/07/matriarchy-mother-right-and-vindication-of-the-female-principle-3/.

Eller, Cynthia. *Gentlemen and Amazons: The Myth of Matriarchal Prehistory, 1861–1900.* Berkeley: University of California Press, 2011.

———. *The Myth of Matriarchal Prehistory: Why an Invented Past Won't Give Women a Future.* Boston: Beacon Press, 2000.

Elster, Ernestine S. "Marija Gimbutas, 1921–1994." *American Journal of Archaeology* 98, no. 4 (October 1994): 755–57.

Engels, Friedrich. *Origin of the Family, Private Property, and the State.* 1884. https://www.marxists.org/archive/marx/works/download/pdf/origin_family.pdf.

Engels, "Socialism: Utopian and Scientific." 1880. https://www.marxists.org/archive/marx/works/1880/soc-utop/.

Erisman, Fred. "L. Frank Baum and the Progressive Dilemma." *American Quarterly* 20, no. 3 (Autumn 1968): 616–23.

Etherington, Norman, ed. *The Annotated She: A Critical Edition of H. Rider Haggard's Victorian Romance Novel.* Bloomington: Indiana University Press, 1991.

Evans, James. "Joseph Francois Lafitau: A Disciple of Herodotus Amongst the Iroquois," https://www.academia.edu/6171003/Lafitau.

Evans, Taliesen. *All about the MidWinter Fair, San Francisco.* 2nd edition. San Francisco: W. B. Bancroft & Co., 1894.

Falkner, Julie. "Molly Brant, Mohawk Loyalist." *History's Women,* http://www.historys-women.com/earlyamerica/mollybrant.htm.

Faludi, Susan. *Backlash: The Undeclared War Against American Women.* New York: Crown, 1991.

Feest, Christian F. "Father Lafitau as Ethnographer of the Iroquois." *Native American Studies* 15, no. 2 (2001): 19–25.

Feldman, Anne E. "Women and the Press at the 1893 World's Columbian Exposition." In *World's Fair Notes: A Woman Journalist Views Chicago's 1893 Columbian Exposition,* by Marian Shaw, 97–99. St. Paul: Pogo Press, 1992.

Feldstein, Ruth. *Motherhood in Black and White: Race and Sex in American Liberalism, 1930–1965.* Ithaca, NY: Cornell University Press, 2000.

Fenton, William N. "Introduction" to Lewis Henry Morgan, *League of the Haudenosaunee: A Classic Study of an American Tribe with Original Illustrations.* New York: Citadel Press, 1984.

Fillingim, David. "By the Gods—Or Not: Religious Plurality in *Xena: Warrior Princess.*" *Journal of Religion and Popular Culture* 21, no. 3 (Fall 2009): n.p.

Firestone, Shulamith. "The Dialectic of Sex." In *Radical Feminism: A Documentary Reader.* Edited by Barbara A. Crow, 90–97. New York: New York University Press, 2000.

Fishbane, Jonathan David. *Mother-Right, Myth, and Renewal: The Thought of Johann Jakob Bachofen and Its Relationship to the Perception of Cultural Decadence in the Nineteenth Century.* PhD diss., University of Michigan, 1981.

Flexner, Eleanor, and Ellen Fitzpatrick. *Century of Struggle, The Woman's Rights Movement in the United States.* Cambridge, MA: Harvard University Press, 1996.

Flinn, John J. *Official Guide to the Midway Plaisance.* Chicago: The Columbian Guide Co., 1893.

Forbes, Caille F. *Introducing Bert Williams: Burnt Cork, Broadway, and the Story of America's First Black Star.* New York: Basic Books, 2008.

Fortes, Meyer. *Kinship and Social Order: The Legacy of Lewis Henry Morgan.* Chicago: Aldine, 1969.

Frank, Susanne. "Gender Trouble in Paradise: Suburbia Reconsidered." In *Gender in an Urban World.* Edited by Judith N. DeSana, 127–48. Bingley, UK: Emerald Group Publishing, 2008.

Frazier, E. Franklin. *The Negro Family in the United States.* Chicago: University of Chicago Press, 1939.

French Sheldon, May. "An African Expedition." Reprinted in *The Congress of Women: Held in the Women's Building, World's Columbian Exposition, Chicago, U.S.A., 1893.* Edited by Mary Kavanaugh Oldham Eagle. Chicago: Monarch Book Co., 1894.

———. "Customs Among the Natives of East Africa, from Teita to Kilimegalia, with Special Reference to Their Women and Children." *Journal of the Anthropological Institute of Great Britain and Ireland* 21 (1892): 358–90.

———. *Sultan to Sultan: Adventures Among the Masai and Other Tribes of East Africa.* Boston: Arena Publishing, 1892.

Friedan, Betty. *The Feminine Mystique.* New York: Laurel, 1963.

Fromm, Erich. "The Theory of Mother Right and Its Relevance to Social Psychology." In *Erich Fromm: Love, Sexuality, and Matriarchy—About Gender.* Edited by Rainer Funk. New York: International Publishing, 1997.

Gage, Matilda Joslyn. "To the Daughters of 1986." In Sally Roesch Wagner, *A Time of Protest: Suffragists Challenge the Republic, 1870–1887, 107–11.* Aberdeen, SD: Sky Carrier Press, 1988.

———. *Women, Church and State.* New York: The Truth Seeker Co., 1893.

Gasmna, Daniel. *The Scientific Origins of National Socialism.* London: McDonald, 1971.

Geary, Daniel. *Beyond Civil Rights: The Moynihan Report and Its Legacy.* Philadelphia: University of Pennsylvania Press, 2015.

General Laws, Memorials, and Resolutions of the Territory of Wyoming, c. 31. Cheyenne, WY: S. Allen Bristol, Public Printer, Tribune Office, 1869.

Giddings, Paula. *When and Where I Enter: The Impact of Black Women on Race and Sex in America.* New York: W. Morrow, 1984.

Gilbert, James. *Men in the Middle: Searching for Masculinity in the 1950s.* Chicago: University of Chicago Press, 2005.

Gilbert, Sandra M., and Susan Gubar. *No Man's Land: The Place of the Woman Writer in the Twentieth Century.* Vol. 2: *Sexchanges.* New Haven, CT: Yale University Press, 1989.

Gillmore, Inez Haynes. *Angel Island.* London: G. Bell, 1914. Project Gutenberg e-book, 2009. http://www.gutenberg.org/files/4637/4637-h/4637-h.htm.

Gilman, Charlotte Perkins. *In This Our World.* Oakland, CA: McCombs & Vaughan, 1893.

———. *The Living of Charlotte Perkins Gilman: An Autobiography.* Madison: University of Wisconsin Press, 2014.

———. *The Man-Made World: Or, Our Androcentric Culture.* New York: Charlton Co., 1911.

———. *Moving the Mountain.* In *The Herland Trilogy.* New York: Start Publishing, 2012.

————. *Unpunished: A Mystery*. New York: Feminist Press at CUNY, 1998.

————. "Why I Wrote 'The Yellow Wallpaper.'" *Forerunner* 4, no. 10 (October 1913). https://csivc.csi.cuny.edu/history/files/lavender/whyyw.html.

————. *Women and Economics: A Study of the Economic Relation Between Men and Women as a Factor in Social Evolution*. Boston: Small, Maynard, 1898.

————. *The Yellow Wallpaper*. New York: Bedford/St. Martin's, 1998.

Gimbutas, Marija. *The Civilization of the Goddess: The World of Old Europe*. Edited by Joan Marler. San Francisco: HarperSanFrancisco, 1991.

————. *The Goddesses and Gods of Old Europe, 6500–3500 B.C.: Myths and Cult Images*. London: Thames and Hudson, 1974. Reprint, Berkeley: University of California Press, 2007.

————. *The Language of the Goddess*. London: Thames and Hudson, 1989.

————. *The Living Goddesses*. Berkeley: University of California Press, 2001.

Gingrich, Newt. *To Renew America*. New York: HarperCollins, 1999.

Ginsburg, Carl. *Race and Media: The Enduring Life of the Moynihan Report*. New York: Institute for Media Analysis, 1989.

Gitlin, Marty. *Wounded Knee Massacre*. Denver: Greenwood Press, 2011.

Golden, Catherine J. "Looking Backward: Rereading Gilman in the Early Twenty-First Century." In *Charlotte Perkins Gilman: New Texts, New Contexts*. Edited by Jennifer S. Tuttle and Carol Farley Kessler, 44–68. Columbus: Ohio State University, 2011.

Goldman, Adria Y., Vanetta S. Ford, Alexa A. Harris, and Natasha R. Howard, eds. *Black Women in Popular Culture: The Conversation Continues*. New York: Rowman and Littlefield, 2014.

Goodall, Jane. *Performance and Evolution in the Age of Darwin: Out of the Natural Order*. London: Routledge, 2002.

Goode, G. Brown. *First Draft of a Classification for the World's Columbian Exposition*. Washington, DC: Government Printing Office, 1893.

Gordon, Joan, and Suzy McKee Charnas. "Closed Systems Kill: An Interview with Suzy McKee Charnas," *Science Fiction Studies* 26, no. 3 (November 1999): 447–68.

Gordon, Linda. *Pitied But Not Entitled: Single Mothers and the History of Welfare, 1890–1935*. New York: Free Press, 1994.

Gossman, Lionel. "Orpheus Philologus: Bachofen versus Mommsen on the Study of Antiquity." *Transactions of the American Philosophical Society* 73, no. 5 (1983): 1–89.

Gottner-Abendroth, Heide. "Why the Term Matriarchy?" International Academy HAGIA, 2009, ahttp://www.hagia.de/en/matriarchy/why-the-term-matriarchy.html.

Gow, Iain. "Review, *From the Realm of the Ancestors*." *Canadian Journal of Political Science* 31, no. 4 (December 1998): 837–39.

Green, Gretchen L. "Gender and the Longhouse: Iroquois Women in a Changing Culture." In *Women and Freedom in Early America*. Edited by Larry D. Eldridge, 7–25. New York: New York University Press, 1997.

Grube, Melinda. "Religious Freedom Room." Matilda Joslyn Gage Foundation. http://www.matildajoslyngage.org/gage-home/religious-freedom-room/.

Haase, Wolfgang, and Reinhold Mayer, eds. *European Images of the Americas and the Classical Tradition*. Berlin: De Gruyter, 1993.

Haggard, H. Rider. *Ayesha: The Return of She*. Mineola, NY: Dover Publications, 2012.

———. *She: A History of Adventure*. IndoEuropeanPublishing.com e-book, 2010.

Handy, M. P. *World's Columbian Exposition Official Catalogue*. Chicago: W. B. Conkey Co., 1893.

Hanley, Tim. *Wonder Woman Unbound: The Curious History of the World's Most Famous Superheroine*. Chicago: Chicago Review Press, 2014.

Haraway, Donna. "A Manifesto for Cyborgs: Science, Technology, and Socialist Feminism in the 1980s." In *Coming to Terms: Feminism, Theory, Politics*. Edited by Elizabeth Weed, 173–204. New York: Routledge, 2013.

Harper's Weekly. Pictorial History of the Chicago Fair. New York: May 13, 1893.

Harris, Marvin. *The Rise of Anthropological Theory: A History of Theories of Culture*. Lanham, MD: AltaMira Press, 2001.

Harris, Trudier. *From Mammies to Militants: Domestics in Black American Literature*. Philadelphia: Temple University Press, 1982.

Harris-Perry, Melissa. *Sister Citizen: Shame, Stereotypes, and Black Women in America*. New Haven, CT: Yale University Press, 2011.

Harvey, David Allen. "Living Antiquity: Lafitau's *Moeurs des Sauvages Amériquains* and the Religious Roots of the Enlightenment Science of Man." *Proceedings of the Western Society for French History* 36 (2008): 75–92.

Hausman, Bernice L. "Sex Before Gender: CPG and the Evolutionary Paradigm of Utopia." *Feminist Studies* 24, no. 3 (Autumn 1998): 488–510.

Hearn, Michael Patrick. "The Wizard Behind the Plate. In *Baum's Road to Oz: The Dakota Years*. Edited by Nancy Koupal, 5–44. Pierre: South Dakota State Historical Society Press, 2000.

Hewitt, Marsha Aileen. *Critical Theory of Religion: A Feminist Analysis*. Minneapolis: Fortress Press, 1995.

Hiltz, Roxane. "Reviewed Work: *Mothers and Amazons*." *Contemporary Sociology* 4, no. 1 (January 1975): 669–80.

Hinsley, Curtis. "Ambiguous Legacy: Daniel Garrison Brinton at the International Congress of Anthropology." In *Coming of Age in Chicago: The 1893 World's Fair and the Coalescence of American Anthropology*, 99–109. Edited by Curtis M Hinsley and David R. Wilcox (Lincoln: University of Nebraska Press, 2016).

———. "Anthropology as Education and Entertainment: Frederic Ward Putnam at the

Fair." In *Coming of Age in Chicago: The 1893 World's Fair and the Coalescence of American Anthropology*, 1–77. Edited by Curtis M. Hinsley and David R. Wilcox (Lincoln: University of Nebraska Press, 2016).

Holmes, Rachel. *The Hottentot Venus: The Life and Death of Saartjie Baartman*. London: Bloomsbury, 2007.

hooks, bell. *Ain't I a Woman: Black Women and Feminism*. New York: Routledge, 2015.

———. *Feminist Theory: From Margin to Center*. Boston: South End Press, 1980.

Howard, Sidney *The Silver Cord: A Comedy in Three Acts*. New York: Samuel French, 1926.

Hudak, Jennifer. "The 'Social Inventor': Charlotte Perkins Gilman and the (Re)Production of Perfection." *Women's Studies* 32 (2003): 455–77.

Hull, Akasha Gloria, Patricia Bell Scott, and Barbara Smith, eds. *All the Women Are White, All the Blacks Are Men, But Some of Us Are Brave*. New York: Feminist Press, 1982.

Hull, Akasha Gloria, and Barbara Smith. "Introduction: The Politics of Black Women's Studies." In *All the Women Are White, All the Blacks Are Men, But Some of Us Are Brave: Black Women's Studies*. 2nd edition. Edited by Akasha Gloria T. Hull, Patricia Bell Scott, and Barbara Smith. New York: Feminist Press, 2015. Kindle e-book.

In Remembrance of the Midwinter International Exposition, San Francisco, California. San Francisco, 1894.

Irwin, Inez Haynes. *Amazons and Angels*. New York: Doubleday, Doran, 1933.

Islas, Alfredo Ruiz. "Hernán Cortés y la Isla California." *Iberoamericana* 27 (September 2007): 39–58.

Jacknis, Ira. "Refracting Images: Anthropological Display at the Chicago World's Fair, 1893." In *Coming of Age in Chicago: The 1893 World's Fair and the Coalescence of American Anthropology*. Edited by Curtis M. Hinsley and David R. Wilcox, 261–336. Lincoln: University of Nebraska Press, 2016.

Jackson, Jacquelyne. "Black Women in a Racist Society." In *Racism and Mental Health*. Edited by Charles Willie, Bernard Kramer, and Bentram Brown, 185–268. Pittsburgh: University of Pittsburgh Press, 1972.

Jackson, Kenneth T. *Crabgrass Frontier: The Suburbanization of America*. New York: Oxford University Press, 1985.

Jacobs, Naomi. "Reviewed Works: *Mizora: A Prophecy* by Mary E. Bradley Lane and Jean Pfaelzer." *Utopian Studies* 12, no. 1 (2001): 210–12.

Jastrow, Joseph. "The Pathology of Emotion." *The Saturday Review*, May 4, 1929, 978. http://www.unz.org/Pub/SaturdayRev-1929may04–00978a03?View=PDF.

Jenks, Tudor. *The Century World's Fair Book for Boys and Girls, Being the Adventures of Harry and Philip with their Tutor, Mr. Douglass at the World's Columbian Exposition*. New York: Century Co., 1893.

Jensen, Joan M. "All Pink Sisters: The War Department and the Feminist Movement in the 1920s." In *Decades of Discontent: The Women's Movement, 1920–1940.* Edited by Lois Scharf and Joan M. Jensen, 199-222. Boston: Northeastern University Press, 1987.

Johnson, Lyndon B. "To Fulfill These Rights: Remarks of the President at Howard University." June 4, 1965. http://www.presidency.ucsb.edu/ws/?pid=27021.

Johnson, W. Fletcher. *The Red Record of the Sioux: The Life of Sitting Bull and the History of the Indian War.* New York: Union Publishing House, 1891.

Johnston, Georgia. "Three Men in *Herland:* Why They Enter the Text." *Utopian Studies* no. 4 (1991): 55–59.

Jones, Libby Falk, and Sarah Webster Goodwin, eds. *Feminism, Utopia, and Narrative.* Knoxville: University of Tennessee Press, 1990.

Jones, Sara Gwenllian. "Histories, Fictions, and *Xena: Warrior Princess.*" *Television and New Media* 1, no. 4 (November 2000): 403–18.

Jordan, June. "Memo to Daniel Patrick Moynihan." In June Jordan, *New Days: Poems of Exile and Return.* New York: Emerson Hall, 1974.

Kandiyoti, Deniz. "Bargaining with Patriarchy." *Gender and Society* 3 (Sept. 1988): 274–90.

Kaufman, Polly. *National Parks and the Woman's Voice: A History.* Albuquerque: University of New Mexico Press, 2006.

Keats, John. *The Crack in the Picture Window.* Boston: HoughtonMifflin, 1957.

Kerber, Linda. *Women of the Republic: Intellect and Ideology in Revolutionary America.* Chapel Hill: University of North Carolina Press, 1980.

Kessler, Carol Farley. *Charlotte Perkins Gilman: Her Progress Toward Utopia with Selected Writings.* Syracuse, NY: Syracuse University Press, 1995.

———. "Consider Her Ways: The Cultural Work of Charlotte Perkins Gilman's Pragmatopian Stories." In *Utopian and Science Fiction by Women: Worlds of Difference.* Edited by Jane L. Donawerth and Carol A. Kolmerten, 126–36. Syracuse, NY: Syracuse University Press, 1994.

Kimmel, Michael. *Angry White Men: American Masculinity at the End of an Era.* New York: Nation Books, 2013.

Kipnis, Ira. *The American Socialist Movement, 1897–1912.* Chicago: Haymarket Books, 2005.

Kirby, W. H. "The Universal Brotherhood of Humanity." *Theosophic Messenger* 12 (March 1911): 344–45.

Klaus, Alisa. "Depopulation and Race Suicide: Maternalism and Pronatalist Ideologies in France and the United States." In *Mothers of a New World: Maternalist Politics and the Origins of Welfare States.* Edited by Seth Koven and Sonya Michel, 188–212. New York: Routledge, 1993.

Kleinbaum, Abby. "Introduction." In *Baum's Road to Oz: The Dakota Years*. Edited by Nancy Koupal, 1–4. Pierre: South Dakota State Historical Society, 2000.

——. "On the Road to Oz: L. Frank Baum as Western Editor." In *Baum's Road to Oz: The Dakota Years*, ed. Nancy Koupal (Pierre: South Dakota State Historical Society Press, 2000): 49–71.

——. *Our Landlady*. Lincoln: University of Nebraska Press, 1999.

——. *The War Against the Amazons*. New York: New Press, 1983.

——. "Wonderful Wizard of the West: L. Frank Baum in South Dakota, 1888–1891." *Great Plains Quarterly* (1989). http://digitalcommons.unl.edu/cgi/viewcontent. cgi?article=1387&context=greatplainsquarterly.

Koven, Seth, and Sonya Michel. "Womanly Duties: Maternalist Politics and the Origins of Welfare States in France, Germany, Great Britain, and the United States, 1880–1920." *American Historical Review* 95, no. 4 (Oct. 1990): 1076–1108.

Koven, Seth, and Sylvia Michel, eds. *Mothers of a New World: Maternalist Politics and the Origins of Welfare States*. New York: Routledge, 1993.

Kroeber, Theodora. *Alfred Kroeber: A Personal Configuration*. Berkeley: University of California Press, 1970.

——. *Ishi in Two Worlds: A Biography of the Last Wild Indian in North America*. Berkeley: University of California Press, 1961.

Kunzel, Regina. "White Neurosis, Black Pathology: Constructing Out of Wedlock Pregnancy in the Wartime and Postwar United States." In *Not June Cleaver: Women and Gender in Postwar America, 1945–1960*. Edited by Joanne Meyerowitz, 304–334. Philadelphia: Temple University Press, 1994.

Kuper, Adam. *The Reinvention of Primitive Society: Transformations of a Myth*. New York: Routledge, 2005.

Ladd-Taylor, Molly. *Mother-Work: Women, Child Welfare, and the State, 1890–1930*. Urbana: University of Illinois Press, 1994.

Laderman, Gary, and Luis Leon, eds. *Religion and American Cultures: Tradition, Diversity, and Popular Expression. Vol. 1*. Santa Barbara, CA: ABC-CLIO Press, 2003.

Lafitau, Joseph Francois. *Customs of the American Indians Compared with the Customs of Primitive Indians*. Edited and translated by William N. Fenton and Elizabeth L. Moore. Toronto: Champlain Society, 1974.

Lamberti, Elena. *Marshall McLuhan's Mosaic: Probing the Literary Origins of Media Studies*. Toronto: University of Toronto Press, 2012.

Lane, Ann J. *To Herland and Beyond: The Life and Works of Charlotte Perkins Gilman*. New York: Pantheon, 1990.

Lane, Mary E. Bradley. *Mizora: A Prophecy. A manuscript found among the papers of Princess Vera Zarovitch*. New York: G. W. Dillingham, 1989. Kindle e-book.

Lanser, Susan S. "Feminist Criticism, 'The Yellow Wallpaper,' and the Politics of Color in America." *Feminist Studies* 15, no. 3 (Autumn 1989): 415–41.

Lant, Kathleen Margaret. "The Rape of the Text: Charlotte Gilman's Violation of Herland." *Tulsa Studies in Women's Literature* 9, no. 2 (Autumn 1990): 291–308.

Larson, Erik. *The Devil in the White City: A Saga of Magic and Murder at the Fair that Changed America.* New York: Vintage, 2004.

Lee, Harper. *Go Set a Watchman.* New York: HarperCollins, 2015.

———. *To Kill a Mockingbird.* New York: HarperCollins, 1960.

Le Guin, Ursula K. *The Farthest Shore.* In *The Earthsea Quartet.* New York: Penguin Books, 1992.

———. "Is Gender Necessary?" 1976. https://americanfuturesiup.files.wordpress.com/2013/01/is-gender-necessary.pdf.

———. "Is Gender Necessary Redux?" 1988. Accessed June 24, 2017. https://americanfuturesiup.files.wordpress.com/2013/01/is-gender-necessary.pdf, accessed June 24, 2017.

———. *The Left Hand of Darkness.* New York: Ace Books, 1987.

———. *Tehanu,* in *The Earthsea Quartet.* New York: Penguin Books, 1992.

———. *The Tombs of Atuan.* In *The Earthsea Quartet.* New York: Penguin Books, 1992.

———. *The Wizard of Earthsea.* In *The Earthsea Quartet.* New York: Penguin Books, 1992.

Leonard, Thomas C. "Origins of the Myth of Social Darwinism: The Ambiguous Legacy of Richard Hofstadter's *Social Darwinism in American Thought.*" *Journal of Economic Behavior and Social Organization* 71 (2009): 37–51.

di Leonardo, Micaela. *Exotics at Home: Anthropologies, Others, and American Modernity.* Chicago: University of Chicago Press, 1998.

Leon-Portilla, Miguel. "California: Land of Frontier." In *Common Border, Uncommon Paths: Race, Culture, and National Identity in U.S.-Mexican Relations.* Edited by Jaime E. Rodriguez O. and Kathryn Vincent, 15–26. Wilmington, DE: Scholarly Resources, 1997.

Lepore, Jill. *The Secret History of Wonder Woman.* New York: Vintage, 2014.

Leslie, Amy. *Amy Leslie at the Fair.* Chicago: W. B. Conkey Co., 1893. "Lester Frank Ward." American Sociological Association. http://www.asanet.org/about/presidents/Lester_Ward.cfm.

Levi-Strauss, Claude. *The Naked Man: Mythologiques.* Chicago: University of Chicago Press, 1981.

Levy, David M. *Maternal Overprotection.* New York: Columbia University Press, 1943.

Lincoln, Abbey. "To Whom Will She Cry Rape?" In *The Black Woman: An Anthology.* New York: New American Library, 1970. Kindle e-book.

Lindfors, Bernth. *Africans on Stage: Studies in Ethnological Show Business.* Bloomington: Indiana University Press, 1999.

Lindner, Robert M. *Rebel Without a Cause: The Hypnoanalysis of a Criminal Psychopath.* New York: Grove Press, 1944.

Lindsey, Kay. "Poem." In *The Black Woman: An Anthology.* New York: New American Library, 1970. Kindle e-book.

Littlefield, Henry M. "The Wizard of Oz: Parable on Populism." *American Quarterly* 16, no. 1 (Spring 1964): 47–58.

Lomax, Tamura A., and LeRhonda Manigault-Bryant. "Introduction." In *Womanist and Black Feminist Responses to Tyler Perry's Productions.* Edited by LeRhonda Manigault-Bryant, Tamura A. Lomax, and Carol B. Duncan, 1–13. New York: Palgrave Macmillan, 2014.

Long, Lisa A. "*With Her in Ourland:* Herland Meets Heterodoxy." In *Charlotte Perkins Gilman and Her Contemporaries: Literary and Intellectual Contexts.* Edited by Cynthia J. Davis and Denise D. Knight, 171–93. Tuscaloosa: University of Alabama Press, 2004.

Lopate, Phillip. "Sidney Lumet, or the Necessity for Compromise." *Film Comment* 33, no. 4 (July–August 1997): 50–53.

Lorde, Audre. "The Master's Tools Will Never Dismantle the Master's House." In *This Bridge Called My Back: Writings By Radical Women of Color.* Edited by Cherrie Moraga and Gloria Anzaldua, 25–28. New York: Kitchen Table Press, 1983.

Lubiano, Wahneema. "Black Ladies, Welfare Queens, and State Minstrels: Ideological War by Narrative Means." In *Race-ing Justice, En-gendering Power: Essays on Anita Hill, Clarence Thomas, and the Construction of Social Reality.* Edited by Toni Morrison, 323–63. New York: Pantheon Books, 1992.

Lundberg, Ferdinand, and Marynia F. Farnham. *Modern Woman: The Lost Sex.* New York: Grosset and Dunlap, 1947.

MacKinnon, Catherine. *Toward a Feminist Theory of the State.* Cambridge, MA: Harvard University Press, 1991.

The Magic City: A Portfolio of Original Photographic Views of the Great WF and Its Treasures of Art, including a Graphic Representation of the Famous MP, Historical Fine Arts Series. Vol. 1, no. 2, Jan. 22, 1894. Philadelphia: H. S. Smith and C. R. Graham for Historical Publishing Co., 1894.

Maguire, Gregory. *A Lion Among Men.* New York: William Morrow, 2008.

———. *Out of Oz.* New York: HarperCollins, 2011.

———. *Son of a Witch.* New York: HarperCollins, 2005.

———. *Wicked: The Life and Times of the Wicked Witch of the West.* New York: William Morrow, 1996.

"Man and His Works: Ethnological Exhibits at the Fair." Reprinted in *Coming of Age in*

Chicago: The 1893 World's Fair and the Coalescence of American Anthropology. Edited by Curtis M Hinsley and David R. Wilcox, 91–98. Lincoln: University of Nebraska Press, 2016).

Manigault-Bryant, L., T. Lomax, and C. Duncan, eds. *Womanist and Black Feminist Responses to "The Help."* New York: Palgrave Macmillan, 2014.

Manring, Maurice M. *Slave in a Box: The Strange Career of Aunt Jemima.* Charlottesville: University of Virginia Press, 1998.

Marilley, Suzanne M. "Frances Willard and the Feminism of Fear." *Feminist Studies* 19, no. 1 (1993): 123–46.

Marshall, Paule. "Reena." In *The Black Woman: An Anthology.* New York: New American Library, 1970. Kindle e-book.

Marston, William Moulton. *Emotions of Normal People.* New York: Harcourt, Brace, 1928.

———. *March On!* New York: Doubleday, Doran, 1939.

———. *Try Living!.* New York: Thomas Y. Crowell, 1937.

———. *Venus With Us: A Tale of the Caesar.* New York: Sears Publishing, 1932.

———. "Why 100,000,000 Americans Read Comics." *American Scholar* 13, no. 1 (Winter 1943): 35–44.

Marx, Karl, and Friedrich Engels. *The Communist Manifesto,* Section III. http://www.historyguide.org/intellect/manifesto.html.

"Matriarchy." *The American Heritage Dictionary of the English Language.* https://ahdictionary.com/word/search.html?q=matriarchy&submit.x=45&submit.y=34.

"Matriarchy." *Merriam-Webster.* https://www.merriam-webster.com/dictionary/matriarchy.

"Matriarchy." *Oxford English Dictionary.* http://www.oed.com.

May, Elaine Tyler. *Homeward Bound: American Families in the Cold War Era.* New York: Basic Books, 1988.

McClintock, Anne. *Imperial Leather: Race, Gender, and Sexuality in the Colonial Context.* New York: Routledge, 1995.

McCluskey, Audrey T. "Telling Truth and Taking Names: An Interview with Spike Lee." *Black Camera* 19, no. 1 (Spring/Summer 2004): 1–11.

McLennan, John Ferguson. *Primitive Marriage: An Inquiry into the Origin of the Form of Capture in Marriage Ceremonies.* Edinburgh: Adam and Charles Black, 1865.

Merril, Judith. *Better to Have Loved: The Life of Judith Merril.* Toronto: Between the Lines, 2002.

Meyerowitz, Joanne. *Not June Cleaver: Women and Gender in Postwar America, 1945–1960.* Philadelphia: Temple University Press, 1994.

Midway Types and Scenes: A Book of Illustrated Lessons about the People of the Midway Plaisance, World's Fair. Chicago: American Engraving Co., 1894.

Miller, Francesca. *Latin American Women and the Search for Social Justice*. Lebanon, PA University Press of New England, 1991.

Mink, Gwendolyn. *The Wages of Motherhood: Inequality in the Welfare State, 1917–1942*. Ithaca, NY: Cornell University Press, 1995.

Mohr, Dunja M. "Parity, with Differences: Suzy McKee Charnas Concludes the Holdfast Series." *Science Fiction Studies* 26 (1999): 468–72.

Molina, Natalia. *Fit to Be Citizens?: Public Health and Race in Los Angeles, 1879–1939*.

Moore, Raylyn. *Wonderful Wizard, Marvelous Land*. Bowling Green, KY: Bowling Green University Press, 1974.

Morgan, Lewis Henry. *Ancient Society, or Researches into the Lines of Human Progress From Savagery to Barbarism to Civilization*. Cambridge: Harvard University Press, 1964.

———. *League of the Haudenosaunee: A Classic Study of an American Tribe with Original Illustrations*. New York: Citadel Books, 1984.

———. *Systems of Consanguinity and Affinity of the Human Family*. Washington: Smithsonian Institution, 1870.

Morris, Susana M. *Close Kin and Distant Relatives: The Paradox of Respectability in Black Women's Literature*. Charlottesville: University of Virginia Press, 2014.

Moskin, "Why Do Women Dominate Him?." In *The Decline of the American Male*, edited by *Look* magazine (New York: Random House, 1958): 3–24.

Moynihan, *Family and Nation: The Godkin Lectures, Harvard University*. San Diego: Harcourt Brace, 1986.

Muccigrosso, Robert. *Celebrating the New World: Chicago's Columbian Exposition of 1893*. Chicago: Ivan R. Dee, 1993.

Murphy, Patricia. "The Gendering of History in *She*." *Studies in English Literature, 1500–1900* 39, no. 4 (Autumn 1999747–772.

Nash, Gerald D. "The Census of 1890 and the Closing of the Frontier." *Pacific Northwest Quarterly* 71, no. 3 (July 1980): 98–100.

National Black Feminist Organization. "Statement of Purpose." http://www-personal. umd.umich.edu/~ppennock/doc-BlackFeminist.htm.

National Woman's Rights Convention. "Resolutions, Washington, DC, January 1869." http://www.lehigh.edu/~dek7/SSAWW/writWRDRWashingR.htm.

Ness, Immanuel. *Encyclopedia of American Social Movements*. London: Routledge, 2004.

Newman, Louise Michele. *White Women's Rights: The Racial Origins of Feminism in the United States*. New York: Oxford University Press, 1999.

Northrop, H. D. *The World's Fair as Seen in One Hundred Days, containing a complete history of the World's Columbian Exposition; captivating descriptions of the magnificent buildings and marvelous exhibits, such as works of art, textiles fabrics, machinery, natural products, the latest inventions, discoveries, etc., etc., including a full description of Chicago, its wonderful buildings, parks, etc.* Philadelphia: Ariel Book Co., 1893.

Norton, "For Sadie and Maude." In *Sisterhood is Powerful: An Anthology of Writings from the Women's Liberation Movement,* edited by Robin Morgan (New York: Random House, 1970): pp.

Nye, Russell B. "An Appreciation." In *L. Frank Baum: The Wizard of Oz,* ed. Michael Patrick Hearn. (New York, NY: Schocken, 1983): 162–175.

Office of Policy Planning and Research. *The Negro Family: The Case for National Action.* Washington: U.S. Department of Labor, 1965. https://web.stanford.edu/~mros-enfe/Moynihan%27s%20The%20Negro%20Family.pdf.

Official Catalogue of Exhibits on the Midway Plaisance: Department M-Ethnology, Group 176: isolated exhibits, Midway Plaisance (digital version). http://scholarship.rice.edu/jsp/xml/1911/22074/1/aa00144.tei.html#div1037.

Official Guide to the Midwinter Exposition in Golden Gate Park. San Francisco: G. Spaulding & Co., 1894, 115.

Official History of the California Midwinter International Exposition. H. S. Crocker Co., 1894.

Ong, Walter. "Comics and the Super State." *Arizona Quarterly* 1 (1945): 34–48.

Ormrod, Joan. "Cold War Fantasies: Testing the Limits of the Familial Body." In *The Ages of Wonder Woman: Essays on the Amazon Princess in Changing Times,* ed. Joseph J. Darowski (Jefferson, NC: McFarland, 2014): 52–65.

Qureshi, Sadiah. "Displaying Sara Baartman, 'The Hottentot Venus.'" *History of Science* 43 (2004): 233–257.

Parham, Thomas A. Adisa Ajamu, Joseph L. White, *Psychology of Blacks: Centering Our Perspectives in the African Consciousness.* New York: Psychology Press, 2010.

Parker, Arthur C. *The Life of General Ely S. Parker: The Last Grand Sachem of the Iroquois and General Grant's Military Secretary.* Buffalo: Buffalo Historical Society, 1919.

Parker, David B. "Oz: L. Frank Baum's Theosophical Utopia." http://www.mindspring.com/~daveh47/OzFiles/wiztheos.txt.

———. "The Rise and Fall of *The Wonderful Wizard of Oz* as a 'Parable on Populism.'" *Journal of the Georgia Association of Historians* 15 (1994): 49–64.

Parkhurst, Jessie W. "The Role of the Black Mammy in the Plantation Household." *Journal of Negro History* 23, no. 3(1938): 349–369.

Pascoe, Peggy. *Relations of Rescue: The Search for Female Moral Authority in the American West.* New York: Oxford University Press, 1990.

Patton, Sandra. *Birthmarks: Transracial Adoption in Contemporary America.* New York: New York University Press, 2000.

Peoples, Whitney. "(Re)Mediating Black Womanhood: Tyler Perry, Black Feminist Cultural Criticism, and the Politics of Legitimation." In *Womanist and Black Feminist*

Responses to Tyler Perry's Productions, eds. LeRhonda Manigault-Bryant, Tamura A. Lomax, and Carol B. Duncan (Palgrave Macmillan, 2014): 147–162.

Pfaelzer, Jean. *The Utopian Novel in America, 1886–1896*. Pittsburgh: University of Pittsburgh Press, 1985.

Phillips, Julie. *James Tiptree Jr.: The Double Life of Alice B. Sheldon*. New York: St. Martin's, 2006.

The Photographic World's Fair and Midway Plaisance: The Main Buildings, the Entrances, the Foreign, State and Territorial Buildings; The Charming Water Views, Statuary and Paintings, and the Most Striking Scenes of the Midway Plaisance: The Most Extensive and Perfect Collection Yet Published of the Marvels and Beauties of the World Columbian Exposition. Chicago: The Monarch Book Co., 1894.

Picturesque World's Fair: An Elaborate Collection of Colored Views, published with the endorsement and approval of George R. Davis, Director-General of the World's Columbian Exposition. Comprising Illustrations of the Greatest Features of The World's Columbian Exposition and Midway Plaisance; Architectural, Artistic, Historical, Scenic and Ethnological. The Magnificent Water and Landscape Effects and Charming Vistas Made Realistic by Authentic Reproduction In All of the Colors of Nature and Art. Chicago: W.B. Conkey Co., 1894.

Piercy, Marge. *Woman on the Edge of Time*. London: Women's Press, 1976. Reprint, New York: Ballantine Books, 1997.

Plant, Rebecca Jo. *Mom: The Transformation of Motherhood in Modern America*. Chicago: University of Chicago Press, 2010.

———. *The Repeal of Mother Love: Momism and the Construction of Motherhood in Philip Wylie's America*. Ph.D. dissertation, Johns Hopkins University, 2001.

Plant, Rebecca Jo, and Marian van der Klein. "Introduction." In *Maternalism Reconsidered: Motherhood, Welfare and Social Policy in the Twentieth Century*, edited by Marian van der Klein, Rebecca Jo Plant, Nichole Sanders, and Lori R. Weintraub, (New York: Berghahn Books, 2012).

Polakow, Valerie. *Lives on the Edge: Single Mothers and Their Children in the Other America*. Chicago: University of Chicago Press, 1993.

Portfolio of Photographs of the World's Fair. Chicago: Werner Co., 1893.

Pugh, Tison. "'There lived in the Land of Oz two queerly made men': Queer Utopianism and Antisocial Eroticism in L. Frank Baum's Oz Series." *Marvels and Tales: Journal of Fairy-Tale Studies* 22, no. 2 (2008): 217–239.

Putnam, Frederic Ward. "Introduction." In *Oriental and Occidental Northern and Southern Portrait Types of the Midway Plaisance: A Collection of Photographs of Individual Types of various nations from all parts of the World who represented, in the Department of Ethnology, The Manners, Customs, Dress, Religion, Music and other distinctive traits and peculiarities of their Race, with interesting and instructive descriptions accompa-*

nying each portrait, together with an Introduction by Prof. F.W. Putnam, of Harvard University, Chief of the Department of Ethnology at the WCE. St. Louis: N.D. Putnam Publishing Co., 1894.

Raab, Mark, Jim Cassidy, Andrew Yatsko, and William J. Howard. *California Maritime Archaeology: A San Clemente Island Perspective.* Lanham: Altamira Press, 2009.

Rafferty, Edward C. *Apostle of Human Progress: Lester Frank Ward and American Political Thought, 1841–1913.* New York: Rowman & Littlefield, 2003.

Railton, Benjamin. *Redefining American Identity: From Cabeza de Vaca to Barack Obama.* London: Palgrave, 2011.

Rainwater, Lee and William L. Yancey. *The Moynihan Report and the Politics of Controversy.* Boston: MIT Press, 1967.

Ralph, Julian. *Harper's Chicago and the World's Fair: The Chapters on the Exposition Being Collated from Official Sources and Approved by the Department of Publicity and Promotion of the World's Columbian Exposition.* New York: Harper & Brothers, 1893.

Randall, Alice. *The Wind Done Gone.* New York: Houghton Mifflin Harcourt, 2001.

Rapp, Rayna, and Ellen Ross. "The 1920s: Feminism, Consumerism, and Political Backlash in the United States." In *Women in Culture and Politics: A Century of Change.* Edited by Judith Friedlander, Blanche Wiesen Cook, Alice Kessler-Harris, and Carroll Smith-Rosenberg (Bloomington: Indiana University Press, 1986).

———. "The Twenties' Backlash: Compulsory Heterosexuality, the Consumer Family, and the Waning of Feminism." In *Class, Race and Sex: The Dynamics of Control,* edited by Amy Swerdlow and Hanna Lessinger (New York: Barnard College Women's Center, 1983): 93–107.

Rashley, Lisa Hammond. "Revisioning Gender: Inventing Women in Ursula K. Le Guin's Nonfiction." *Biography* 20, no. 1 (Winter 2007): 22–47.

Redstockings. "Redstockings Manifesto." In *Radical Feminism: A Documentary Reader* Ed. Barbara A. Crow (New York: New York University Press, 2000), 223–25.

Reed, Christopher. *"All the World Is Here": The Black Presence at White City.* Bloomington: Indiana University Press, 2002.

Reid, Julia. "'She-who-must-be-obeyed': Anthropology and Matriarchy in H. Rider Haggard's *She.*" *Journal of Victorian Culture* 20, no. 3 (2015): 357–74.

Richards, Olive Byrne, "Emotions of Normal People (Review)." *Journal of Abnormal and Social Psychology* 24, (April 1929): 135–138.

Riesman, David. *The Lonely Crowd. A Study of the Changing American Character.* New Haven: Yale University Press, 1950.

Riis, Thomas, ed. *The Music and Scripts of In Dahomey.* Madison: A-R Editions Inc., 1996.

Riley, Michael O'Neal. *Oz and Beyond: The Fantasy World of L. Frank Baum.* Lawrence: University Press of Kansas, 1997.

Ritter, Gretchen. "Silver Slippers and a Golden Cap: L. Frank Baum's *The Wonderful Wizard of Oz* and Historical Memory in American Politics." *Journal of American Studies* 31, no. 2 (August 1997): 171–202.

Ritzer, George and Jeffrey Stepnisky, eds. *The Wiley-Blackwell Companion to Major Social Theorists.* Wiley-Blackwell, 2011.

Roberts, Robin. *A New Species: Gender and Science in Science Fiction.* Urbana: University of Illinois Press, 1993.

Robinson, Julian. *Gynecocracy: A Narrative of the Adventures and Psychological Experiences of Julian Robinson Under Petticoat Rule, Written by Himself.* 1893. Reprint, London: Locus Elm Press, 2014. Kindle e-book.

Rogers, James Allen. "Darwinism and Social Darwinism." In *Herbert Spencer: Critical Assessments. Vol. 2.* Edited by John Offer (London: Routledge, 2000): 149–64.

Rogers, Katherine M. *L. Frank Baum, Creator of Oz.* New York, NY: St. Martin's Press, 2002.

Ruddick, Nicholas. *The Fire in the Stone: Prehistoric Fiction from Charles Darwin to Jean M. Auel.* Middletown, CT: Wesleyan University Press, 2009.

Russ, Joanna. *The Female Man.* Boston: Beacon Press, 2000.

———. *The Image of Women in Science Fiction.* Andover, MA: Warner Modular Publications, 1973.

———. "Recent Feminist Utopias." In *Future Females: A Critical Anthology,* ed. Marleen S. Barr (Bowling Green: Bowling Green University Press, 1981), 71–85.

———. "When It Changed." http://boblyman.net/englt392/texts/When%20It%20Changed.pdf.

Russell, Michele. "Black-Eyed Blues Connections: Teaching Black Women." In *All the Women Are White, All the Blacks Are Men, But Some of Us Are Brave.* Edited by Akasha Gloria Hull, Patricia Bell Scott, and Barbara Smith. New York: Feminist Press, 1982. Kindle e-book.

Ryan, Melissa Ann. "(Un)natural Law: Women Writers, the Indian, and the State in Nineteenth-Century America." PhD diss., University of Arizona, 2004.

Rydell, Robert W. *The Books of the Fairs: Materials About World's Fairs, 1834–1916, in the Smithsonian Institution Libraries.* Chicago: American Library Association, 1992.

———. "'Darkest Africa': African Shows at America's World's Fairs, 1893–1940." In *Africans on Stage: Studies in Ethnological Show Business.* Edited by Bernth Lindfors, 135–55. Bloomington: Indiana University Press, 1999.

Sackett, S. J. "The Utopia of Oz." In *L. Frank Baum: The Wizard of Oz.* Edited by Michael Patrick Hearn, 207–20. New York: Schocken, 1983.

Sanday, Peggy Reeves. "Matriarchal Values and World Peace: The Case of the Minangkabau." Second World Congress of Matriarchal Studies, 2005. http://www.second-congress-matriarchal-studies.com/sanday.html.

———. *Women at the Center: Life in a Modern Matriarchy.* Ithaca, NY: Cornell University Press, 2002.

Sanders, Fran. "Dear Black Man." In *The Black Woman: An Anthology.* Edited by Toni Cade. New York: New American Library, 1970. Kindle e-book.

Sanderson, Stephen K. *Evolutionism and Its Critics: Deconstructing and Reconstructing as Evolutionary Interpretation of Human Society.* Boulder, CO: Paradigm Publishers, 2007.

Sanger, Margaret. *Happiness in Marriage.* Oxford: Pergamon, 1926.

———. *Women and the New Race.* 1920. Kindle e-book.

Sapphire. *Push.* New York: Vintage, 1996.

Saros, Daniel E. *Labor, Industry, and Regulation During the Progressive Era.* London: Routledge, 2008.

Savion, Susan. *Quoting Matilda.* Bloomington, IN: AuthorHouse, 2014.

Sayre, Nora. *Running Time: Films of the Cold War.* New York: Doubleday, 1982.

Schmidt, Regin. *Red Scare: FBI and the Origins of Anticommunism in the United States, 1919–1943.* Copenhagen: Museum Tusculanum Press, 2000, 26.

Scholes, Robert. "A Footnote to Russ's 'Recent Feminist Utopias.'" In *Future Females: A Critical Anthology.* Edited by Marleen S. Barr. Bowling Green, KY: Bowling Green State University Press, 1981, 86–87.

Schram, Sanford F., and Jose Soss. "Success Stories: Welfare Reform, Policy Discourse, and the Politics of Research." *Annals (The American Academy of Political and Social Science)* 577 (2001): 49–65.

Schwartz, Evan I. *Finding Oz: How L. Frank Baum Discovered the Great American Story.* New York: Houghton Mifflin Harcourt, 2009.

Schwarz, Judith. *Radical Feminists of Heterodoxy, Greenwich Village, 1912–1940.* Norwich, VT: New Victoria Publishers, 1986.

Scott, Gertrude M. "Village Performance: Villages at the Chicago World's Columbian Exposition." PhD diss., New York University, 1991.

Scott, Patricia Bell. "Debunking Sapphire: Toward a Non-Racist and Non-Sexist Social Science." In *All the Women Are White, All the Blacks Are Men, But Some of Us Are Brave.* Edited by Akasha Gloria Hull, Patricia Bell Scott, and Barbara Smith. New York: Feminist Press, 1982.

Seaver, James E. *A Narrative of the Life of Mary Jemison* (1824). Project Gutenberg e-book. http://www.gutenberg.org/files/6960/6960-h/6960-h.htm.

Sebald, Hans. *Momism: The Silent Disease of America.* Chicago: Nelson-Hall, 1976.

Shange, Ntozake. *for colored girls who have considered suicide/when the rainbow is enuf.* New York: Macmillan, 1975. Reprint, New York: Scribner, 2010.

Sharp, Gwen. "Vintage Anti-Suffrage Postcards." *Sociological Images.* https://thesocietypages.org/socimages/2012/11/08/vintage-anti-suffrage-postcards/.

Shaw, Marian. *World's Fair Notes: A Woman Journalist Views Chicago's 1893 Columbian Exposition*. St. Paul: Pogo Press, 1992.

Shelley, Martha. "Lesbianism and the Women's Liberation Movement." In *Radical Feminism: A Documentary Reader*. Edited by Barbara A. Crow, 305–9. New York: New York University Press, 2000.

Shoemaker, Nancy. "The Rise or Fall of Iroquois Women." *Journal of Women's History* 2, no. 3 (Winter 1991): 39–57.

Sklar, Kathryn Kish. "The Historical Foundations of Women's Power in the Creation of the American Welfare State, 1830–1930." In *Mothers of a New World: Maternalist Politics and the Origins of Welfare States*. Edited by Seth Koven and Sonya Michel, 43–93. New York: Routledge,1993.

Skocpol, Theda. *Protecting Soldiers and Mothers: The Political Origins of Social Policy in the United States*. Cambridge, MA: Harvard University Press, 1992.

Smith, Barbara. "Racism and Women's Studies." In *All the Women Are White, All the Blacks Are Men, But Some of Us Are Brave*. Edited by Akasha Gloria Hull, Patricia Bell Scott, and Barbara Smith. New York: Feminist Press, 1982. Kindle e-book.

Snider, Denton Jacques. *World's Fair Studies*. London: Forgotten Books, 2013.

Sotiropoulos, Karen. *Staging Race: Black Performers in Turn-of-the-Century America*. Cambridge, MA: Harvard University Press, 2006.

Spretnak, Charlene. "Beyond the Backlash: An Appreciation of the Work of Marija Gimbutas." *Journal of Feminist Studies in Religion* 12, no. 2 (Fall 1996): 91–98.

Stagl, Gerry. "Bachofen, Johann J." In *Theory in Social and Cultural Anthropology*. Edited by R. Jon McGee and Richard L. Warms. Thousand Oaks, CA: Sage Publications, 2013. http://sk.sagepub.com/reference/theory-in-social-and-cultural-anthropology/n17.xml.

Stange, Mary Zeiss. "The Once and Future Heroine: Paleolithic Goddesses and the Popular Imagination." *Women's Studies Quarterly* 21, no. 1 (Spring 1993): 55–66.

Stanton, Elizabeth Cady, Susan B. Anthony, and Matilda Joslyn Gage. *History of Woman Suffrage. Vol. 1*. Rochester, NY: Charles Mann, 1887.

Staples, Robert. "The Myth of Black Macho: A Response to Angry Black Feminists." *Black Scholar* 10, no. 6/7: 24–33.

———. "The Myth of the Black Matriarchy." *Black Scholar*. November–December (1981): 26–34.

Steele, Ian K. *Setting All the Captives Free: Capture, Adjustment, and Recollection in Allegheny County*. Montreal: McGill-Queen's University Press, 2013.

Steinem, Gloria, and Phyllis Chesler, eds. *Wonder Woman*. New York: Outlet, 1972.

Stern, Bernhard J., ed. "The Letters of Asher Wright to Lewis Henry Morgan." *American Anthropologist* (1933): 138–45.

Stockett, Katherine. *The Help.* New York: Penguin Books, 2009.

Stocking, George W. Jr. *Victorian Anthropology.* New York: Free Press, 1987.

Stone, Merlin. *When God Was a Woman.* New York: Harcourt Brace Jovanovich, 1976.

Strecker, Edward. "Motherhood and Momism: Effect on the Nation." *University of West Ontario Medical Journal* (March 1946): 59–77.

———. *Their Mothers' Sons: The Psychiatrist Examines an American Problem.* Philadelphia: Lippincott, 1946.

Stuller, Jennifer K. *Ink-Stained Amazons and Cinematic Warriors: Superwomen in Modern Mythology.* London: I. B. Tauris, 2010.

———. "What Is a Female Superhero?" In *What Is a Superhero?* Edited by Robin S. Rosenberg and Peter Coogan, 19–24. New York: Oxford University Press, 2013.

Stump, Melinda. "'The Most Deadly Spot on the Face of the Earth': The United States and Antimodern Images of 'Darkest Africa,' 1880–1910." MA thesis, University of Northern Iowa, 2013.

Superson, Anita M., and Ann E. Cudd, eds. *Theorizing Backlash: Philosophical Reflections on the Resistance to Feminism.* Lanham, MD: Rowman & Littlefield, 2002.

This, Craig. "Containing Wonder Woman: Frederic Wertham's Battle Against the Mighty Amazon." In *The Ages of Wonder Woman: Essays on the Amazon Princess in Changing Times.* Edited by Joseph Darowski, 30–41. Jefferson, NC: McFarland, 2013.

Thompson, Denise. *Radical Feminism Today.* London: SAGE Publications, 2001.

Thompson, Ethan. *Parody and Taste in American Television Culture.* New York: Routledge, 2011.

Thurber, Cheryl. "The Development of the Mammy Image and Mythology." In *Southern Women: Histories and Identities.* Edited by Virginia Bernhard, Betty Brandon, Elizabeth Fox-Genovese, and Theda Perdue, 87–108. Columbia: University of Missouri Press, 1992.

Thurber, James. "The Wizard of Chittenango." In *L. Frank Baum: The Wizard of Oz.* Edited by Michael Patrick Hearn, 159–61. New York: Schocken, 1983.

Tickner, Lisa. *The Spectacle of Women: Imagery of the Suffrage Campaign, 1907–1914.* Chicago: University of Chicago Press, 1988.

Tiptree, James Jr. *Houston, Houston, Do You Read?* New York: Doubleday, 1996.

Tretault, Lisa. *The Myth of Seneca Falls: Memory and the Women's Suffrage Movement, 1848–1898.* Chapel Hill: University of North Carolina Press, 2014.

Trigger, Bruce G., and Wilcomb E. Washburn. *The Cambridge History of the Native Peoples of the Americas, Part 2.* Cambridge: Cambridge University Press, 1996.

Turner, Frederick J. "The Significance of the Frontier in American History." Address to the American Historical Association, 1894. http://www.historians.org/about-aha-and-membership/aha-history-and-archives/archives/the-significance-of-the-frontier-in-american-history.

Tuttle, Jennifer S., and Carol Farley Kessler, eds. *Charlotte Perkins Gilman: New Texts, New Contexts.* Columbus: Ohio State University Press, 2011.

van den Oever, Roel. *Mama's Boy: Momism and Homophobia in Postwar American Culture.* New York: Palgrave Macmillan, 2012.

Van der Spek, Inez. *Alien Plots: Female Subjectivity and the Divine in the Light of James Tiptree's "A Momentary Taste of Being."* Liverpool: Liverpool University Press, 2000.

Wagenknecht, Edward. "Utopia Americana." In *L. Frank Baum: The Wizard of Oz.* Edited by Michael Patrick Hearn, 142–56. New York: Schocken, 1983.

Wagner, Sally Roesch. *Matilda Joslyn Gage: She Who Holds the Sky.* Aberdeen, SD: Sky Carrier Press, 1999.

———. "That Word is Liberty: A Biography of Matilda Joslyn Gage." PhD diss., University of California at Santa Cruz, 1978.

Walby, Sylvia. "Backlash in Historical Context." In *Making Connections: Women's Studies, Women's Movements, Women's Lives.* Edited by Mary Kennedy, Cathy Lubelska, and Val Walsh, 76–87. London: Taylor & Francis, 1993.

Walkowitz, Judith R. *City of Dreadful Delight: Narratives of Sexual Danger in Late Victorian London.* Chicago: University of Chicago Press, 1992.

Wallace, Michele. *Black Macho and the Myth of the Superwoman.* New York: Dial Press, 1979. Reprint, New York: Verso, 1990.

Wallace-Sanders, *Mammy: A Century of Race, Gender, and Southern Memory.* Ann Arbor: University of Michigan Press, 2008.

Walsh, Correa Moylan. *Feminism.* New York: Sturgis and Walton, 1917.

Ward, Lester Frank. "Our Better Halves." *Forum* (November 1888), https://gynocentrism.com/2015/05/15/our-better-halves-1888/.

———. *Pure Sociology: A Treatise on the Origin and Spontaneous Development of Society.* New York: Macmillan, 1903.

Ware, Susan. "American Women in the 1950s: Nonpartisan Politics and Women's Politicization." In *Women, Politics, and Change.* Edited by Louise A. Tilly and Patricia Gurin, 281–99. New York: Russell Sage Foundation, 1990.

———. *Beyond Suffrage: Women in the New Deal.* Cambridge, MA: Harvard University Press, 1981.

Warren, Kim. "Gender, Race, Culture, and the Mythic American Frontier." *Journal of Women's History* 19, no. 1 (Spring 2007): 234–41.

Warren, Louis S. *Buffalo Bill's America: William Cody and the Wild West Show.* New York: Random House, 2007.

Watts, Jill. *Hattie McDaniel: Black Ambition, White Hollywood.* New York: Amistad, 2007.

Webb, Michael. "The City in Film." *Design Quarterly* no. 136 (1987): 3–32.

Weimann, Jeanne Madeline. *The Fair Women.* Chicago: Academy Press, 1981.

Weinbaum, Alys Eve. *Wayward Reproductions: Genealogies of Race and Nation in Transatlantic Modern Thought.* Durham, NC: Duke University Press, 2004.

———. "Writing Feminist Genealogy: Charlotte Perkins Gilman, Racial Nationalism, and the Reproduction of Maternalist Feminism." *Feminist Studies* 27, no. 2 (Summer 2001): 271–302.

Weiner, Lynn Y. "Maternalism as Paradigm: Defining the Issues." *Journal of Women's History* 5, no. 2 (Fall 1993): 95–130.

———. *Seduction of the Innocent.* New York: Rinehart, 1954.

Weir, James Jr. "Domesticity or Matriarchy, Which?" *The American Practitioner* 18 (1894): 419–23. https://archive.org/stream/mobot31753002158159/mobot31753002158159_djvu.txt.

———."The Effect of Female Suffrage on Posterity." *American Naturalist* 29, no. 345 (Sept. 1895): 815–25.

Welter, Barbara. "The Cult of True Womanhood: 1820–1860." *American Quarterly* 18, no. 2 (1966): 151–74.

White, Trumbull. *The World's Columbian Exposition, Chicago, 1893.* Chicago: International Publishing, 1893.

Whitfield, Stephen J. *The Culture of the Cold War.* Baltimore: Johns Hopkins University Press, 1996.

Whyte, William H. *The Organization Man.* New York: Simon and Schuster, 1956.

Wilcox, Clyde. "The Not-so-Failed Feminism of Jean Auel." *Journal of Popular Culture* 28, no. 3 (Winter 1994): 63–70.

Wilcox, David R. "Anthropology in a Changing America: Interpreting the Chicago 'Triumph' of Frank Hamilton Cushing." In *Coming of Age in Chicago: The 1893 World's Fair and the Coalescence of American Anthropology.* Edited by Curtis M. Hinsley and David R. Wilcox, 125–52. Lincoln: University of Nebraska Press, 2016.

Williams, Brooke. "The Retreat to Cultural Feminism." In *Feminist Revolution.* Edited by Redstockings of the Women's Liberation Movement, 65–68. New York: Random House, 1978.

Williams, Fannie C. "A 'White Queen' at the World's Fair." *Chautauquan* 18 (1893): 342.

Williams, Keira V. *Gendered Politics in the Modern South: The Susan Smith Case and the Rise of a New Sexism.* Baton Rouge: Louisiana State University Press, 2012.

Willie, Charles V., and Richard J. Reddick. *A New Look at Black Families.* Lanham, MD: Rowman & Littlefield, 2010.

Willis, Ellen. "Radical Feminism and Feminist Radicalism." *Social Text* no. 9/10 (Spring–Summer 1984): 91–118.

Wilson, Sloan. *The Man in the Gray Flannel Suit.* New York: Four Walls Eight Windows, 1955.

The Wonders of the World's Fair: Only the Most Superb Views. Chicago: W. B. Conkey Co., 1894.

Wood, Robert C. *Suburbia: Its People and Their Politics.* Boston: Houghton Mifflin, 1958.

"World's Columbian Exposition Records, 1891–1895." Special Collections Research Center, University of Chicago, Box 2, Folder 5.

"World's Fair Number, The Youth's Companion." Boston, Thursday, May 4, 1893.

Wright, Bradford W. *Comic Book Nation: The Transformation of Youth Culture in America.* Baltimore: Johns Hopkins University Press, 2003.

Wright, Gwendolyn. *Building the Dream: A Social History of Housing in America.* Boston: MIT Press, 1981.

Wylie, Philip. *Generation of Vipers.* Normal, IL: Dalkey Archive Press, 1996.

Yaszek, Lisa. "The Domestic SF Parabola." In *Parabolas of Science Fiction.* Edited by Brian Attebury and Veronica Hollinger, 106–24. Middletown, CT: Wesleyan University Press, 2013.

———. "Feminism." In *The Oxford Handbook of Science Fiction.* Edited by Rob Latham, 537–48. New York: Oxford University Press, 2014).

INDEX